Telling Travels

Telling Travels

Selected Writings by Nineteenth-Century
American Women Abroad

Edited by

Mary Suzanne Schriber

Northern Illinois

University Press

DeKalb

1995

© 1995 by Northern Illinois University Press

Published by the Northern Illinois University Press, DeKalb,
Illinois 60115

Manufactured in the United States using acid-free paper

Design by Julia Fauci

∞ ✪

Library of Congress Cataloging-in-Publication Data

Telling travels : selected writings by nineteenth-century
American women abroad / edited by Mary Suzanne Schriber.

p.   cm.

Includes bibliographical references.

ISBN 0-87580-195-1. — ISBN 0-87580-561-2 (pbk.)

1. Travelers' writings, American—Women authors.
2. American prose literature—Women authors. 3. American
prose literature—19th century. 4. Americans—Travel—Foreign countries. 5. Voyages and travels. 6. Women travelers.
I. Schriber, Mary Suzanne, 1938– .

PS648.T73T45   1994   94-28678

818'.409355—dc20   CIP

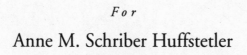

For

Anne M. Schriber Huffstetler

Contents

Acknowledgments

I am indebted to the staff of the Interlibrary Loan Service of Founders Memorial Library, Northern Illinois University, under the direction of Tobie Miller. Their patient and persistent work in locating numerous and obscure texts of travel enabled me to select the representative few included in this collection. I am indebted, as well, to Jitka Hurych, Head of the Science and Engineering division of Founders Memorial Library, and to William Baker, Professor of English and Humanities bibliographer of Founders Memorial Library, for their assistance in locating bibliographical and biographical information on specific women travelers. My thanks to Craig Abbott, Professor of English, for his advice on editorial matters. I owe particular thanks to Dolores Henry, of Manuscript Services of the College of Liberal Arts and Sciences under the direction of Karen Blaser, for her swift and careful preparation of the many dusky pages of nineteenth-century books from which the manuscript of this anthology evolved. Finally, my thanks to Anthony E. Scaperlanda for his encouragement.

"The woman has been set free. . . . One had but to pass a week in Florida, or on any of a hundred huge ocean steamers, or walk through the Place Vendôme, or join a part of Cook's tourists to Jerusalem, to see that the woman had been set free."

—Henry Adams,
The Education of Henry Adams
(1907)

"I am developing a high opinion of myself as a traveler. I consider that I excel most masculine travelers, for I travel in all countries without arms to protect me, without Baedecker and Bradshaw to inform me, and without boon companion or tobacco to console me."

—Lilian Leland,
Traveling Alone: A Woman's Journey Around the World
(1890)

Introduction

Looking back on the challenge he faced in 1881 when writing *The Portrait of a Lady*, Henry James recalls asking himself just what Isabel Archer, his heroine, would do. "Why, the first thing she'll do," he thought, "will be to come to Europe. . . . Coming to Europe is even for the 'frail vessels,' in this wonderful age, a mild adventure." Some thirty years later, in 1913, the narrator of Edith Wharton's *The Custom of the Country* describes the "drifting hordes" of Americans "scattered to the four corners of the globe," swelling "the spring mob of trans-Atlantic pleasure-seekers" descending on "the incredible number of the hotels and their simply incalculable housing capacity."[1] While the adventure of traveling in Europe and other destinations was much more than a "mild" experience for many nineteenth-century American women, it is indisputable that during the nineteenth century, American women, the majority of them white and middle or upper class, began to travel abroad in significant numbers for the first time in history. Beginning in the 1820s and continuing through the turn of the century and beyond, the prototypes of Daisy Miller, Isabel Archer, and Undine Spragg set out by the hundreds to see Europe, Africa, the Middle East, China, and the rest of the world. Missionaries and novelists, archaeologists and journalists, nurses and teachers, reformers and society matrons, musicians and artists, wives, widows, and single women, the curious, the young, and the old—all steamed into the British Isles and Europe and fanned out around the globe.

Statistics tell part of the story of the travels of nineteenth-century white American women. As early as 1835, according to Paul R. Baker, some fifty women were among the three hundred Americans who visited Rome during Holy Week. Between 1848 and 1850, excluding American residents and family members, Roman newspapers listed nine hundred names of visiting Americans, many of them women.[2] After the Civil War, "hundreds and then thousands of less-known, now long-forgotten Americans swarmed over the Atlantic," many women among them, as among the fifty thousand Americans who, in 1866 alone, traveled to Europe.[3] Mrs. John Sherwood wrote in 1890 that there were "more than eleven thousand virgins who semi-yearly migrate[d] from America to the shores of England and France."[4] These "virgins" and their mothers, as chronicled in the fiction of Henry James and Edith Wharton, came to shop for dresses at Worth's in Paris, to mingle with nobility in England and elsewhere, and to bask in the sun and society at Swiss watering holes such as Vevey and Geneva. Other visitors, such as Emma Hart Willard and Harriet Beecher Stowe, came seeking knowledge of the Old World and fresh insights into reform and education to take back to the New World.

Continents other than Europe were also traveled by great numbers of women. Figures compiled from the itineraries of those women who published book-length accounts of their journeys (far fewer than the numbers that traveled) provide a sense of their movements. The more than 195 book-length accounts of foreign travel published by women before 1900 include sections on the following places: 538 on travel in Britain and Europe; 20 on travel in China; 17 on travel in Palestine; 11 on travel in India; 22 on travel in Egypt; 2 on travel to the East Indies; 20 on travel in Greece; 3 on travel in Arabia; 6 on travel in Algeria; and 4 on travel in Africa.[5] Women ventured, as well, to Chili, Cuba, the Yucatan, Jamaica, and Alaska—virtually everywhere accessible to the traveler.

While John Straiton, writing in 1881 of his wife and daughter's trip to India, Asia Minor, Egypt, the Holy Land, Turkey, and Greece, correctly observed, "It is still quite novel for two American ladies to go half-way around the world, as these have done, on a journey of intelligence, recreation, and health,"[6] it is also true that women increasingly traveled for reasons sometimes conventional and sometimes innovative. Women such as Henrietta Shuck were sent off by church mission boards to convert the peoples of the Middle East and the Far

East to Christianity. Many others set off to seek adventure or to prove that the weaker sex was capable of traveling the world over without the protection of a man. In the process, they often suffered excruciating mal de mer and endured other severe hardships. As early as 1829, Abby Morrell left a child at home and sailed with her husband on a sealing vessel to the Philippines, where she was subject to sexual harassment by an American consul.[7] Elizabeth B. Dwight, a representative missionary figure dispatched with her husband to Constantinople, found herself in the midst of a raging plague and of "dreadful fires, which have driven hundreds of people to beggary and thrown multitudes of others into scenes of distress."[8] Caroline Paine tolerated lizards in her rooms, sandstorms in the desert, and life in a tent for forty days, carrying with her from America into foreign fields the spirit of the pioneer woman.[9] Travelers to the Middle East and the Far East were victims of disease, erratic shipping schedules, red tape, and especially quarantines. Once they had reached their destinations, they found hotels to be "invariably wretched"; if they were in Jerusalem, they found no hotels at all before 1850.[10] Travelers persistently expressed annoyance with beggars, thieves, and filth. Even after the railroad offered more comfort and ease to the continental traveler than the old diligence, women as well as men chose to explore backroads by whatever means available. Fanny Bullock Workman threw prudence to the winds and toured Algeria by bicycle (or "rovers") with her husband William in the 1890s. As they passed "farmhouses and native habitations," Workman reports, "the dogs would rush out at us, sometimes singly, sometimes in twos and threes, barking furiously, snapping and showing their teeth in a most threatening manner. . . . What would have happened to us had we not been provided with steel-cored whips, it is not difficult to predict."[11] In the light of such experiences, the etymology of the word *traveler* seems entirely accurate and appropriate: a traveler is "one who suffers *travail,* a word deriving in its turn from Latin *tripalium,* a torture instrument consisting of three stakes designed to rack the body."[12]

Women nevertheless continued to abandon their domestic routine and to set out to see the world. The proportions of this female exodus were without historical precedent. Prior to the nineteenth century, women travelers were ordinarily, to borrow Anne Tyler's title, "accidental tourists" undertaking travel for religious or practical purposes: to get from one place to another, to domesticate new territories in the wake of male exploration, to fill out an entourage organized by men, or to accompany husbands or fathers attached to embassies or military forces.[13] While colonial American women had traveled by necessity, simply to reach the shores of the New World, travel in other directions, from America to other continents, was relatively rare and primarily undertaken in the role of daughter or wife. Abigail Adams, for example, traveled with her father and mother in England and France from 1784 to 1787, and Martha Bayard, wife of a diplomat attached to the Jay mission, lived in England from 1794 to 1797, but such women were exceptions to the rule.

Early in the nineteenth century, however, technology conspired with challenges to ideology to set a record number of American women afloat on the high seas and ashore on other continents in diligences, railway cars, and jinrickshas and on donkeys, camels, bicycles, and foot. The advent of steam-powered ships and eventually of the "steam palace" changed dramatically the conditions, speed, and practicality of travel and with it women's exposure to foreign lands. The wooden sailing ships of the early nineteenth century, woefully outfitted with wooden berths and cramped quarters and subject to fire, mechanical failures, and the perils of the deep, took from twenty-four days to six weeks to cross the Atlantic. These vessels were replaced by the "tea kettles" or "steam kettles" of the 1840s and 1850s, which were equipped with what Harriet Beecher Stowe christened "sea-coops," narrow cabins with narrow berths and a single communal bathroom. In the 1840s, the luxuriously outfitted "steam palace" or "naval mansion" mercifully made its debut. By 1867, over one hundred of them were daily plowing the Atlantic, and by 1875, Cunard and eleven other lines with excellent safety records crossed the Atlantic in a matter of days.[14]

While the "steam palace" increased comforts for all travelers, capitalist entrepreneurs heeded opportunities to reap profits from the ranks of the ladies, and they invested in shipboard appointments that catered to women in particular. Public dining halls, boasting fresh flowers and ceilings of stained glass in turquoise, amethyst, and topaz, were furnished with silk upholstered chairs of richly carved solid mahogany. These were complemented by private "boudoirs of soft blue and gold where lights admitted by the 'ports' became iridescent through man-tinted glasses." There were "innumerable bath and toilet rooms in every section and on every deck."[15] Together with the advent of the Thomas Cook "package" tour, available at relatively moderate cost, such accommodations enabled women to travel across oceans comfortably and in ladylike fashion.

Technology and gender ideology, the system of understandings invoked by the term "ladylike," cooperated to serve the nineteenth-century American woman. Having been hobbled in the practical sense by the oceans between themselves and other continents, American women were further hobbled by ideological constrictions pertaining to gender. Indeed, it took more effort to escape from these ideological constrictions than to sail from the shores of New York or San Francisco. Limited by perceived divine design to the contingencies of her biological being, defined by her ability to bear children, and assigned to the domestic sphere, the "frail vessel" that was Woman was expected to remain close to her own front door. As entrepreneurs seized financial opportunities in catering to women, so women seized ideological opportunities from the taste for profits that motivated the captains of industry. The steam palace made it increasingly difficult to argue that the so called weaker sex belonged at home. Next to its speed, the great virtue of the steam palace was, after all, its status as a traveling home, complete with all the comforts—a fact that was not lost on women travelers. As Mrs. A. E. Newman, marshaling a characteristic trope, wrote in 1861: "Let us turn now to our 'life on the ocean wave, and our home on the rolling deep.'"[16]

Moreover, gaps in the ideology of gender, the social construct that defines femininity and masculinity and their proper domains, were being opened throughout the nineteenth century as what Sara Mills calls the discourse of femininity [17] mushroomed. Constricting definitions of "woman's sphere" were challenged and the roles of women in the public arena were expanded by a powerful surge of activities: women's quest for public rights of citizenship early in the century; women's work for causes such as abolition and their discovery of their own strengths in the process; women's press for suffrage in the aftermath of 1848 and the Seneca Falls women's convention; women's union in numerous voluntary associations such as Sorosis and the WCTU; and women's entrance into colleges, the professions, and the workplace.

Between the 1850s and the 1890s, the New Woman emerged from these initiatives. Carroll Smith-Rosenberg describes the attitudes of women identified as the New Woman: "Rejecting conventional female roles and asserting their right to a career, to a public voice, to visible power, [women] laid claim to the rights and privileges customarily accorded bourgeois men."[18] Emboldened by the ferment around them, even women who would not classify themselves among the ranks of the New Woman[19] moved out of their cultural confinement within domestic and local boundaries and moved into national and international spaces, seizing for themselves the freedom of movement that has been the historical prerogative of the male. They issued themselves passports to freedoms that threatened to change the borders of the mind even as those thrown up around the body were breached. Pursuing destinations both psychological and geographical, women were transformed from accidental tourists into what Paul Fussell defines as *travelers:* those who, although visiting places already discovered, retain in the process the "excitement of the unpredictable" that accompanies exploration and the "pleasure of 'knowing where one is' that belongs to tourism."[20]

Apparently aware on some level that women's passports would change their lives as well, many men were rendered uncomfortable by the wanderlust of the ladies. Lucy Seaman Bainbridge mimics such men in the voice of a provincial friend who insists, "'A woman's business is to stay to home and look after things and save. . . . My girls are a paintin' old jugs and saucers, and talkin' about art, and wantin' to go to Europe. Why can't people be satisfied to stay at home and keep to the good old ways!'"[21] When women accomplished daring feats, their veracity was sometimes impugned. Take the case of Fanny Bullock Workman, who climbed the Himalayas and explored the mountains and glaciers of eastern Karakoram. Asked "by staunch and indignant women-friends to deny publicly at lectures" the assertion that she "did not really climb the peaks and passes" she lectured and wrote about but was instead "hauled to the summits by coolies," Workman declared it "beneath [her] notice to deny such a trivial accusation."[22]

Public skepticism and alarm about women's new liberties, together with a desire to cling to conventional notions of woman's domestic calling, were sufficiently loud and widespread, however, to gnaw at the confidence even of those who were themselves in the category of the New Woman. Ida Tarbell, for example, living in Paris to study the life of Madame Roland, wrote, "There was a disturbing number of [American women in Paris] compelling me to ask myself again and again if this break for freedom, this revolt against security in which I myself was taking part was not a fatal adventure bound to injure the family, the one institution in which I believed more than any other, bound to produce a terrible crop of wretchedness and abnormality."[23]

Nevertheless, in the teeth of carping, criticism, and sometimes nagging self-doubts, women seized the historical moment to pursue their thirst for knowledge and adventure, often strategically invoking an allegiance to Womanhood as they explained their desire to travel. Thus Ella W. Thompson began her book of travels, in 1874:

> I want to say, to begin with, that the writer of this book is one of "the few, the immortal few," left of her sex in America, who would rather have an India shawl any day than the suffrage; but in dark moments, when both have seemed equally unattainable, it has occurred to her that most women's lives are passed, so to speak, in long, narrow galleries, built about with customs and conventionalities more impervious than stone. Sometimes they contract to a hot little kitchen, and the owner might as well be a Vestal Virgin, and done with it, her whole life being spent in keeping up the fire. . . . Plenty of doors lead out of these galleries, but only those marked "Church," "Visits," and "Shopping," move easily on their hinges.
>
> Most of us . . . cast longing eyes at the door marked with the magical word "Europe," and it has opened freely enough when the husband said the "Open, sesame;" it is only of late years that women have made the amazing discovery that they can say it themselves with like success, but it is well to keep the hinges well oiled, and the rubbish cleared away from the threshold. When my turn came, I felt as if I had been taken into a high mountain and been promised all the kingdoms of the earth, and had at once accepted the offer.[24]

As Leo Hamalian puts it,

For most women, immobilized as they were by the iron hoops of convention, the term "abroad" had a dreamlike, talismanic quality. It conjured up a vision composed of a whole cluster of myths, half-myths, and truths—of sunlight, of liberty, of innocence, of sexual freedom, of the fantastic and the healing, of the unknown and the mysterious—all those concepts that stood in direct confrontation to domesticity. When women did buy tickets to sail on ships to India or to ride the Orient Express to Baghdad, their real destination, more often than not, was a restorative idea rather than a place on the map.[25]

Wherever a white middle-class woman is to be found in the nineteenth century, an advice book to assist her in navigating the tempestuous sea of gender cannot be far behind. Nineteenth-century anxiety over gender took form in conduct books of travel, trunkloads of printed advice about how to dress, what to take abroad, and how to behave that swelled the discourses of femininity in America even as they swelled the pocketbooks of publishers. Florence Hartley's *Ladies' Book of Etiquette and Manual of Politeness* (1872) includes chapters on "Traveling" and on "How to Behave at a Hotel," perhaps because, as she says, "To be truly polite, remember you must be polite at *all* times, and under *all* circumstances."[26] One of the prodigious number of popular travel books by Thomas W. Knox includes, in addition to advice on "Traveling with Camels and Elephants" and "Traveling with Reindeer and Dogs," a chapter entitled "Special Advice to Ladies, by a Lady" (1881). The first of a two-volume collection, *The Woman's Book* (1894), includes a chapter by the journalist and traveler Elizabeth Bisland entitled "The Art of Travel," in which not only female and male travelers but also unmarried and married female travelers are offered separate advice, evidently in keeping with their different stations in life.

In counsel typical of conduct manuals, a publication of the Women's Rest Tour Association cautioned women to "forswear shabbiness" in their shipboard clothing because, "unless entirely lacking in the natural feminine desire to look your best, you will then deeply regret masquerading as a guy." The manual continues, "Take for travelling a new, stout, plain, and pretty dress. . . . If any woman questions the need of beauty in such a serviceable gown, let her remember that the consciousness of being well and appropriately dressed will double the pleasure of her trip."[27] The orientation toward gender that Nancy Cott finds in the diaries and letters of New England women from 1780 to 1835[28] governed the female traveler's reading of herself and her sex through the nineteenth century, as when Ella W. Thompson points out that "men have dressed sensibly for many years" but "Women never can be really happy in any condition where they lose their good looks."[29] Immersion in the ideology of gender often had tangible effects, even on otherwise practical women such as Fanny Bullock Workman, one of the most adventurous and daring of American women travelers. At the end of the century and nearly sixty years after Amelia Bloomer, Workman wore full skirts as she traveled by bicycle and skirmished with dogs snapping at her ankles and legs.[30] Perhaps the most pervasive, invasive, and overarching issue in the lives of nineteenth-century American women, gender was a steamer trunk of paraphernalia that women were unable or unwilling or reluctant to leave behind or to jettison from some foreign pier.

While the possibilities of international travel for African American women were at best severely limited, some from among the population of Free Blacks did undertake foreign ventures.[31] The ferment in connection with abolition, the "woman question," suffrage, and the professions that rendered white women more mobile and bold as the century progressed found a parallel in the activities of African American women who organized, participated in abolitionist groups, and sought education and professions. But while affluent white women who took to travel escaped the confinement of their own kitchens and parlors, African American women who found their way abroad escaped the confinement of labor in fields and kitchens and parlors owned by (white) others. White women were charged with domesticity; black women were domestics. Nancy Gardner Prince escaped the drudgery of service jobs, for example, when she married Nero Prince, a footman at the court of the Russian tsar, and traveled to Russia. While affluent white women were circumscribed by convention, African American women were enslaved by racism and by poverty.

The feel of freedom that accompanied travel was, therefore, radically different for each race. White women could anticipate a sense of freedom and adventure from the moment they arrived at the pier and then boarded ship. For African American women, the voyage itself was painful, no matter how luxurious the vessel. Sarah Parker Remond (1824–1894), for example, about to depart for England, Scotland, and Ireland under the sponsorship of the Ladies and Young Men's Anti-Slavery societies, wrote to a friend in 1858: "I hope to reach London before winter, but I dread starting for many reasons. I do not fear the wind nor the waves, but I know that no matter how I go, the spirit of prejudice will meet me." The "dread" she feels arises from the fact that she would be forced to cross the Atlantic in steerage.[32] Once arrived on foreign shores, however, African American women in the nineteenth century, as in the twentieth century, were liberated from the burden of race under which they labored in the United States. Josephine Brown, who was barred from school in Buffalo because of segregation, traveled with her sister Clara to London and France in the 1850s and wrote in a letter in 1854: "On our arrival in this country, we spent the first year in France, in a boarding-school . . . and never once heard our color alluded to in disrespectful terms. We afterwards returned to London, and entered a school . . . and here, too, we were always treated with the greatest kindness and respect." Training to be teachers and afraid that "color would be a barrier against employment," the Browns were "happily disappointed" and taught in schools in England, where, Josephine wrote, "[B]oth my assistant and pupils are all white. Should I return to America, it is scarcely probable that I could get a school of white pupils, and this makes me wish to remain here, for I am fond of teaching."[33]

The lists of African American women who made international journeys include Sarah Parker Remond, whose crossing of the Atlantic was without a "male protector." She remained in Britain to study at Bedford College for Ladies, returned to the United States in 1866 "to lecture on behalf of the Equal Rights Association," and then "returned to Europe and its unsegregated society" eventually to study medicine and to practice in Florence, where in 1885 her sisters, Maritcha Remond and Caroline Remond Putnam, joined her in her self-imposed exile.[34] Edmonia Lewis (1845–c. 1911), supported by abolitionists, studied sculpture in Boston and in 1865 went to Rome where, more ambitious and successful than Henry James's Roderick Hudson, she founded a studio that employed twenty workers. Her artistic endeavors met considerable success in the 1870s.[35] The Jubilee Singers of Fisk University, many women among them, twice toured abroad in the 1870s, singing for Queen Victoria and the royal family, the Russian czarina, and members of the British Parliament; on the Continent, they sang for the king and queen of the Netherlands, Kaiser Wilhelm and Crown Prince Frederick of Germany, and the duke and duchess of Saxony. According to Dorothy Sterling, "The Jubilee Singers were the first of a long procession of black artists who won recognition in Europe that they could not find in the United States. The absence of race prejudice during their years abroad transformed their lives, making it difficult for them to live in the South again. Two male members of the troupe remained in Europe; three others, including Maggie Porter, returned for concert tours from time to time."[36] Reform and missionary activities as well as the arts sometimes required African American women to travel: Harriet Jacobs (1818–1896) traveled to England in 1868 to solicit funds for a home for orphans and aged freedpeople in Savannah; Fanny Jackson Coppin (1837–1913) went to the Cape of Good Hope Colony with her husband and talked to African women on "the subjects of righteousness, temperance and the judgment to come."[37]

Having invaded the historically male territory of travel with their womanliness in tow, white women took to telling travels voluminously, in print. They converted travel into a passport to the hitherto predominantly masculine domain of the travel book. Of more than 1,800 books (in addition to innumerable articles in periodicals) of foreign travel by Americans published in America before 1900, some 195, as stated before, were the work of women. The number of travel books published by women escalates as the century, the technologies of travel and print, and economic affluence evolve: women published approximately 27 books of foreign travel before and 168 after the Civil War.[38] Perhaps half of these were, remarkably, the work of women who did not routinely aspire to print. While it is predictable that women devoted to the power of the word—poets and novelists such as Lydia Sigourney and Harriet Beecher Stowe and reformers such as Margaret Fuller and Julia Ward Howe—would publish their travels, and while it was a job requirement that women such as Kate

Field, inserting themselves into the world of journalism, would write on assignment, there were other, "miscellaneous" women such as Abby Morrell and Adelaide L. Harrington who were somehow empowered by travel to come before the public in print. Although the "steam palace" together with challenges to the ideology of Woman eased the tensions surrounding women and travel, technology and ideology do not account entirely for women's decisions to publish. Why did otherwise private, domestic women pursue what was for them the exceptional and public activity of publishing travel accounts?

The obvious but insufficient answer to this question is that in the nineteenth century women finally came into possession of the raw material for travel writing: travel itself. Once having traveled, women wrote for the same reason as many American men; that is, they wrote to promote the superiority and the manifest destiny of American political and spiritual values, for which the travel book was a fit form. Paul R. Baker explains that American travelers of either gender judged American life superior to any other, whether in religion or in morality, particularly as they expressed themselves on the topics of the American family; the treatment of women; the work ethic; the system of commerce; and, above all, the American system of government.[39] American women travel writers would refashion the world, particularly in its treatment of women, on the American plan. They undertook what Mary Louise Pratt, in connection with European women travelers, calls the "Imperial Quest *par excellence:* the Civilizing Mission,"[40] but in reverse, carrying salvation to their parent civilization. (Witness, for example, Julia Ward Howe presiding over a Congress on Women's Rights in Paris in 1877.) Often marshaling the discourse of colonialism, these travel writers "produced" in their texts the European, African, and Middle Eastern, among "Other" natives, particularly the native Woman, and then reveled in the privileges and superiority of American womanhood. Abby Morrell, for example, anticipating Alexis de Tocqueville, dedicates her *Narrative of a Voyage* in 1833 to her countrywomen, "the happiest of their sex." Often working to realize the vision of what was called, earlier in the century, republican motherhood and its successor, "a maternal commonwealth that fused public and private concerns, domesticity and politics,"[41] they cast themselves as *exploratrices sociales*[42] and studied foreign institutions and reforms with which to instruct the people at home. Thus Emma Hart Willard, founder of Troy Seminary, toured Europe examining the state of women's education in France and subsequently published her *Journal and Letters* (1833); Margaret Fuller visited institutions dedicated to the amelioration of the lot of the poor and the lives of women and children—schools, prisons, a bathing establishment, a washing house, crèches—and reported on these in letters to the *New York Tribune;* and Harriet Beecher Stowe, having been invited abroad by English abolitionists, returned home to write her impressions of European reform movements in *Sunny Memories of Foreign Lands* (1854).

Beyond the "womanly," civilizing mission, travel accorded the ordinarily homebound nineteenth-century white American woman the sense of a story to be told, an experience that warranted public record, and an important and therefore legitimate occasion to write. The genre of travel writing offered an inviting vehicle to meet the occasion. Certain features of the genre combined with women's salvific role to encourage women to take up the pen. Historically a remarkably elastic genre, travel writing is something of a literary carpetbag into which travelers pack all that they need for their travels and all that they collect along the way. It holds everything from history to art, to anecdotes, to the topical and the trivial within a potpourri of forms ranging from letters to journals, to poems and dialogues, to essays and narratives.[43] The travel book is commodious and informal, a discontinuous form of writing similar to the journal, the memoir, the letter, and the diary, all of which women have produced from the earliest times.[44]

Women travelers proceed to play on the fit between gender roles and genre, between the rhythm of women's domestic lives and travel. Like home life, travel and journal-keeping móve by fits and starts, subject to delays and interruptions. Women use domestic metaphors to explain the form of their travel accounts and to flavor them, as well, in a market awash with accounts of travel. Delight Sweetser, for example, wrote in 1898, "I may go zigzagging from one topic to another with as little regard for order as Japanese fields have when they go zigzagging over the landscape."[45] Helen Hunt Jackson calls one of her entries "a kind of washing-day-dinner letter" and continues, "You'll eat it because you can't get any other, and you won't be hungry as if you had eaten nothing; but don't we all hate Monday dinners?"[46] Mabel Loomis Todd claims that her book about the Amherst Eclipse expedition to Japan "necessarily makes divers small branchings in its course, like a sort of ornamental needlework much affected by our grandmothers," and she asserts, "I have, as it were, feather-stitched my way to Yezo and back again."[47]

Furthermore, there was a healthy market for travel writing in nineteenth-century America, a fact unlikely to have escaped women travelers. Despite the ritual protests that greeted the appearance of new books of travel, publishers saw a market for them and published some 325 such books between 1800 and 1850 and some 1,440 between 1851 and 1900.[48] Ronald J. Zboray finds that in the late 1840s, 19 percent of the books charged from the New York Society Library by men and 15 percent of those charged by women were books on travel, which, while valued by merchants engaged in international trade, were valued for psychological reasons as well. In the midst of the cultural change and fragmentation that characterized the Victorian period in America, travel books provided "models of individual characters . . . mastering alien environments" that were even more foreign than the environment of early capitalism, yet they were comforting because of their adhesion to precapitalist values.[49]

The connection between travel books and history also created an audience and a market. Travel accounts provided lessons in history, offering opportunities to measure the place and progress of America, the land of millennial hopes, against the rise and fall of other civilizations.[50] Moreover, Americans were eager for travel books because of international events. The revolution in Italy, the July Monarchy in France, the challenge to slavery in the British empire and elsewhere, the adventures of Henry Morton Stanley and David Livingston in Africa, the opening of Chinese markets to the goods of an industrializing America—all of these kept the world in the minds of Americans and whetted their appetites for news and analysis of foreign lands. There was literary business to be done, and women travelers, like women who wrote fiction in the nineteenth century, were ready to do it.[51]

Encouraged by travel and by the market for travel writing, women became increasingly comprehensive in their declared reasons for publishing travel books as the century progressed and as the "woman's sphere" pushed further into the public domain. At mid-century, Henrietta Shuck introduces her book of experience in China with the most modest of prefaces: "Whatever be the imperfection of the following miscellaneous notices. . . . Their preparation was originally undertaken for the special perusal of young friends."[52] By the end of the century, women travelers are considerably more bold. Adelaide Hall claims to write *Two Women Abroad* (1897) for an entirely secular reason: to encourage women to travel. Other writers are nakedly topical and ambitious. Adelaide Rosalind Kirchner writes *A Flag for Cuba* (1897) and Mary Hannah Krout writes *Hawaii and a Revolution* (1898) for political reasons: the one to appeal for Cuban independence and the other to plead for the annexation of Hawaii by the United States. The commodiousness and elasticity of the genre offered a public space in which women made their voices heard on national and international issues. The genre also offered an arena in which women could practice a public voice and become progressively more confident and critical in its use. In keeping with this mounting assertiveness, the apologies with which antebellum women conventionally prefaced their travel accounts diminish over time, becoming rare in postbellum accounts.

The waning and eventual disappearance of the apology may be connected with another postbellum phenomenon in travel writing: a reordering of motives for creating texts of travel. Before the Civil War, women's accounts of journeys were by-products of travel. Emma Hart Willard, for example, who traveled abroad for reasons of health and in the interests of Troy Seminary, collected what became her *Journal and Letters from France and Great Britain* (1833) ostensibly as an afterthought and at the behest of friends. After the Civil War, however, travel was sometimes the by-product of a professional decision to write and to publish books and articles. Kate Field, for example, conceived journalistic travel projects and then traveled to execute them, eventually publishing *Hap-Hazard* (1873) and *Ten Days in Spain* (1875). Elizabeth Bisland and Nellie Bly traveled around the world in competition with one another and with Jules Verne's Phileas Fogg to produce newspaper copy. In the wake of mass

tourism and a consequent wave of travel books, touring "solely in order to write tour-memoirs," James Buzard finds, "was a familiar
charge, one often made against women on the basis of their proverbial garrulousness and exhibitionism."[53] This insidiously gendered
perception registers, of course, a manly discomfort with the increasing frequency of a female public voice. It registers something else as
well: a significant initiative on the part of women. Undertaking travel
with the intention to write tour-memoirs, and splicing these with critiques on public issues, women actively created occasions to "go public" instead of passively waiting on chance to deliver such occasions to
their doorsteps. Female travelers, that is, quietly slipped into the available public space of the travel genre in the first half of the nineteenth
century; but in the latter part of the century they deliberately carved
out ever more territory in which to make themselves heard.

Whether a desire to travel produced writing or a desire to write
produced travel, women's accounts, far from being solely devoted to
reports of travel, are compendia of discourses about national and international issues (one being the "woman question") authorized by the
act of travel. Use of the travel genre to forward a gender agenda is perhaps the most intriguing feature of women's travel writing in the nineteenth century. Women travelers united gender and the travel genre to
accomplish two ends. First, they used gender to sell their travel writing in a market increasingly inundated with travel writing. In 1857 an
American reviewer lamented, "[T]he subject of European travel is so
hackneyed that only a first-rate ability is competent to make a new
book on the subject interesting."[54] By 1897, the situation had further
deteriorated; the publishers' preface to Adelaide S. Hall's *Two Women
Abroad* declares,

> We realize that in introducing to the public "Two Women Abroad,"
> with the expectation of holding the reader's interest from beginning to
> end, we have undertaken no easy task. The dangers, discomforts and ex-
> pense of travel have been so lessened that thousands of Americans now
> cross the ocean in palatial steamers to see for themselves what was once
> attainable only through the medium of books. The columns of the daily
> press report current events from every part of the globe almost as soon
> as they occur. Therefore, to publish a book describing the scenes and in-
> cidents of a six months' tour in foreign lands seems almost absurd.[55]

Women travelers and their publishers cleverly yoked the liability of a saturated market to the liabilities of gender and converted both into assets. Gender difference offered itself as material to distinguish the travel books of women from those of their male counterparts. In more than one-tenth of the travel books by American women published in the United States during the nineteenth century, the writer's gender is emphasized. This sometimes occurs in the book's title—for example, *A Woman's First Impressions of Europe* (Mrs. E. A. Forbes, 1865) or *Europe Through a Woman's Eye* (Lucy Yeend Culler, 1883). A subtitle sometimes introduces gender, as in *Adventures in East Africa or Sultan to Sultan: The Narrative of a Woman's Adventures among the Masai and Other Tribes of East Africa* (May French-Sheldon, 1892). Also, remarks that serve to italicize gender may appear in preliminaries or elsewhere in the text. In Lucy Yeend Culler's book, for example, the gender inflection of the title is magnified in the book's conclusion by its repetition in boldface and upper-case type. It reads, "If any of my readers wonder why I have said so little concerning the agriculture, manufactures, commerce, customs and habits of the people and political affairs of the countries which we visited, please remember that this is EUROPE THROUGH A WOMAN'S EYE"[56]

The culture's discourse on femininity claimed a distinction between a woman's view of the world and the perspective of a man, and subjects were divided along gender lines. A woman's view, excluding subjects presumed by the culture to be the province of the male, would focus on "womanly" interests. Playing on difference as early as 1839, Sarah Haight writes, "I think I hear you say, away with all such *bas bleu*-ism [charters, history, and tribal commanders], and talk to me rather of shawls and robes, turbans and slippers, pearls and emeralds. Talk of Circassians and Georgians, harems and baths, sherbets and sweetmeats, pipes and coffee." Two years later, in 1841, Catharine Sedgwick writes, "Do not fear that I am about to give you a particular description [of docks and warehouses]. . . . Our 'woman's sphere,' the boundaries of which some of my sex are making rather indefinite, does not extend to such subjects." Forty-one years later, in 1882, Lucy Bainbridge writes of her adventures in China, "Life everywhere is made up of little things. This is especially true with women; hence if I write of trivial matters, leaving to others of the opposite sex the

broad, comprehensive opinions of peoples and politics, it must be remembered that the writer is looking at the world with a woman's eyes.
After years of dealing with butcher, grocer, and the milkman, it is a
matter of real interest to a housewife how these things are managed
round on the other side of the world."[57] Women travelers capitalized
on the ideological construction of their gender to advertise their work
as different from men's; thus in a crowded market they distinguished
their works for readers.

Yet feminist irony, overt compliance and covert violation of
codes and systems, is clearly at work in women's accounts of travel.
From the first appearance of American women's books of travel in
1833, the subject matter that women chose to treat encompasses far
more than the "shawls and robes, turbans and slippers" that Sarah
Haight mentions. Abby Morrell pleads in 1833 for "the amelioration of the lot of seamen," and Elizabeth Banks calls at the end of
the century for the amelioration of the lot of British working
women.[58] Women's accounts of travel show that all issues were
women's issues. Protests to the contrary are, as often as not, rhetorical strategies, the mounting of a performance on the stage of gender consciousness rather than an expression of conviction. The performance was calculated, in all likelihood, to draw an audience—to
sell books.

Capitalizing further on the ideology of difference, women travelers
sometimes make an issue of traveling solo, turning to their own purposes a pervasive nineteenth-century discourse that invades travel, as
other, narratives: female vulnerability. James Buzard observes that particularly before 1850 "[o]nly great wealth or great courage to ignore
social disapprobation, or both, could give women the opportunity to
travel," by which he means "simply to move—unladen and unaccompanied." Buzard explains,

> [British] men in touring parties that included women were ex-
> horted to constant vigilance, because it was commonly acknowledged
> that women required shielding from a host of perils large and small:
> women travelling alone (or in groups without men) were referred to as
> "unprotected" and looked at askance; young women travelling any dis-
> tance alone were almost never to be encountered. . . . By mid-century

male escorts were being aided or supplanted by the comforting paternalism of Cook, Murray, Baedeker, and their competitors.[59]

By emphasizing the act of traveling alone, as Lilian Leland does in the epigraph to this introduction, women may be engaging in entrepreneurial play with a feature of the travel genre that became more prominent with the escalating numbers of female travelers. Yet behind their play, and that of their male counterparts, lurks the shadow of female sexual vulnerability. These texts of the "lone" female traveler (which in the nineteenth century means "unaccompanied by a male" rather than literally "alone"), when situated in the nineteenth-century discourses of femininity, implicitly flirt with the titillating. In an era in which "the American girl" was an object of marital (and material) interest to financially straitened foreign nobility, an era in which Henry James could build a novella from the compromising "indiscretions" of Daisy Miller, these texts suggest a seduction motif and the narrative suspense the motif constructs. Operating against this cultural backdrop of female vulnerability to seduction and sexual violation, however, the texts of male and female travelers differ. Whereas the texts of males insist on defending the female body of the presumably naive female traveler from alien invasions, the texts of female travelers, stressing the choice to travel alone, implicitly insist that women can take care of themselves even as they speak for themselves in their texts of travel. In effect, women's textualizing of "solo" travel is women's writing of the story of James's Daisy Miller and Winterbourne. Furthermore, the texts of women who traveled solo accomplish one more task as they quietly evoke the specter of seduction and a tarnished reputation: they reorder androcentric priorities established by the courtly male. They value experience and adventure over virginity and intactness or they insist that it is possible to have both. The order of the world they construct, in other words, is feminocentric.

Women travelers, even when conservatively affirming an androcentric order rather than urging a feminist view, accomplish a major purpose in their texts of travel: they rewrite the culture's story of Woman. As even the most conservative of these travelers inscribe in their texts the culture's idea of Woman, they also construct women who differ from Woman as defined by the culture. They rewrite themselves, other women, and the entire sex. Even as they protest the desire to come before the public, they proceed to present themselves in print, talking of politics as well as potatoes. They undermine the image of Woman as a frail and dependent creature at risk when traveling solo by first drawing the reader's attention to the notion and then demonstrating that women, unlike Woman, travel solo intrepidly and with gusto. They rewrite culture and history by writing women into them, making speak the silences of male travel texts on the subject of women. This serves to revise the idea of Woman, the culture's abstraction that substitutes for women, and replace it with women. In short, women transmute narratives of travel, traditionally androcentric, into gynocentric narratives of their lives and narratives of gender, using the travel book as a structure within which to embed a major agenda: the politics of gender.

Women have historically made use of diaries and letters, private and personal forms, to record their lives and opinions. Among the most significant changes in the nineteenth century, however, was the emergence into the public arena of the voices of American women, who in addition to their work in journalism and fiction made the travel genre into a vehicle to carry women's critiques of public issues. I have selected for inclusion in this anthology, therefore, those texts of travel prepared for publication by the traveler herself and constructed for public rather than for private consumption. Although many women travelers, such as Emma Hart Willard, avow that their published letters preserve the unvarnished, pristine state of materials intended only for the eyes of friends at home rather than for public consumption, such protests are largely conventional, registered even as the travelers prepare their texts for entry into the public domain. I have sought to represent, from the first book of travel in 1833 until the turn of the century, those books most revelatory of American cultural discourses written by a cross section of women, from journalists and novelists to reformers and "miscellaneous" women. Some, such as Harriet Beecher Stowe, Catharine Maria Sedgwick, and Constance Fenimore Woolson, are names with which we are familiar; others, such as Abby Jane Morrell, Nancy Gardner Prince, and Lucy Seaman Bainbridge, have been largely lost to many of us. I have also attempted to select excerpts representing the range of places and subject matter about which women wrote: England and Japan; beggars and priests; mountains and flatland; politics and religion; dignitaries, common people, and, of course, other women. The full texts from which these excerpts are taken offer the pleasures traditionally associated with the travel genre. They carry us to foreign destinations on generally conventional itineraries. They offer historical information; sagas of adventures and hardships; tales of lodgings and modes of transportation; impressions of foreign peoples; and descriptions of nature's grandeur. In the background, the hum and buzz of nineteenth-century American culture can be overheard. Simultaneously inside and outside of the dominant and majority male practice in the travel genre, these telling travels of American women, constructing a feminocentric world, are important in the history both of travel writing and of women's writing in nineteenth-century America.

Note on the Text

In preparing the selections for this volume, I have retained, to the greatest extent possible, the original texts as they were printed while bringing them into conformity with current publishing practices. I have therefore preserved characteristics such as archaic spellings and comma usage (for example, commas before verbs), symbols and abbreviations, and idiosyncratic language usage in order to preserve the flavor of each selection. I have replaced archaic printing conventions with current practices in some matters of punctuation, in order to facilitate the modern reader's access to the texts. For example, I have omitted commas before dashes (such as ,—) and reversed the order of quotation marks and semicolons (such as ;"), quotation marks and commas (such as ",), and some quotation marks and exclamation points (such as "!) to reflect current American publishing standards. I have corrected spelling and typographical errors, and I have changed words originally containing ligatures to reflect modern spelling practices. I have provided numbered notes at the end of the volume to clarify the more obscure terms, names of persons, and historical events that appear in the selections. Asterisks in the texts refer to footnotes originally supplied by the authors. Omissions of text within extracts are marked by ellipses in square brackets.

Telling Travels

1

Emma Hart Willard

ॐ

Emma Hart Willard (1787–1870) was a pioneer in women's education, a founder of the Troy Female Seminary (1821), a lecturer, and a writer of history, science, and geography books. She traveled to Paris, England, and Scotland in 1830 and 1831 for reasons of health. Later, she compiled and annotated her letters and journal entries, which she wrote while she was abroad, and published them as *Journal and Letters, from France and Great-Britain* (1833). She contributed the royalties from sales of the book to the Troy Society for the Advancement of Education in Greece, a society Willard founded to raise funds to train teachers for service in Greece.

The following selection from Willard's *Journal and Letters*, a chronological account, contains the Preface and four letters written from Le Havre and Paris to her sister and to another correspondent. These letters appear in Willard's book among other letters describing St. Denis, the Tuileries, and the Louvre and addressing such subjects as politics, topography, shopkeepers, and the French language. The Preface, an elaborate accounting for her decision to travel and to write, exemplifies the conventional practice of many antebellum American women who undertook to publish their travels. Her descriptions of lodgings and of social events, her portrayals of the situation of women abroad, and her reflections on a variety of cross-cultural topics are also characteristic of women's accounts of travel, suggesting that despite rhetoric to the contrary, all issues were women's issues in the nineteenth century.

Journal and Letters, from France and Great-Britain

Preface

When in consequence of ill health, I was obliged to leave my institution in the care of my sister, and go abroad, I intended making observations not only for myself, but for my country women; especially for those who were, and who had been my pupils. Arrived in Europe, and introduced into society in Paris, my views on this subject changed. Seeing so much that was new to me, I felt that what I could learn in my short stay abroad, would not be worth presenting to the public. The difficulty too, of giving candid statements, without betraying implied confidence, was present to my mind—and to make up common place accounts from Guide Books, did not suit my vein. From these considerations then, I lost sight of the public in my observations, and in the descriptions which I gave in letters to my friends, or kept in my private journal. This was hastily written in pencil, amidst many other avocations.

Of matter thus put together, I had two considerable volumes. When I collected, and added to these the letters I had written home, especially those to my sister, I found a bulk of papers, if not of information, quite sufficiently ample to make a book. My friends at home were urging to see my journal; and those abroad, particularly my former pupils, that I should publish my travels. I thought I could about as readily prepare a book for the press, as to put my papers in a condition to be read by my friends.

In the mean time, by the marriage of my sister, which occurred soon after my return, the cares of my school fell more heavily upon me than formerly; and other literary occupations, commenced before my departure, and connected with my plans of education, demanded my attention, and filled up my few leisure hours.*

---

* I refer here to the plan of a volume, or universal history, with an atlas, which I expect ere long to offer to the public

During the prevalence of the cholera, in the month of July following my return, my school was discontinued a fortnight, previous to the regular close of the term. My teachers preferred remaining, and during the time, they copied out my pencil written journal, and I verily thought that one fortnight of my own time spent upon my papers, would have been sufficient to fit them for the press.

But from several considerations, I was undecided as to the expediency of publishing them. I believed that God had devoted me to a special calling, that of female education, and that my time was not my own to bestow upon objects that might amuse me, or gratify my private friends. Early in the month of January last, an affecting appeal was made to me, in behalf of female education in Greece.

From my earliest youth, my mind has dwelt with mingled sorrow and indignation, on the degradation to which my sex are subjected, in Mahometan lands, and those regions adjoining, which are infected by their customs. It appeared, and now appears clear to me, that a time has come, when a door may be opened in Greece for their deliverance, if the means can be found.[1] I no longer hesitated concerning the publication of my papers, since a channel was now presented, through which I could turn my labors to account, in the cause of female education.

But on examining them, to prepare them for the press, I found that I had miscalculated the time required, and greatly undervalued the difficulties of my task, which arose mainly from the circumstance, that they were not originally written for the public, but merely for myself, and my confidential friends—and much of the character which they now bear, be it for the better or the worse, originates in this circumstance—and I must now say to my readers, that as I have made them parties in my confidential communications, so I hope they will treat me with indulgence.

To this I feel myself entitled on several accounts. I have given my labors in a generous cause, and I have toiled in the completion of my work, under the burden of heavy cares, which I bear not for my own sake. I have been obliged, in so doing, sometimes to write and examine papers at late hours, and I have thus so weakened my eyes (I hope however not permanently) that I have been unable to give my work that last examination in reference to style and punctuation, which I should otherwise have done; nor have I been able to correct it in the press, by personal inspection.

That it is not without some diffidence I come before the public, (as these papers must necessarily show me the writer, of a year of my own life,) may appear from a further circumstance. When I first gave them to promote the cause of female education in Greece, I had taken it up, calculating mainly on the support of my former pupils, to whom I intended to dedicate, and send my book of travels. Subsequently, when my beloved townswomen came generously forward, and took an equal responsibility, I proposed to the society then formed, that I should substitute in the place of my journal and letters, a volume, developing more fully my views of female education, than any thing I had yet written; and which I had while in Europe engaged, at some future period, to write. I told the ladies of our society, that in detailing my movements in foreign countries, and in expressing my honest sentiments on the various subjects before me, I should undoubtedly incur censures from those whose opinions differed from mine; and it would injure my feelings, if any portion of such censures should fall upon them.

After a few days consideration, the society decided, that as some public expectation had then been excited, the original plan must be pursued, and the journal and letters published. I have wished to make the work an offering worthy so good a cause—with what success, a candid public must determine. I have written in the spirit of truth and honesty, and have been exceedingly careful in all facts of importance, to state nothing but what I know to be true. But in filling up from memory, some minor articles of description—and in trifling incidental circumstances—the various images of my brain, perchance,

"Confus'dly bound in memory's ties,"

may have been in some instances, incorrectly joined—though I am not aware that such is the fact.

Wishing, if possible, that my book might possess pecuniary value, I have in particular instances dwelt with more minuteness than some might think advisable, on circumstances relating to subjects and persons, which have, as I believe, a permanent hold on the affections of my countrymen. This is particularly the case with regard to those connected with Gen. La Fayette and his family. On the other hand, I have omitted to mention many objects of curiosity, that came under my observation, because they have been generally noticed by other travellers. I am sensible that I have sometimes advanced opinions, which are scantily sustained by the facts which I have mentioned; and I prefer to leave such, standing with whatever foundation my general character may give them, to substantiating them at any sacrifice of the ties of gratitude, or the obligations of implied confidence.

If it be asked why, in such cases, I have not omitted the opinions, as well as the facts on which they were founded, I would answer—because they are such as I deem it important should be known in my own country. I trust that to those who read these pages, it will be apparent, that though I would willingly interest and amuse, yet that I have had at the same time an honest desire, in presenting to the American public, the little knowledge I acquired abroad, that it should be turned to good account in the service of one class or another of our citizens; or more generally go to correct, what I consider false standards of public opinion, or erroneous estimates of ourselves, and others.

Letter to Mrs. A. H. Lincoln
Havre, Oct. 30th

Dear Sister:
I will now come to plain matters of fact on the question, how things here compare with those at home.

To begin with the room in which I write, which is the sleeping apartment of Miss D. and myself. I write upon a round table, covered with a red and blue cotton cloth, not much unlike the same sort of things at home. Just under the table, is the centre piece of a polished oaken floor—an octagon of perhaps eight inches in diameter. Around this, the boards, all of an exact width, and about as broad as a man's hand, continue to be ranged till the whole floor is completed. This is however a different pattern from the other floors in the house, although of the same material, and in the same general style of building. The parlor and dining-room floors are made of parallelograms of oaken plank, about the width and twice the length of a brick, and laid like bricks in a pavement. The stairs are also of oak. The servants clean these stairs and floors every morning, first by sweeping, and then by rubbing with a waxed brush.*

But my chamber—let us look again at that. Sit down by my round table; and lest the slippery oaken floor provoke your patience, put your feet on this comfortable hearth-rug, which, thanks to the kind attention of Mr. D. has been sent us by our landlady. The room we find is about twenty feet square—up four pair of stairs—a moderate heighth, as we are told, for a room in a French city. It fronts the Rue de Paris, which is the principal street in Havre. Examine the two windows, and you will find them different from ours. They open laterally like double doors, swinging inwards. Three large panes of glass, one above the other, fill each of the two moveable sashes. A thin, full muslin curtain is attached to them at bottom and top, moving as they move. A loose drapery of thick muslin, as is common with us, is also fastened above each window, and may at pleasure be thrown over brass curtain pins at the sides. Between the windows stands a bureau not much unlike ours. Chairs are ranged along the wall as we have them, but the form is lighter and less clumsey.

Now let us turn to our left. We find on this side of the apartment (except at the fire-place near the centre) heavy pannel-work of pine. Over the fireplace, which is of moderate size, but immoderate depth, is a looking-glass, large enough, we should suppose, for a parlor, framed into the wall. The fireplace has a marble finish. On the mantel-piece stands a waxen candle, in a flat chamber candle-stick, for which we pay a round price. Below it is a fire-board covered with paper, representing a landscape and lovers, which I believe are common every where. Now look closely at the pannel-work, which I have spoken of, and you will discover that two of the pannels open, and disclose a fine convenient *armoire*, or closet with shelves.

Now let us wheel round, and examine the part of the room opposite the windows. You see nothing but a pannelled wall again—but in it are two pair of large double doors, opening towards us. Look within

---

* This part of house-keeping, though common in warm and moist countries, is not much known to us, of the northern portion of the United States.

these, and you will discover two beds, which you will find somewhat novel in their formation. They are fashioned a little like what in some parts of our country are called *bunks*, although the mahogany work of which they are made is carried down with a graceful sweep, and hollowed out upon the sides. The head and foot of the bedstead are alike. The bottom is of boards, and so near the floor that a broom has only space to pass beneath it. Notwithstanding the bedstead is so low, yet the bed is as high as ours. The distance is filled up with at least three different beds—the first is very thick, of straw—the second, I believe of feathers—and the third of wool. The pillow is very large, and square, coming below the shoulders. If you sleep in one of these beds, settle yourself with discretion, exactly in the middle. You will find there is a delightful elasticity about it, without any of that stifling sensation which one feels from the centre of a full, soft, feather bed.

We have now inspected three sides of the room, and the fourth has nothing worthy of note but the door, which leads into a corridor. But before we go out, let us take a look from the window, which you see opens like a double door, and as easily. The street below is of a sufficient width, and grows wider towards the south. In that direction on the opposite, or east side of the way, is the market. What a motley group are hurrying to and fro! The well-dressed look much like those of our own country, but what odd sights strike us among the peasantry! How strange that the nation most noted for changing fashions among the high, should be the one to keep most tenaciously the old manners and costumes among the low. The Norman peasants are noted for this adherence to ancient customs. Their animals are as singular to our eyes as their dresses. The enormous dray-horses—the little patient asses under burdens of twice their own bulk—the odd sorts of carts little and great, with the queer looking harnesses for the beasts—in short, every thing amuses us—because every thing is new.

One may discover even by looking on this throng of peasantry, that this is the land of gallantry. It is a grave affair, of which all are rather proud than ashamed. Observe that couple of Norman peasants of middle age! On the man, a long frock, woollen cap, and sabots; and on the woman a steeple cap—her sunburnt face and forehead bare, while the ruffle commencing by the ears, grows to a hand's breadth behind. A long waisted short-gown and a striped woollen petticoat, blue and white, complete her costume. Let these two figures go through the whole affair of meeting, bowing, and walking off arm in arm like a dandy and dandizette of Broadway, and it will serve as a specimen of what we are constantly seeing in the streets.

Before we turn from the windows we will remark the houses on the opposite side of the way. The material is of hewn stone, originally a blueish tint, but now blackened by time. The style of building is far more massy and solid than ours, and the houses are higher. What we call the first story, or what in England is called the ground floor, is here called the *rez-de-chaussée;* and is used entirely for the purposes of merchandize. In the hotel where we are, the back rooms of *rez-de-chaussée* are used as kitchens, while the front are occupied for shops. The story above, which we call the second, and which in England is called the first, is here called the entre-sol; and ordinarily it is not so high between joints as the one above, which we should call the third story, but which in French cities is called "*le premier*," (the first) and generally "*la belle étage*," it being the common locality for the saloon, and suite of apartments for receiving company. By examining the opposite houses, we see that the largest windows and most elegant curtains are on this *premier*, or *belle étage*. Above this are sometimes three and sometimes four stories.

Having now examined the interior of my apartment, and learned what we can by looking out of the windows, let us range about the house. From observing, first the doors which open into the corridor on this floor, and then by examining the stories above and below, you will remark, that exactly the same arrangement of apartments takes place on every story throughout the house. The stairs also occupy the same situation, each flight as you ascend being exactly above the others. In massy buildings the main partitions must of course be carried up, on account of the strength of the edifice. Setting out from my room, if you go up two pair of stairs, you will land in the garret, where you will find some small apartments for servants, taken from the general space. But the most attractive object is a flight of stairs by which we can ascend to the top of the house, and have a view of the city, and the neighboring country. It is not however very pleasant to see black roofs of houses, and smoking chimneys. Yet there are here some objects of interest. The sea is on the west, while winding around to the opposite side come up the enormous basins in which lie vast quantities of shipping, where the gay pennon of many a nation floats. From this point of view the houses and ships seem curiously mingled together. On the north, is a beautiful glimpse of the hill of Ingouville, where are discernable at the distance of perhaps a mile and a half, the most elegant mansions which we have yet seen in France. We have visited one of them, the chateau which Bonaparte used to inhabit when at Havre. The grounds are pleasantly laid out, and of the most exquisite verdure, with roses and other beautiful flowers yet in bloom. My companion and myself plucked a small bouquet, but our poor *cocher* was so horrified, that I thought I would never dare the same offence again in France. The French, I have always been told, are remarkable for their abstinence from the least depredation of this kind; and they are rewarded for it by the freedom of access which they enjoy, to gardens and fine grounds, that in other countries are closed to the multitude.

In descending from the top of the house, take care and not step backwards through the trap-door, otherwise you may not escape so well as I did in performing the same feat.

But our warning bell rings, and I must dress for dinner. You won't dine with us then? Well, good-bye! When I return, I will give you some account of the entertainment.

The tables of Madame Lebourg, are arranged a little like ours at the Seminary. There are two of considerable length, crossed at one end by a third. At the centre of this sits Madame Lebourg, performing, with dignity and decision the honors of the repast. Our party, as the latest comers, are seated at some distance from this centre of honor. This is a *table d'hôte*, and as I am told more after the American, than the French fashion. There were but few ladies besides Miss D. and myself, with perhaps thirty gentlemen—and oh! the deafening racket made by these Frenchmen, as they went on with their meal, and became animated in their conversation. Such jabbering— there were a dozen talking at once, each striving to be heard above the rest—with such differences of tone, from the grave bass up to the long-drawn treble squeak, into which French speakers not unfrequently run their voices at the close of a sentence. When the tumult

and the din increased beyond all bearing, our dignified hostess inter-
posed and these boisterous elements for a while were hushed.

Politics seem the absorbing subject. Accounts are brought of recent
fires occurring in the vicinity, doubtless the work of incendiaries. The
Liberals attribute them to the Carlistes. Liberalism is altogether the
order of the day here, and really I was so much occupied with the subject, that I cannot be so minute with regard to the dinner as you
might expect. The changes of the great political drama, affect me
more than those of the dishes. But to tell you what I recollect; the
manner of setting the table does not differ much from the American.
A white table-cloth is spread; there is placed for each person a dining-
plate, and one for soup within it; a large silver fork with a well-sharp-
ened knife; a large napkin, with a small roll of bread; a tumbler, and
a wine-glass. You find upon the table, some substantial dishes—but
before they are served, a waiter brings you soup. If there is fish, that
is offered next. Then each person takes his choice in calling for a dish
that suits him. Not a great quantity is sent at a time, and be it what it
may—boiled beef, roast chickens, mutton cotelets, or veal *fricandeau*,
he takes it with bread alone, (the Americans, however, eat potatoes
with meat,) he then changes his plate, and is helped to a small quantity of some other dish. Perhaps the second change will be some kind
of vegetables, which are elegantly prepared, and called *entremets*, as
being generally taken between the meats. A Frenchman, whatever he
eats never puts his knife to his mouth. After cutting his meat, he lays
it down and eats with his fork.

After dinner we go to the salon, and there, are offered hot coffee
and *liqueurs*, that is cordials, noyeau, &c., in very small elegant
glasses. I found the coffee delicious, and highly refreshing. We used
sugar with it, but never cream or milk, which is not even offered. The
candles are by this time lighted; and the salon of Madame Lebourg is
cheerful and pleasant, and we are here made to feel at home. When I
see this lady in the morning, with a cap and *robe du matin*, arranging
her house, I would take her for a careful matron of forty. But when
she is dressed for dinner, her hair elegantly coiffed, curled high at the
angles of the forehead, and set up in fine taste with a high comb behind, a genteel dress exactly fitting her shape, with a suitable kerchief,
I then should think mine hostess might be a belle under thirty. A con-

siderable part of the gentlemen we meet at table seem to be boarders from the city. One of them a lively Frenchman of perhaps twenty five, appears duly sensible of the charms of Madame L. While she is carving at table, which she does in a most *masterly* manner, he is ever helpful; or if she looks as if there is too much noise, he is ever ready to increase it by crying out against it. He generally remains in the salon, where Madame sits engaged working a chair cushion—in a beautiful pattern, in crewels of different colors. The lady is gracious, but I never saw her give the least token of being particularly pleased with this homage.

The men we meet here, have many of them such enormous whiskers and moustaches, that their appearance is quite hideous. I hope it will be long before American gentlemen adopt this barbarous fashion. There is a young Portuguese that we call Don Miguel, who has really a terrific look. Although he is a young man of a handsome person, (but that the snout is uncovered) you might take his head for that of an enormous black bear.

Madame Lebourg is a politician—a liberal—full of feeling for the good La Fayette—the common father of the French and Americans—and loving what he loves. She was speaking in raptures of the American institution and government, to some young gentlemen who are here from the United States. One of them told her that her admiration was altogether misplaced—that ours was the mere government of the mob, which fortunately however would not last long; as it was now waning to its dissolution. We should doubtless in the end have something better, but must expect troublesome times first. That is—we should have the light and blessings of royalty, after we had first toiled through the slough of anarchy. All this was too much for me. I told Madame Lebourg, who expressed much surprise, that such sentiments were not very common among us—that on the contrary, we believed that the old governments of Europe were to assimilate to our own, as being more agreeable to natural justice, and the improved state of the world.

By the way, this young American, although agreeable, respectable and gentlemanly, yet on this subject often vexed and grieved me. The English government was his theme—the English nobility his models—while our own institutions were treated with undisguised contempt. "Now," said I, "if these are your real sentiments, I advise you by all means, as you are going to visit England, to stay in that country. You like the government, and the order of things there. Very well—you have a right to do so; and if you remain there, you will make a good citizen. Your opinions will then be useful to yourself, and the country which sustains you; but such opinions in America, will render you uncomfortable—will make you a bad citizen—and either drive you to mean duplicity, or debar you from political preferment."*

December 30, 1830

Dear Sister:

Last evening, I went with my son to Gen. La Fayette's *soirée*. Mr. Rives, who happened to be near the door of the first apartment of the suite which contained the General's company, joined us. The rooms were unusually full. We edged along, conversing together—expecting to find the General in the next room; when suddenly the countenance of the blessed patriot, full of benevolence, was beaming upon us. After answering his enquiries about my health, I told him I hoped he was not the worse, for the dissipation of the last evening. "Oh no," said he, "I am all the better for having spent the evening with you!" This he said, not emphasising the *you*, but in just such a way that it might mean, "I am the better for having been amused last evening"— and I told him I was happy that he had been entertained. It may look like vanity for me to tell you of these things; but it is not my pride alone; it is my deeply filial affection, my reverential love, that is gratified thus to meet a return, where I had so little reason to expect it.

I must now tell you, how it was that we spent the evening together. It was at the *Opéra Français*, usually called the Grand Opera. You will remember that he told me he had not been at a theatre since the revolution, and the first time he did go, he would go with me. One

---

* This young gentleman preceded us, by a few days, in our journey to Paris. Having called at my lodgings one day when I was out, he said he had a message to leave which would please me. "Tell Mrs. Willard," said he, "that I am already twenty per cent, more of an American than when I landed in France." He is a sensible young man, and I think he will return an American above par.

evening before had been appointed, and failed from the illness of one of the performers. It was the evening before last that we finally went. I expected that the people would have cheered him as he entered. But he was in a citizen's dress, and went with a determination, as it appeared, not to be known.

The two boxes next, and each side the king's, were for the evening taken by the La Fayette family. There are places in each for six persons, two in front, and three deep. The General, Mrs. S—— of Baltimore, (a particular friend of Madame George La Fayette,) two of the General's grand-daughters, Col. C——, an officer of his household, and myself, filled the box to the left of the king's. Mrs. S—— and myself were placed in the front seats, notwithstanding our entreaties that the General would take one of them; two of his grand-daughters had the two next, and the General was quite back where it was impossible for any one below to see him.

The first piece was an opera, "*Le Dieu et la Bayadère.*" In this I saw the performance of M'lle Taglioni, the first dancer in the world. Much of this French opera dancing is what it should not be; but of Taglioni, though expected much, yet her performance perfectly astonished me; and I exclaimed in a *pas seul,* where she seemed divested of terrestrial gravity, and to fly, rather than dance, "this is the sublime of dancing!"

The scenery of the theatre—the splendor of the dresses and decorations—the crowds of actors, all capital in their parts—the perfection of instrumental music displayed by the grand orchestra, who were all so perfect in time, that it was as if one spirit played the numberless instruments—all this was admirable.

After we had been in the theatre about half an hour, an officer entered the box, bowed very low, and presented the General a paper, containing a few lines, written, as I observed, in an elegant hand. He looked rather grave, and perplexed for a moment as he read the paper; then said— "the king has sent for me to come to him. I must go, but I will return." I begged him not to return on my account, if it would incommode him; but he said he could not consent to lose all the pleasure of the evening. Before he returned, the first piece was over; and those of the La Fayette family, in the other box, came in the interval, to greet us. Their countenances seemed a little shaded, and I thought they were uneasy that he had insisted on sitting so far back. Mrs. S——, then took her place behind my chair, and all appeared determined that he should take the front seat, when he returned. Just as they had completed the arrangement, he came in, but he refused to go forward. Mrs. S—— now refused to take the seat, as did the other ladies also, who were in the box with us. Just then the sweet Mathilde La Fayette came from the other box to speak to her grand father. He told her to take the seat; and though she would not for the world have done so impolite thing by voluntarily taking the precedence of older ladies; yet she did not a moment dispute, what she saw was her grand-father's will.

Thus seated and arranged, we went through another dancing piece. It was the *ballet* pantomime of *Manon Lescaut*. The scenery and the dresses, represented the court of Louis XV. The stiff bows and curtsies—and hoops and trains, and elbow cuffs—the frizzed and powdered heads, and enormous head-dresses—the silk-velvet, gold-trimmed, long-skirted coats, and silver embroidered white satin vests—the little boys and girls dressed like their fathers and mothers, and curtsying and bowing as stiffly—the dancing of minuets—slow, and graceful, and formal—it was all pleasing: and the representation was historically true.

Gen. La Fayette was much amused. "Why," said he, "this is exactly my time!" "Voilà ce petit enfant!" exclaimed Mathilde, as a little boy, a sprig of nobility, in a long embroidered coat, and flapped vest, with his hair queued and powdered, appeared upon the stage. Said the General, "I was dressed *just so* when I was of that age!" "*Just so.*"

That piece went off. But I observed that the eyes of the people, were ever and anon, turning towards our box—and when at another interval, we rose from our seats, as every body did, suddenly there was a shout, "*Vive La Fayette! Vive La Fayette!*" It resounded again and again, and was echoed and re-echoed by the vaulted roof. In the enthusiasm of the moment, I exclaimed, "you are discovered—you must advance!"—and I handed him over the seats, unconscious at the moment that I was making myself a part of the spectacle. He advanced, bowed thrice, and again retreated—but the cries continued. Then the people called out "*la Parisienne! la Parisienne!*" You know it is the celebrated national song of the last revolution.

The curtain rose. Nourrit, an actor who, in the former piece had the principal male part, came forward. He was dressed as a Parisian gentleman. His figure was bold, and he bore in his hand an ample standard, which he elevated, waving the tri-colored flag. He had himself, been one of the heroes of the three days.[2] He sung the song in its true spirit, amidst repeated applauses. When he came to the part where it speaks of La Fayette, with his white hairs, the hero of both worlds, the air was rent with a sudden shout. I looked at him, and met his eye. There was precisely the same expression as I marked, when we sung to him in Troy; and again I shared the sublime emotions of his soul, and again they overpowered my own. My lips quivered, and irrepressible tears started to my eyes. When the song was over, the actor came and opened the door of the box, and in his enthusiasm embraced him. "You sung charmingly," said La Fayette. "Ah General, you were here to hear me!" was the reply.

When we descended to leave the theatre, the thronging multitude reminded me of the time, when crowds for a similar purpose assembled in America. The grand opera house is an immense building. In the lower part is a large room, supported by enormous pillars, and used as a vestibule. To this room the crowd had descended, and here they had arranged themselves on each side of a space, which they had left open for La Fayette, that they might see, and bless him as he passed. There was that in this silent testimonial of their affection, more touching, than the noisy acclaim of their shouts. There was something too, remarkable in the well defined line which bounded the way left open. A dense crowd beyond—not even an intruding foot, within the space, which gratitude and veneration had marked. I can scarcely describe my own feelings. I was with him, whom from my infancy I had venerated as the best of men; whom for a long period of my life I had never hoped even to see in this world. Now I read with him his noble history, in the melting eyes of his ardent nation. And I saw that he was regarded as he is, the father of France—aye, and of America too. America! my own land! It was for her sake I was thus honored, and it was for me to feel her share in the common emotion. My spirit seemed to dilate, and for a moment, self-personified as the genius of my country, I enjoyed to the full his triumph, who is at once her father, and her adopted son.

There are rumours of wars. I think the people of France, especially the young men, desire it. This, and the trial of the ministers, are the theme of conversation, go where I will.[3]

Some of my best hours are spent with Mr. Cooper and his family. I find in him, what I do not in all who bear the name of Americans, a genuine American spirit. His conversation on various subjects, particularly his descriptions of scenery, are delightful. He sometimes sets before me the vales of Italy; sometimes he makes me see the white spectral form, of a distant mountain among the Alps; or hear amidst their profound gulfs, the roar of a cataract, which falls to some viewless chasm below. I often tell him, that I hope he will give us a work, whose scene shall be laid in Switzerland, so deeply does its scenery seem impressed upon his mind, and so finely do his words delineate it. One day I told him the report, with regard to his having borrowed the plot of his "Wish-ton-Wish" from Miss Sedgewick's "Hope Leslie." He said, that he had never read "Hope Leslie" in his life, nor had he heard of the subject of it at the time of writing his book. This would perhaps be considered incredible, but for the fact, that he reads little. He prefers originals to copies, and studies nature. My last minute for writing has come. God's blessing be with all my dear household.

Yours, ever.

Letter to Mrs. A. H. Lincoln, Continued

We may make many valuable improvements from the instruction of French women in regard to dress, which after all, is no unimportant affair to a woman. They certainly observe economy in some things, beyond the women of our country. Their nice things are not put on in the morning, or worn in patrolling the streets. They regard a *grande toilette* in the morning, as decidedly vulgar; at the same time I must exonerate them from the charge, as far as I have had opportunity to observe, of wanting neatness.

A plain dress of calico, or of some cheap material, made close—a kerchief of plain Jaconet muslin or *tulle*,* finished at the neck with ruffles exquisitely quilled or plaited, and a cap of tulle, completes the

---

* Cotton lace.

morning costume of a French lady. The queen of France would not be so ungenteel as to wear a cap of blonde, or the princesses, her daughters, to wear dresses very low in the neck, or of slight material, before dinner; which here is ordinarily at six o'clock.

In the care taken of their dresses, the French ladies observe economy. I have learned many useful things in the manner of folding dresses to lay away, and packing them to travel. If a good dress was to be laid on a closet shelf for only a day, it would be folded with the utmost nicety, and pinned in a large napkin. It then comes out unwrinkled, and apparently fresh.

The use of large napkins at the dinner table, is another way by which they display care in this particular. The practise too, of covering the chairs and sofas of salons, with covers of brown linen, which are kept clean by frequent changing, has no doubt its origin in the same spirit of nicety, though it saves the elegant cushions of the chairs also, which are often of beautiful figured material, of some delicate color.

More regard is paid to convenience and health in morning costumes in France, than with us in America. It being now winter, their morning dresses are generally made with linings throughout, and frequently with a slight wadding inserted. Ladies here never walk the streets with thin shoes, unless they have a pair of clogs over them.

In what I have said of the neatness of the French ladies, I judge more particularly from those I have lived with. Madame B—— and her two daughters are models in this respect. Their bed-rooms are as neat as their persons. In most of the French families where I am in the habit of making morning visits, I find the ladies in neat and becoming, though simple attire, but I see some opposite examples.

The ladies, as they walk the streets, sometimes make a sorry figure. The trimmings of their hats, from the humidity of the climate, are apt to get a stringy crestfallen look. A kind of cloak is now quite in vogue, and worn by the most respectable ladies, made of a sort of woollen cloth, which looks like a thin inner blanket of a New-England housewife—dyed in the yarn, and woven like kerseymere; presenting checks of about an inch square, of different colors. Some of these cloaks, have these checks alternately of deep and pale blue; some of deep and pale red; and though a Parisian lady wears such a cloak to church, and in the streets, I am sure a New-England woman would not, on account of its vulgar appearance.

What I have said of their dress for the streets, is to be understood mainly of their shopping excursions, which take them through narrow and muddy walks. All make these when they have real business. The newspapers, which give an account of all the out-door proceedings of the King's family, frequently say, that at such an hour, Madame Adelaide, the king's sister, and his two oldest daughters went out to make purchases.

I never knew a French woman guilty of making a shop-keeper, show her things merely for her own diversion. When the ladies go out for morning visits, for a promenade in the garden of the Tuileries, or take the fashionable drive two or three miles west of Paris in the *Bois de Boulogne*, they dress with care, yet suitably to the occasion.

Although I did not intend when I came to Paris, to change much the fashion of my dresses, yet as I find real improvements, I am pleased to adopt them, for the sake of utility and health, and besides, I find myself in a manner obliged, in the circle in which I am, to conform in a degree to the modes here.

Yet though I endeavour so far to conform to the customs, as not to disgrace my acquaintances, still in some things, I will have my own ways. If I happen to hit upon something a little new, which takes, they give me more credit for it, than if I had written a good book; but if it does not, then I have trials. You know I would never have my ears bored. Of course I do not wear ear-rings, and it really requires no small independence of character to get along with it. On a subject of such importance as this, even French politeness sometimes fails. The ladies seem to speak of it, as if it were a kind of deformity; and one advised me, to fasten ear-rings by strings passing over my ears. Sometimes, when I am asked the reason of my singularity in this respect, I say, (speaking according to the rule for answering questions, given in the book of Proverbs,) that I always fancied, I had an uncommonly well-shaped ear, and could not bear to spoil it. If I had had a homely one, I should not have minded making a hole in it, and drawing it down to an acute angle. One gentleman asked me if it was unfashionable in America to wear ear-rings. "Oh no," I told him. "Men as well as women wore them there; not only at the bottom of the ear, but throughout the whole rim, and in their noses besides."

One evening, after I was dressed to go out, I stepped into the salon to wait for a carriage. Among other company, there was a great beau of an old bachelor, who knows almost every thing; speaks four languages, sings, and plays the piano, makes speeches that would grace a novel to us all in our turns, sometimes standing and sometimes kneeling: and who is as renowned for impudence, as for learning and accomplishments. After making his elegant bow, "Madam," said he, "if you were my wife, I should order you to change that turban for a cap, since you refuse to wear ear-rings." "When I am your wife," said I, "you will find me very obedient. I hear the carriage—bon soir."

It is incredible what a nice eye, a French woman has, for dress and personal appearance. It is like a musician, whose ear has become so acute, that he discovers discords, where to ordinary persons, there seems perfect harmony. But they are not in dress, what they are sometimes supposed in our country to be, dashing and finical; but they really understand the matter, and their taste is chaste and correct, and though I will not relinquish my fixed principles, either of morals or taste, yet I endeavor to profit by it; for whatsoever things are really lovely, are to be thought of. Besides, they invent a thousand convenient methods, which I like to learn; many of which I hope to show you when I return. I go through all the shops where various articles of dress are made, and when I see something new, which is promising, buy a specimen to carry home.

Whatever they may have been in times past, the French women at this day, are more simple and natural in their dress in many respects, than the American. They dress their own hair without false curls; and this is considered, (truly I think) more becoming, even when their locks are partially changed by age. At first, the grey hair of ladies, past their youth, elegantly curled and put up, and worn in evening parties without hat or cap; or if these were used appearing in front; had something unpleasing in its aspect. But in truth, the hair, the complexion, and the figure each suit the other; and why should ladies conceal grey hairs more than gentlemen? Some of these ladies, prove as I am told, the most dangerous of coquettes. Yet notwithstanding the assertion of a young gentleman, made in the height of his passion for a woman of twice his age, that he considered a lady's beauty materially improved

by her hair's becoming a little grey; yet I am far from believing that
this opinion is generally held. I am told there are persons in Paris who
earn their living by plucking the white hairs from ladies heads; and
gentlemen's too, for aught I know. One day my consequential French
hair-dresser, who comes regularly before dinner, fell into a grave discourse with my sewing woman, on the point, how far in the case of
female beauty, art would make up for the deficiencies or decays of nature; and he ended by uttering, "*des cheveux et les dents! voilà l'essen-
tiel!*"* [. . .]

Apropos to affectation—the French ladies sometimes accuse the
American women of this fault. They praise most those here, who are
the most entirely free from it. Mrs. S——, of B——, they often speak
of, on account of the sweet simplicity of her manners and dress.
American gentlemen they admire. There is some truth in these distinctions. In France there is more affectation among the men than the
women; with us, more among the women than the men. But general
rules, you know, have their exceptions.

Letter to Mrs. ——
Paris, March 22d, 1831

Dear Madam:
You wish to know, when I speak of the danger into which our
young American women may fall in Paris, what I mean; and whether
any thing appears, on the face of society, other than the most perfect
decency.

Not generally, unless you reckon as out of its pale, very low-necked
dresses, and such dances as the waltz and galopade. These dances may
do for girls, who are guarded as the French females are before marriage—never being left alone, with those who might seek to repeat, in
private, the freedoms taken with their persons in public.

But the danger lies in associating with those, who, while they are
living in the transgression of God's commands, have all the fascina-
tions of accomplished manners; and whom they see received exactly
as others. They may occasionally, too, hear shocking principles ut-

---

* The hair and the teeth! These are the essentials!

tered, by those whose opinions they see no reason for not respecting. We never hear characters scanned in Paris, as with us, as to the moral tendency of their actions. The standard of good society has nothing to do with such trifling circumstances; and it is the height of impertinence to inquire into them, or make any remarks concerning them. Not that a French woman does not take into consideration respectability—right and wrong; but respectability, concerns a person's connections, style of living, &c., and right and wrong, relate to the right and wrong of caps and hats, dresses and ribbons.

In this state of affairs, if we go into promiscuous society, you see how impossible it must be for a young woman, to form any kind of judgment, as to the real characters of those she may meet. Perhaps among the splendid dames, I met at court, was she, who was once Madame Tallien: now married to an Italian prince, and, as I am told, well received there. You will, I dare say, recollect her as the infamous woman, who was drawn shamefully through the streets of Paris, during the old revolution, to personate the goddess of reason. I heard a respectable lady speak of her, and laughing at so witty a story, relate how she used to introduce to her visiters, her numerous group of children, (no two of which she probably named after the same father) telling them to "look at her little sins."

A single lady, of great personal elegance, whom I often met, I learnt, by indubitable circumstances (which came to my knowledge many weeks after my introduction to her) was the *chère amie* of a married man: and among my acquaintances, other cases of the same nature, as far as morality is concerned, rose to my suspicion, if not to my knowledge.

In general, however, nothing can be more modest than the demeanor, in society, of all we meet. But once in a while, one may chance to see an adroit maneuvre of a different complexion. Once, in a room where few were present, I saw, by a sudden turn, a lady of whom I never heard ill, touch her lips to the neck of a gentleman, as he stooped for some object beside her.

As a specimen of the principles one may chance to be edified with in Paris, I will tell you what I heard said by a French lady, who was perhaps piqued by the rude remark of a gentleman, who, after praising the American females, said he would not dare to trust French women as wives. The lady, whose own correctness I never heard impeached, observed: Well, I own I am no friend to marriage—how absurd to make one promise to love the same person forever! Why, it is impossible. Give me nothing to eat, but a leg of mutton all my days, and I should starve to death.

Is not this enough to show you, that American women, especially if young and inexperienced, are better off at home, than here. True, a young woman, under the care of a watchful matron, and guarded by dignity of manners and innate purity, may escape these dangers.

Yet Heaven forbid, that I include all French women in this censure—and as I have before remarked, there are some better signs in these times. The two families now most placed in the public eye, are those of Louis Phillippe, and La Fayette. The Queen is believed by all, to be a pattern of conjugal virtue; and nothing appears, but that her daughters will emulate her worthy example. The La Fayettes are as much American, as French, in their manners, and could they give the tone to society, France would be not less indebted to them, than to the venerated Patriarch of the family. And many other ladies, I know, of whom I am equally confident, that their cast of moral character is such, as cannot dwell with depravity in its vilest form.

That I am not severe beyond truth, a fact which stares in the face of a stranger, as soon as he opens his guide book, is sufficient evidence. More than one third of the children, born in Paris, are born out of wedlock. And what is wedlock here, in too many instances, but a license to sin with the greater impunity? Yet, while thus iniquity is abroad, the obligations of virtue are known, and tacitly acknowledged; else, why the hypocritical decency which the general face of society presents? Why the convenient accommodations to give privacy to sin, and to its consequences?

How shocking are those consequences to the innocent beings who are cursed for their parents' guilt! Never did I see a sight which so afflicted my heart, as the infants at the Hospital of the Foundlings. Here were hundreds of babes ranged along in little beds, or laid on inclined couches to receive the warmth of a stove. Young nurses were feeding them with pap, or standing carelessly around; while moanings and shriekings were in my ears, from the little pallid sufferers, which, as it were, withered my soul within me. And where, ye little innocents, I mentally exclaimed, where are the fathers, who should have shielded your helpless infancy! Where the mothers, whose bosoms should have warmed and fed you! Perchance they shine in the court, or are charioted along the streets, engaged in new intrigues. Surely, God will bring these things into judgment.

In walking through an apartment where were many beds for the infants, I came to one place, where were thirty or forty, which had the white curtains suspended from the frame work above, dropped; and the little bed was entirely enclosed. These, said a lady, who pulled me by the sleeve, as I was about to raise one of the curtains—these, contain the dead! I turned away, heartstricken, and left the Hospital as soon as I could. It is true, these dismal sights were sometimes relieved, by a Sister of Charity, who seemed really intent upon her charge: and here and there an infant, apparently healthy, smiled, unconscious of its condition, and the life of servitude and degradation, to which it was abandoned.

I know that benevolent intentions, were in the hearts of those who founded this institution; and now actuate those devoted women, who thus give their days and nights to labor and watchfulness. It is said, these Hospitals prevent the crime of infanticide. But they cannot save the lives of the infants, who perish by hundreds, deprived of their natural aliment. If we urge that such institutions encourage crimes of another kind, we are told that these infants are often the children of the virtuous poor, who cannot support them. Why, then, if they are the children of the virtuous poor, are they thus mysteriously received in a basket, at the entrance, and no questions asked? I am no friend to disguises—they betoken no good—and think it is wrong in the outset to encourage them. Let vice wear her own colors. The virtuous part of society are not responsible for those crimes, which they denounce and discourage, but when men undertake to do, or countenance evil, that good may come, they always, in the long run, do more hurt than good.

The French are certainly worthy of imitation, in the facility with which persons of either sex, adapt themselves to their situation. No matter who their relations are, or what their former situation may have been—if poverty comes, or if they see it approaching, they betake themselves to some profitable occupation, not concealing their situation, and living on in splendor, at the expense of others.

Much evil among us, originates in a prejudice from which the French seem, in a great measure, free—that there is something degrading in a woman's doing any thing to earn money. In families with us, where the father employs his hands from morning till night in cutting off yards of calico, as tying up pounds of tea, not for charity—but for profit—his daughters would consider it a shocking degradation to employ theirs, to earn money, by making caps, or hats, or dresses for others.

Though I have been sometime in Paris, and I have not been an inattentive observer of the frame of society here, especially in cases where my own sex are concerned, yet I am sensible that I do not understand it sufficiently, to pronounce with decision on points, in which as a woman, desirous to promote the good of my sex, I feel an interest. Women here, as is well known, act a more conspicuous part in business affairs, than is common in Great Britain or America. The laws too are different; a married woman not being here a nullity. In so far as this may lead to profligacy of manners, I should condemn it.

But in order that the experiment should be fairly tried here, it would be necessary that Paris should be divested of other causes of profligacy, and then we should know whether a woman's coming forward in mercantile and other business, would of itself produce it. Take from the city its indecent pictures and statues. Let men take their consciences into their own hands. Let them no longer believe that sin can be paid for in money; but believe that it is an account to be settled with the just and omniscient Judge, every man for himself, without other Mediator than the man Christ Jesus; and see then if the useful, though it might be the more public industry of women, than that which is common with us, would produce disorders in society. I do not say it would not, but of this I am confident—that in our frame of society, by going to the opposite extreme, the evils are often produced, which it would seem to be the leading tendency of our customs to avoid.

For example, suppose with us a young man with sufficient experience in business to conduct it, but without property, becomes acquainted with a young woman, it may be well educated, but also without property. He loves her, but it checks the native impulse of his affections, because he fancies that his pretty wife must be kept dressed like a doll, and in an elegant parlor, and he has not the means. So he looks out for a woman who has money, and marries her, though he loves her not—or he lives unmarried—but in either case, he is the man to resort to the haunts of vice—perchance to seduce the innocent. And the woman he loved—perhaps had understood the language of his eyes—felt that his heart was hers, and given her own in return—and she now secretly pines in solitary celibacy. In a country like ours, where industry is rewarded, such things betoken something wrong in custom concerning our sex. Our youth thus throw away their individual happiness; and incur the chance of becoming bad members of society. And the fault does not lie with the men, other than this, that they seem not to have the courage to endeavor to break wrong customs. They are willing to be industrious in their calling, but custom prohibits the woman from becoming that meet and suitable help to the man, for which her Creator designed her. An educated woman, might become to a merchant, his bookkeeper, and as it were a silent partner in his business—keeping a watch over other agents during his absence—giving him notice of important events, which concern the state of markets—and in fine, she might render a thousand important services in his affairs, without neglecting the care of her household concerns, the drudgery of which might be performed by uneducated persons, the value of whose time would be trifling to the family, compared with what hers might be made. Understanding the business affairs, and taking an interest in the advancement of the family property, more than in the finery of her dress and furniture, she would need no stern mandate to keep in the ways of economy. If her husband is taken away by death, he parts in peace, as to the condition of his wife and children, for she will know how to settle his affairs, or continue his business.

These reflections I have been led to make by what I remark here. There are shops which I frequent to make purchases, where great order prevails, and which I am told are wholly under the direction of the mistress, in their interior arrangements. One I recollect, a little out of the northwestern Boulevard, where there are two rooms—one below, and the other above. The mistress, a grave and decided woman, keeps her stand behind a counter on one side the door, with a female assistant by her side. They do all the writing in the books. The clerks, of whom there are several, do the selling part; but whatever articles I bought, they were not made into a parcel, till they were carried with the bill, and the money to her, and the three compared. Then she and her assistant put down in their books the articles, and the account received. And I am told that the whole is compared with the state of the shop, before it is closed, so that the clerks have no chance of purloining goods or money. I asked where were the husbands of these women, and was told that they were abroad making purchases—attending to the payments, and watching the state of the markets. Now I do not believe that a woman in a situation like that, industriously employed, is in a more dangerous place than when she is idle in her parlor, or reading novels, or receiving calls from gossips, or lounging fops. But I think a middle course between public exposure and the utter uselessness of some of the wives of our shopkeepers, especially those who board, instead of keeping house, might be devised; particularly where they are women of intelligence and education.

But this is a subject on which I could write a book, if I had time. Indeed, this letter will become one, if I do not bring it to a speedy close.

Adieu, dear Sister.

2

Abby Jane Morrell

࿔

At the age of twenty-four, Abby Jane Wood Morrell (born 1809) left her son at home in the care of her mother and set off on a commercial expedition to hunt seals with her husband, Benjamin, a mercantile seaman and the captain of the schooner *Antarctic*, in which they sailed. Her adventure, which began on 2 September 1829 and ended on 27 August 1831, carried her to New Zealand, New Guinea, the Philippines and other islands in the South Pacific, the Antarctic, Madagascar, Singapore, the Cape of Good Hope, St. Helena, the Azores, and France. She dedicates her account of this voyage, entitled *Narrative of a Voyage to the Ethiopic and South Atlantic Ocean, Indian Ocean, Chinese Sea, North and South Pacific Ocean, in the Years 1829, 1830, 1831* (1833), "To my countrywomen, the happiest of their sex, born in a land of liberty, educated in a knowledge of virtue and true independence, single by choice, or wedded with their own consent, friends to the brave, and patrons to the enterprising."

The selection that follows reproduces the Advertisement and Preface for Morrell's book and Chapters 2, 8, and 12 in their entirety. In her descriptions of foreign lands, Morrell focuses on such features as birds (including the albatross), flowers, and ambergris. Colonizer and proponent of international trade, she discusses aspects of transculturation: the conduct of missionaries, the hostility of natives, the conditions for seamen, the effects of intoxicating liquor, the progress of discovery and colonization, and the restriction of trade. Her Advertisement and her Preface typify the assumption of separate spheres of activity for men and women that informs many accounts of travel, for either rhetorical or philosophical reasons.

Narrative of a Voyage

Advertisement

The reader will perceive a similarity, at least of outline, between this work and a part of the larger volume of Capt. Benjamin Morrell,[1] published in December last, containing a narrative of the four voyages of that adventurous navigator; in the last of which he discovered several groups of hitherto unknown islands, and had the misfortune to lose a portion of his crew by the treachery of the savage inhabitants. [. . .]

The narrative of Capt. Morrell is essentially practical and descriptive; and its contents are the results of a sailor's observations: the present work is of a more reflective character, and exhibits the impressions made upon the mind of an educated female by scenes and occurrences so different from those which it is the lot of women generally to encounter. [. . .]

The scenes and adventures of which Mrs. Morrell was a witness were highly interesting in their nature, and it is believed that an account of them, divested of nautical technicalities and descriptions purely maritime, will be read with pleasure, especially by readers of her own sex and country.

Preface

When I took up my pen to prepare my journal for publication, I intended to make nothing more than a plain narrative of the events of my voyage, interspersed with such general remarks as might suggest themselves to my mind. But as I proceeded, I felt an irrepressible desire to make some observations on a subject which has become an object of no small interest to philanthropic sympathy—I mean the amelioration of the condition of American seamen. I believe that their habits can be reformed, and it requires no arguments to prove how much this reformation would subserve the best interests of commerce.

It may be thought strange that a woman should take up a subject so foreign to those which generally occupy the attention of her sex. It was, however, deeply impressed on my mind that, being a woman, I was in some measure better qualified to offer a few suggestions on this subject than any one engaged in the navy or the merchant service. A writer so situated might be suspected of wishing to effect promotion or of seeking employment; and knowing the dislike the public have to remarks coming from a quarter where interest or prejudice may be mingled with the information offered, I thought they might at least expect sincerity from me. With all my earnestness to make these remarks, I tremble when I think I am about to offer them for the consideration of the public. Perhaps they will listen to me kindly. It has been said, that when Napoleon was brooding over his disasters no one dared approach him but a pet child, who played around him and induced him to take nourishment and repose. Let the public therefore consider me in the capacity of the child; and if there be any force in my suggestions, they will go for what they are worth; if there be none, why they will pass off with a smile.

It is seldom, indeed that a female can know any thing upon this subject; but as I have had some opportunity of becoming acquainted with it, I hope I may be excused for venturing to give my opinion. I should be proud to be one of the humble instruments in improving the condition and raising the moral and intellectual standard of that race of men which ever has and ever will share in the prosperity and glory of our country. In life I would ask no higher gratification than to learn that the work of reform was going on successfully; and desire no other earthly honour after death than an inscription on my tombstone declaring that the ashes of the mariner's friend repose beneath.

Narrative

[Chapter 2]

Frequently on our passage from the island of Desolation to Lord Auckland's group, we could not keep a fire to cook any thing, for the waves often swept over us; and our sails were splitting and spars were falling around us every day. It was on the 29th of December that we reached this group, and at eleven in the morning the crew went on shore to get shellfish and other things that we wanted, while the vessel was riding safely at anchor in a fine harbour. I amused myself in listening to the sweet notes of the ten thousand beautiful birds warbling among the forest trees, within fifty yards from the stern of the

Antarctic. I had been assisted to the deck by my husband and brother, and weak as I was, I felt new life at the scene. In the ecstasy of the moment, I felt that all the flowers were opening to receive me—that the birds sang a joyous welcome for me—and the "incense-breathing morn" was charming to my senses. To one who has escaped the dangers of the sea—who has been long prostrate upon a sick-bed—a gleam of sunshine is reviving; but now all my senses were banqueting at once. If ever gratitude to my Maker penetrated my heart, it was at this moment; if ever I poured out that heart, it was at such enjoyments as I now felt. Such moments as these are an equivalent for long days and nights of pain. The sea around me was full of albatrosses and aquatic birds of all sorts which are found in a temperate climate. The land was picturesque—the hills beginning to rise almost from the water's edge, with deep valleys between them, each terminating at the shore in small caves. The forests were very luxuriant, and showed the strength and fertility of the soil, which was covered with numerous plants not common to my own country. I noticed several that I was acquainted with, and many that I did not know. One plant here deserves to be particularly mentioned: it is a species of flax that bears a yellow flower, and grows near the seashore, and sometimes far up the hills. The threads of the heart are silky; and, in the opinion of my husband, it might be raised in our southern states, and by its abundant growth and easy cultivation soon supersede hemp-fields, as well as those of flax. The season here at this time answers to our July; though not uncomfortably warm at any part of the day, the thermometer not rising above 65° at noon. The land-birds were large brown and green paroquets, large wood-pigeons, and a great variety of small birds. Among the latter there is a green bird, about the size of a robin whose melody is so fine, and his notes so varied, that one might imagine himself regaled by a hundred different sorts of songsters at once. The animals here are mostly strangers to man, and have but little fear of him. It is seldom that they hear the murderous gun of the sportsman; and the ornithologist in his rambles around the globe has, perhaps, never been here to write the biographies of these tenants of the forest. The fish here are good, and can be had at all times.

On the 4th of January we sailed from the Auckland group; our vessel was in fine order, and we seemed to set out as on a new voyage.

The group at which we were so much refreshed lies in south latitude 50° 40′, and 166° 4′ east longitude.

In the 6th of this month we saw the south cape of New-Zealand. The boats were sent to examine the shore, but found no fur-seal upon them, the obtaining of which was one object of the voyage. The boats continued to examine the shores of the south-east and east sides of Night Island. The winds were light and the weather fair, and on the 12th of January, at noon, we had a visit from the natives, who came off to us in a war-canoe, which contained about fifty men, two of whom were principal chiefs, from Flat Point. These chiefs were whimsically tattooed; their ears marked, and their bodies stamped with red or blue. From all that we could learn, their chief occupation is war. They carry about them greater variety of offensive and defensive weapons than most other savages. Their looks are bold and fierce, and they have no small share of martial dignity. Like other savages they delight in the war-song, and carry their phrensy and fury to the greatest excess. They have been, as near as I could learn, cannibals, and now, when prisoners are taken, they frequently cut from them while alive pieces of flesh and masticate it, to show their fury and fiendish joy at their success. Their dexterity in the use of their war-clubs, spears, &c., is said to be surprising. Their affections are strong; they mourn their dead with all those marks of phrensy so often described to us as belonging to savage life. They cut themselves—tear their flesh—and utter the most piercing cries. Polygamy is allowed among them; a chief having two or three wives, or perhaps as many as he wishes to maintain; or it may be that the number marks the rank of the warrior or chief. The females are generally quite young, many of them mothers at the age of twelve or fourteen. Ignorance is the mother of superstition, and these savages have it to a great extent. Their priests are arbitrary, and keep them in fear, being under that bondage themselves. I have marked that they observe their fasts and their prayers from impressions of fear. The love of God is not known where ignorance abounds; it is that love, properly known, that casteth out all fear. Some of these superstitions make them vigilant and daring, as well as cautious; they believe that the spirit of him who was killed and devoured by his enemies suffers everlasting punishment in the world of spirits, but if rescued and buried his spirit ascends to the abode of their gods. This opinion generally prevails throughout all the southern hemisphere among savages. These savages have more curiosity than our North American Indian are said to have, for they examined the Antarctic [the ship] with great scrutiny and apparent delight, and took their departure in the most peaceful manner. We continued the examination of the shores, holding frequent intercourse with the natives.

On the 19th of January we saw Cape Briton, and soon after came to anchor in the Bay of Islands, about five miles east of the missionary establishment, where we found several English whaling-ships, viz. the ship George, Captain Gray, from London: the Royal Sovereign, Captain King, and the Thetis, Captain Gray, from the same place. These were skilful, enterprising navigators, and very gentlemanly men. They all treated us with the greatest kindness, and I dined on board of each in turn, and received every attention that could be paid to a female in a distant country, whose very situation excites some sympathy and great courtesy. It is pleasant, if it is even at the farthest side of the globe, to be where national prejudices are forgotten, and all are of the same family. It is impossible for those who speak the same language not at times to love one another.

On the 29th of January, 1830, the English captains, my husband, and myself, went to pay our respects to the good people of the missionary establishment. My heart was overflowing at being once more in the embraces of Christian friends. Oh! there is religion in the world, said I mentally, when I saw the accomplished females who had left all the comforts of society and the charms of friendship in England, to come to these shores of heathenish ignorance and ferocity, for the sake of extending the Redeemer's kingdom, putting their trust in him, and overcoming the vanities of this world. Their labours were incessant; for they did not allow themselves more than eight hours out of the twenty-four for repose and meals. All the rest were devoted to civilizing and Christianizing the natives. The male missionaries work many hours in the field, clothed in duck frocks and trousers, with the natives, learning them to cultivate their lands. They then spend several hours in the day in teaching the natives to read and write, and to understand the precepts of our holy religion. The wives and daughters of these pious labourers are engaged in teaching the females to sew and to read. The natives are devout and tractable. These missionaries seemed to have as many under their care as they could readily teach, and their influence was spreading far and near, and is now extremely powerful. A few years ago not a ship's crew could land without arms and a guard, and perchance, some of them were massacred in attempting to get a little wood or water; but now they may travel anywhere to the extent of a hundred miles around the missionary dwellings, and eat and sleep in security, without guard or arms, or without fear. When a vessel arrives the natives are seen flocking to the shore, extending their arms to receive the white men from a distant country, bringing with them the fruits of their agriculture in great quantities, at the lowest prices. A quarter of a dollar here, I am positive, would purchase more than could be had in the New-York market for two dollars.

The common kitchen-garden vegetables are excellent, and in fine variety; some apples may be had, and the small meats and poultry are supplied in abundance. Beef is not as yet much in use, but soon will be raised, as much as will be required. When I thought of these changes, produced by such feeble means, I wondered how any one could doubt the truth and efficacy of the Christian religion. Here, without the shedding of one drop of blood, Christianity had been planted; it had been as the tree of life in a forest of the upas, and the healing in its leaves had brought out and spread abroad light and salubrity where once darkness and pestilence reigned.

The whole party remained with these good people until about four o'clock in the afternoon, when we proposed leaving; but they were anxious to have us all stay with them while we were on the coast. The captains declined, as they did not think it proper to sleep away from their vessels, for the wind often blows hard here, and sudden squalls are common, but my husband consented that I might stop for one night. Often when joining with them in their devotions I asked myself, can there be any thing selfish in this? is it not pure and undefiled religion before God? It can hardly be called before man, for there were no civilized men to observe them. How happy they seemed! Indeed, how happy they were, although so far removed from the dear country of their birth and the friends of their childhood. Even prayer itself is purified on such an occasion and in such a place; it was no great stretch of the imagination for me to think myself joining in the devotions of those who had lived in paradise in primitive innocence.

I now felt myself recruiting very fast, for I could walk a few rods without assistance, my limbs beginning to come to a natural state of feeling; but inflexible duty would not suffer my husband to linger here on any account. He came for me on the following day, and I was obliged to take a painful farewell of these holy people. Mr. Davis and his daughters, Mr. Williams and his wife and daughters, and some of the natives, came to take their leave of me. They prayed for my temporal and eternal happiness, and for my friends, and then sang a hymn that went to my soul, and waked up all its sympathies. They all accompanied me to the beach, and with tears, embraces, and kisses, I and my female friends parted—they to attend to duties, and I to be tossed again by the winds and waves, to encounter new hardships, and to enjoy new adventures. On my reaching the deck of the Antarctic I was received by my brother and our brave tars with three hearty cheers, which were repeated by the crews of the English ships alongside of us, and to close the scene these cheers were echoed and re-echoed by a thousand native voices, in the canoes and on shore.

The next day we could not sail as we expected, the wind blowing too fresh from the north. The natives, seeing this, were desirous that we should again come on shore, and an invitation for us to visit them came from the king and queen, which was accepted. This was the 23rd day of January, 1830. The boats of the Antarctic were prepared, and those of the ships joined, amounting in all to twelve whale-boats, handsomely manned. The natives had expected us, and came in myriads to see us. On touching the shore we were met by Kippy-Kippy, the king; the queen then approached, and extended her hand most courteously to welcome an American woman to her territory. Her appearance was affable and kind. After our greeting was passed, she waved a fan she held in her left hand, and at this signal more than seven thousand of her train, of both sexes, broke out into a song of joyous welcome; after which they gave three cheers that made the welkin ring. They then formed two double parallel lines, the females composing the inner, and the males the outer sections. As we advanced the females fell on their knees, and the males on one knee. I was carried on a sort of stage or chair, by six of their principal warriors, who proceeded with great state and solemnity, decorated with feathers of different kinds. Some of their ornaments were of surpassing beauty. The women all bore a green branch in their hands, and the heads of the men were ornamented with branches and feathers. When we came within fifty yards of the king's palace, the pathway was strewed with beautiful wild flowers, quite to the door, where we found elegant mats spread for at least ten yards square. The king now spread before us a superb banquet of the choicest fruits of his clime, and the young women entertained us with many songs, of no ordinary melody; after which the warriors gave us a war-dance for our amusement. There were at least two hundred of them. The king then came forward and made us a speech, and to my surprise, he spoke very good English. The substance of the oration was in praise of the missionaries. He said that before these good men came they knew nothing, but that now they were good men; that they could now lie down and sleep without fear of being killed by their enemies; that now they could sleep in peace; and that before these good men came, they had eaten human flesh, and thought it acceptable to their gods. The night coming on, I could not obtain all the information I could wish. I acquainted the queen that I must now leave her and go on board; at which she clasped me in her arms, and kissed me several times. She made me many presents of elegant mats and delicate shells, when I took my departure, and was attended to the boats with great ceremony. The bows being directed to our vessels, the tars, both English and American, dropped their oars at a signal, and the boats were propelled like dolphins through the water.

As soon as we left the beach, the natives gave three cheers, which were answered by our men with great glee. In a few minutes we reached the Antarctic, where we found a great many canoes alongside, loaded with potatoes and hogs in abundance, presents from the king and queen. It would be difficult after this to make me believe that missionaries could do no good among savages; such as we saw would do good anywhere. In a few short years all within their influence had been softened, and every one was anxious to be more enlightened. Some had all the gentleness that attends the polite and good in any country. The terrific monarch of fierce warriors was now as courteous as a man could be, brought up in the bosom of polished society, and at the very first opportunity made an open acknowledgement of his obligations to religion and letters. I did not consider that these honours were paid to me as an individual, but to all females of my own country and to those of the English nation.

The next morning, January 24th, we took leave of all our English friends and the natives, got under way, and put to sea with a fresh breeze and a light rain, bound to Manila. We continued on our voyage with occasionally thick weather and brisk breezes, until we reached the latitude of 1° 23' north, and longitude 170° 2' east. We now, February 16th, found ourselves in the north-east trade-winds, with fair weather, and on the 19th, in the morning, we saw Strong's Island, which lies in latitude 5° 58' north, and longitude 162° 55' east.

[Chapter 8]

Tercera is one of the Azores, which group is nine in number; some writers make more of them, by taking into the account some large rocks, but there are only nine islands of consequence, the principal one of which is called Tercera, measuring twenty-five miles in length, fifteen in breadth, and about fifty-four in circumference, the figure being, of course, rather elliptical than circular. This group lies in the Atlantic Ocean, about 36° to 40° north latitude, and from 25° to 35° west longitude. The Portuguese took possession of these islands in about 1446; some historians fix the date earlier and some later, and no precise time can be fixed for their discovery or possession. In former ages nature appears to have been at work in raising islands by volcanic power; but in later days she seems to have lost her vigour, or is disposed to quit her labours, for no island of importance has been thrown from the deep beds of ocean for the cultivation of man since the discovery of these islands by the Portuguese. The soil is productive, and oranges and grapes grow in great profusion. The climate is healthy, and though earthquakes sometimes terrify the inhabitants, still it is seldom that they cause any essential injury. It is the opinion of some philosophers that these islands are supported by volcanic arches, whose vast ovens are burning with perpetual fires; this is no very comfortable thought for those who keep it in mind, but the inhabitants here think this the garden of the world, or at least the place where it might be made; and it is most assuredly true that a finer climate can hardly be found than that of the Azores. The government, though arbitrary, is mild, and I could find no instances of oppression. These islands were once supposed to belong to Africa, by geographical position, but of late years they have been classed as European, for it is certain that the new race of inhabitants are Portuguese. Portugal has always held them in affection, because they were first known to them in modern times, and have been constantly under the protection of that government.

The whole island of Tercera, as far as I could see it, and we made frequent tours into the country, is but an exhausted volcano. So far as I have seen the islands of the sea through more than three hundred degrees of longitude, they appear to have been brought forth by volcanoes in the oceans of the east and west. It is true that they are at work now, but they must have been more active in former times than at present. The Portuguese here are a quiet and inoffensive people, but they are hardly acquainted with the growth of our country; they still think that we are in our infancy, as they measure all growths by length of years. They had heard of our settlement on the coast of Africa,[2] and spoke of it as a feeble attempt to get rid of our surplus black population; they think it will not last long, but we indulge in other hopes; and I feel persuaded that this is one of the most important colonies even planted since the settlement of North America. Its climate is as healthy as any we have ever known, notwithstanding the location. The settlement has flourished as well, and is increasing as fast, as did any of the American colonies, and their commerce is greater in proportion to the number of inhabitants. None are more attentive to the cultivation of mind and morals and their territory is unbounded, for the tenth part of Africa is not at present under cultivation. Most of this fifth part of the globe is wild as it was when the beasts of the field and birds of the air were its lords-proprietors. I can see nothing to prevent this colony from being the nucleus of nations; flourishing in arts and sciences, in commerce, in civil freedom, and all that constitutes a state. What can be more rational than these noble efforts to advance the interests of man, particularly degraded man? My nation and people are now doing something to wipe off a dark spot from their escutcheon.

If this colony is cherished, the United States will reap the advantages of it; they will get rid of their surplus population of blacks, and at the same time be planting a colony from whence great commercial results may be expected. I conceive that there is to be a change in a great portion of the globe, and that change will take place speedily. The agents and governors of the colonization society have been men of talents and perseverance: the most remarkable man, however, among them, was an African. The Rev. Lot Carey, who died not long since at Monrovia, was an extraordinary man. While he was a slave in Virginia, by his own industry and anxiety for knowledge, he learned to read and to write, and acquired so much general information that he was intrusted with the management of a large tobacco warehouse. In this business, by his perquisites and his industry in the time allowed him, he accumulated a sufficient sum of money to purchase, not only his own freedom, but that of his wife and children also. He was discreet, sober, and religious, and became a preacher of the gospel while yet a slave. Many who heard his discourses thought his views of the Bible were excellent. When the colonization society was formed, and Liberia purchased, he was ready at the commencement of the settlement to depart with the earliest settlers, and took his share in every labour. He acted not only as a spiritual guide, but as a civil magistrate, as deputy agent, and for a while, in the absence of Mr. Ashmun,[3] as chief magistrate of Liberia. In every situation which he was called to fill, he not only evinced the high powers of a gifted mind, but the pure spirit of a righteous man. If such specimens of intellect and virtue can be found rising up among slaves, what may we not expect from these people in a state of civil and religious freedom, enlightened by schools in every branch of knowledge?

This must be effected by exploring expeditions, by missionary societies, and by a universal temperance, which is rapidly pervading the whole population of the globe. These exploring expeditions should be got up by individual enterprise, assisted by government. Their failure the government will not be answerable for, but their success must of course be a national benefit. According to the present law of nations, discovery gives the right of possession, so far as it relates to any other power than the aborigines; if this should be considered of consequence, certainly the trade of lands discovered would for some time be of advantage to our commercial people. It were well, too, that we should do something for the world whose commerce we enjoy; we have now a name to support, and what have we done to raise its glory? Our whalers have done something worthy of remembrance, but this is all. To Nantucket, New-Bedford, Stonington, and a few other places, is most of the credit due for all the discoveries we have made in the Pacific Ocean. These enterprising men have traversed every sea in search of whales, and they have generally communicated to the world what they have found new or profitable. When the government has wanted information, they have been ready to communicate it from their very accurate and satisfactory journals; if no advantage has been taken of their discoveries, it is not their fault.

The next step to finding where savage men live is that of furnishing them the means of instruction; and this can only be done by sending enlightened missionaries to teach them civilization and Christianity. Wherever an intelligent missionary establishment is to be found, there good results have been witnessed, notwithstanding the abuse of some, and the fear of others; there is no exception to the rule. Civilized nations have heretofore carried intoxicating liquors to those they visited, and while they opened up the light of mind and religion to them, have taught them the vices found in corrupt associations of the civilized world. The poor wretches had acquired all the vices before they had been taught to practise a single virtue that they had not before known; thus civilization has heretofore been to them a curse instead of a blessing. But now it is otherwise; the refinements of society are taught them without its vices.

Ardent spirits have in general been an article of traffic in these regions, and the poor wretches have been cheated by proffering to their lips the intoxicating draught. It is the sweet recollection of our little voyage that we have never offered to the lips of primitive man one drop of ardent spirits; we have met them and drink the waters of their springs, and never said to them that there was any thing that an Indian would like better. I never saw an Indian inebriated, because we never gave him any thing to steal away his senses. It has been, as far as I am informed, the universal practice to carry ardent spirits to the people of these rude islands, and the baneful effects no one ever doubted while engaged in the traffic. Why should it not be made a penal, as it is a moral, offence to teach them drunkenness? There is a new and a better era to come than has as yet been known; for even the pilgrims of New-England gave the aborigines these strong waters in traffic. The visitors to these benighted regions should never let them know that such a thing as a drunken man ever existed. It is said by some that they already have inebriating delights among them; but this is true only to a certain extent, and that a very small one. They seldom make use of narcotics, or of any thing that entirely destroys their senses. The process of distillation they are unacquainted with, and but few simple juices are very inebriating. Of all the natives unaccustomed to Europeans, I never saw one who had any marks of intemperance about him. Travellers may say what they please of these natives in regard to intemperance, but they never bear any of the marks of it until they become acquainted with civilized man. The ava-root and other narcotics produce a stupefaction, but they leave no blotch, no laxity of muscle, no disgusting redness of the eyes, and all the wretched symptoms induced by the use of ardent spirits.

Missionaries, who should be at first school-masters, and then preachers, should be sent to every isle of the sea as well as to the continent. Letters should be first taught, with domestic arts; and then the high principles of morality and religion. If day-schools for children, and Sunday-schools for men, women, and children, should be established, I firmly believe that the work of refinement and morals would go rapidly on in any of those islands which we have visited, and which are now in darkness. The natural capacity of these savages, I believe, is not inferior to that of any people in the world. It is, I think—I go to no theorist for the doctrine—a law of nature, that wherever there is a fine physical organization among mankind, there mental capacity will be found also. This may be a mortifying doctrine to proud man in the old clans, tribes, or nations, but it is nevertheless true. I believe there is as much genius in some of the islanders we saw as can be found in France, England, or America. These new regions hardly ever see "The tenth transmitter of a foolish face"; but the natives are quick of perception in all the ordinary duties of life, and are also acute observers of passing events; they compare and combine most rapidly in every instance where they are called upon to act. I do not believe that He who made man has given any particular gifts to any one race. If there be any superiority, it is in giving to some of the islanders we saw a larger corporeal frame than to any race of men which history has ever enumerated. The progress of the improvement of these people depends on us; and we shall be answerable in future for the intelligence and virtue they shall possess. Much may be done at a little expense, for there are persons of good education who are willing to settle at these places if they could have the protection of government and the assistance of the charitable in their exertions. English will in a few years be the language of all the islanders where English or American missionaries are established; for as soon as the natives become more enlightened, they will find that their own scanty language will be insufficient to express their ideas; and picking up a little English from common intercourse with those who have come to teach them, they will be anxious to gain something more from day to day until they become proficients in English literature. They are, as I have said, imitative, and of course soon learn to write well: the chirography of Pomaré, which has been shown in the United States, was elegant—such as a professor of penmanship might be proud of. The missionaries are, at least all that I have seen, satisfied with the quickness and assiduity of the natives, and also with their docility when they become impressed with the idea that they are receiving some benefit from instruction, and that their teachers have no other object than to do them good. The missionaries should have nothing to do with trade; that must be left to others; for if these people once get the idea into their heads that the missionaries are labouring to gain wealth, that moment their influence is at an end, and their only protection will be a resort to arms. It is not from a sanguinary disposition that the natives make attacks on vessels that visit them, but from a desire to obtain what others have at the easiest rate.

On the 10th of June we arrived at Cadiz. The harbour is a noble one; the city is one of the finest in Spain, and, if properly garrisoned, must be capable of sustaining obstinate defence. I make these observations, begging the reader to understand that I know, or think I do, which is perhaps of quite as much importance, a good deal about the subject of defence, from hearing an almost perpetual conversation about the capability of defence of one place or another in parts of the world where there were no guns or castles, as well as in those which were strongly fortified. In this bay rode the proud navies of Spain in every age of Spanish greatness, from the invincible armada to the time Villeneuve sailed to be beaten at the battle of Trafalgar. This was the rendezvous of the navies of the New World. The Earl of Essex, the favourite of Queen Elizabeth, took this city in 1596; it has sustained several sieges, but was taken by the French in a late period of history. It is an old city, and no doubt is full of those things that interest a traveller whose views are directed to objects less superficial than those which strike the eye of the common observer. Our tastes change with our experience: at first we look at whatever stands most prominent, such as great and magnificent buildings, or striking peculiarities of the people; but we afterward direct our attention to more minute matters, which do not lie on the surface, and in all probability find more satisfaction in these researches than in gazing at what everybody sees, or has examined. But I was deprived of the pleasure of describing this city, as we were not permitted to stay there. This was at first surprising to me, for I could not conceive of any cause why I should not see the people of Cadiz; and I grieved the more at it, as I had informed my female friends at Manila that I was to visit Cadiz, and therefore was under various commands from them to some of their friends in the city. We were not permitted to stay in the port when it was known that we had come from Manila many months before, and that the cholera was there; our journals, also, showed that two of our men had died of this disorder. The authorities were very peremptory on this point, and threatened to fire into us if we did not depart instantly. This was silly as it was timid and arbitrary, for after so many months, if the disease had been contagious we were free from any infection, and could not have communicated it to the people of Cadiz. When we bring matters home to us, how much better do we reason than when our remarks are general. How ridiculous were these quarantine laws to us, who had been out of danger over the distance of nearly fifteen thousand miles of ocean! Not having a single man sick of any contagious disease, nor of any other, except accidental indisposition, we were forced to leave this port without discharging a particle of cargo, and to direct our course to Bordeaux. The sickness called the cholera, it is true, had been on board of our vessel, and carried off two of the crew, but those who early made known their sickness to my husband and myself were cured; these two were beyond assistance when we were informed of their sickness.

This disease did not then appear in my eyes as it since has. I considered it entirely an Asiatic disorder, and one that would be confined to that country. It had passed from the Hoogly and the Ganges to Manila, and was fatal among the lower classes of society, but was by no means confined to them; still the higher classes in Manila thought so little of it, or rather, perhaps, said so little about it, that I did not think much of its deadliness. The mortality among our sailors was less than usual, and therefore their deaths by this disease made no very deep impression on my mind. It was only after we were denied the hospitalities of Christians that I began to reflect on the selfishness of people in their fear of an epidemic.

I was aware that this sweeping disorder had entered Europe by way of Astracan, and had been very deadly, but little did I think it would ever spread over my own dear country; causing so great a panic that for nearly a mile in the principal street of New-York, at noonday, not half a dozen people could be seen.[4] Desolation had extended over all my native city; and while looking over my journal to prepare it for publication, every hour the house was filled with bulletins of the progress of this mighty scourge of mankind. The different symptoms and the different treatment were sufficient to distract every one. It was difficult to know what course to pursue when a person was attacked; and until the disease was far advanced, it was almost impossible to tell whether the patient was sick with it or not. The symptoms were almost as various as the patients; cramps, diarrhoea, and occasional spasms are general premonitions of the disease; no headache or dizziness marks its coming on, but rather, like the apoplexy, its forerunner was a high state of animal spirits. I never left New-York during the whole time it was raging in the city, and had an opportunity of witnessing its disorganizing effects on society, as well as the sufferings of those whom it has attacked. The deaths were numerous, and the disease came as a thief at night; but the disease, and even the deaths, were nothing to the alarm. This spread through all circles, and seemed to be a disease of itself, more malignant than the cholera. The constituted authorities did much, and the rich subscribed large sums of money, but if individuals in common life had not made exertions, personal and pecuniary, the sufferings would have been more intense than they were. Such sweeping calamities have a sad effect in many instances on the human mind; they dry up all the generous currents of the heart, and destroy all the wholesome ceremonies of burial and funeral honours. Although there are frequently unnecessary expenses attending a funeral, yet there is something dreadful in having a friend die in such a manner as to be hurried to the grave as a vile suicide who had no objects or wishes to live for. To have a being whom we love this hour well—sick the next—dead the next—and hurried to the grave before his ashes are cold—is too much for human nature. I believe if every one was obliged to live in the city during the rage of the sickness, that many evils would be avoided. The natural ties between the rich and the poor and the middle classes of society would not be sundered; one could give relief to others, and all, depending on Heaven, would go on as usual in most things. The great evils of this disease have sprung from alarms; fear has slain more than disease itself. In future days the folly of flying from the cholera will be evident to all, and the great mass of the inhabitants of every city will come to the truth with the fact—

"I ran from trouble, and trouble ran and overtook me."

All the individual miseries which have flowed from the cholera will never be known. The tears and prayers of widows and orphans have had their influence with the God of mercies, and another scourge may not, perhaps, overtake them. This disease has touched the rich, but it has dwelt with the poor; it does, indeed, sweep off vice, but it does not keep always with the vicious; the temperate, the abstemious, the cautious, and even the extremely scrupulous have fallen victims to its ravages. "*Be ye ready*" is a maxim for all who live among men.

[Chapter 12]
I now felt that I was drawing near my native land, and began to question myself as to what purpose I had spent my time during the long and to me interesting voyage. Had I treasured up all the knowledge that I might have done was a natural question. It is hard to satisfy one's self upon such an inquiry; but I had done something to-

wards it. I was not prepared by education or habits to make the most of my situation, but still the consoling reflection arose that I had never distrusted Providence; had never repined; and, as far as I was able, cheered my husband in all his misfortunes—and they were not a few. I felt myself a much graver matron than when I embarked, and had more settled and, as I thought, more rational opinions for the government of life. I had suffered much, but enjoyed more; I had laid up a stock to reflect and reason upon during my future days; I had left my child a short time to him, a long one indeed to me, but I thought I had learned enough to balance the pain of this absence in the attainment of that discretion which a mother should have in bringing up a child. It is by the kindness of Heaven that mothers do as well as they are found to do; for most of them in the early part of their days can have only the philosophy of the heart to direct them, not that of the head. My adventurous course was not a source of pride to me—it was not for any specific purpose that I became a voyager, but simply to be a companion of my husband: my feelings or reasonings were uncontrolled, and the views I have taken of things, if not deep, are just as an unlearned mind would see them. Every thing was rare and strange to me, and necessarily excited my curiosity. If I had ever contemplated taking such a voyage, I think I should have been better prepared to bring home something more worthy of myself and my countrywomen; but as it is, they must take my intention for my deeds. The great difficulty we women feel in collecting information, is the want of order and classification of our thoughts; and we therefore labour much harder to arrive at true conclusions than those who have a regular pigeon-hole in which to place all sorts of information. Perhaps those who cabinet whatever they think worth preserving, do not enjoy them so much as we who think only of amusing ourselves, without enlightening others. I doubt whether a scientific observer would have had more thoughts than passed through my teeming brain; but he would have known how to arrange them, and have drawn conclusions tending to establish known truths, or elicit new ones; while whatever observations or conclusions I might make were liable to be dispersed for not knowing where to preserve them. The unstudied and unpractised mind, however, observes many things that might escape the notice of the best educated.

Every vessel we met I amused myself with considering as a messenger to bring us some tidings from the friends we left at our departure; but they often passed us at too great a distance to speak to them, and as it was a time of peace and the weather fair, we left each other with a pleasurable sensation, certain that each was well provided with necessaries for the remainder of the voyage. These sights thickened as we came nearer our own shores, and afforded new proofs that commercial enterprise was the characteristic of our countrymen.

On arriving so near the termination of my voyage, and taking a retrospective view of what had principally fixed my attention during its continuance, I felt my mind drawn to the contemplation of the regions we had visited in the Southern Pacific. I hope to live to see the islands in this ocean inhabited by my countrymen, under the protection of my country. There is no obstacle in the way of this. That the Kings of Portugal or Spain first erected their standard in those seas is nothing, or that the pope issued his bull in their favour is now nothing; but that they who discover should possess, if they choose, is the common sense law of nations. Settlements might be made on some of the islands we have discovered, with every prospect of securing the commerce of those seas, or at least with sharing it with other nations. We have existed at all only about two centuries, and as an independent and free nation, acknowledged and received into the great family about half a century; and yet we are considered the third commercial people on the globe. We were prosperous as carriers of the commodities of other nations; and we shall be so in carrying our own. Agriculture and manufactures have increased with commerce and added to our independence, and will serve to support it if we do not have too much of what is termed the protecting system. Differences will arise in the minds of men how far each should be carried, and legislative power should assist either when it can be done without prejudice to the others; but it is certain that where all are active, and industrious, and intelligent, these things will be kept nearly right, although a few may complain on both sides. It is a subject of great consideration, and should engage the attention of every thinking being, and each should do a part to assist in the great work of building up a nation. We have now some copy of every great and excellent institution that time has produced, though many of them as yet are but outlines, and want filling up.

The first step to be taken in order that all the benefits may be derived from the islands of the Pacific which they are capable of affording, must be to spread the light of the gospel and civilization among them, which can only be done through the medium of missionaries. For this purpose I hope I shall not call in vain on my countrywomen, who have contributed so largely in supporting missionary establishments, and other works of charity, both at home and abroad; I implore them to continue their exertions, not only as matters of charity, but of knowledge also, and to assist all in their power to aid the great cause of true national glory. The rising generation are to be educated and directed, and the females of our country have much to do with this. That we possess the requisite capabilities, Hannah More, Miss Edgeworth, Mrs. Hemans—and our own countrywomen, Mrs. Sigourney and Miss Sedgwick[5]—may be adduced; and in those branches of which mathematics is the basis, Mrs. Somerville has transcended all who have attempted to instruct youth in these matters before. A hundred others, on both sides of the water, may be brought forward to prove what women are doing in the great work of advancing the social and intellectual condition of mankind. This little enterprise of mine—little as it regards society—has taught me what my sex can do if called to act in the business of life.

I feel myself now wedded to the seas as much as the Chief of Venice was to the Adriatic. I love to contemplate its immensity, its sameness, its power as a medium of communication from one nation to another. The ocean has all the attributes of sublimity, immensity, and fearfulness; all the properties of usefulness; as affording food for man, and ten thousand pathways for the world.

3

Sarah Rogers Haight

Sarah Rogers Haight (1808–1881) was the wife of a wealthy merchant of New York, Richard K. Haight, and a leader of New York society known for her lavish entertainments. According to *Pelletreau's Records of Smithtown, Long Island,* "on her frequent trips to Europe she was attended by a retinue like a princess. Her portrait in the 'Book of Beauty' shows her to have been a person of surpassing elegance."[1]

In 1836 and 1837, Haight traveled from Paris through Switzerland, Austria, Prussia, Holland, Denmark, Sweden, Norway, and Finland to Russia and down to Odessa, contributing letters on her travels to the *New York American.* Although this "first series" of letters was projected for publication by Harper and Brothers, it was never printed in book form. Another travel book, *Over the Ocean; or Glimpses of Travel in Many Lands* (1846) has also been attributed to her.

The selection that follows is taken from Haight's two-volume collection entitled *Letters from the Old World. By a Lady of New York* (1840). The first volume includes accounts of travel to Odessa, the Bosphorus, Constantinople, Alexandria, Cairo, and Thebes; the second chronicles her travels to Sidon, Tyre, Nazareth, Jerusalem, Damascus, Beyrout, Constantinople, Stamboul, Athens, Venice, and Paris. In addition to cataloging the discomforts and hardships of travel, the excerpts contained in this selection, taken from Volume 1, Letters 2, 3, 12, and 13; and Volume 2, Letters 25 and 26, capture the tendency of the American travel writer to cast the Orient in the discursive formation of Orientalism and to see the contemporary world as decayed and inferior to the splendors of the past. Haight's raptures concerning the Holy Land are also typical of her era.

Letters from the Old World

[I, Letter 2]
Constantinople, —.

Coming now, as I did, from a modern European city (Odessa), but recently built, and peopled by persons a majority of whom are from western Europe—stepping, as it were, from the streets of Paris or Marseilles, and their gay saloons—in two days I found myself in Turkey, with everything differing so materially from what I had ever before seen. The turban in lieu of the hat, flowing robes and wide trousers in place of short coats and pantaloons, red and yellow slippers instead of boots, long beards and curled mustaches instead of shorn faces, and veiled heads in lieu of the female face divine. The stately sycamore after the stunted birch, the dense cypress forests after naked "steppes"; minarets in the place of towers and steeples, and the cry of the Muezzim instead of bells; Saracenic verandahs, latticed windows, and low fancy-painted wooden structures of Asiatic origin, instead of the straight lines of the severer Grecian architecture which prevails in Russia.

These and a hundred minor opposites, and the sudden transition from scenes familiar with earliest observation to those hitherto existing only in the fancy, and recollections of poetry and romance, reminiscences of Moore, Byron, and Scott, cause the contrast to take one by surprise, and work one up into a state of excitement too much allied to exaggeration to admit of calm investigation and impartial judgment. Yet to such feelings, so new, so agreeable, so undefinable, I delight at times to give way; and have never before found myself under circumstances where romance seemed so nearly akin to reality, or imagination to matter of fact, as when sailing down the Bosphorus, and feeling myself surrounded by everything Oriental and Asiatic. I can thus account for the very many extravagant eulogiums we often read in the accounts of many travellers, suddenly arriving from western countries, and sailing up the Bosphorus for the first time. These feelings being, "like angels' visits, few and far between," it seems a pity to shut one's heart against the sweet intrusion, but rather to court the ecstatic pleasure they induce, and by gentle embraces endeavour to arrest their fleeting course. The sad and sober realities of life are but too apt to claim dominion over us, and chase away those bright and pleasant dreams. Not caring to divest myself of the delightful emotions I experienced, I floated down the Bosphorus with Europe and Asia on either hand, having fresh in my mind the reminiscences of Greek and Persian struggles which these shores once beheld, of crusading armies with pike and pennon, lance and oriflamme, "in all the pride and panoply of war," careering on in thousands, with victory in their van, and returning across this strait in wretched decimals, rallying under the walls of the treacherous Greek, and craving protection and food from that emperor who had betrayed them among the defiles of the Taurus into the hands of their barbarous foe, whence few ever reached their own firesides or the halls of their ancestors. Now and then a holy palmer returned to tell the tale of their sad defeat, or the "gallant troubadour" chanted in ladye's chamber or at the festive board the wonders of the East and the exploits of the departed great.

Long after the flood of Deucalion burst these mountain barriers, and the furious Eusine spread desolation along the shores of Greece, causing the plains of Muscovie to rise from beneath the waters, and the Caspian to recede into its retired basin, refusing communication with the briny sea; long after these events the adventurous Argive drove his bright prow against this rapid current, and felt his way around the Euxine in search of the golden fleece.

Xenophon, with his ten thousand veterans, here consummated his famous retreat from Asia. First the Greek, and then the warlike Roman claimed dominion over these waters and these hills.

In later times the merchant of Venice and his rival of Genoa strove for the ascendency; the latter fixed himself firmly upon the mountain top, where his eagle nests remain almost intact to this day. At last the turbaned Turk, debouching from the "Caspian Gates," came thundering down the plains of Asia Minor, and seated himself upon the throne of the last Caesar.

While dwelling upon these and similar reminiscences, and indulging in reflections incident to them, we were hurried along by steam and current until, on turning an angle in the strait, the "Queen of the East" greeted my enraptured sight. While the gentlemen were on shore in quest of lodgings I had an opportunity of observing at my leisure the scene around me, and a friend who came on board had the politeness to explain to me the details of this unique picture. From no one point can this wonderful panorama be viewed with so much satisfaction as from the one at which we were anchored, a little to the east of Seraglio Point.

I am told that there are several points of view from the tops of the surrounding hills, where the prospect is far more grand, but the singular details which go to fill up the great outline are there lost in the distance.

From our position I first faced the south, and had the shore of Asia directly before me, with the great suburb of *Scutary* extending a long distance to the east and west, and far inland, with its immense forests of cypress covering the rear. A little to the right of it is the site of ancient Chalcedon. On either hand I had the Bosphorus for miles to the eastward, and the sea of Marmora, with its numerous islands, as far as the eye could reach to the westward.

Turning round and facing the north, the whole city of Stamboul rose in front of me, from the water's edge to the top of the hills around; and the Golden Horn, filled with thousands of all sorts of curious craft, from a light four-oared caique to the proud four-decker of 150 guns.

After gazing with wonder and mute astonishment on this immense and truly extraordinary amphitheatre, the imagination, by a very slight though perfectly natural effort at amplification, could continue the illusion and convert the whole scene into a vast "Coliseum," with its arena overflowed with water, and the moving objects on its surface acting out to the life scenes of a splendid *naumachia*, worthy of the greatest Caesar that ever catered for the insatiate desires of a Roman world. The first object of importance near to me is Seraglio Point, which always attracts the stranger's earliest attention; but I must acknowledge that, however great my impatience had been to see this celebrated spot, my disappointment exceeded it. Instead of the stately palaces and Oriental grandeur which most travellers describe as belonging to this renowned residence of so many sultans, I saw only a mass of irregular buildings, thrown together without any architectural rule, and in defiance of all good taste, be that taste Eastern or Western. The only redeeming quality it has is that the barbarism of its exterior *ensemble* is in perfect keeping with the bloody and ferocious scenes which have been so often enacted within. The style of architecture is neither Grecian, Egyptian, Moresque, nor Gothic; and in grandeur it falls far short of the ancient seat of the Czars of Russia, the Kremlin of Moscow. Its interior I may describe to you hereafter. A very interesting association is attached to this spot: on the extremity of this cape was situated the ancient city of Byzantium, showing the tact of its founders in the selection of a site. There is a historical anecdote which says that when the founders of Byzantium were about to "locate" their city, they of course consulted the oracle. The reply, as usual, was obscure, though full of meaning when rightly applied. "*Let it be over against the country of the blind men.*" Now where was to be found a country of "blind men"? Another largesse to the priests, and another rich offering to the shrine of the popular oracle, brought this solution to the enigma: That the men of Chalcedon were blind, inasmuch as they had overlooked this unrivalled site for a city when they were founding their own. All eyes being now open to the advantages of this promontory, the beautiful and sheltered harbour of the Golden Horn, and its sweet water river—the former for defence, and the latter for its navies and commerce—the city of Byzantium soon rose into magnificence, power, and grandeur unequalled in those days; so that when the Western capital of the Caesars became too insecure for them, they, as you very well know, adopted this as the capital of the Roman empire.

The cape, bounded by the Golden Horn on one side and the Sea of Marmora on the other, is in form very like the lower half of Manhattan Island, and the site of Byzantium like the site of New Amsterdam, at the extreme point.

The ground is quite undulating, and in several places rises into hills, which are now each adorned by a separate mosque. Would that the level and chain of our engineers, and the spade and scraper of the labourer, had not done their murderous work upon the green mounts of Manhattoes, else we might now have seen another seven-hilled city in the West. There is nothing left of Byzantium save its history. [. . .]

On the moment of our landing there was one of the greatest cannonadings I ever heard in my life. All the vessels of war in the harbour poured out their thunders from hundreds of brazen mouths, and some of such enormous size that they seemed to shake the very waters under us. It was some fête day; and the sultan, going to mosque, was being saluted, as is the custom here.

At the quay I found that there were oilcloth cloaks provided for us, in order to prevent contact with any person who might possibly communicate the plague to us.

We had to scramble up the steep hill through Galata to Pera, where our hotel is situated. That, and the excitement and fatigue of this most eventful day of my life, have so exhausted my mental faculties and prostrated my physical strength, that I am sure no other excuse need be given you for the many exceptions you will have reason to take with this present tedious letter.

Once more, good-night.

[I, Letter 3]
Constantinople, —.

You doubtless expect me now to enter into much detail respecting the interior of Stamboul; but I am sorry to say that I fear your anticipations on that point will meet with some disappointment, for it would ill become me to pretend to give you even a faint idea of things which in themselves are to me so new and as yet unstudied; besides, it would be altogether superfluous to waste your valuable time in repeating over, in my hurried and discursive manner, that which you can at any moment find so much better done by abler pens than mine. Would you not consider as unworthy of acceptance any gleanings which I might gather from a field so lately and so faithfully harvested by such a master-hand as that of our present worthy and able minister at the Sublime Porte, Commodore Porter? The commodore has just presented us with a copy of his valuable and interesting work on Constantinople;[2] and, besides the thanks we owe him for his politeness, I feel doubly indebted to him for having thus put me in possession of a mass of information which I might have sought for elsewhere in vain. In addition to which, also, this agreeable book, of which, until this day, I had no knowledge (it having been published since I left home), will spare me the necessity of going into many details with which I had proposed to myself to furnish you.

However, as no two persons ever take exactly the same view of that which comes under their observation, I will record some of my impressions, merely for your own private gratification, referring you for details to the commodore's book, which I am sure will suit your taste better than all the dry volumes that have appeared on this interesting subject since that now obsolete work of Lady Mary Wortley Montague.

Since my last we have made our first journey and voyage of discovery in this amphibious world of Stamboul. No excursion can be made without two or three, or more, trips across the water, and that in those little eggshell *caïques*, which seem every moment as though they would topple over. Apropos of a "*caïque*": as I shall frequently have to mention it, better now that I should try to describe one to you. They are of various sizes, with one to four pairs of oars, and sometimes more. All over three pairs of oars are reserved especially for persons of some importance in the state and diplomatists; no plebeians like ourselves may pretend to encroach upon the dignity of those grandees, by assuming the privileged number of oars, under penalty of some punishment: just as the custom prevails in Russia, that none save the family of the Czars are permitted to wear the imperial ermine, or in Tuscany, as I am told, to drive more than four in hand. The caiques are all, large and small, built upon the same model, extremely light and long, with a round bottom and no keel. They are quite as light and tottering as our Indian bark canoes, and extremely dangerous to those unaccustomed to their management. They are generally handsomely carved within, and kept extremely neat and clean. There is but one elevated seat for passengers, and that is for one person only; it is in the extreme stern. The other part of the company must be seated "*à la Turque,*" on a carpet in the *bottom* of the boat, in order to keep the greatest weight below the centre of gravity. The least unskillfulness in the manner of sitting alters so much the trim of the boat, that the surly boatmen will not dip an oar until we "Giaours" place ourselves just as they direct; and we, of course, must needs submit to the dictation of these dingy Charons, or we should have to wait until Doomsday to be ferried over.

I felt the full force of the old saw that says, when in Turkey one must do as Turks do, and I am now beginning to lose my national importance and impatience, and am becoming as resigned and apathetic in matters of discomfort and inconvenience as the most devoted follower of the Prophet. Before we ventured to dive into the dark and mysterious labyrinths of Stamboul, we thought it best to take our usual precaution, that of ascending some tower to observe well how the land lies, and to take a fair departure. We have always found, by so doing when we first enter any foreign city and when we are about to leave it, that we obtain an indelible impression of its general location, form, and extent, the proportionate size and peculiar appearance of its principal monuments and other prominent features. I would recommend all young and persevering travellers to adopt this practice, although too fatiguing a one, perhaps, for the listless tourist, who, like his portmanteau, is carried along by the current from place to place, indifferent to anything which is certain to require personal exertion, or induce the least mental or bodily fatigue, satisfied if he can but return home and say "Veni, vidi," "Vincit" belonging not to the same category of his associations.

The tower of the Genoese being very near our hotel, just below the summit of the hill of *Pera*, we hastened to ascend its giddy height. And oh! such a *glorious* sight as here burst upon my view what pen can describe! At this moment my fingers refuse to do their office, and my trembling pencil does not aspire even to trace the outline of this wonderful and gorgeous picture. My impressions and opinions, however, belong to myself. The former you desire always to participate in; and as you are ever generous enough to respect the latter, however erroneous they may be at times, I shall suppress my timidity, and give you an unreserved expression of both whenever I think they will in the least contribute to your amusement and satisfaction. I now say, without fear of contradiction, that the view from *this* point of Stamboul is far more magnificent than any other view that Europe can present. I am informed by persons here, who have travelled the wide world over, that they never have seen anything to compare with this view of the Queen of the East, as she is seated in Oriental majesty upon her seven-hilled throne. Her back towards Europe, her fixed regard on Asia, her either arm reaching from the Euxine to the Marmora, and, surpassing *Canute*, presents her either foot to *two seas at once*, saying, "Thus far shalt thou come, and no farther." And to all the nations that may venture in peace upon her glorious waters, she says, Bow thy head, pay tribute, and pass on! Should an enemy have the foolhardy temerity to attempt a passage of her threshold, she would laugh in derision at his puny efforts and bid defiance to the navies of the world. It was a glorious morning when I looked out for the first time in my life upon this rich and extended Oriental landscape, in the midst of which is enshrined the mightiest city of the East. Every feature marks it as a truly Oriental scene. The domes and minarets of the mosques, the star and crescent waving over the ships, the cypress forests, the vine-clad hills, all betokened this the land of the *East*, the very personification of poetry, even brighter and more enchanting than those beautiful lines of Byron, wherein he asks,

> "Know ye the land where the cypress and myrtle
> Are emblems of deeds that are done in their clime?
> Where the rage of the vulture, the love of the turtle,
> Now melt into sorrow, now madden to crime?
> Know ye the land of the cedar and vine,
> Where the flowers ever blossom, the beams ever shine,
> Where the light wings of Zephyr, oppress'd with perfume,
> Was faint o'er the gardens of Gul in her bloom;
> Where the citron and olive are fairest of fruit,
> And the voice of the nightingale never is mute;
> Where the tints of the earth, and the hues of the sky
> In colour though varied, in beauty may vie,
> And the purple of ocean is deepest in dye;
> Where the virgins are soft as the roses they twine,
> And all, save the spirit of man, is divine?
> 'Tis the clime of the East, 'tis the land of the Sun."

Who is there that, looking down upon this peculiar scene, can feel other than a tumult of contending emotions, powerful as they are opposite, and intensely interesting from the high excitement which they produce and the glow of satisfaction which they inspire, arising from this rare privilege of visiting a spot fraught with so many, so great, and such extraordinary associations. Has not the poet just said,

> "Know ye the land of the cedar and vine,

Where the flowers ever blossom, the beams ever shine?"

Yet is not this also the land of *pestilence* and plague?

"Where the virgins are soft as the roses they twine,"

and yet is it not also the land where "man is a despot and woman a *slave*," and sold as cattle in the market-place?

Is not this the land by Nature blessed beyond her pale, and where "all save the spirit of man is divine?" and yet is it not here that those blessings are least appreciated, and left to run fallow through the sheer neglect and inanity of the lazy and stupid possessors of the soil? Is not this once splendid capital of a Roman empire now the mere rendezvous of a horde of beastly Tartars?

The palace of a Constantine and the stately temples of a Theodosius, are they not levelled with the dust; and from their discordant materials have not sprung the Vandalian structures of a barbarous race of Turcomans? The Christian temple, once dedicated to the service of the God of peace, has it not been sacked, and its priests passed over with the bloody cimeter, and its sacred altar profaned by the worship of the murderous Moslem?

Does not the *crescent* now wave where first in all the East the *cross* was raised as a nation's standard?

Are not the intrigues of a polluted hareem now directed by a sultan mother, on the very spot where an Empress Helena once moved the splendid court of her all-powerful son in favour of the gospel of Christ, and the pure religion which it inculcates? In short, this capital, intended by Nature to be the key of the East, and the seat of empire and of power, has it not now become a proverb among the nations for its weakness and imbecility?

From the halls of that palace, whose ruined walls lie scattered around, went forth the mandates which called into existence those stately structures whose domes and arches now serve to mark those sacred spots in Palestine, rendered "Holy Land" by the birth, the life, the death and resurrection of our Christ, and the acts and martyrdom of his apostles. Shade of Helena! couldst thou but rise and see thy loved Sophia's shrine, desecrated by the infidel, her altars polluted by the hands of a guilty and benighted priesthood, her sacred cross displaced by Islam's crescent, and the bloody banner waving over God's holy fane, in despair wouldst thou return to thy resting-place, to await that judgment-day when a just retribution may be expected upon those who now trample under foot the sacred emblem of our holy religion. But, before that day arrives, we are promised a millennium of peace, when all men shall be of one religion. God's peculiar people will again be gathered into one fold. The Turk and all the Moslem race will ere then have disappeared; the days of the evil to come will have passed away; and the seven golden candlesticks be once more replaced, and lighted in the midst of Asia.

At that perhaps not distant epoch the crescent will fall from each proud minaret, and the emblem of the Christian faith resume its former place, and these swelling domes shall again resound with loud *Hosannas to the Lord of Hosts.*

[I, Letter 12]
Grand Cairo, —.

Our place of rest for the night was a large tomb, excavated in the solid rock, in the side of the hill, with one end opening upon a sort of terrace. Being well swept out, and spread with carpets and mattresses around the sides, it formed a tolerably comfortable parlour, with divans, &c. In the centre a table was arranged, by placing several canteen boxes side by side, which, with a clean white table-cloth and sundry articles of dinner furniture, wore quite a promising aspect.

My impatience for dinner led me to make a domiciliary visit to the quarters of Monsieur François, who I found had appropriated to himself another of these chambers of the dead, which he had transformed into a pretty good *restaurant* for the living, and in which, with the aid of a little charcoal from Cairo, and sundry portions of *mummy* from a neighbouring pit, he made out to produce for us several courses of viands in his best style. This was the first time in my life that I ever *bivouacked* for a night, or made a meal seated *à la Turc* upon the ground.

A good appetite, good company, light hearts, and a consciousness of perfect security, caused our dinner and *soirée* in the tomb to pass off delightfully. The evening conversation turned unfortunately upon tombs, mummy-pits, and mummies.

My sleeping apartment, separated by a curtain from the dining-room in front, was the nook where had been the sarcophagus of some Pharaoh or other. My mattress and its occupant filled up the sacred space; nor was I at all disturbed by the wandering spirit whose three thousand years of metempsychosis can scarcely yet be over, and which might very probably have been guarding my couch in the body of the trusty dog at my feet, unconscious that my dinner had been, perhaps, cooked with its former earthly tenement.

After a day of such unusual fatigue, it is not singular that I desired to seek an early repose; and when the light of my taper disclosed to me the *locale* of my couch, its arrangements were not uncomfortable; but then, "*to sleep, perchance to dream, ay, there's the rub.*" The gentle-men spread their carpets, and, rolling themselves in their cloaks, were soon unconscious of the noisy revelry of our servants in the next-door tomb, or the unceasing jargon of the loquacious Bedouins, prowling round to catch the crumbs that fell from the tables.

As soon as the hunger of our servants was appeased and their liba-tions had ceased, nature asserted her rights, and not a soul of them but was as silent as their companions, the mummies; none, save myself, appeared to be awake.

Whether from motives of curiosity, or from a troubled conscience like another Lady Macbeth, I seized the burning taper, drew aside my curtain, and, stepping lightly over the sleepers, reached the terrace in front of the tomb, where the night breeze instantly extinguished my light. My first impulse was to retreat; but, aware that my husband and his friends lay within ten feet of the door, I was reassured.

The first near object that arrested my attention was our *trusty* Mustafa, sitting on a stone, with a firelock across his arm, but fast asleep. The night was one of truly *Egyptian darkness*. Such a back-ground, together with what I then saw, formed the very *beau ideal* of a subject for the pencil of De la Notte. In the distance, a few dying embers served to throw an uncertain light on sundry forms lying about, so like the human as easily to be mistaken for man or mummy. In the foreground were several camp-fires, around which were seated the half-naked Bedouins, silently and voraciously devouring some fragments of food.

While gazing at these hideous creatures, my imagination trans-formed the hooded females who flitted by the blaze into Hecates and witches, the swarthy myrmidons into devils incarnate, and the half-consumed mummy-fuel into some victim they were tormenting. Now and then a shrill ejaculation from a female, or a coarse laugh from the savage-looking beings by the fire, with their lank bodies, shaved heads, sunken eyes, and endless mouths, gave the whole a more sepulchral and demoniacal appearance than anything I had ever seen before in real life, or in the mock horrors of *Der Freischutz*.[3] To give the last finishing touch to the picture, and to exalt my excited feelings to the highest pitch, in every direction lay fragments of mummies. Their resinous cerements were scattered in all directions; each puff of wind drove them across the embers, where, instantly igniting, they caused a transient blaze to flash a lurid glare upon hundreds of "*death's heads and cross-bones.*" At each step of these busy demons was heard the sharp crackling of dried human skeletons; a sound which, together with my already surcharged vision, so overcame all my remaining courage, that I tottered back to my sepulchral couch, and there endeavoured to overcome my excitement, and, if possible, partake of the repose around me. Restless and uneasy, my thoughts wandering from one lugubrious object to another, I endeavoured to drown them all in ineffectual attempts to force a sleep; but all my expedients failing, I relighted my taper, and determined to while away the remainder of the night, either in reading, or in the most agreeable reflections I could conjure up. To me, who had never before passed a night out of a house, it was not a very amusing matter to be thus lying in a *cavern of the Libyan rocks*, in the very centre of the greatest Necropolis the world ever knew, where were entombed countless millions of human bodies, scarcely changed in feature, the accumulated relics of ages, and the unbroken ranks of nations and people existent more than three thousand years ago. Not only the Egyptian, but the most distinguished individuals from many nations lie here entombed; for such was the celebrity of this sacred spot, such the known skill of its adepts in the art of embalming; such the gorgeousness of the funeral habiliments; such the luxury and splendour of the obsequies, that no higher honour could be conferred, nor a more consoling promise made, than that contained in the significant words of Scripture, "Memphis Shall Bury Thee."

Endeavouring to abstract my ideas from the contemplation of this city of the dead, my thoughts would constantly recur to its stupendous monuments. Passing over the countless minor erections and excavations of the great families of the Pharaohotic age, the mind dwells with awe upon those artificial mountains of stone, cemented with the blood of a hundred thousand victims, and built for the mere purpose of hiding the body of an individual, while its soul was performing the descending and ascending series of *transmigrations*, until, its appointed *cycle* revolving, it should reclaim its former human habitation. From these monuments of human error and folly, my imagination carried me to the vast artificial caverns immediately beneath me, down whose perpendicular shafts I had been previously looking. I had been informed that many of them are computed to contain each a *million* of bodies, standing tier upon tier, until they reach within a few feet of the spot where I then lay. I inquired of myself, with such a Necropolis, what must have been the city of the living?

[I, Letter 13]
Grand Cairo, —.

Yes, Grand Cairo! And why not Grand Cairo as well as grand duke, or grand sultan, or any of the other grand names of these grandiloquent days? [. . .]

The novelty of my first impressions begins to wear off, and Cairo of the nineteenth century stands out in bold relief from the few beautiful remains of *El Cahira*, of poetic and romantic memory, of which we always delight to read and which we still more desire to visit.

Of the latter there now only remain a few stately mosques, with their Saracenic domes and minarets, going fast to decay; some curious tombs in the environs, several ruined palaces of former wealthy individuals, remarkable only for their interior structure and ornament, and their stained glass windows, from which were derived those beautiful windows of the Gothic cathedrals of western Europe; several singular Persian fountains and numerous arabesque sculptures on the imposts and lintels of the doors of private houses, apparently once much in fashion, and no doubt of very high antiquity for Cairo.

The reason for my latter supposition is, that all the houses of Cairo have the first story built of strong cut stone, and all upper stories of wood, or lath and plaster, and something of unburned bricks; the superstructure being of such mean materials and so slightly put together, that they decay much sooner than the basement. The nature of the climate, however, protects these card-houses much longer than in more northern and humid climates. But the stonework rarely decays, and fashion in building never changes in the East. I send you some sketches of these singular door-ways, which, together with the other drawings, will serve to convey to your mind some of the impressions of travelling in the palmy days of *El Cahira*, under its Fatimite sovereigns, and previous to the reign of the barbarous and destroying Turk. The times when the princely merchants of Arabia and India met here on common ground with those of Fez and Cordova, Genoa and Venice, by whose traffic this city became so wealthy and so powerful that it obtained among the Eastern nations the appellation of "*greatest among the great*," &c., &c.

The ruins of Saladin's palace, and those of the subsequent Mameluke beys, are connecting links between the good old times of *El Cahira*, those of its reverses under the Turks, of its subsequent retrograde march in the reign of anarchy, and that of its complete degradation in the nineteenth century, when Western Europe chose to make the fields of Egypt its battle-ground.

There is here at present an extraordinary contrast between the architectural possessions of the governors and the governed. Wooden palaces of a semi-Italian style, gayly painted, whitewashed cotton-mills, arsenals, and military schools, huge warehouses and commercial depots, are the types of power. Dilapidated buildings, their exterior covered with the dust of decayed stucco, their lath fibres and timber ribs protruding through the lacerated skin of mud plaster; wooden lattice-work without paint, brown with age and dust, together with filthy entrances, are the exterior characteristics of the dwellings of the people. Two or three handsome English and French gardens, belonging to the pacha and his son, contrast singularly with the general absence of all such private pleasure-grounds as are seen within and around perhaps every other city in the world; at least I have never before seen an instance to the contrary during my few wanderings.

The pacha and a few other dignitaries retain the old Turkish costume; many of his native satellites have adopted the semi-European dress of the Constantinople government officers and dependants—tight pantaloons, vest, and frock-coat, the common under-boot of Europe, and sometimes white stockings and shoes, and even the long outside boot is sometimes seen to adorn their nether man. The only thing not European is the scarlet *fez* (a fashion adopted from Morocco) in place of the old turban, and instead of the round Frank hat. [...]

A heavy slouching turban, a greasy silk gown, kept together with a faded French imitation cotton shawl, a pair of dirty red or yellow slippers, and a tattered embroidered cotton handkerchief peeping out of pocket, make up the outer man of ninety and nine out of every hundred natives one meets in the streets and bazars of Cairo. I am perfectly aware that some of this class of persons present a far more agreeable exterior when at home, and one more in conformity with their general urbane and graceful manners and manly features. But then the proportion here of those who creep along in tatters through the public streets, that they may the more uninterruptedly and securely worship their *penates* in Babylonish garments, and in all the pride of Oriental luxury, is small indeed in comparison with that found in the little world of Constantinople. Here there are not so many roads to opulence, and the streams of wealth are all ravenously swallowed up by the huge leviathan who holds the sceptre of Egypt.

One of the most amusing things in Cairo is to observe the physiognomy and costume of the motley tribe of *Franks* whom one sees stealing about the purlieus of the bazars and market-places. (Of course I except the few European gentlemen who either belong to the diplomacy, or are residents here for some scientific object, and also the foreign officers of rank in the army and household of the pacha.) Twenty times in a day I am reminded by the razor face, lizard form, and rueful countenance of some Italian, French, Perotte, or Smyrniote Frank, of the luckless wight in the play who styles himself "Sylvester Daggerwood,"[4] and I cannot restrain my merriment when I see him pull out his ragged pocket furniture. It pictures in such a graphic manner the scene where poor Sylvester, in rehearsing Othello, displays his tattered cambric, and in the most inflated style exclaims, "This handkerchief an Egyptian to my mother gave."

If one were desirous of making a *recueil* of all the various costumes of Western Europe, from the days of Beau Nash to those of the immortal Brummel, one need but sit down with his sketch-book at the corner of Frank-street in Cairo. The pencil of a Hogarth would find full employment there.

From the ill-assorted and grotesque Frank costumes seen here at all times, one would suppose that the last fifty years' sweepings of all the old clothes shops in Europe had been collected in the great square, in a heap as high and as universally assorted as the mountain of cast-off deformities before the throne of Rhadamanthus.

Then, as many impatient unfortunates waiting around as there were at that famous scramble, each one, not choosing, but taking what he could get. And he who is curious in languages need walk but a few times past the door of a Frank *café* to become upon terms of intimacy with that child of many fathers, the *lingua Franca* of the East; a language of as many dialects as there are places between Trieste and Trebizonde, and from Moscow to Mocha. [. . .]

[II, Letter 25]
Tyre, —.

[. . .] In some parts of Mount Lebanon there is a sect of Christians called Maronites, but whose religion, I am informed, is a curious mixture of Christianity and paganism. I probably shall see more of them another time, when I may give you some account of them.

I have seen some of the women of this tribe, and will endeavour to describe to you a part of their very singular costume. From their foreheads projects a long silver tube, or *horn*, which is about twenty inches long, resembling the head ornament of the fabled unicorn.

The real purpose for which they carry this exceedingly uncouth and inconvenient appendage, or whether it is connected with the doctrines of their religion, I know not.

The object ostensibly is, to hang on it the veil which covers their faces; and, while it completely conceals them from observation, it allows room for the circulation of fresh air, which is not the case with the tight kerchief worn by the Turk and Arab women generally.

In order to counterpoise this formidable and heavy protuberance, there are attached to its base a number of silken cords, which hang down their backs to the ground, and to which are suspended silver balls and large crimson silk tassels.

In reflecting on this curious ornament, it called to my mind the various passages of Scripture, of which it is a striking illustration; and one can almost believe that the fashion was brought in the most ancient times from Ur of the Chaldees, by the followers of Zidon. In 1 Samuel ii., 1, we read, "And Hannah prayed, and said, My heart rejoiceth in the Lord, mine horn is exalted in the Lord." Job says, "I have defiled my horn in the dust." Psalm lxxv., 4, "I said to the wicked, Lift not up the horn." Again, lxxxix., 17, "And in thy favour our horn shall be exalted." Also in lxxxix., 24, "And in my name shall his horn be exalted." Various similar passages are to be found throughout the Bible, possibly having reference to this unique ornament of the ancient daughters of Shem.

In the course of the day's ride we met a caravan, consisting of the hareem and led horses of an officer of Ibrahim Pacha's army, following to the field their warlike lord. If we could have supposed the ladies (?) as handsome as the Arabian horses (of which there were a dozen very beautiful ones), we should have regretted the vile practice that prevented us from seeing their faces. The women in these countries all use *two* stirrups when riding, for an obvious reason.

Scarcely had this cavalcade passed, when we met another of a very different character; it was that of two *Jews* returning from a pilgrimage to Jerusalem, whither they had been to visit the tombs of their forefathers, and the various relics which they still cling to with religious veneration. Having performed so pious and soul-saving an act, as they verily believe, they were returning to lay their bones in the land of their adoption, which was Bucharest on the Danube.

One was a very old and venerable-looking man, and doubtless no imperfect representation of one of the ancient patriarchs.

I do not deem it an idle speculation, as I journey through this land, consecrated by the residence of the patriarchs and the labours of the apostles, keenly to scrutinize the countenance of all I meet, for the chance of discovering some lineal descendants of those distinguished men; and really I have seen many who, from their venerable appearance, hoary locks, and snow-white beards (almost down to the waist), added to peculiar gravity of manner, might be adopted as no improbable resemblance. In fact, I can at every hour of the day see countenances so familiar to me, that sometimes I am startled at the sudden apparition of an old friend. They are no less than the fac-simile of those inspired features delineated on canvass with such surprising truth by the old Italian masters, in their scriptural subjects.

[. . .]

This day will be the fifth of our pilgrimage in Syria, and so far I have been much gratified with what I have seen, and much interested in the reminiscences which attach to everything around me. Besides, I am highly delighted with this mode of travelling; so independent, so exciting, so conducive to health, and to me so novel and amusing.

A hundred little incidents daily occur, too trifling to notice separately, but, as a whole, making a sum total of amusement and enjoyment which I never experienced when rolling over the Macadamized roads of Europe in a well-appointed chariot and four. I hope the long route I have yet before me may prove equally pleasant with the beginning, but that I can scarcely expect. When we get more into the interior, I must look for greater fatigue and privations, if not some positive dangers; yet my every want is anticipated and provided for by my kind conductors, whose increasing watchfulness is ever on the alert, that no discomfort may annoy, and no harm reach me. But my chief dependance is on that kind *Providence* which has carried me thus far through so many dangers, and has so frequently preserved my life in times of imminent peril. May he continue to be the guide of my footsteps, and the guardian of my welfare unto the end; and may he sanctify to me the inestimable privilege that I am about to enjoy, that of treading the same paths, and taking shelter under the same rocks which, in their wanderings through the Holy Land, my Redeemer and his apostles were wont to frequent.

And may I return from my pilgrimage to the place of the birth, the death, the resurrection, and the ascension of my Saviour, both wiser and better than at present! I know that you will sincerely join with me in desiring such a consummation; and I once more bid you adieu.

[II, Letter 26]
Nazareth, —.

Although two days have elapsed since my last short epistle, yet I have gathered but little wherewith to amuse you. Were it not that you will expect something from this place, I should defer writing until I had collected more materials. [. . .]

The nearer we approached to Nazareth, the greater became our anxiety to see it. As firm believers in the narrative of the important events which occurred during the sojournment of the blessed Jesus upon earth (the scene of many of which was in this place), as well as in the incalculable benefit which the world has derived from his life and his death, how could we approach a place consecrated by his residence for many years without feelings of reverential awe?

At noon we came in sight of the town, our first view of which was from the summit of a very high hill at the foot of which it is built. In a moment I could almost realize all the interesting accounts I had been reading from my earliest youth. My imagination carried me back to those days when the Saviour of the world condescended to make his abode in that very place upon which my eyes were then gazing, and I almost fancied I could see him mingling with his fellow-citizens in their daily occupations, while his sacred lips were imparting the counsels of a God, and uttering the deep instructions of the gospel.

As soon as our tent was pitched, for which we selected a favourable position, commanding a view of the town, with a glimpse of the plain of Esdraelon beyond the valley, and the tall head of Tabor lifting itself above the surrounding hills, we proceeded to examine those objects and places pointed out as being connected with the history of Jesus Christ.

Most of them are under the care of the Franciscan convent, to which they must be a source of some revenue.

The first place to which we were taken was the church of the Annunciation, built over the spot where they say the angel appeared to Mary, announcing that a Saviour should be born, adding these important words: "He shall be great, and shall be called the Son of the Highest; and the Lord God shall give unto him the throne of David; and he shall reign over the house of Jacob for ever, and of his kingdom there shall be no end."

The place is a small cave in the side of the valley, and may possibly have been used as an interior apartment to some building placed immediately in front of it, as I frequently see practiced at present all over the East. A place so important as this could hardly escape the notice of the early Christians, and by them it was, perhaps, handed down to the times when monuments were erected over all the most sacred spots of the Holy Land. To say that I am a believer in the truth of this tradition, would perhaps be venturing more than you would be willing implicitly to receive; but yet I am sure you would neither scorn my faith nor despise my weakness, as would those who are skeptical in all that concerns our holy creed. If the latter were worthy of notice, and if argument were not lost upon them, one might reply to their sneers respecting the identity of this and other sacred spots by putting to them these queries.

Do you now think it probable, or even possible, that when, three hundred years hence, the disciples of civil liberty from the Old World shall visit the shores of our native land, where it first had its birth, and shall ask the then inhabitants of America to point out to them a Bunker Hill, the rock of Plymouth, the site of the Hall of Independence in Philadelphia, or even that of our old Federal Hall of New-York, these places will have passed away from the memory of man? Ay, and the birthplace, the residence, and tomb of the immortal Washington, will that, too, be so soon forgotten? How much less than all these was the memory of the sacred places of Palestine likely to be engraven on the hearts of the true followers of Christ? And when Helena visited them in order to perpetuate for ever the identity of these holy localities, I *do* believe (all scorners to the contrary notwithstanding) that she received the truth in very substance, and with no alloy of interested bigotry or priestly deception, so far as the fixing of positive localities. As for the pretended discoveries of *relics* in various places, I doubt if ever she believed or sanctioned them, whatever the fathers of the church of Rome may say in defence thereof.

I find that we have entered upon a field which, though a fruitful one in matters of divine truth, is sadly overrun with the weeds of monkish fiction; but he that would attempt with a rude hand to uproot the latter, before the great harvest day arrives, would do more injury to the good cause than a legion of modern railroad reformers and patent creed inventors could repair in ages. It is to these very monks that we are indebted for the preservation of the identity of all the sacred localities in the Holy Land and elsewhere. And during the barbarous era of the middle ages, when the myriads of Europe overran the hills and valleys of Palestine in search of relics, what wonder is it that a mercenary race of pretended holy men sprang up, who, taking advantage of the confiding simplicity and zealous credulity of the Crusaders, drove a profitable trade upon an unlimited capital of *timber* and *iron* in the shape of the *True Cross*, the nails, and the spear? Such we all know to have been the fact to a great extent; and it is still practised in a retail way in the *holy* warehouses which their predecessors erected in the form of chapels, on a hundred spots of very apocryphal sanctity. Even in our Saviour's time the great temple was converted into "a den of thieves," and so the sublime monuments of Helena dwindled into mere bazars for the sale of relics, and into theatres for the representation of mock-holy puppet-shows.

When these powerful competitors took the field to run the race of cupidity against each other, they soon distanced all the earlier pretenders in the arena of traffic. The latter now only serve to furnish subsistence each for one or two miserable friars, who keep the keys, and serve as *custodi* and *ciceroni*, doling out for a few *paras* cheap editions of their traditionary lore in bad Spanish or worse Italian. Of these I will give you one or two specimens, which, among many others, have come under my observation during this first day spent upon truly holy ground.

While the cave of the *Annunciation* (over which a splendid monument was very early erected) even now supports in ease and luxury a whole convent of priests and monks, all the numerous fungi which sprang up around it in the hotbed of early fanaticism serve at present only as primary schools for young novitiates in the science of ancient priestcraft.

One of these is "the *very house* occupied by *Joseph* when he followed his occupation of carpenter." A chapel is built over it, on the walls of which hang several pictures, one representing Joseph holding by one hand Jesus when a child six or eight years old, and in the other the implements of his trade, saw, square, and hammer.

In the area, enclosed by another chapel, we were called on to do reverence to "the *very table* on which Christ supped with his disciples both before and after his resurrection."

It is a flat rock with a smooth surface, and of sufficient dimensions to accommodate twelve or thirteen persons. According to a by-law of the Romish Church (perhaps of the Greek also), those who visit this relic are entitled to an indulgence of *seven* years, which, no doubt, at one time *paid very well* (according to mercantile parlance).

About a fourth of a mile from the town is "the identical fountain at which Mary used to draw water," and at which a rival tradition says "the angel appeared to her with the annunciation."

As to the truth of the latter, I will leave it to the schools to dispute or confirm; but the former (that of its being the identical fountain where the wife of Joseph was in the habit of procuring the family supplies of one of the prime necessities of life) I am very ready to believe, for, in the first place, it is a most bountiful spring, co-existent with the hills around, and still supplying the whole town; and in the second, I am informed there is *no other* near Nazareth.

Another runner for the convent showed us the "precise spot on the '*brow of the hill*' whence the enraged Jews were about to precipitate our Saviour into the valley below": in the rock are shown the *marks of his fingers* by which he clung and saved himself.

These, with many other absurdities, one must listen to with all due reverence. It is impossible to scoff or sneer at the recital of these monkish legends, when they proceed from such lips as I have heard utter them, with a meekness and humility, and, I verily believe, with a *perfect sincerity*, which showed that the speakers were, at the very worst, but humble and ignorant tools of a crafty brotherhood. I have watched the countenances of some of them when they were enthusiastically expatiating upon various touching themes immediately connected with the sacred relics and localities under their charge, and if ever the features are indicative of what is passing in the heart, I could *not* mistake the simple *sincerity* and *honest* devotedness of the Italian novitiate, particularly when I see him draw from his bosom what he believes to be a piece of the true "*santa croce*," and, kissing it, let fall upon the sacred relic the involuntary tear. Whatever may be the error in the *creed* of these individuals, their *faith* is manifestly strong. In this, how much *safer* are they than the "*smart freethinker*," who has no faith at all? It is recorded that "by grace are ye saved, through *faith*."

The town of Nazareth is at present, like all the other towns I have seen in these countries, a congregation of poor miserable hovels, thrown together without order or regularity. Its present condition is the same as when its very meanness drew from Nathaniel the significant expression, "Can there come any good thing out of Nazareth?" It is built partly in a narrow valley, and partly on the sloping side of one of the hills by which it is closely environed. Most of the houses (upon nearer inspection than I at first made) I found to be built of stone; they are square, with flat roofs, covered with earth.

"The Christian inhabitants of Nazareth enjoy a degree of toleration unknown elsewhere in Syria or the Holy Land."

More anon. Adieu!

4

Catharine Maria Sedgwick

ॐ

Catharine Maria Sedgwick (1789–1867) published twelve novels, including *Hope Leslie; or Early Times in the Massachusetts* (1827), *Live and Let Live; or Domestic Service Illustrated* (1837), and *Married or Single?* (1857). In 1839, she traveled abroad, visiting Britain, France, Italy, Switzerland, Germany, and Belgium and eventually gathered her travel letters in two volumes entitled *Letters from Abroad to Kindred at Home* (1841) and signed "By the Author of 'Hope Leslie,' 'Poor Rich Man and the Rich Poor Man,' 'Live and Let Live,' &c., &c."

Sedgwick knew that her travel book entered a densely populated territory. European travel, she wrote, is a field "so thoroughly reaped that not an ear, scarcely a kernel, remains for the gleaner." Sedgwick's text, informed by an interest in the question of American identity, reveals as well her gender anxieties. In a footnote, for example, she first praises the "rare gifts, attainments, and the almost unequalled richness and charm" of the conversation of Mrs. Anna Jameson, author of *Characteristics of Women* (1832); then, as if fearful that attainments will undermine women's nature, she adds, "[W]ith all these a woman may be, *after all*, but a kind of monster; how far they are transcended by the virtues and attractions of her domestic life, it was our happiness to know from seeing her daily in her English home."

Letters from Abroad proceeds chronologically, in epistolary form. Volume 1 is introduced with a conventional prefatory apology begging for "indulgence for the following pages . . . published rather with deference to the wishes of others than from any false estimate of their worth." While Volume 1 consists largely of letters from Britain, Volume 2 consists of letters from the continent. The excerpts that follow, taken from Volume 1 and written to Sedgwick's brother, Charles, from London, typify the tendency of American travelers to use travel as an occasion to write about America and to report on visits with literary figures and other notable people.

Letters from Abroad to Kindred at Home

My dear C.,

[. . .] I believe of all my pleasures here, dear J. will most envy me that of seeing Joanna Baillie,[1] and of seeing her repeatedly at her own home: the best point of view for all best women. She lives on Hempstead Hill, a few miles from town, in a modest house, with Miss Agnes Baillie, her only sister, a most kindly and agreeable person. Miss Baillie—I write this for J., for we women always like to know how one another look and dress—Miss Baillie has a well-preserved appearance; her face has nothing of the vexed or sorrowing expression that is often so deeply stamped by a long experience of life. It indicates a strong mind, great sensibility, and the benevolence that, I believe, always proceeds from it if the mental constitution be a sound one, as it eminently is in Miss Baillie's case. She has a pleasing figure—what we call lady-like—that is, delicate, erect, and graceful; not the large-boned, muscular frame of most Englishwomen. She wears her own gray hair: a general fashion, by-the-way, here, which I wish we elderly ladies of America may have the courage and the taste to imitate; and she wears the prettiest of brown silk gowns and bonnets fitting the beau ideal of an old lady: an ideal she might inspire if it has no pre-existence. You would, of course, expect her to be, as she is, free from pedantry and all modes of affectation; but I think you would be surprised to find yourself forgetting, in a domestic and confiding feeling, that you were talking with the woman whose name is best established among the female writers of her country; in short, forgetting everything but that you were in the society of a most charming private gentlewoman. She might (would that all female writers could!) take for her device a flower that closes itself against the noontide sun, and unfolds in the evening shadows.*

---

* In the United States Mrs. Barbauld would perhaps divide the suffrages with Miss Baillie; but in England, as far as my limited observation extended, she is not rated so high or so generally read as here. She has experienced the great disadvantage of being considered the organ of a sect. Does not the "Address to the Deity" and the "Evening's Meditation" rank with the best English poetry? and are not her essays, that on "Prejudice" and that on the "Inconsistency of Human Expectations," unsurpassed?

We lunched with Miss Baillie. Mr. Tytler the historian and his sister were present. Lord Woodhouselie, the intimate friend of Scott, was their father. Joanna Baillie appears to us, from Scott's letters to her, to have been his favourite friend; and the conversation among so many personally familiar with him naturally turned upon him, and many a pleasant anecdote was told, many a thrilling word quoted.

It was pleasant to hear these friends of Scott and Mackenzie talk of them as familiarly as we speak of W., B., and other household friends. They all agreed in describing Mackenzie[2] as a jovial, hearty sort of person, without any indication in his manners and conversation of the exquisite sentiment he infused into his writings. One of the party remembered his coming home one day in great glee from a cockfight, and his wife saying to him, "Oh, Harry, Harry, you put all your feelings on paper!"

I was glad to hear Miss Baillie, who is an intimate friend of Lady Byron, speak of her with tender reverence, and of her conjugal infelicity as not at all the result of any quality or deficiency on her part, but inevitable.* Strange this is not the universal impression, after Byron's own declaration to Moore that "there never was a better or even a brighter, a kinder or a more amiable and agreeable being than Lady B."

After lunch we walked over to a villa occupied by Miss Baillie's nephew, the only son of Dr. Baillie. It commands a view almost as beautiful and as English as that from Richmond Hill; a view extending far—far over wide valleys and gently-swelling hills, all standing thick with corn. Returning, we went to a point on Hampstead Hill overlooking the pretty "vale of 'ealth," as our coachman calls it, and which has been to us the vale of hospitality and most homelike welcome. This elevation, Miss B. told me, was equal to that of the ball on

---

* I should not have presumed, by a public mention of Lady Byron, to have penetrated the entrenchments of feminine delicacy and reserve which she has with such dignity maintained, but for the desire, as far as in my humble sphere I might do it, to correct the impression so prevailing among the readers of Moore's biography in this country, that Lady B. is one of those most unlovely of women who, finding it very easy to preserve a perpendicular line, have no sufferance for the deviations of others, no aptitude, no flexibility. How different this image from the tender, compassionate, loveable reality! the devoted mother, the trusted friend, the benefactress of poor children.

the dome of St. Paul's. We could just discern the dome penetrating far into the canopy of smoke that overhangs all London. Miss B. says Scott delighted in this view. It is melancholy, portentous, better suited, I should think, to the genius of Byron. I have seen sublime sights in my life, a midnight thunder-storm at Niagara and a "gallant breeze" on the seashore, but I never saw so spirit-stirring a spectacle as this immense city with its indefinite boundaries and its dull light. Here are nearly two millions of human beings, with their projects, pursuits, hopes, and despairs, their strifes, friendships, and rivalries, their loves and hates, their joys and anguish, some steeped to the lips in poverty, others encumbered with riches, some treading on the confines of Heaven, others in the abysses of sin, and all sealed with the seal of immortality. [. . .]

You will perhaps like to know, my dear C., more definitely than you can get them from these few anecdotes of my month in London, what impressions I have received here; and I will give them fairly to you, premising that I am fully aware how imperfect they are, and how false some of them may be. Travellers should be forgiven their monstrous errors when we find there are so few on whose sound judgments we can rely, of the character of their own people and the institutions of their own country.

In the first place, I have been struck with the *identity* of the English and the New-England character—the strong family likeness. The oak-tree may be our emblem, modified, but never changed by circumstances. Cultivation may give it a more graceful form and polish, and brighten its leaves, or it may shoot up more rapidly and vigorously in a new soil; but it is always the oak, with its strength, inflexibility, and "nodosities."

With my strong American feelings, and my love of home so excited that my nerves were all on the outside, I was a good deal shocked to find how very little interest was felt about America in the circles I chanced to be in. The truth is, we are so far off, we have so little *apparent* influence on the political machinery of Europe, such slight relations with the literary world, and none with that of art and fashion, that, except to the philosopher, the man of science, and the manufacturing and labouring classes, America is yet an undiscovered country, as distant and as dim as Heaven. It is not, perhaps, to be wondered at. There are new and exciting events every day at their own doors, and there are accumulations of interests in Europe to occupy a lifetime, and there are few anywhere who can abide Johnson's test when he says that, "whatever withdraws us from the power of our senses; whatever makes the past, the *distant*, or the future predominate over the present, advances us in the dignity of thinking beings." Inquiries are often put to me about my country, and I laugh at my own eagerness to impart knowledge and exalt their ideas of us, when I perceive my hearers listening with the forced interest of a courteous person to a teller of dreams.

One evening, in a circle of eminent people, the question was started, "what country came next in their affections to England?" I listened, in my greenness expecting to hear one and all say "America"; no, not one feeble voice uttered the name. Mrs. ——, with her hot love of art, naturally answered, "Italy is *first* to us all." "Oh, no," replied two or three voices, "England first, and next—Germany." "England first," said Mrs. A., "Germany next, and I think my third country is—Malta!" I thought of my own land, planted from the English stock, where the productions of these very speakers are most widely circulated, and, if destined to live, must have their longest life; the land where the most thorough and hopeful experiment of the capacity of the human race for knowledge, virtue, happiness, and self-government is now making; the land of promise and protection to the poor and disheartened of every country; and it seemed to me it should have superseded in their affections countries comparatively foreign to them.

I have seen instances of ignorance of us in quarters where you would scarcely expect it; for example, a very cultivated man, a bishop, asked K. if there were a theatre in America! and a person of equal dignity inquired "if the society of Friends was not the prevailing religious sect in Boston!" A literary man of some distinction asked me if the Edinburgh and Quarterly Reviews were read in America; and one of the cultivated women of England said to me, in a soothing tone, on my expressing admiration of English trees, "Oh, you will have such in time, when your forests are cut down, and they have room for their limbs to spread." I smiled and was silent; but if I saw in vision our graceful, drooping, elm-embowering roods of ground, and, as I looked at the stiff, upright English elm, had something of the pharisaical "holier than thou" flit over my mind, I may be forgiven.

I was walking one day with some young Englishwomen, when a short, sallow, broad man, to whom Nature had been niggardly, to say the least of it, passed us. "I think," said I, "that is a countryman of mine; I have seen him in New-York." "I took him for an American," said one of my companions, with perfect nonchalance. "Pray tell me why." "He looks so like the pictures in Mrs. Trollope's book!" It is true, this was a secluded young person in a provincial town, but I felt mortified that in one fair young mind Mrs. Trollope's vulgar caricatures should stand as the type of my countrymen.[3]

I have heard persons repeatedly expressing a desire to visit America—for what? "To see a prairie"— "to see Niagara"— "to witness the manner of the help to their employers; it must be so very comical!" but, above all, "to eat canvass-back ducks!" The canvass-backs are in the vision of America what St. Peter's is in the view of Rome. But patience, my dear C. In the first place, it matters little what such thinkers think of us; and then things are mending. The steamers have already cancelled half the distance between the two continents. "The two worlds are daily weaving more closely their interests and their friendships. I have been delighted with the high admiration expressed here in all quarters of Dr. Channing,[4] and, above all, to find that his pure religion has, with its angel's wings, surmounted the walls of sectarianism. I have heard him spoken of with enthusiasm by prelates as much distinguished for their religious zeal as for their station. Prescott's History[5] is spoken of in terms of unqualified praise. I have known but one exception. A reviewer, a hypercritic "dyed in the wool," sat next me at Mrs. ——'s dinner. He said Mr. Prescott must not hope to pass the English custom-house unless he wrote purer English, and he adduced several words which I have forgotten. I ventured to say that new words sprung out of new combinations of circumstances;* that, for example, the French revolution had created

---

* I was struck with the different views that are taken of the same subject in different positions, when afterward, in a conversation with the celebrated Manzoni, he asked me if America, in emancipating herself from political dependence, had also obtained intellectual freedom; if, unenslaved by the classic models of England, we venture to modify the language, and to use such new phrases and words as naturally sprung from new circumstances.

many words. "Yes," he replied, "and American words may do for America; but America is in relation to England a province. England must give the law to readers and writers of English." After some other flippant criticisms, he ended with saying that the History of Ferdinand and Isabella was one of the best extant, and that Mr. Prescott had exhausted the subject.

He said, what was quite true before the habits of colonial deference had passed away, but is no longer, "that an American book has no reputation in America till it is stamped with English authority, and then it goes off edition after edition." He uttered sundry other impertinences; but, as he seemed good-natured and unconscious that they were so, I sat them down to the account of individual ignorance and prejudice, not to nationality, which has too often to answer for private sins.

Society, as I have before told you, has the same general features here as with us. The women have the same time-wasting mode of making morning visits, which is even more consuming than with us, inasmuch as the distances are greater. What would Mrs. —— do in London, who thought it reason enough for removing from New-York to the country, that she had to spend one morning of every week in driving about town to leave visiting-cards? One would think that the proposition which circulates as undeniable truth, that time is the most valuable of possessions, would prevent this lavish expenditure. But it is not a truth. Nothing is less valuable to nine tenths of mere society people, or less valued by them, than time. The only thing they earnestly try to do is to get rid of it.

I have seen nothing here to change my opinion that there is something in the Anglo-Saxon race essentially adverse to the spirit and grace of society. I have seen more invention, spirit, and ease in one soirée in a German family at New-York, than I have ever seen here, or should see in a season in purely American society. An Englishman has an uncomfortable consciousness of the presence and observation of others; an immense love of approbation, with either a shyness or a defiance of opinion.

Thoroughly well-bred people are essentially the same everywhere. You will find much more conventional breeding here than with us, and, of course, the general level of manners is higher and the surface more uniform.

"Society is smoothed to that excess,
That manners differ hardly more than dress."

They are more quiet, and I should say there was less individuality, but from a corresponding remark having been made by English travellers among us. I take it the impression results from the very slight revelations of character that are made on a transient acquaintance. There is much more variety and richness in conversation here, resulting naturally from more leisure and higher cultivation. But, after all, there seems to me to be a great defect in conversation. The feast of wit and reason it may be, but it is not the flow and mingling of soul. The Frenchman, instructed by his *amour propre*, said truly, "*tout le monde aime planter son mot.*"* Conversation seems here to be a great arena, where each speaker is a gladiator who must take his turn, put forth his strength, and give place to his successor. Each one is on the watch to seize his opportunity, show his power, and disappear before his vanity is wounded by an indication that he is in the way. Thus conversation becomes a succession of illuminations and triumphs—or failures. There is no such "*horreur*" as a bore; no such bore as a proser. A bore might be defined to be a person that must be listened to. I remember R. saying that "kings are always bores, and so are royal dukes, for they must not be interrupted as long as they please to talk." The crowning grace of conversation, the listening with pleased eagerness, I have rarely seen. When Dr. C. was told that Coleridge pronounced him the most agreeable American he had ever seen, he replied, "Then it was because he found me a good listener, for I said absolutely nothing!" And yet, as far as we may judge from Coleridge's Table-Talk, he would have been the gainer by a fairer battle than that where

"One side only gives and t'other takes the blows."

A feature in society here that must be striking to Americans, is the great number of single women. With us, you know, few women live far beyond their minority unmated, and those few sink into the

---

* "Every man likes to put in his word."

obscurity of some friendly fireside. But here they have an independent existence, pursuits, and influence, and they are much happier for it; mind, I do not say happier than fortunate wives and good mothers, but than those who, not having drawn a husband in the lottery of life, resign themselves to a merely passive existence. Englishwomen, married and single, have more leisure and far more opportunity for intellectual cultivation, than with us. The objects of art are on every side of them, exciting their minds through their sensations and filling them with images of beauty. There is, with us, far more necessity, and, of course, opportunity, for the development of a woman's faculties for domestic life, than here; but this, I think, is counterbalanced by women's necessary independence of the other sex here. On the whole, it seems to me there is not a more loveable or lovely woman than the American matron, steadfast in her conjugal duties, devoted to the progress of her children and the happiness of her household, nor a more powerful creature than the Englishwoman in the full strength and development of her character.

Now, my dear C., a word as to dress for the womankind of your family. I do not comprehend what our English friends, who come among us, mean by their comments on the extravagance of dress in America. I have seen more velvet and costly lace in one hour in Kensington Garden than I ever saw in New-York; and it would take all the diamonds in the United States to dress a duchess for an evening at L—— house. You may say that lace and diamonds are transmitted luxuries, heir-looms (a species of inheritance we know little about); still you must take into the account the immense excess of their wealth over ours, before you can have a notion of the disparity between us.

The women here up to five-and-forty (and splendid women many of them are up to that age) dress with taste—fitness; after that, abominably. Women to seventy, and Heaven knows how much longer, leave their necks and arms bare; not here and there one, "blinded, deluded, and misguided," but whole assemblies of fat women—and, O tempora! O mores!—and *lean*. Such parchment necks as I have seen bedizzened with diamonds, and arms bared, that seemed only fit to hold the scissors of destiny, or to stir the caldron of Macbeth's witches. —— dresses in azure satins and rose-coloured silks, and bares her arms as if they were as round and dimpled as a cherub's, though they are mere bunches of sinews, that seem only kept together by that nice anatomical contrivance of the wristband on which Paley expatiates.[6] This post-mortem demonstration is perhaps, after all, an act of penance for past vanities, or perhaps it is a benevolent admonition to the young and fair, that to this favour they must come at last! Who knows?*

The entire absence of what seems to us fitness for the season may in part result from the climate. In June and July, you know, we have all our dark and bright colours, and rich stuffs—everything that can elicit the idea of warmth, laid aside; here we see every day velvets and boas, and purple, orange, and cherry silks and satins. Cherry, indeed, is the prevailing colour; cherry feathers the favourite headdress. I saw the Duchess of Cambridge the other evening at the opera with a crimson-velvet turban! Remember, it is July!

We have seen in the gardens plenty of delicate muslins over gay-coloured silks; this is graceful, but to us it seems inappropriate for an out-of-door dress.

The absence of taste in the middling classes produces results that are almost ludicrous. I am inclined to think taste is an original faculty, and only capable of a certain direction. This might explain the art of dress as it exists among the English, with the close neighbourhood of Paris, and French milliners actually living among them; and this might solve the mystery of the exquisite taste in gardening in England, and the total absence of it in France.

As you descend in the scale to those who can have only reference to the necessities of life in their dress, the English are far superior to us. Here come in their ideas of neatness, comfort, and durability. The labouring classes are much more suitably dressed than ours. They may have less finery for holy-days, and their servants may not be so *smartly* dressed in the evening as are our domestics, but they are never shabby or uncleanly.† Their clothes are of stouter stuffs, their shoes stronger, and their dress better preserved. We have not, you know, been into the

---

* It is to be hoped that Mrs. ——, in her promised essay on the philosophy of dress, will give some hints to our old ladies not to violate the harmonies by wearing auburn hair over wrinkled brows, and some to our young women on the bad taste of uniformity of costume without reference to individual circumstances or appearance. Her own countrywomen do not need these suggestions.

† Would it not be better if our rich employers would persuade their women-servants to wear caps, and leave liveries to countries whose institutions they suit?

manufacturing districts, nor into the dark lanes and holes of London, where poverty hides itself; but I do not remember, in five weeks in England, with my eyes pretty wide open, ever to have seen a ragbed or dirty dress. Dirt and rags are the only things that come under a rigid sumptuary law in England.

Order is England's, as it is Heaven's, first law. Coming from our head-over-heels land, it is striking and beautiful to see the precise order that prevails here. In the public institutions, in private houses, in the streets and thoroughfares, you enjoy the security and comfort of this Heaven-born principle. It raises your ideas of the capacities of human nature to see such masses of beings as there are in London kept, without any violation of their liberty, within the bounds of order. I am told the police system of London has nearly attained perfection. I should think so from the results. It is said that women may go into the street at any hour of the night without fear or danger; and I know that Mrs. —— has often left us after ten o'clock, refusing the attendance of our servant as superfluous, to go alone through several streets to the omnibus that takes her to her own home.*

The system of ranks here, as absolute as the Oriental *caste*, is the feature in English society most striking to an American. For the progress of the human race it was worth coming to the New World to get rid of it. Yes, it was worth all that our portion of the human family sacrificed, encountered, and suffered. This system of castes is the more galling, clogging, and unhealthy, from its perfect unfitness to the present state of freedom and progress in England.

Travellers laugh at our pretensions to equality, and Sir Walter Scott has said, as truly as wittily, that there is no perfect equality except among the Hottentots. But our inequalities are as changing as the surface of the ocean, and this makes all the difference. Each rank is set about here with a thorny, impervious, and almost impassable hedge. We have our walls of separation, certainly; but they are as easily knocked down or surmounted as our rail-fences.

---

*When we had been in London some weeks, one of my party asked me if I had not missed the New-York stacks of bricks and mortar, and if I had observed that we had not once heard a cry of "fire!" In these respects the contrast to our building and burning city is striking. In fifteen months' absence I never heard the cry of fire.

With us, talents, and education, and refined manners command respect and observance, and so, I am sorry to say, does fortune; but fortune has more than its proverbial mutability in the United States. The rich man of to-day is the poor man of to-morrow, and so vice versa. This unstableness has its evils, undoubtedly, and so has every modification of human condition; but better the evil that is accidental than that which is authorized, cherished, and inevitable. That system is most generous, most Christian, which allows a fair start to all; some must reach the goal before others, as, for the most part, the race is ordained to the swift, and the battle to the strong.

But you would rather have my observations than my speculations; and as, in my brief survey, I have only seen the outside, it is all I can give you, my dear C. I have no details of the vices of any class. I have heard shocking anecdotes of the corruption prevailing among the high people; and men and women have been pointed out to me in public places who have been guilty of notorious conjugal infidelities, and the grossest violations of parental duty, without losing caste; and this I have heard imputed to their belonging to a body that is above public opinion. I do not see how this can be, nor why the opinion of their own body does not bear upon them. Surely there should be virtue enough in such people as the Marquis of Lansdowne and the Duchess of Sutherland[7] to banish from their world the violators of those laws of God and man, on which rest the foundations of social virtue and happiness.

Those who, from their birth or their successful talents, are assured of their rank, have the best manners. They are perfectly tranquil, safe behind the entrenchments that have stood for ages. They leave it to the aspirants to be the videttes and defenders of the outworks. Those persons I have met of the highest rank have the simplest and most informal manners. I have before told you that Lord L—— and the Bishop of —— reminded me of our friends Judge L—— and Judge W——, our best-mannered country-gentlemen. Their lordships have rather more conventionalism, more practice, but there is no essential difference. Descend a little lower, and a very little lower than those gentry who by birth and association are interwoven with the nobility, and you will see people with education and refinement enough, as you would think, to ensure them the tranquillity that comes of self-respect, manifesting a consciousness of inferiority; in some it appears in servility, as in Mrs. ——, who, having scrambled on to ——'s shoulders and got a peep into the lord-and-lady world, and heard the buzz that rises from the precincts of Buckingham Palace, entertained us through a long morning visit with third or fourth hand stories about "poor Lady Flora"; or in obsequiousness, as in the very pretty wife of ——, whose eyes, cheeks, and voice are changed if she is but spoken to by a titled person, though she remains as impassive as polar ice to the influence of a plebeian presence. Some manifest their impatience of this vassalage of caste in a petulant but impotent resistance, and others show a crushed feeling, not the humility of the flower that has grown in the shade, but the abasement and incapacity ever to rise of that which has been trodden under foot. Even the limbs are stiffened and the gait modified by this consciousness that haunts them from the cradle to the grave.

A certain great tailor was here yesterday morning to take R.'s directions. His bad grammar, his obsequiousness, and his more than once favouring us with the information that he had an appointment with the Duke of ——, brought forcibly to my mind the person who holds the corresponding position in S——. I thought of his frank and self-respecting manner, his well-informed mind, his good influence, and the probable destiny of his children. I leave you to jump to my conclusion.

The language of the shopmen here indicates a want of education, and their obsequiousness expresses their consciousness that they are the "things that live by bowing." And, by-the-way, I see nothing like the rapidity of movement and adroitness in serving that you find in a New-York shop. You may buy a winter's supply at Stewart's while half a dozen articles are shown to you here. If you buy, they thank you; and if you refuse to buy, you hear the prescribed automaton, "Thank you!" I say "prescribed," for you often perceive an undercurrent of insolence. You will believe me that it is not civility to which I object.

As you go farther down from the tradesman to the servant, the marks of caste are still more offensive. Miss —— took me to the cottage of their herdsman. He had married a favourite servant, who had lived, I believe, from childhood in the family. The cottage was surrounded and filled with marks of affection and liberality. Miss ——

had told me that the woman belonged to a class now nearly extinct in England. "I verily believe," she said, "she thinks my mother and myself are made of a different clay from her"; and so her manner indicated, as she stood in a corner of the room, with her arms reverently folded, and courtesying with every reply she made to Miss ——, though nothing could be more kindly gracious than her manner. I thought of that dear old nurse who, though wearing the colour that is a brand among us, and not exceeded in devotedness by any feudal vassal of any age, expressed in the noble freedom of her manner that she not only felt herself to be of the same clay, but of the same spirit with those she served.

I confess I do see something more than "urbanity" in this "homage." I do not wish to be reminded, by a man touching his hat or pulling his forelock every time I speak to him, that there is a gulf between us. This is neither good for him nor me. Have those who pretend to fear the encroachments and growing pride of the inferior classes never any conscientious fears for their own humility? Do their reflections never suggest to them that pride is the natural concomitant of conscious superiority? But to return to these demonstrations of respect; they are not a sign of real deference. I have seen more real insolence here in five weeks in this class of people than I ever saw at home. At the inns, at the slightest dissatisfaction with the remuneration you offer, you are sure to be told, "Such as is *ladies* always gives more." This is meanness as well as insolence.

As we drove off from Southampton a porter demanded a larger fee than we paid. H. called after us to be sure and give the fellow no more. The fellow knew his quarry; he mounted on the coach, and kept with us through a long street, demanding and entreating with alternate insolence and abjectness. He got the shilling, and then returning to the homage of his station, "Do you sit quite comfortable, ladies?" he asked, in a sycophantic tone. "Yes." "Thank you." "Would not Miss —— like better this seat?" "No." "Thank you." Again I repeat it, it is not the civility I object to. I wish we had more of it in all stations; but it is the hollow sound, which conveys to me no idea but the inevitable and confessed vassalage of a fellow-being.

I am aware that the sins we are not accustomed to are like those we are not inclined to, in the respect that we condemn them heartily and en masse. Few Englishmen can tolerate the manners of our trades-people, our innkeepers, and the domestics at our public houses. A lit-tle more familiarity with them would make them tolerant of the defi-ciencies that at first disgust them, and after a while they would learn, as we do, to prize the fidelity and quiet kindness that abound among our servants without the expectation of pecuniary reward; and they would feel that it is salutary to be connected with this large class of our humble fellow-creatures by other than sordid ties.

If I have felt painfully that the men and women of what is called "good society" in America are greatly inferior in high cultivation, in the art of conversation, and in accomplishments, to a corresponding class here, I have felt quite assured that the "million" with us occupy a level they can never reach in England, do what they will with penny magazines and diffusive publications, while each class has its stall into which it is driven by the tyranny of an artificially constructed society.

While the marks No. 2, No. 3, and so on, are seen cut in, there cannot be the conscious power and freedom, and the self-respect brightening the eye, giving free play to all the faculties, and urging on-ward and upward, which is the glory of the United States, and a new phase of human society.

With your confirmed habits, my dear C., you might not envy the English the luxuries and magnificence of their high civilization; but I am sure you would the precise finish of their skilful agriculture, and the all-pervading comfort of their everyday existence. *If you have money*, there is no human contrivance for comfort that you cannot command here. Let you be where you will, in the country or in town, on land or on water, in your home or on the road, but signify your desires, and they may be gratified. And it is rather pleasant, dear C.—it would be with your eye for order—to be in a country where there are no bad—bad!—no imperfect roads, no broken or unsound bridges, no swinging gates, no barn-doors off the hinges, no broken glass, no ragged fences, no negligent husbandry, nothing to signify that truth omnipresent in America, that there is a great deal more work to do than hands to do it. And so it will be with our uncounted acres of unsubdued land for ages to come. But we are of English blood, and we shall go forward and subdue our great farm, and make it, in some hundreds of years, like the little garden whence our fathers came. In the mean time, we must expect the English travellers who come among us to be annoyed with the absence of the home-comforts which habit has made essential to their well-being, and to be startled, and, it may be, disgusted with the omission of those signs and shows of respect and deference to which they have been accustomed;[8] but let us not be disturbed if they growl, for "'tis their nature to," and surely they should be forgiven for it.*

---

*It is difficult for an American to appreciate the complete change that takes place in a European's position and relations on coming to this country; if he did, he would forgive the disgusts and uneasiness betrayed even by those who have the most philanthropic theories. He who was born in an atmosphere of elegance and refinement, far above the masses of his fellow-beings; who has seen them eager to obey his slightest signal, to minister to his artificial wants, ready to sit at his feet, to open a way for him, or to sustain him on their shoulders; who is always so far above them as to be in danger of entirely overlooking them, finds suddenly that all artificial props are knocked from under him, and he is brought down to a level with these masses, each individual elbowing his own way, and he obliged to depend on his own merit for all the eminence he attains. M. de Tocqueville is a striking illustration of the conflict between a democratic faith and the habits and tastes engendered by a European education. Perhaps some observation and reflection on this subject would convince parents of the injudiciousness of rearing children in Europe who are to live in America.

5

Caroline Kirkland

ॐ

Caroline Matilda Stansbury Kirkland (1801–1864) visited England, France, and Italy in 1848 with three friends. She later published a two-volume account of these travels as *Holidays Abroad; or Europe from the West* (1849). Already an established author at the time of her travels, Kirkland is identified on the title page for her book as "Mrs. Kirkland, author of 'A New Home,' 'Forest Life,' etc." After the publication of *A New Home—Who'll Follow?* (1839) and *Forest Life* (1842), a series of essays, came *Western Clearings* (1845), a collection of stories.

In the preface to her travel account, Kirkland declares her intention "to give a simple, personal narrative," in order that, taking the reader with her "through the medium of sympathy," she might "succeed in suggesting what may be advantageously accomplished by the traveller." Declaring that she writes for Americans, she claims, "I did not know, until I had begun to write down my impressions of European travel, how much audacity it requires to offer one's poor thoughts of these great and beautiful things, after all that has been well said about them." Addressing the plethora of travel materials on the market, she explains, "I was obliged to make a compromise with modesty, by secretly vowing to resist all temptation to put anything in my book which could be suspected of an intent to convey information, properly so called. A faithful reading of Murray's Guide Books will give more of that than one can use."

The format of Kirkland's text is chronological and erratic. She sometimes heads entries with dates as well as place names and sometimes omits dates altogether. In the selection that follows, taken from the end of Volume 2, Kirkland reflects on the English. In addition to manifesting the plurality of cultural discourses that comes into play in the travel genre, the excerpt typifies the work of antebellum women travelers on two counts: the effort to define American culture through its difference from England and the attempt to defend the United States from the attacks of British travelers to America.

Holidays Abroad

It is difficult to give one's views of a foreign country in the simple style of truth, without appearing to assume the office of the satirist. I must be allowed to insist on the difference between sarcastic remark, and a plain, unvarnished statement of facts or impressions. I am too sincere an admirer and lover of England to have a thought of sarcasm or depreciation in my heart, while I recall the pleasant days spent within her borders. But, on the other hand, I owe it to myself and my readers to state as plainly as possible the result of my observations, and particularly the conclusions to which I could not help coming, when comparison with our own country was suggested.

It might seem, at first view, that a long residence in a foreign country, was required to enable one to form a rational opinion of its characteristic features, and in some sense this may be true. For some descriptive purposes, it would, indeed, be necessary to become a denizen. But the broader and more general characteristics of a strange land are, perhaps, more fully within the observation of the mere tourist than of the closer student. We assimilate ourselves so rapidly with the people among whom we live, that in a short time their peculiarities are no longer such to us. It is by contrast with previous impressions and habits that we best discover them; and the traveller who would ascertain the points which distinguish his own country from that which he visits, must carefully note down his earliest impressions. To form a general estimate of the merits of the difference is quite another thing, and requires all the candor and good sense and sympathy we are able to bring to the work. In the remarks which follow I attempt nothing but to show how certain things in England seem to an American after a few weeks' observation. It is proverbially safe to believe one's own eyes, and the English are anything but cameleons.

The American in England is irresistibly prompted to comparisons. The language he hears on every side is essentially his mother tongue, yet it is spoken with such differences that it seems to him almost like another; or, if he be not accustomed to take much note of peculiarities of language, he is constantly reminded by the manner of those whom he addresses, that his natural talk is in some respects foreign to their ears. He recognizes in the national temperament a strong resemblance to what he had considered to be the prevailing tone at home; yet when he is in company with individual Englishmen, he is ready to suspect himself of being half French, and discovers, in his own looks, tones, and manner, a vivacity and demonstrativeness of which he had been before quite unconscious. The national maxims and sentiments are such as he loves and honors; they are just what make his pride and glory at home; just what form the favorite material for Fourth of July orations; yet the institutions which are supposed consonant with these maxims in England are those against which he has been a sworn enemy from his cradle. The most ordinary observation shows him that there are no people on earth more substantially free than the English; more free to act, speak, write, abuse their governors, hatch treason, preach agrarianism, burn haystacks, or do anything else that may pertain to the privileges of a self-governed people; but the same observation makes evident the fact that no people are more dazzled by rank, more servile to titled, or even merely wealthy insolence; more ambitious of the smallest rise in the social scale; more anxious to keep the downs down; more ready to swell with all their breath, the sails of success. He drops in at a county meeting where he hears a nobleman of immense wealth pouring out the overflowing of his honest soul in sentiments of brotherhood—of devotion to the interests of the laboring classes, of contempt for the shows and appliances of fortuitous exaltation; and he goes back to London in a perfect glow of delight, writes home his discovery that he has been all along mistaken in his ideas of the English aristocracy; that they are fine fellows, after all: as good democrats as can be found even at Albany. The next day he happens to be standing in St. James's Park when the company is passing to the Queen's drawing-room; and in one of the most gorgeous of all the equipages, round which hang clustering footmen in the most absurd and degrading of all the liveries, he recognizes his democrat of the county meeting. What wonder that he goes home and tears up yesterday's letter?

It is thus that the American in England walks in a sort of mystification. His ideal of the mother country was made up from books— not to-day's books, but books hallowed by time, and sealed by the whole world's love and gratitude. He did not, to be sure, expect to find Shakespeares; but he had unconsciously endowed the whole nation with something of Shakespeare's universality—the opposite of mean and narrow prejudice. He knew that a Milton is

"The single wonder of a thousand years,"

but he had, by a pleasant illusion, admitted a vague notion that the dignity and independence of Milton were national traits—at least we may take the liberty to express by this figure the somewhat romantic expectations with which we approach for the first time the land of our literature. It is a matter of feeling, not judgment—an impression— one of the illusions that we act upon without believing. It is natural for us to suppose that the great bond of a common literature is an effective bond; that souls fed on the same food must have some constitutional resemblance, some fruitful sympathies. We love England for her mighty ones, for her greatness, for being our mother; and we imagine that she loves us in return, for the sake of our common origin, for what we have done thus far, for our love of her.

But she does not love us. With all the large exceptions that we well know and remember—with all the private kindness that is accorded to a portion of the Americans who visit her shores, by a few of her noble spirits—

"Spirits that live inspher'd
In regions mild of calm and serene air
Above the smoke and stir of this dim spot—"

and whose more expanded sympathies enable them to receive us in the spirit in which we come—England, social England, looks upon her American children with contempt only half veiled; prizes not their love, scorns their admiration, views their efforts at improvement with a lofty disdain, and studiously avoids recognizing their claims to respect. Arrogating to herself a superiority that is never to be questioned, she cannot forgive our showing in her presence any other quality beside docility. If we come as mere learners—if we begin with an acknowledgment of hopeless inferiority—if we are willing to allow that to differ from England in any particular, important or trifling, is

to be wrong—she will look upon us with a certain sort of compla-
cency, abate a little of her superciliousness, and acknowledge that we
are not quite irredeemably benighted. But even then, the good sense
which perceives English infallibility is considered rather as an individual exception. America—the vague, disagreeable something which
universal England means by that word—still lies in darkness, at an
immeasurable distance; despising dignities—wild after every kind of
unrespectable novelty in politics and religion—abetting all sorts of
revolutions—repudiating—self-glorifying—stealing English books—
loving slavery for the pleasure of flaying slaves—chewing tobacco—
eating eggs out of wine-glasses!

Ideas must have original materials, as well as worlds; and the materials for this monstrous idea of our country are various. England will
not (yet) take the trouble of asking herself what they are, but no
American who has much intercourse with English society can be at a
loss to enumerate the leading ones. The corner of our rock of offence
is, of course, that old rebellion, so vexatiously successful, and, moreover, so particularly galling because brought on by the excessively
blind and blundering arrogance of the mother country, which, by a
little politic kindness, could have held her sprightly child in leading
strings for half a century more at least. She is practising every day the
lesson we taught her, and may thank this dear-bought wisdom for the
present stability of St. James's, such as it is. It is for want of such effectual teaching that the ex-king of the French is now her guest. But
we do not always appreciate this description of good offices.

The next stratum—for this is one of the cases in which we must
look deep for the foundations of an airy fabric—is perhaps not unlikely to be the war of 1812, which broke the spell of England as "mistress of the seas," and awakened her to the fact that Americans against
Englishmen makes very different fighting from Frenchmen against
Englishmen. So much of England's arrogance is founded upon her
past success in all matters dependant on physical force, that a blow in
that quarter tells deeply. She would be better content that we should
produce a new Shakespeare, though she would be very slow to acknowledge him. In the department of mind, she has not quite forgotten her ancient nobleness, for here it is her glorious ones that give
tone to public sentiment. Military and naval defeats and disgraces are
comprehensible by a quite different order of men, and serve to

awaken the enmity of the unquestioning crowd who make up the mass of every nation.

As to further material, it is hard to say whether slavery or repudiation is oftenest thrown in the teeth of Americans who venture to have opinions upon any subject in England. And if these matters be considered in the abstract, this is right enough. Nobody could say too much in condemnation of either; and the American who goes abroad ignorant, or perverted, or indifferent on either point, deserves whatever mortification he may encounter, and should bless Englishmen, or anybody else, for showing him the true aspect of such things. But it is quite another affair to receive with submission the impertinence of those who affect to treat slavery and repudiation as *American* sins; putting on an air of immaculate, insphered dignity; looking down, as it were, from an unapproachable height of virtue, upon our incomprehensible transgressions; wondering that we can look honest, pious people in the face, while we indulge our wicked propensities to oppression and fraud. As these subjects are always prominent in the English mind when Americans are present, it is quite natural that frequent allusion should be made to them; and it is quite as natural that the foreigner who feels the insolence of the imputations and implications never omitted on such occasions, should, yielding the ground entirely as to abstract right, defend himself and his country from contemptuous insult, by reminding his assailants of some favorite national sins of their own—for in England such sins are national, while here they are often, as in the present case, only sectional—sins which in their practical results outrun all the miseries and wrongs of slavery, and all the dishonesty of repudiation so far, that nothing but wilful blindness could mistake their enormity.

The mere abolition of the legalized slave-trade, which it took Wilberforce and Clarkson and their associates[1] twenty years to worry Great Britain into, is now the foundation of a self-glorification which throws ours out of the question; and the purchase of her West India slaves—that miserable expedient which, leaving the slave still at the mercy of the master, while their interests are more at variance than ever, has so signally failed of producing the true benefits of a hearty abolition—this mere drop of ill-managed concession to the opinions of the day, is considered a counterbalance for all the grinding and desolating oppression allowed in India, where slavery is still encouraged, because it fills the pockets of impoverished nobles and needy soldiers, who might else prove troublesome at home.

These are truths which our natural and hereditary reverence and affection for England would induce us to forget, if we were not forced to snatch up weapons of defence against unprovoked and ungenerous attacks.[2] To enter upon explanations and apologies with regard to the accusations brought against us were a hopeless task; for our good neighbors care only just enough about us to be sharp-sighted to our faults, not enough to take any pains to inform themselves as to our difficulties. It is easier to condemn than to examine.

Repudiation is but a minor item in the list of excuses for dislike; and if it could be visited upon those to whom it properly belongs, we should have nothing to say. But to insist on charging it upon the whole United States, is simply a piece of stolid ill-temper. The English are, to be sure, proverbially slow in the reception of foreign ideas, and doggedly set against the value of new ones; but they could easily, if they were desirous of doing justice, come at some notion of the nature of our confederacy, and our State independence; and so lay repudiation at its proper door, instead of pretending to consider it the bantling of republicanism. But they are peculiarly sensitive in the region of the pocket, and as they can only get three or four per cent. for money at home, it must doubtless have been a cruel disappointment to find that there was any uncertainty attending the reception of ten or twenty from us. We ought to feel very patient under their anger about repudiation.

With regard to that particular sort of national dishonesty which systematically appropriates other men's property and means of living, because it happens to be of a kind easily stolen, I confess to an humbled silence under British objurgation.[3] If anybody thinks that to write and publish a book, which others read, is not creating a property on which the author has a right to depend as a means of subsistence, I cannot agree with him; and I have never yet seen an argument on the subject which convinced me that it was less dishonest to steal a book than a pair of shoes. If an author has no right to live by his works, a clergyman can have no claim on account of his public teaching, or a legislator because he devotes his time to debate and the preparation for it. People who perform intellectual labor must form the single exception to the law which appoints that men shall enjoy that place in society to which their ability and industry entitle them. So absurd an idea I cannot advocate, even for the sake of defending the land I love against the angry taunts of our English neighbors. They are right in despising the moral coarseness which can think a wrong justified by the ease with which it can be perpetrated. They are quite right in feeling that the American people ought not to be willing to be amused and instructed without rendering some equivalent, merely because the creditor is so placed that he has no power to collect his dues. All that the American in England can say, when the sore subject is mentioned, is, that he hopes the day for such meanness is passing away. A higher general cultivation, and a nobler appreciation of the blessings and claims of mind, will undoubtedly set us right on this subject. May the time be not far distant!

But besides these larger causes of dislike, and leaving out of the account youth, prosperity, fame, growth—we have a vast number of petty successes to answer for—rivalries in inventions, improvements, commerce, navigation—everything which contributes to the material greatness of nations. To England we seem to be rioting in all the insolence of youthful strength, while she is conscious within herself of the symptoms of decadence. The curiosity, the vivacity, the activity, the restlessness, the forwardness, the want of reverence for age, which characterizes a young people, is offensive to her dignity. It is as if an old lady, seated in her quiet drawing-room, surrounded by all the cherished mementos of her youth, and all the acquisitions of her rich prime, should suddenly suffer the irruption of a parcel of school-boys—her brother's children, from the country; whose relationship she could not deny, and to whose well-developed limbs and good-looking faces her heart would warm under other circumstances; yet whose untamed sprightliness and unconscious nonchalance fill her with alarm. One spies out the darns in her well-saved carpet; another begins twirling the music-stool, soon discovers that its screw is out of order, and offers to mend it for her; another strikes the old harpsichord, and bursts into a gay laugh at its jingling. There may be others, meanwhile, who are quietly admiring the works of art which adorn her walls and pedestals, and yet more who are disposed to sit at her footstool, listening to her lessons of practical wisdom and experience. But she wishes them all gone! Their presence reminds her of the encroachments of a new generation; their strength is a reproach to her weakness—their vivacity is oppressive to the quiet self-complacency in which she had enshrined herself. A visit from one of her ancient gossips—whom sympathy would prevent from disturbing her thoughts, and whose elegant decrepitude, being greater than her own, would bring with it a certain amount of consolation—would be far more agreeable. The promise of her stout nephews is acknowledged, perhaps, but the approbation is very cold and unfruitful; especially if their father had imprudently connected himself, in early life, with "a young person not fit for good society"—which is the position our American freedom holds with regard to the liberty so much boasted of by the English. We have gone beyond the standard, and are wrong, of course. If we had contented ourselves with the exact measure and model of liberty enjoyed by our great mother, we might hope for her approbation. A step in advance is license, and vulgarizes us. Captain Hall,[4] a pretty fair exponent of the leading sentiment of his country, said that Americans must forever lack "the ennobling sentiment of *loyalty*." He meant loyalty to a man or an idea; he had no conception of loyalty to a principle, which is a far more ennobling sentiment.

The English feeling towards us is so natural, and so pardonable under the circumstances, that it is the silliest thing in the world to be vexed and made cross and spiteful by it. Personal experience of it is provoking, and I am far from advocating a tame submission in individual instances. But a national feeling of anger on such grounds, is totally unjustifiable and unworthy. The nation treats us with all the respect we can desire. Governments are not so reckless as to indulge contempt for their equals. The dislike and pretended contempt of which I speak, is a wholly private and social matter. It is closely akin to the Chinese feeling with respect to "outer barbarians," heightened, as that is, by fear, and by the necessity for a certain amount of outward civility. There is this difference, however—that the English have, after all, a vast fund of good sense and good feeling—a fund that must, in the long run, suffice for all exigencies, though it is not always available, or ready for small occasions. For this reason we shall never cease to love and honor them; and for the same they will be ready, in due time, to love and honor us. We can surely afford, therefore, to be patient.

6

Margaret Fuller Ossoli

૨♦

Margaret Fuller Ossoli (1810–1850), author, critic, feminist, Transcendentalist, and revolutionary, was educated according to the classical curriculum of her day. This was provided by her father, Timothy, who, disappointed that Sarah Margaret, as she was called, was not a boy, allowed her a masculine education. A formidable conversationalist, her most famous conversations were with such personages as Ralph Waldo Emerson, Orestes Brownson, George Ripley, Elizabeth and Sophia Peabody, Theodore Parker, Lydia Maria Child, and Ellen and Caroline Sturgis.

Fuller produced, with Emerson and others, *The Dial* and published *Summer on the Lakes* (1844) and *Papers on Literature and Art* (1846). Perhaps her most famous book is *Woman in the Nineteenth Century* (1845), a mature consideration of the political, intellectual, economic, and sexual aspects of feminism. In 1836 she wrote, "How am I to get the information I want, unless I go to Europe?" Her chance came a decade later when, in 1846, Horace Greeley of the *New York Tribune* (for whom Fuller had been writing articles on such institutions as Sing Sing and promoting the foundation of such institutions as a house of refuge for discharged women convicts) appointed her the *Tribune*'s foreign correspondent. She sailed for England on 1 August 1846 and, in the ritual fashion of American travelers, visited noteworthy people, including Wordsworth, Joanna Baillie, and the Italian patroit Mazzini, who was then in exile in England. In November of that year she crossed to France and visited George Sand and Chopin, among others. She arrived in Rome in April 1847 and became active in the revolutionary movement there; bore a son in 1848; married Giovanni Angelo, Marchese d'Ossoli, in 1849; and on her return voyage to the United States in 1850 died in a shipwreck off Fire Island, near New York.

Fuller's letters to the *Tribune* from Italy sometimes include conventional comment on tourist sites. For example, she declares in a letter from Rome dated 17 December 1847 that "like others," she "went through the painful process of sight-seeing, so unnatural everywhere, so counter to the healthful methods and true life of the mind." But she was in Italy during a period of revolutionary activity, when the Roman Republic was proclaimed, when the French laid seige to the city, and when the Republic was overthrown. These events, together with her own character and her role as a correspondent, dictate letters heavily concerned with political issues.

The excerpts in this selection are from Fuller's correspondence sent to the *Tribune* between 1847 and 1849. They appear as Letters 18 and 30 in *At Home and Abroad; or, Things and Thoughts in America and Europe* (1856; second edition 1895), edited and published by her brother Arthur after her death. Letter 18, undated, takes its place among the many nineteenth-century American texts of travel whose authors, absorbed with the United States and with American identity, find in European travel an occasion to express that preoccupation. Letter 30 reflects Fuller's attention to political and historical events and, documenting her republican fervor, places her solidly and vociferously in the revolutionary camp. As she pleads with her compatriots for the cause of the Italian republic, she reveals, again, that travel writing is inescapably about two worlds—home and abroad. Her text focuses on the revolution in Italy, but its subtext addresses America and the republican principles and millenial hope nurtured there.

At Home and Abroad

[Letter 18]

[. . .] This letter will reach the United States about the 1st of January; and it may not be impertinent to offer a few New-Year's reflections. Every new year, indeed, confirms the old thoughts, but also presents them under some new aspects.

The American in Europe, if a thinking mind, can only become more American. In some respects it is a great pleasure to be here. Although we have an independent political existence, our position toward Europe, as to literature and the arts, is still that of a colony, and one feels the same joy here that is experienced by the colonist in returning to the parent home. What was but picture to us becomes reality; remote allusions and derivations trouble no more: we see the pattern of the stuff, and understand the whole tapestry. There is a gradual clearing up on many points, and many baseless notions and crude fancies are dropped. Even the post-haste passage of the business American through the great cities, escorted by cheating couriers and ignorant *valets de place*, unable to hold intercourse with the natives of the country, and passing all his leisure hours with his countrymen, who know no more than himself, clears his mind of some mistakes—lifts some mists from his horizon.

There are three species. First, the servile American—a being utterly shallow, thoughtless, worthless. He comes abroad to spend his money and indulge his tastes. His object in Europe is to have fashionable clothes, good foreign cookery, to know some titled persons, and furnish himself with coffee-house gossip, by retailing which among those less travelled and as uninformed as himself he can win importance at home. I look with unspeakable contempt on this class—a class which has all the thoughtlessness and partiality of the exclusive classes in Europe, without any of their refinement, or the chivalric feeling which still sparkles among them here and there. However, though these willing serfs in a free age do some little hurt, and cause some annoyance at present, they cannot continue long; our country is fated to a grand, independent existence, and, as its laws develop, these parasites of a bygone period must wither and drop away.

Then there is the conceited American, instinctively bristling and proud of—he knows not what. He does not see, not he, that the history of Humanity for many centuries is likely to have produced results it requires some training, some devotion, to appreciate and profit by. With his great clumsy hands, only fitted to work on a steam-engine, he seizes the old Cremona violin, makes it shriek with anguish in his grasp, and then declares he thought it was all humbug before he came, and now he knows it; that there is not really any music in these old things; that the frogs in one of our swamps make much finer, for they are young and alive. To him the etiquettes of courts and camps, the ritual of the Church, seem simply silly—and no wonder, profoundly ignorant as he is of their origin and meaning. Just so the legends which are the subjects of pictures, the profound myths which are represented in the antique marbles, amaze and revolt him; as, indeed, such things need to be judged of by another standard than that of the Connecticut Blue-Laws.[1] He criticises severely pictures, feeling quite sure that his natural senses are better means of judgment than the rules of connoisseurs—not feeling that, to see such objects, mental vision as well as fleshly eyes are needed and that something is aimed at in Art beyond the imitation of the commonest forms of Nature. This is Jonathan[2] in the sprawling state, the booby truant, not yet aspiring enough to be a good school-boy. Yet in his folly there is meaning; add thought and culture to his independence, and he will be a man of might: he is not a creature without hope, like the thick-skinned dandy of the class first specified.

The artistes form a class by themselves. Yet among them, though seeking special aims by special means, may also be found the lineaments of these two classes, as well as of the third, of which I am now to speak.

This is that of the thinking American—a man who, recognizing the immense advantage of being born to a new world and on a virgin soil, yet does not wish one seed from the past to be lost. He is anxious to gather and carry back with him every plant that will bear a new climate and new culture. Some will dwindle; others will attain a bloom and stature unknown before. He wishes to gather them clean, free from noxious insects, and to give them a fair trial in his new world. And that he may know the conditions under which he may best place them in that new world, he does not neglect to study their history in this.

The history of our planet in some moments seems so painfully mean and little—such terrible bafflings and failures to compensate some brilliant successes—such a crushing of the mass of men beneath the feet of a few, and these, too, often the least worthy—such a small drop of honey to each cup of gall, and, in many cases, so mingled that it is never one moment in life purely tasted—above all, so little achieved for Humanity as a whole, such tides of war and pestilence intervening to blot out the traces of each triumph—that no wonder if the strongest soul sometimes pauses aghast; no wonder if the many indolently console themselves with gross joys and frivolous prizes. Yes! those men *are* worthy of admiration who can carry this cross faithfully through fifty years; it is a great while for all the agonies that beset a lover of good, a lover of men; it makes a soul worthy of a speedier ascent, a more productive ministry in the next sphere. Blessed are they who ever keep that portion of pure, generous love with which they began life! How blessed those who have deepened the fountains, and have enough to spare for the thirst of others! Some such there are; and, feeling that, with all the excuses for failure, still only the sight of those who triumph gives a meaning to life or makes its pangs endurable, we must arise and follow.

Eighteen hundred years of this Christian culture in these European kingdoms, a great theme never lost sight of, a mighty idea, an adorable history to which the hearts of men invariably cling, yet are genuine results rare as grains of gold in the river's sandy bed! Where is the genuine democracy to which the rights of all men are holy? where the child-like wisdom learning all through life more and more of the will of God? where the aversion to falsehood, in all its myriad disguises of cant, vanity, covetousness, so clear to be read in all the history of Jesus of Nazareth? Modern Europe is the sequel to that history, and see this hollow England, with its monstrous wealth and cruel poverty, its conventional life, and low, practical aims! See this poor France, so full of talent, so adroit, yet so shallow and glossy still, which could not escape from a false position with all its baptism of blood! See that lost Poland, and this Italy bound down by treacherous hands in all the force of genius! See Russia with its brutal Czar and innumerable slaves! See Austria and its royalty that represents nothing, and its people, who, as people, are and have nothing! If we consider the amount of truth that has really been spoken out in the world, and the love that has beat in private hearts—how genius has decked each spring-time with such splendid flowers, conveying each one enough of instruction in its life of harmonious energy, and how continually, unquenchably, the spark of faith has striven to burst into flame and light up the universe—the public failure seems amazing, seems monstrous.

Still Europe toils and struggles with her idea, and, at this moment, all things bode and declare a new outbreak of the fire, to destroy old palaces of crime! May it fertilize also many vineyards! Here at this moment a successor of St. Peter, after the lapse of near two thousand years, is called "Utopian" by a part of this Europe, because he strives to get some food to the mouths of the *leaner* of his flock.[3] A wonderful state of things, and which leaves as the best argument against despair, that men do not, *cannot* despair amid such dark experiences. And thou, my Country! Wilt thou not be more true? Does no greater success await thee? All things have so conspired to teach, to aid! A new world, a new chance, with oceans to wall in the new thought against interference from the old!—treasures of all kinds, gold, silver, corn, marble, to provide for every physical need! A noble, constant, starlike soul, an Italian, led the way to thy shores, and, in the first days, the strong, the pure, those too brave, too sincere, for the life of the Old World, hastened to people them. A generous struggle then shook off what was foreign, and gave the nation a glorious start for a worthy goal. Men rocked the cradle of its hopes, great, firm, disinterested men, who saw, who wrote, as the basis of all that was to be done, a statement of the rights, the *inborn* rights of men, which, if fully interpreted and acted upon, leaves nothing to be desired.

Yet, O Eagle! whose early flight showed this clear sight of the sun, how often dost thou near the ground, how show the vulture in these later days! Thou wert to be the advance-guard of humanity, the herald of all progress; how often hast thou betrayed this high commission! Fain would the tongue in clear, triumphant accents draw example from thy story, to encourage the hearts of those who almost faint and die beneath the old oppressions. But we must stammer and blush when we speak of many things. I take pride here, that I can really say the liberty of the press works well, and that checks and balances are found naturally which suffice to its government. I can say that the minds of our people are alert, and that talent has a free chance to rise. This is much. But dare I further say that political ambition is not as darkly sullied as in other countries? Dare I say that men of most influence in political life are those who represent most virtue, or even intellectual power? Is it easy to find names in that career of which I can speak with enthusiasm? Must I not confess to a boundless lust of gain in my country? Must I not concede the weakest vanity, which bristles and blusters at each foolish taunt of the foreign press, and admit that the men who make these undignified rejoinders seek and find popularity so? Can I help admitting that there is as yet no antidote cordially adopted, which will defend even that great, rich country against the evils that have grown out of the commercial system in the Old World? Can I say our social laws are generally better, or show a nobler insight into the wants of man and woman? I do, indeed, say what I believe, that voluntary association for improvement in these particulars will be the grand means for my nation to grow, and give a nobler harmony to the coming age. But it is only of a small minority that I can say they as yet seriously take to heart these things; that they earnestly meditate on what is wanted for their country, for mankind—for our cause is indeed the cause of all mankind at present. Could we succeed, really succeed, combine a deep religious love with practical development, the achievements of genius with the happiness of the multitude, we might believe man had now reached a commanding point in his ascent, and would stumble and faint no more. Then there is this horrible cancer of slavery, and the wicked war that has grown out of it. How dare I speak of these things here? I listen to the same arguments against the emancipation of Italy, that are used against the emancipation of our blacks; the same arguments in favor of the spoliation of Poland, as for the conquest of Mexico. I find the cause of tyranny and wrong everywhere the same—and lo! my country! the darkest offender, because with the least excuse; forsworn to the high calling with which she was called; no champion of the rights of men, but a robber and a jailer; the scourge hid behind her banner; her eyes fixed, not on the stars, but on the possessions of other men.

How it pleases me here to think of the Abolitionists! I could never endure to be with them at home, they were so tedious, often so narrow, always so rabid and exaggerated in their tone. But, after all, they had a high motive, something eternal in their desire and life; and if it was not the only thing worth thinking of, it was really something worth living and dying for, to free a great nation from such a terrible blot, such a threatening plague. God strengthen them, and make them wise to achieve their purpose!

I please myself, too, with remembering some ardent souls among the American youth, who I trust will yet expand, and help to give soul to the huge, over-fed, too hastily grown-up body. May they be constant! "Were man but constant, he were perfect," it has been said; and it is true that he who could be constant to those moments in which he has been truly human, not brutal, not mechanical, is on the sure path to his perfection, and to effectual service of the universe.

It is to the youth that hope addresses itself; to those who yet burn with aspiration, who are not hardened in their sins. But I dare not expect too much of them. I am not very old; yet of those who, in life's morning, I say touched by the light of a high hope, many have seceded. Some have become voluptuaries; some, mere family men, who think it quite life enough to win bread for half a dozen people, and treat them decently; others are lost through indolence and vacillation. Yet some remain constant;

> "I have witnessed many a shipwreck,
> Yet still beat noble hearts."

I have found many among the youth of England, of France, of Italy, also, full of high desire; but will they have courage and purity to fight the battle through in the sacred, the immortal band? Of some of them I believe it, and await the proof. If a few succeed amid the trial, we have not lived and loved in vain.

To these, the heart and hope of my country, a happy new year! I do not know what I have written; I have merely yielded to my feelings in thinking of America; but something of true love must be in these lines. Receive them kindly, my friends; it is, of itself, some merit for printed words to be sincere.

[Letter 30]
Rome, May 27, 1849

I have suspended writing in the expectation of some decisive event; but none such comes yet. The French, entangled in a web of falsehood, abashed by a defeat that Oudinots[4] has vainly tried to gloss over, the expedition disowned by all honorable men at home, disappointed at Gaeta,[5] not daring to go the length Papal infatuation demands, know not what to do. The Neapolitans have been decidedly driven back into their own borders, the last time in a most shameful rout, their king flying in front. We have heard for several days that the Austrians were advancing, but they come not. They also, it is probable, meet with unexpected embarrassments. They find that the sincere movement of the Italian people is very unlike that of troops commanded by princes and generals who never wished to conquer and were always waiting to betray. Then their troubles at home are constantly increasing, and, should the Russian intervention quell these to-day, it is only to raise a storm far more terrible to-morrow.

The struggle is now fairly, thoroughly commenced between the principle of democracy and the old powers, no longer legitimate. That struggle may last fifty years, and the earth be watered with the blood and tears of more than one generation, but the result is sure. All Europe, including Great Britain, where the most bitter resistance of all will be made, is to be under republican government in the next century.

"God moves in a mysterious way."

Every struggle made by the old tyrannies, all their Jesuitical deceptions, their rapacity, their imprisonments and executions of the most generous men, only sow more dragon's teeth; the crop shoots up daily more and more plenteous.

When I first arrived in Italy, the vast majority of this people had no wish beyond limited monarchies, constitutional governments. They still respected the famous names of the nobility; they despised the priests, but were still fondly attached to the dogmas and ritual of the Roman Catholic Church. It required King Bomba, the triple treachery of Charles Albert, Pius IX, and the "illustrious Gioberti," the naturally kind-hearted, but, from the necessity of his position, cowardly and false Leopold of Tuscany, the vagabond "serene" meannesses of Parma and Modena, the "fatherly" Radetzsky, and, finally, the imbecile Louis Bonaparte, "would-be Emperor of France,"[6] to convince this people that no transition is possible between the old and the new. *The work is done;* the revolution in Italy is now radical, nor can it stop till Italy becomes independent and united as a republic. Protestant she already is, and though the memory of saints and martyrs may continue to be revered, the ideal of woman to be adored under the name of Mary, yet Christ will now begin to be a little thought of; *his* idea has always been kept carefully out of sight under the old *régime;* all the worship being for the Madonna and saints, who were to be well paid for interceding for sinners—an example which might make men cease to be such, was no way coveted. Now the New Testament has been translated into Italian; copies are already dispersed far and wide; men calling themselves Christians will no longer be left entirely ignorant of the precepts and life of Jesus.

The people of Rome have burnt the Cardinals' carriages. They took the confessionals out of the churches, and made mock confessions in the piazzas, the scope of which was, "I have sinned, father, so and so."

"Well, my son, how much will you *pay* to the Church for absolution?" Afterward the people thought of burning the confessionals, or using them for barricades; but at the request of the Triumvirate they desisted, and even put them back into the churches. But it was from no reaction of feeling that they stopped short, only from respect for the government. The "Tartuffe" of Molière has been translated into Italian, and was last night performed with great applause at the Valle. Can all this be forgotten? Never! Should guns and bayonets replace the Pope on the throne, he will find its foundations, once deep as modern civilization, now so undermined that it falls with the least awkward movement.

But I cannot believe he will be replaced there. France alone could consummate that crime—that, for her, most cruel, most infamous treason. The elections in France will decide. In three or four days we shall know whether the French nation at large be guilty or no— whether it be the will of the nation to aid or strive to ruin a government founded on precisely the same basis as their own.

I do not dare to trust that people. The peasant is yet very ignorant. The suffering workman is frightened as he thinks of the punishments that ensued on the insurrections of May and June. The man of property is full of horror at the brotherly scope of Socialism. The aristocrat dreams of the guillotine always when he hears men speak of the people. The influence of the Jesuits is still immense in France. Both in France and England the grossest falsehoods have been circulated with unwearied diligence about the state of things in Italy. An amusing specimen of what is still done in this line I find just now in a foreign journal, where it says there are red flags on all the houses of Rome; meaning to imply that the Romans are athirst for blood. Now, the fact is, that these flags are put up at the entrance of those streets where there is no barricade, as a signal to coachmen and horsemen that they can pass freely. There is one on the house where I am, in which is no person but myself, who thirst for peace, and the Padrone, who thirsts for money.

Meanwhile the French troops are encamped at a little distance from Rome. Some attempts at fair and equal treaty when their desire to occupy Rome was firmly resisted, Oudinot describes in his despatches as a readiness for *submission*. Having tried in vain to gain this point, he has sent to France for fresh orders. These will be decided by the turn the election takes. Meanwhile the French troops are much exposed to the Roman force where they are. Should the Austrians come up, what will they do? Will they shamelessly fraternize with the French, after pretending and proclaiming that they came here as a check upon their aggressions? Will they oppose them in defence of Rome, with which they are at war?

Ah! the way of falsehood, the way of treachery—how dark, how full of pitfalls and traps! Heaven defend from it all who are not yet engaged therein!

War near at hand seems to me even more dreadful than I had fancied it. True, it tries men's souls, lays bare selfishness in undeniable deformity. Here it has produced much fruit of noble sentiment, noble act; but still it breeds vice too, drunkenness, mental dissipation, tears asunder the tenderest ties, lavishes the productions of Earth, for which her starving poor stretch out their hands in vain, in the most unprofitable manner. And the ruin that ensues, how terrible! Let those who have ever passed happy days in Rome grieve to hear that the beautiful plantations of Villa Borghese—that chief delight and refreshment of citizens, foreigners, and little children—are laid low, as far as the obelisk. The fountain, singing alone amid the fallen groves, cannot be seen and heard without tears; it seems like some innocent infant calling and crowing amid dead bodies on a field which battle has strewn with the bodies of those who once cherished it. The plantations of Villa Salvage on the Tiber, also, the beautiful trees on the way from St. John Lateran to La Maria Maggiore, the trees of the Forum, are fallen. Rome is shorn of the locks which lent grace to her venerable brow. She looks desolate, profaned. I feel what I never expected to—as if I might by and by be willing to leave Rome.

Then I have, for the first time, seen what wounded men suffer. The night of the 30th of April I passed in the hospital, and saw the terrible agonies of those dying or who needed amputation, felt their mental pains and longing for the loved ones who were away; for many of these were Lombards, who had come from the field of Novarra to fight with a fairer chance—many were students of the University, who had enlisted and thrown themselves into the front of the engagement. The impudent falsehoods of the French general's despatches are incredible. The French were never decoyed on in any way. They were received with every possible mark of hostility. They were defeated in open field, the Garibaldi legion rushing out to meet them; and though they suffered much from the walls, they sustained themselves nowhere. They never put up a white flag till they wished to surrender. The vanity that strives to cover over these facts is unworthy of men. The only excuse for the imprudent conduct of the expedition is that they were deceived, not by the Romans here, but by the priests of Gaeta, leading them to expect action in their favor within the walls. These priests themselves were deluded by their hopes and old habits of mind. The troops did not fight well, and General Oudinot abandoned his wounded without proper care. All this says nothing against French valor, proved by ages of glory, beyond the doubt of their worst foes. They were demoralized because they fought in so bad a cause, and there was no sincere ardor or clear hope in any breast. [. . .]

It is most unfortunate that we should have an envoy here for the first time, just to offend and disappoint the Romans. When all the other ambassadors are at Gaeta, ours is in Rome, as if by his presence to discountenance the republican government, which he does not recognize. Mr. Cass,[7] it seems, is required by his instructions not to recognize the government till sure it can be sustained. Now it seems to me that the only dignified ground for our government, the only legitimate ground for any republican government, is to recognize for any nation the government chosen by itself. The suffrage had been correct here, and the proportion of votes to the whole population was much larger, it was said by Americans here, than it is in our own country at the time of contested elections. It had elected an Assembly; that Assembly had appointed, to meet the exigencies of this time, the Triumvirate. If any misrepresentations have induced America to believe, as France affects to have believed, that so large a vote could have been obtained by moral intimidation, the present unanimity of the population in resisting such immense odds, and the enthusiasm of their every expression in favor of the present government, puts the matter beyond a doubt. The Roman people claims once more to have a national existence. It declines further serfdom to an ecclesiastical court. It claims liberty of conscience, of action, and of thought. Should it fall from its present position, it will not be from internal dissent, but from foreign oppression.

Since this is the case, surely our country, if no other, is bound to recognize the present government *as long as it can sustain itself.* This position is that to which we have a right: being such, it is no matter how it is viewed by others. But I dare assert it is the only respectable one for our country, in the eyes of the Emperor of Russia himself.

The first, best occasion is past, when Mr. Cass might, had he been empowered to act as Mr. Rush[8] did in France, have morally strengthened the staggering republic, which would have found sympathy where alone it is of permanent value, on the basis of principle. Had it been in vain, what then? America would have acted honorably; as to our being compromised thereby with the Papal government, that fear is idle. Pope and Cardinals have great hopes from America; the giant influence there is kept up with the greatest care; the number of Catholic writers in the United States, too, carefully counted. Had our republican government acknowledged this republican government, the Papal Camarilla[9] would have respected us more, but not loved us less; for have we not the loaves and fishes to give, as well as the precious souls to be saved? Ah! here, indeed, America might go straightforward with all needful impunity. Bishop Hughes himself need not be anxious. That first, best occasion has passed, and the unrecognized, unrecognizing Envoy has given offence, and not comfort, by a presence that seemed constantly to say, I do not think you can sustain yourselves. It has wounded both the heart and the pride of Rome. Some of the lowest people have asked me, "Is it not true that your country had a war to become free?" "Yes." "Then why do they not feel for us?"

Yet even now it is not too late. If America would only hail triumphant, though she could not sustain injured Rome, that would be something. "Can you suppose Rome will triumph," you say, "without money, and against so potent a league of foes?" I am not sure, but I hope, for I believe something in the heart of a people when fairly awakened. I have also a lurking confidence in what our fathers spoke of so constantly, a providential order of things, by which brute force and selfish enterprise are sometimes set at naught by aid which seems to descend from a higher sphere. Even old pagans believed in that, you know; and I was born in America, Christianized by the Puritans—America, freed by eight years' patient suffering, poverty, and struggle—America, so cheered in dark days by one spark of sympathy from a foreign shore—America, first "recognized" by Lafayette.[10] I saw him when traversing our country, then great, rich, and free. Millions of men who owed in part their happiness to what, no doubt, was once sneered at as romantic sympathy, threw garlands in his path. It is natural that I should have some faith.

Send, dear America! to thy ambassadors a talisman precious beyond all that boasted gold of California. Let it loose his tongue to cry, "Long live the Republic, and may God bless the cause of the people, the brotherhood of nations and of men—the equality of rights for all." *Viva America!*

Hail to my country! May she live a free, a glorious, a loving life, and not perish, like the old dominions, from the leprosy of selfishness. [. . .]

7

Nancy Prince

ॐ

Nancy Gardner Prince (born 1799), opening her account with a personal family history, highlights the family ties between autobiography and travel writing. She tells the reader of her narrative that her grandmother was a Native American captured by the English; that her grandfather, who fought at the battle of Bunker Hill, was a slave stolen from Africa when a lad; and that her stepfather, with whom her mother had six children, escaped from a slave ship arriving from Africa by swimming ashore—a story he often recounted. She adds that her own father died and left her mother with two children when Nancy was three months old. Her stepfather was impressed into service as a mariner, and Nancy's brother, too, followed the sea, making it probable that in her youth, during which she lived in Massachusetts, Nancy Prince heard tales of travel and adventure.

In 1824, Nancy married Nero Prince, who was attached to the court of the tsar of Russia, and on 14 April 1824 they embarked for Russia, where they lived until 1833. She returned to America for seven years before setting out in 1840 to work as a missionary in Jamaica. In 1841 she returned to the United States and for nine months solicited aid in Philadelphia for Jamaicans; in 1842, she returned to Jamaica for a period of four months. From these collective experiences came a pamphlet on Jamaica (1841) and a book entitled *A Narrative of the Life and Travels of Mrs. Nancy Prince*, which first appeared in 1850 and which was followed by a second, expanded edition in 1853 and by a third and final edition in 1856.[1]

The format of Prince's book is chronological, the content heavily autobiographical. The first and second excerpts presented in this selection address Russian manners and customs. These excerpts follow a sketch of Prince's early life, her marriage, and her voyage to Russia. The third excerpt, about Jamaica and Prince's activities there, follows further descriptions of Russia and its climate; Prince's departure from St. Petersburg in 1833; her return to Boston and her occupational pursuits there; and her voyage to Jamaica. The last excerpt, about her final return to the United States, follows Prince's account of an earlier return in 1841 and a description of the history, topography, and climate of the West Indies. Prince concludes her narrative with thanks to God and with a poem entitled "The Hiding Place." Taken from the second edition of her narrative, these excerpts show Prince's attention to ethnographic detail, and they document the perils to which travel exposed a free Black.

A Narrative of the Life and Travels of Mrs. Nancy Prince

[. . .] The palace where the imperial family reside is called the court, or the seat of Government. This magnificent building is adorned with all the ornaments that possibly can be explained; there are hundreds of people that inhabit it, besides the soldiers that guard it. There are several of these splendid edifices in the city and vicinity. The one that I was presented in, was in a village, three miles from the city. After leaving the carriage, we entered the first ward; where the usual salutation by the guards was performed. As we passed through the beautiful hall, a door was opened by two colored men in official dress. The Emperor Alexander, stood on his throne, in his royal apparel. The throne is circular, elevated two steps from the floor, and covered with scarlet velvet, tasseled with gold; as I entered, the Emperor stepped forward with great politeness and condescension, and welcomed me, and asked several questions; he then accompanied us to the Empress Elizabeth; she stood in her dignity, and received me in the same manner the Emperor had. They presented me with a watch, &c. It was customary in those days, when any one married, belonging to the court, to present them with gifts, according to their standard; there was no prejudice against color; there were all castes, and the people of all nations, each in their place.

The number of colored men that filled this station was twenty; when one dies, the number is immediately made up. Mr. Prince filled the place of one that had died. They serve in turns, four at a time, except on some great occasions, when all are employed. Provision is made for the families within or without the palace. Those without go to court at 8 o'clock in the morning; after breakfasting, they take their station in the halls, for the purpose of opening the doors, at signal given, when the Emperor and Empress pass.

First of August, we visited the burying-ground where the people meet, as they say, to pay respect to their dead. It is a great holiday; they drink and feast on the grave stones, or as near the grave as they can come; some groan and pray, and some have music and dancing. At a funeral no one attends except the invited; after the friends arrive, a dish of rice, boiled hard, with raisins, is handed round; all are to take a spoonful, with the same spoon, and out of the same dish; in the meanwhile the priest, with his clerk, performs the ceremony, perfuming the room with incense. The lid is not put on to the coffin, the corpse being laid out in his or her best dress. The torch-men (who are dressed in black garments, made to slope down to their feet, with broad brimmed hats that cover their shoulders,) form a procession, with lighted torches in their hands, bowing their heads as they pass along very gravely; then comes one more with the lid on his head; then the hearse with the corpse drawn by four horses, covered with black gowns down to their feet; they all move along with great solemnity. Before entering the grave-yard, the procession goes to an adjoining church, where there are many ladies, placed on benches, side by side, according to their ages; the ladies dressed as if they were going to a ball-room, displaying a most dreadful appearance. Each one has her hands crossed, and holding in one of them a pass to give to Peter, that they may enter into Heaven. At this place they light their candles, and receive their rice in the manner before mentioned. The top is then put on to the coffin, and the procession forms and repairs to the grave; the priest sanctifies the grave, then casts in dust, and the coffin is consigned to its narrow-house; then commence the yells; they drink, eat cake, black bread, and finish their rice, when the party return back to dinner, where every thing has been prepared during their absence. This is the Greek mode of burying their dead. On the birth of a child, the babe is not dressed until it is baptized; it is immersed all over in water; a stand with an oval basin, is brought for the purpose by the clerk. The mother is presented with gifts, which are placed under her pillow. Should the babe die before this rite is performed, it is not placed with the others; but should it die having been baptized, although not more than two hours old, it is dressed and placed on the bench at church with the rest. In this manner, the common people bury their dead.

When any of the imperial family dies, they are laid in state forty days, and every thing accordingly. There is a building built expressly for the imperial families, where their remains are deposited. In the front part of it, the criminals that have rebelled against the imperial family are placed in cells, thus combining the prison and the tomb;

and in sailing by, these miserable creatures are exposed to the careless gaze of unfeeling observers.

St. Petersburg was inundated October 9th, 1824. The water rose sixteen feet in most parts of the city; many of the inhabitants were drowned. An island between the city and Cronstadt, containing five hundred inhabitants, was inundated, and all were drowned, and great damage was done at Cronstadt. The morning of this day was fair; there was a high wind. Mr. Prince went early to the palace, as it was his turn to serve; our children boarders were gone to school; our servant had gone of an errand. I heard a cry, and to my astonishment, when I looked out to see what was the matter, the waters covered the earth. I had not then learned the language, but I beckoned to the people to come in. The waters continued to rise until 10 o'clock, A.M. The waters were then within two inches of my window, when they ebbed and went out as fast as they had come in, leaving to our view a dreadful sight. The people who came into my house for their safety retired, and I was left alone. At four o'clock in the afternoon, there was darkness that might be felt, such as I had never experienced before. My situation was the more painful, being alone, and not being able to speak. I waited until ten in the evening; I then took a lantern, and started to go to a neighbor's, whose children went to the same school with my boarders. I made my way through a long yard, over the bodies of men and beasts, and when opposite their gate I sunk; I made one grasp, and the earth gave away; I grasped again, and fortunately got hold of the leg of a horse, that had been drowned. I drew myself up, covered with mire, and made my way a little further, when I was knocked down by striking against a boat, that had been washed up and left by the retiring waters; and as I had lost my lantern, I was obliged to grope my way as I could, and feeling along the walk, I at last found the door that I aimed at. My family were safe and they accompanied me home. At 12 o'clock, Mr. Prince came home, as no one was permitted to leave the palace, till his majesty had viewed the city. In the morning the children and the girl returned, and I went to view the pit into which I had sunk. It was large enough to hold a dozen like myself, where the earth had caved in. Had not the horse been there, I should never again have seen the light of day, and no one would have known my fate. Thus through the providence of God, I escaped from the flood and the pit.

My helper, God, I bless thy name;
The same thy power, thy grace the same;
I 'midst ten thousand dangers stand,
Supported by thy guardian hand.

[. . .]

May, 1825. I spent some time visiting the different towns in the vicinity of St. Petersburg. In the fall of the same year, the Emperor retired to a warmer climate for the health of the Empress Elizabeth. January, 1826, the corpse of Alexander was brought in state, and was met three miles from the city by the nobles of the court; and they formed a procession, and the body was brought in state into the building where the imperial family were deposited. March, of the same year, the corpse of Elizabeth was brought in the same manner. Constantine was then king of Poland, he was next heir to the throne, and was, unanimously voted by the people, but refused and resigned the crown in favor of his brother Nicholas. The day appointed the people were ordered to assemble as usual, at the ringing of the bells; they rejected Nicholas; a sign was given by the leaders that was well understood, and the people great and small rushed to the square and cried with one voice for Constantine. The emperor with his prime minister, and city governor, rode into the midst of them, entreating them to retire, without avail; they were obliged to order the cannons fired upon the mob; it was not known when they discharged them that the emperor and his ministers were in the crowd. He was wonderfully preserved, while both his friends and their horses were killed. There was a general seizing of all classes, who were taken into custody. The scene cannot be described; the bodies of the killed and mangled were cast into the river, and the snow and ice were stained with the blood of human victims; as they were obliged to drive the cannon to and fro in the midst of the crowd, the bones of those wounded, who might have been cured, were crushed. The cannon are very large, drawn by eight horses, trained for the purpose. The scene was awful; all business was stopped. This deep plot originated in 1814, in Germany, with the Russian nobility and German, under the pretence of a Free Mason's Lodge. When they returned home they increased their numbers and presented their chart to the emperor for permission, which was granted. In the year 1822, the emperor being suspicious that all was not right, took their chart from them. They carried it on in small parties, rapidly increasing, believing they would soon be able to destroy all the imperial branches, and have a republican government. Had not this taken place, undoubtedly they would at last have succeeded. So deep was the foundation of this plot laid, both males and females were engaged in it. The prison-houses were filled, and thirty of the leading men were put in solitary confinement, and twenty-six of the number died, four were burned. A stage was erected and faggots were placed underneath, each prisoner was secured by iron chains, presenting a most appalling sight to an eye-witness. A priest was in attendance to cheer their last dying moments, then fire was set to the faggots, and those brave men were consumed. Others received the knout, and even the princesses and ladies of rank were imprisoned and flogged in their own habitations. Those that survived their punishment were banished to Siberia. The mode of banishment is very imposing and very heart-rending, severing them from all dear relatives and friends, for they are never permitted to take their children. When they arrive at the gate of the city, their first sight is a guard of soldiers, then wagons with provisions, then the noblemen in their banished apparel guarded, then each side, conveyances for the females, then ladies in order, guarded by soldiers.

Preparations were now being made for the coronation of the new Emperor and Empress. This took place September, 1826, in Moscow, 555 miles south-east from St. Petersburg. All persons engaged in the court were sent beforehand, in order to prepare for the coming event. After his majesty's laws were read, as usual on such occasions, those who wished to remain in his service did so, and those who did not were discharged.

After the coronation, the Emperor and his court returned to St. Petersburg. June, 1827, war was declared between Russia and Turkey. They had several battles, with varied success. The Russians surrounded and laid siege to Constantinople. The Sultan of Turkey sued for peace, and a treaty was at last signed, and peace was proclaimed in 1829. In March, of the same year, war was declared with Poland. 1831. The cholera, that malignant disease, made its appearance in Austria, from thence to little Russia, making great ravages, thousands of people falling a prey. It then began to rage in St. Petersburg, carrying off 9,255. This disease first appeared in Madagascar, 1814, where most of the inhabitants died. It is called the plague, that God sent among the people of Israel and other nations, for centuries back. Much might be said of this dreadful disease and others that are but little known in this country. God often visits nations, families, and persons, with judgments as well as mercies.

The present Emperor and Empress are courteous and affable. The Empress would often send for the ladies of the court at 8 o'clock in the evening to sup with her: when they arrive at the court they form a procession and she takes the lead. On entering the hall, the band strikes up; there are two long tables on each side, and in the midst circular tables for the imperial family. The tables are spread apparently with every variety of eatables and desserts, but everything is artificial, presenting a novel appearance. When the company are seated, the Emperor and Empress walk around the tables and shake hands with each individual, as they pass. The prisoners of war who are nobles, are seated by themselves with their faces veiled. There is a tender or waiter to each person, with two plates, one with soup and the other with something else. After a variety of courses, in one hour they are dismissed by the band. They then retire to another part of the palace to attend a ball or theatrical amusements. At the Empress' command they are dismissed. She carries power and dignity in her countenance, and is well adapted to her station. And after her late amusements at night, she would be out at an early hour in the morning, visiting the abodes of the distressed, dressed in as common apparel as any one here, either walking, or riding in a common sleigh. At her return she would call for her children, to take them in her arms and talk to them. "She riseth while it is yet night and giveth meat to her household and a portion to her maidens, she stretcheth out her hands to the poor, yea, she reacheth out her hands to the needy; she is not afraid of the snow, for all her household are clothed in scarlet." Then she would go to the cabinet of his Majesty; there she would write and advise with him.

The Russian ladies follow the fashions of the French and English. Their religion is after the Greek Church. There are no seats in their churches; they stand, bow, and kneel, during the service. The principal church is on the Main street. There are the statues of the great commanders that have conquered in battle. They are clad in brass, with flags in their hands, and all their ancient implements of war are deposited there. The altar is surrounded by statues of the Virgin Mary and the twelve apostles. When Russia is at war, and her armies are about to engage in battle, it is here that the Emperor and his family and court, come to pray for victory over the enemy. The day they engaged in battle against the Poles, the Empress Dowager took her death; she was embalmed and laid in state six weeks in the hall of the winter palace. I went a number of times to see her, and the people pay her homage, and kiss the hands of that lump of clay. All religion is tolerated, but the native Russians are subject to the Greek Church. There are a number of institutions in St. Petersburg where children of all classes have the privilege of instruction. The sailors' and soldiers' boys enter the corps at the age of seven, and are educated for that purpose. The girls remain in the barracks with their parents, or go to some institution where they are instructed in all the branches of female education. There are other establishments, where the higher classes send their children. [. . .]

Sunday, December 6th, at six o'clock in the evening, dropped anchor at St. Ann Harbor, Jamaica. We blessed the Lord for his goodness in sparing us to see the place of our destination; and here I will mention my object in visiting Jamaica. I hoped that I might aid, in some small degree, to raise up and encourage the emancipated inhabitants, and teach the young children to read and work, to fear God, and put their trust in the Savior. Mr. Whitmarsh and his friends came on board and welcomed us. On Tuesday we went on shore to see the place and the people; my intention had been to go directly to Kingston, but the people urged me to stay with them, and I thought it my duty to comply, and wrote to Mr. Ingraham to that effect. I went first to see the minister, Mr. Abbott; I thought as he was out, I had better wait his return. The people promised to pay me for my services, or send me to Kingston. When Mr. Abbott returned he made me an offer, which I readily accepted. As I lodged in the house of one of the class-leaders I attended her class a few times, and when I learned the method, I stopped. She then commenced her authority and gave me to understand if I did not comply I should not have any pay from that society. I spoke to her of the necessity of being born of the spirit of God before we become members of the church of Christ, and told her I was sorry to see the people blinded in such a way.

She was very angry with me and soon accomplished her end by complaining of me to the minister; and I soon found I was to be dismissed, unless I would yield obedience to this class-leader. I told the minister that I did not come there to be guided by a poor foolish woman. He then told me that I had spoken something about the necessity of moral conduct in church members. I told him I had, and in my opinion, I was sorry to see it so much neglected. He replied, that he hoped I would not express myself so except to him; they have the gospel, he continued, and let them into the church. I do not approve of women societies; they destroy the world's convention; the American women have too many of them. I talked with him an hour. He paid me for the time I had been there. I continued with the same opinion, that something must be done for the elevation of the children, and it is for that I labor. I am sorry to say the meeting house is more like a play house than a place of worship. The pulpit stands about the middle of the building, behind are about six hundred children that belong to the society; there they are placed for Sabbath School, and there they remain until service is over, playing most of the time. The house is crowded with the aged and the young, the greater part of them barefooted. Some have on bonnets, but most of the women wear straw hats such as our countrymen wear.

I gave several Bibles away, not knowing that I was hurting the minister's sale, the people buy them of him at a great advance. I gave up my school at St. Ann, the 18th of March. I took the fever and was obliged to remain until the 7th of April. The people of St. Ann fulfilled their promise which they made to induce me to stop with them. On the 11th of April I arrived at Kingston, and was conducted to the Mico Institution, where Mr. Ingraham directed me to find him; he had lost his pulpit and his school, but Mr. Venning, the teacher, kindly received me. I remained there longer than I expected; the next morning he kindly sent one of the young men with me to the packet for my baggage. I then called on the American Consul, he told me he was very glad to see me for such a purpose as I had in view in visiting

Jamaica, but he said it was a folly for the Americans to come to the island to better their condition; he said they came to him every day
praying him to send them home.

He likewise mentioned to me the great mortality among the emigrants. The same day I saw the Rev. J. S. Beadslee, one of our missionaries, who wished me to accompany him forty miles into the interior of the country.

On May the 18th, I attended the Baptist Missionary meeting, in
Queen Street Chapel; the house was crowded. Several ministers spoke
of the importance of sending the gospel to Africa; they complimented
the congregation on their liberality the last year, having given one
hundred pounds sterling; they hoped this year they would give five
hundred pounds, as there were five thousand members at the present
time. There was but one colored minister on the platform. It is generally the policy of these missionaries to have the sanction of colored
ministers, to all their assessments and taxes. The colored people give
more readily, and are less suspicious of imposition, if one from themselves recommends the measure; this the missionaries understand very
well, and know how to take advantage of it. On the 22d and 23d of
June, the colored Baptists held their missionary meeting, the number
of ministers, colored and mulattoes, was 18, the colored magistrates
were present. The resolutions that were offered were unanimously accepted, and every thing was done in love and harmony. After taking
up a contribution, they concluded with song and prayer, and returned
home saying jocosely, "they would turn macroon hunters."

Mack is the name of a small coin in circulation at Jamaica. I called,
on my return, at the market, and counted the different stalls. For vegetables and poultry 196, all numbered and under cover; beside 70 on
the ground; these are all attended by colored women. The market is
conveniently arranged, as they can close the gates and leave all safe.
There are nineteen stalls for fresh fish, eighteen for pork, thirty for
beef, eighteen for turtle. These are all regular built markets, and are
kept by colored men and women. These are all in one place. Others
also may be found, as with us, all over the city. Thus it may be hoped
they are not the stupid set of beings they have been called; here *surely
we see industry;* they are enterprising and quick in their perceptions,
determined to possess themselves, and to possess property besides,

and quite able to take care of themselves. They wished to know why I was so inquisitive about them. I told them we had heard in America that you are lazy, and that emancipation has been of no benefit to you; I wish to inform myself of the truth respecting you, and give a true account on my return. Am I right? More than two hundred people were around me listening to what I said.

They thanked me heartily. I gave them some tracts, and told them if it so pleased God I would come back to them and bring them some more books, and try what could be done with some of the poor children to make them better. I then left them, and went to the East Market, where there are many of all nations. The Jews and Spanish looked at me very black. The colored people gathered around me. I gave them little books and tracts, and told them I hoped to see them again.

There are in this street upwards of a thousand young women and children, living in sin of every kind. From thence I went to the jail, where there were seventeen men, but no women. There were in the House of Correction three hundred culprits; they are taken from there, to work on plantations. I went to the Admiral's house, where the emigrants find a shelter until they can find employment, then they work and pay for their passage. Many leave their homes and come to Jamaica under the impression that they are to have their passage free, and on reaching the island are to be found, until they can provide for themselves.

How the mistake originated, I am not able to say, but on arriving here, strangers poor and unacclimated, find the debt for passage money hard and unexpected. It is remarkable that whether fresh from Africa, or from other islands, from the South or from New England, they all feel deceived on this point. I called on many Americans and found them poor and discontented—ruing the day they left their country, where, notwithstanding many obstacles, their parents lived and died—a country they helped to conquer with their toil and blood; now shall their children stray abroad and starve in foreign lands.

There is in Jamaica an institution, established in 1836, called the Mico Institution. It is named after its founder, Madame Mico, who left a large sum of money to purchase, (or rather to ransom, the one being a Christian act, the other a sin against the Holy Ghost, who expressly forbids such traffic.) Madame Mico left this money to ransom the English who were in bondage to the Algerines; if there was any left, it was to be devoted to the instruction of the colored people in the British Isles.

Beside the Mico establishment, there are in Jamaica twenty-seven church missionary schools, where children are taught gratis. Whole number taught, 952. London Missionary Society Schools, sixteen; the number taught not ascertained. National Schools, thirty-eight. There are also the Wesleyan, Presbyterian and Moravian Schools; it is supposed there are private schools, where three or four thousand are educated in the city of Kingston, and twice the number in the street without the means of instruction. All the children and adults taught in the above named schools, are taxed £1 a year, except the English Church School, this is the most liberal. The Rev. Mr. Horton, a Baptist minister in Kingston, told me he had sent ninety children away from the Baptist school because they did not bring their money. It is sufficient to say they had it not to bring!

Most of the people of Jamaica are emancipated slaves, many of them are old, worn out and degraded. Those who are able to work, have yet many obstacles to contend with, and very little to encourage them; every advantage is taken of their ignorance; the same spirit of cruelty is opposed to them that held them for centuries in bondage; even religious teaching is bartered for their hard earnings, while they are allowed but thirty-three cents a day, and are told if they will not work for that they shall not work at all; an extraordinary price is asked of them for every thing they may wish to purchase, even the Bibles are sold to them at a large advance on the first purchase. Where are their apologists, if they are found wanting in the strict morals that Christians ought to practice? Who kindly says, forgive them when they err. "Forgive them, this is the bitter fruit of slavery." Who has integrity sufficient to hold the balance when these poor people are to be weighed? Yet their present state is blissful, compared with slavery.

Many of the farmers bring their produce twenty or thirty miles. Some have horses or ponys, but most of them bring their burdens on their head. As I returned from St. Andrew's Mountain, where I had been sent for by a Mr. Rose, I was overtaken by a respectable looking man on horseback; we rode about ten miles in company. The story he told me of the wrongs he and his wife had endured while in slavery, are too horrible to narrate. My heart sickens when I think of it. He asked me many questions, such as where I came from? why I came to that Isle? where had I lived, &c. I told him I was sent for by one of the missionaries to help him in his school. Indeed, said he, our color need the instruction. I asked him why the colored people did not hire for themselves? We would be very glad to, he replied, but our money is taken from us so fast we cannot. Sometimes they say we must all bring 1 *l*.; to raise this, we have to sell at a loss or to borrow, so that we have nothing left for ourselves; the Macroon hunters take all—this is a nickname they give the missionaries and the class-leaders—a cutting sarcasm this!

Arrived at a tavern, about a mile from Kingston, I bade the man adieu, and stopped for my guide. The inn-keeper kindly invited me in; he asked me several questions, and I asked him as many. How do the people get along, said I, since the emancipation? The negroes, he replied, will have the island in spite of the d——. Do not you see how they live, and how much they can bear? We cannot do so. This man was an Englishman, with a large family of mulatto children. I returned with my mind fully made up what to do. Spent three weeks at the Mico establishment, and three with my colored friends from America. We thought something ought to be done for the poor girls that were destitute; they consulted with their friends, called a meeting, and formed a society of forty; each agreed to pay three dollars a year and collect, and provide a house, while I came back to America to raise the money for all needful articles for the school. Here I met Mr. Ingraham for the first time; he had come from the mountains, and his health had rapidly declined. Wishing to get his family home before the Lord took him away, he embarked for Baltimore in the Orb, and I sailed for Philadelphia, July 20th, 1841, twenty-one days from Jamaica, in good health. I found there, Fitz W. Sargent's family, from Gloucester, who I lived with when a little girl; they received me very kindly, and gave donations of books and money for that object. [. . .]

After leaving Jamaica, the vessel was tacked to a south-west course. I asked the Captain what this meant. He said he must take the current as there was no wind. Without any ceremony, I told him it was not the case, and told the passengers that he had deceived us. There were two English men that were born on the island, that had never been on the water. Before the third day passed, they asked the Captain why they had not seen Hayti. He told them they passed when they were asleep. I told them it was not true, he was steering south south-west. The passengers in the steerage got alarmed, and every one was asking the Captain what this meant. The ninth day we made land. "By ——," said the Captain, "this is Key West; come, passengers, let us have a vote to run over the neck, and I will go ashore and bring aboard fruit and turtle." They all agreed but myself. He soon dropped anchor. The officers from the shore came on board and congratulated him on keeping his appointment, thus proving that my suspicions were well founded. The Captain went ashore with these men, and soon came back, called for the passengers, and asked for their vote for him to remain until the next day, saying that he could by this delay, make five or six hundred dollars, as there had been a vessel wrecked there lately. They all agreed but myself. The vessel was soon at the side of the wharf. In an hour there were twenty slaves at work to unload her; every inducement was made to persuade me to go ashore, or set my feet on the wharf. A law had just been passed there that every free colored person coming there, should be put in custody on their going ashore; there were five colored persons on board; none dared to go ashore, however uncomfortable we might be in the vessel, or however we might desire to refresh ourselves by a change of scene. We remained at Key West four days.

September 3d, we set sail for New York, at 3 o'clock in the afternoon. At 10 o'clock a gale took us, that continued thirty-six hours; my state-room was filled with water, and my baggage all upset; a woman, with her little boy, and myself, were seated on a trunk thirty-six hours, with our feet pressed against a barrel to prevent falling; the water pouring over us at every breaker. Wednesday, the 9th, the sun shone out so that the Captain could take an observation. He found himself in great peril, near the coast of Texas. All hands were employed in pumping and bailing. On the eleventh, the New Orleans steamer came to our assistance; as we passed up the river, I was made to forget my own condition, as I looked with pity on the poor slaves, who were laboring and toiling, on either side, as far as could be seen with a glass. We soon reached the dock, and we were there on the old wreck a spectacle for observation; the whites went on shore and made themselves comfortable, while we poor blacks were obliged to remain on that broken, wet vessel. The people were very busy about me; one man asked me who I belonged to, and many other rude questions; he asked me where I was born; I told him Newburyport. "What were your parents' names?" I told him my father's name was Thomas Gardner; his countenance changed; said he, "I knew him well"; and he proved friendly to me. He appeared very kind, and offered to arrange my affairs so that I might return to New York through the States. I thought it best to decline his proposal, knowing my spirit would not suffer me to pass on, and see my fellow-creatures suffering without a rebuke. We remained four days on the wreck; the boxes that contained the sugar were taken out; the two bottom tiers were washed out clean. There were a great many people that came to see the vessel; they were astonished that she did not sink; they watched me very closely. I asked them what they wished. In the mean time, there came along a drove of colored people, fettered together in pairs by the wrist; some had weights, with long chains at their ankles, men and women, young and old. I asked them what that meant. They were all ready to answer. Said they, "these negroes have been imprudent, and have stolen; some of them are free negroes from the northern ships"; "and what," I asked "are they there for?" "For being on shore, some of them at night." I asked them who made them Lord over God's inheritance. They told me I was very foolish; they should think I had suffered enough to think of myself. I looked pretty bad, it is true; I was seated on a box, but poorly dressed; the mate had taken my clothes to a washerwoman; why he took this care, he was afraid to send the cook or steward on shore, as they were colored people. I kept still; but the other woman seemed to be in perfect despair, running up and down the deck, wringing her hands and crying, at the thought of all her clothes being destroyed; then her mind dwelt upon other things, and she seemed as if she were deranged; she took their attention for a few minutes, as she was white. Soon the washer-woman came with my clothes; they spoke to her as if she had been a dog. I looked at them with as much astonishment as if I had never heard of such a thing. I asked them if they believed there was a God. "Of course we do," they replied. "Then why not obey him?" "We do." "You do not; permit me to say there is a God, and a just one, that will bring you all to account." "For what?" "For suffering these men that have just come in to be taken out of these vessels, and that awful sight I see in the streets." "O that is nothing; I should think you would be concerned about yourself." "I am sure," I replied, "the Lord will take care of me; you cannot harm me." "No; we do not wish to; we do not want you here." Every ship that comes in, the colored men are dragged to prison. I found it necessary to be stern with them; they were very rude; if I had not been so, I know not what would have been the consequences. They went off for that day; the next day some of them came again. "Good morning," said they; "we shall watch you like the d—— until you go away; you must not say any thing to these negroes whilst you are here." "Why, then, do you talk to me, if you do not want me to say any thing to you? If you will let me alone, I will you." "Let me see your protection," they replied, "they say it is under the Russian government." I pointed them to the 18th chapter of Revelations and 15th verse: "The merchants of these things which were made rich by her, shall stand afar off, for the fear of her torment, weeping and wailing. For strong is the Lord God who judgeth her." They made no answer, but asked the Captain how soon he should get away.

On the 17th, the Captain put eight of us on board the bark H. W. Tyler, for New York; we had about a mile to walk; the Captain was in honor bound to return us our passage money, which we had paid him at Jamaica; he came without it to see if we were there, and went away saying he would soon return with it; but we saw no more of him or our money! Our bark, and a vessel loaded with slaves, were towed down the river by the same steamer; we dropped anchor at the bottom of the bay, as a storm was rising. The 18th, on Sabbath, it rained all day. Capt. Tyler knocked at my door, wishing me to come out; it rained hard; the bulwark of the bark was so high I could not look over it; he placed something for me to stand on, that I might see the awful sight, which was the vessel of slaves laying at the side of our ship! the deck was full of young men, girls, and children, bound to Texas for sale! Monday, the 19th, Capt. Tyler demanded of us to pay him for our passage. I had but ten dollars, and was determined not to give it; he was very severe with all. I told him there were articles enough to pay him belonging to me. Those who had nothing, were obliged to go back in the steamer. Tuesday, the 20th, we set sail; the storm was not over. The 22d the gale took us; we were dismasted, and to save sinking, sixty casks of molasses were stove in, and holes cut in the bulwarks to let it off. All the fowls, pigs, and fresh provisions were lost. We were carried seventy-five miles up the bay of Mexico. The Captain was determined not to pay the steamer for carrying him back to New Orleans, and made his way the best he could.

The 3d of October we arrived again at Key West. The Captain got the bark repaired, and took on board a number of turtles, and a plenty of brandy. Friday, the 7th, set sail for New York; the Captain asked me why I did not go ashore when there in the Comet; "had you," said he, "they intended to beat you. John and Lucy Davenport, of Salem, laid down the first ten dollars toward a hundred for that person who should get you there." The Florida laws are about the same as those at New Orleans. He was very talkative: wished to know if I saw anything of the Creole's crew while at Jamaica. I told him they were all safe, a fine set of young men and women; one dear little girl, that taken from her mother in Virginia, I should have taken with me, if I had had the money. He said his brother owned the Creole, and some of the slaves were his. "I never owned any; I have followed the sea all my life, and can tell every port and town in your State."

October 19th, 1842, arrived at New York, and thankful was I to set my feet on land, almost famished for the want of food; we lost all of our provisions; nothing was left but sailors' beef, and that was tainted before it was salted.

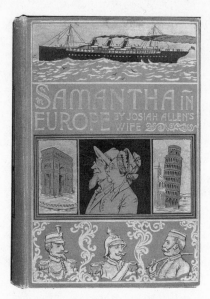

Cover of *Samantha in Europe* (1896), by Josiah Allen's Wife (Marietta Holley). The conventions of travel writing offered humorist Marietta Holley a rich field for satire. Holley herself never married and never set foot outside the United States. Nevertheless, her chararacter Samantha, with her husband Josiah, goes abroad and discovers the absence of women in the laws, histories, and monuments of the world.

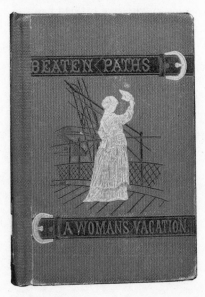

Cover of *Beaten Paths, or A Woman's Vacation* (1874), by Ella W. Thompson. The figure standing alone on the deck evokes the women travelers who made an issue, in travel accounts written in the last quarter of the nineteenth century, of women's ability to travel alone. In January 1889, Charles Dudley Warner writes in *Harper's Magazine*, "It is not long ago that it was thought unsafe for women to travel without a male protector. A brace of spirited girls may now go clear round the world together in entire safety, and without exciting any sentiment more dangerous than admiration."

The frontispiece for *A Woman's Pilgrimage to the Holy Land; or Pleasant Days Abroad, Being Notes of a Tour Through Europe and the East* (1871), by Mrs. Stephen M. Griswold. Women and men are portrayed here seated comfortably on the deck of the *Quaker City*, the ship that in 1867 carried Mrs. Griswold, together with Mark Twain, on the first organized tour to leave American shores.

Two of many categories of dress designed in the 1850s for the various occasions on which a woman would be seen in public. Travel costumes, a great concern of traveling women and their advisers in the nineteenth century, account for the amount of luggage with which women traveled. Costumes such as those pictured here would occupy the better part of a steamer trunk. From *Harper's Magazine* (June–November 1850).

This trunk, described by Elizabeth Bisland as "a great advance" on the "bungling old boxes full of trays," has "a series of drawers both large and small." Bisland recommends also carrying a dressing-bag containing "hairbrush and comb, clothes-brush, nailbrush, and tooth-brush, soap-case, cologne-bottle, portfolio, and travelling inkstand," plus thimbles, needles, thread, tapes, hooks and eyes, pincushions, and safety pins (in both black and white), all of which prepare one "to meet any emergency with calmness." From Bisland's "The Art of Travel," in *The Woman's Book* (1894).

By the 1890s, women's traveling costumes had become more simple. This picture shows Elizabeth Bisland sensibly dressed on her whirlwind tour around the world in competition with Nellie Bly. From *Cosmopolitan* (January 1893).

SHE'S BROKEN EVERY RECORD!

Elizabeth Cochrane Seaman (Nellie Bly) "broke every record" set previously by men by traveling around the world in seventy-two days. She is pictured here with the men she bested. Taking along only one "hand-bag" to carry all that she needed, Bly set not only a speed record but also a clothing and baggage record. From *The World* (26 January 1890).

Elizabeth Bisland forewarns women travelers about "the green spectre of sea-sickness" that "looms up for most women at the very mention of 'the oceans of say' to be faced when they venture off their own continent." She advises, "The whole art of travelling by water is, for eight out of ten, simply a question of evading or assuaging those insufferable pangs." From Bisland's "The Art of Travel," in *The Woman's Book* (1894).

In contrast to Bisland's description of travel by ship, this drawing illustrates the romance of sea travel. In the text that accompanies the illustration, the male writer romanticizes, "We had been enjoying the lovely sunset and now the young moon was shedding a soft, weird light over the water and lighting up the white sails. The ladies had been playing on the guitar and singing." From *Harper's Magazine* (May 1873).

Women rode on donkeys, side-saddle, in order to penetrate remote areas. Travelers reported diligently—sometimes playfully, sometimes earnestly—on modes of transportation. They often made an issue of the odd ways they were transported in order to convey to their readers the strangeness and adventure of travel. From *Mentone, Cairo and Corfu* (1896), by Constance Fenimore Woolson.

In the last quarter of the nineteenth century, women set out on walking tours. Elizabeth Robins Pennell, who with her husband, Joseph, published seven books of travel, reports, "We took many things which we ought not to have taken, and we left behind many things which we ought to have taken. But this matters little, since our advice to all about to start on a walking tour is—*Don't.*" From Pennell's "Our Journey to the Hebrides," in *Harper's Magazine* (September 1888).

Rail travel, which replaced the stagecoach, was common in the second half of the century. This illustration accompanied the serial publication of Elizabeth Bisland's "flying trip." Book, bag, and umbrella are typical accessories of women's travel, and the bouquet recalls the practice of presenting women with flowers upon their departure. From Bisland's "A Flying Trip Around the World," in *Cosmopolitan* (March 1890).

Fanny Bullock Workman and her "trusty rover" in Algeria. The bicycle became a popular mode of travel in the 1880s and 1890s, when cyclists' touring clubs were formed.

Two American women are pictured idyllically above the crowd, looking down on the performance of snake charmers and street musicians hoping to make a few coins. This illustration idealizes what American travelers in fact detested: the aggressiveness of beggars and hawkers in other lands. From *Harper's Magazine* (January 1900).

Fascination with the "exotic" woman of the East, a trope of Orientalism, is invoked in this idyllic representation of a visit to a harem, in which an American woman smokes and chats amicably with a woman of the harem. From *Harper's Magazine* (January 1900).

8

Harriet Beecher Stowe

❦

Following the publication of *Uncle Tom's Cabin; or, Life Among the Lowly* (1852), Harriet Beecher Stowe (1811–1896) was invited by the Glasgow Ladies' Anti-Slavery Society and the Glasgow Female New Association for the Abolition of Slavery to tour Scotland and England. Enlisting Stowe as an ambassador from British to American women, these groups invited Stowe to the British Isles to carry back to America an anti-slavery petition entitled "An Affectionate and Christian Address of Many Thousands of Women of Great Britain and Ireland to Their Sisters the Women of the United States of America," with over half a million signatories. Stowe left New York in March 1853 with her husband, Calvin, and her brother, Charles Beecher, who served as her tour manager and secretary. She arrived in Liverpool after two and one-half weeks on a clipper ship; five months later, in September 1853, she began her voyage back to New York on the steamer *Arctic*. In the British Isles, Stowe was feted and lionized to the point of exhaustion, writing to "Dear Aunt E." shortly after her arrival, "As I saw the way to the cathedral [in Glasgow] blocked up by a throng of people, who had come out to see me, I could not help saying, 'What went ye out for to see? A reed shaken with the wind?' In fact, I was so worn out, that I could hardly walk through the building." After six weeks in the British Isles, she escaped with her brother (Calvin had already returned to the United States) to France, Belgium, Switzerland, and parts of Germany for sight-seeing and rest.

The record of Stowe's journey, *Sunny Memories of Foreign Lands,* published in two volumes in 1854, is the work of three pairs of hands. Harriet Beecher Stowe's edited letters, originally written to children and relatives, make up the bulk of the volumes. Calvin Stowe's introduction and transcriptions of speeches he delivered in the stead of Harriet, who was forbidden to speak in public by conventions governing women, open Volume I. Charles Beecher's journal is interspersed in Volume II. As was conventional in antebellum travel accounts, the format of Volume I is entirely epistolary, and each entry is headed by a letter number. These headings are followed erratically by place and date and consistently by a salutation. Volume I is made up of Stowe's account of the voyage and of travel in England and Scotland. Volume II alternates letters by Stowe and entries taken from the journal of Charles Beecher.

The excerpts in this selection are taken from Volume I, Letter 1, and Volume II, Letters 20 and 28. They document the romance and the hardships of mid-century Atlantic crossings, the social round of the well-placed American tourist, and the work of the "exploratrice sociale" seeking models of social organization—in this case model working-class housing—to address social ills at home as well as abroad. They also include the cultural discourses and cross-cultural critique, such as comments on Americanisms and slavery, that characterize travel writing.

Sunny Memories of Foreign Lands

[I, Letter 1]
Liverpool, April 11, 1853

My Dear Children:—
You wish, first of all, to hear of the voyage. Let me assure you, my dears, in the very commencement of the matter, that going to sea is not at all the thing that we have taken it to be.

You know how often we have longed for a sea voyage, as the fulfillment of all our dreams of poetry and romance, the realization of our highest conceptions of free, joyous existence.

You remember our ship-launching parties in Maine, when we used to ride to the seaside through dark pine forests, lighted up with the gold, scarlet, and orange tints of autumn. What exhilaration there was, as those beautiful inland bays, one by one, unrolled like silver ribbons before us! And how all our sympathies went forth with the grand new ship about to be launched! How graceful and noble a thing she looked, as she sprang from the shore to the blue waters, like a human soul springing from life into immortality! How all our feelings went with her! How we longed to be with her, and a part of her—to go with her to India, China, or any where, so that we might rise and fall on the bosom of that magnificent ocean, and share a part of that glorified existence! That ocean! That blue, sparkling, heaving, mysterious ocean, with all the signs and wonders of heaven emblazoned on its bosom, and another world of mystery hidden beneath its waters! Who would not long to enjoy a freer communion, and rejoice in a prospect of days spent in unreserved fellowship with its grand and noble nature?

Alas! what a contrast between all this poetry and the real prose fact of going to sea! No man, the proverb says, is a hero to his valet de chambre. Certainly, no poet, no hero, no inspired prophet, ever lost so much on near acquaintance as this same mystic, grandiloquent old Ocean. The one step from the sublime to the ridiculous is never taken with such alacrity as in a sea voyage.

In the first place, it is a melancholy fact, but not the less true, that ship life is not at all fragrant; in short, particularly on a steamer, there is a most mournful combination of grease, steam, onions, and dinners in general, either past, present, or to come, which, floating invisibly in the atmosphere, strongly predisposes to that disgust of existence, which, in half an hour after sailing, begins to come upon you; that disgust, that strange, mysterious, ineffable sensation which steals slowly and inexplicably upon you; which makes every heaving billow, every white-capped wave, the ship, the people, the sight, taste, sound, and smell of every thing a matter of inexpressible loathing! Man cannot utter it.

It is really amusing to watch the gradual progress of this epidemic; to see people stepping on board in the highest possible feather, alert, airy, nimble, parading the deck, chatty and conversable, on the best possible terms with themselves and mankind generally; the treacherous ship, meanwhile, undulating and heaving in the most graceful rises and pauses imaginable, like some voluptuous waltzer; and then to see one after another yielding to the mysterious spell!

Your poet launches forth, "full of sentiment sublime as billows," discoursing magnificently on the color of the waves and the glory of the clouds; but gradually he grows white about the mouth, gives sidelong looks towards the stairway; at last, with one desperate plunge, he sets, to rise no more!

Here sits a stout gentleman, who looks as resolute as an oak log. "These things are much the effect of imagination," he tells you; "a little self-control and resolution," &c. Ah me! it is delightful, when these people, who are always talking about resolution, get caught on shipboard. As the backwoodsman said to the Mississippi River, about the steamboat, they "get their match." Our stout gentleman sits a quarter of an hour, upright as a palm tree, his back squared against the rails, pretending to be reading a paper; but a dismal look of disgust is settling down about his lips; the old sea and his will are evidently having a pitched battle. Ah, ha! there he goes for the stairway; says he has left a book in the cabin, but shoots by with a most suspicious velocity. You may fancy his finale.

Then, of course, there are young ladies—charming creatures—who, in about ten minutes, are going to die, and are sure they shall die, and don't care if they do; whom anxious papas, or brothers, or lovers consign with all speed to those dismal lower regions, where the brisk chambermaid, who has been expecting them, seems to think their agonies and groans a regular part of the play.

I had come on board thinking, in my simplicity, of a fortnight to be spent something like the fortnight on a trip to New Orleans, on one of our floating river palaces; that we should sit in our state rooms, read, sew, sketch, and chat; and accordingly I laid in a magnificent provision in the way of literature and divers matters of fancy work, with which to while away the time. Some last, airy touches, in the way of making up bows, disposing ribbons, and binding collarets, had been left to these long, leisure hours, as matters of amusement.

Let me warn you, if you ever go to sea, you may as well omit all such preparations. Don't leave so much as the unlocking of a trunk to be done after sailing. In the few precious minutes when the ship stands still, before she weighs her anchor, set your house, that is to say, your state room, as much in order as if you were going to be hanged; place every thing in the most convenient position to be seized without trouble at a moment's notice; for be sure that in half an hour after sailing an infinite desperation will seize you, in which the grasshopper will be a burden. If any thing is in your trunk, it might almost as well be in the sea, for any practical probability of your getting to it.

Moreover, let your toilet be eminently simple, for you will find the time coming when to button a cuff or arrange a ruff will be a matter of absolute despair. You lie disconsolate in your berth, only desiring to be let alone to die; and then, if you are told, as you always are, that "you mustn't give way," that "you must rouse yourself" and come on deck, you will appreciate the value of simple attire. With every thing in your berth dizzily swinging backwards and forwards, your bonnet, your cloak, your tippet, your gloves, all present so many discouraging impossibilities; knotted strings cannot be untied, and modes of fastening which seemed curious and convenient, when you had nothing else to do but fasten them, now look disgustingly impracticable. Nevertheless, your fate for the whole voyage depends upon your rousing yourself to get upon deck at first; to give up, then, is to be condemned to the Avernus, the Hades of the lower regions, for the rest of the voyage.

Ah, *those* lower regions!—the saloons—every couch and corner filled with prostrate, despairing forms, with pale cheeks, long, willowy hair and sunken eyes, groaning, sighing, and apostrophizing the Fates, and solemnly vowing between every lurch of the ship, that "you'll never catch them going to sea again, that's what you won't"; and then the bulletins from all the state rooms— "Mrs. A. is sick, and Miss B. sicker, and Miss C. almost dead, and Mrs. E., F., and G. declare that they shall give up." This threat of "giving up" is a standing resort of ladies in distressed circumstances; it is always very impressively pronounced, as if the result of earnest purpose; but how it is to be carried out practically, how ladies *do* give up, and what general impression is made on creation when they do, has never yet appeared. Certainly the sea seems to care very little about the threat, for he goes on lurching all hands about just as freely afterwards as before.

There are always some three or four in a hundred who escape all these evils. They are not sick, and they seem to be having a good time generally, and always meet you with "What a charming run we are having! Isn't it delightful?" and so on. If you have a turn for being disinterested, you can console your miseries by a view of their joyousness. Three or four of our ladies were of this happy order, and it was really refreshing to see them.

For my part, I was less fortunate. I could not and would not give up and become one of the ghosts below, and so I managed, by keeping on deck and trying to act as if nothing was the matter, to lead a very uncertain and precarious existence, though with a most awful undertone of emotion, which seemed to make quite another thing of creation.

I wonder that people who wanted to break the souls of heroes and martyrs never thought of sending them to sea and keeping them a little seasick. The dungeons of Olmutz, the leads of Venice, in short, all the naughty, wicked places that tyrants ever invented for bringing down the spirits of heroes, are nothing to the berth of a ship. Get Lafayette, Kossuth, or the noblest of woman born, prostrate in a swinging, dizzy berth of one of these sea coops, called state rooms, and I'll warrant almost any compromise might be got out of them.

Where in the world the soul goes to under such influences nobody knows; one would really think the sea tipped it all out of a man, just as it does the water out of his wash basin. The soul seems to be like one of the genii enclosed in a vase, in the Arabian Nights; now, it rises like a pillar of cloud, and floats over land and sea, buoyant, many-hued, and glorious; again, it goes down, down, subsiding into its copper vase, and the cover is clapped on, and there you are. A sea voyage is the best device for getting the soul back into its vase that I know of.

But at night!—the beauties of a night on shipboard!—down in your berth, with the sea hissing and fizzing, gurgling and booming, within an inch of your ear; and then the steward comes along at twelve o'clock and puts out your light, and there you are! Jonah in the whale was not darker or more dismal. There, in profound ignorance and blindness, you lie, and feel yourself rolled upwards, and downwards, and sidewise, and all ways, like a cork in a tub of water; much such a sensation as one might suppose it to be, were one headed up in a barrel and thrown into the sea.

Occasionally a wave comes with a thump against your ear, as if a great hammer were knocking on your barrel, to see that all within was safe and sound. Then you begin to think of krakens, and sharks, and porpoises, and sea serpents, and all the monstrous, slimy, cold, hobgoblin brood, who, perhaps, are your next door neighbors; and the old blue-haired Ocean whispers through the planks, "Here you are; I've got you. Your grand ship is my plaything. I can do what I like with it."

Then you hear every kind of odd noise in the ship—creaking, straining, crunching, scraping, pounding, whistling, blowing off steam, each of which to your unpractised ear is significant of some impending catastrophe; you lie wide awake, listening with all your might, as if your watching did any good, till at last sleep overcomes you, and the morning light convinces you that nothing very particular has been the matter, and that all these frightful noises are only the necessary attendants of what is called a good run.

Our voyage out was called "a good run." It was voted, unanimously, to be "an extraordinarily good passage," "a pleasant voyage";
yet the ship rocked the whole time from side to side with a steady,
dizzy, continuous motion, like a great cradle. I had a new sympathy
for babies, poor little things, who are rocked hours at a time without
so much as a "by your leave" in the case. No wonder there are so many
stupid people in the world. [. . .]

When the ship has been out about eight days, an evident bettering
of spirits and condition obtains among the passengers. Many of the
sick ones take heart, and appear again among the walks and ways of
men; the ladies assemble in little knots, and talk of getting on shore.
The more knowing ones, who have travelled before, embrace this opportunity to show their knowledge of life by telling the new hands all
sorts of hobgoblin stories about the custom house officers and the difficulties of getting landed in England. It is a curious fact, that old travellers generally seem to take this particular delight in striking conster-
nation into younger ones.

"You'll have all your daguerreotypes taken away," says one lady,
who, in right of having crossed the ocean nine times, is entitled to
speak *ex cathedra* on the subject.

"All our daguerreotypes!" shriek four or five at once. "Pray tell,
what for?"

"They *will* do it," says the knowing lady, with an awful nod; "unless you hide them and all your books, they'll burn up ——"

"Burn our books!" exclaim the circle. "O, dreadful! What do they
do that for?"

"They're very particular always to burn up all your books. I knew
a lady who had a dozen burned," says the wise one.

"Dear me! will they take our *dresses?*" says a young lady, with increasing alarm.

"No, but they'll pull every thing out, and tumble them well over, I
can tell you."

"How horrid!"

An old lady, who has been very sick all the way, is revived by this
appalling intelligence.

"I hope they won't tumble over my *caps!*" she exclaims.

"Yes, they will have every thing out on deck," says the lady, delighted with the increasing sensation. "I tell you you don't know these custom house officers."

"It's too bad!" "It's dreadful!" "How horrid!" exclaim all.

"I shall put my best things in my pocket," exclaims one. "They don't search our pockets, do they?" "Well, no, not here; but I tell you they'll search your *pockets* at Antwerp and Brussels," says the lady.

Somebody catches the sound, and flies off into the state rooms with the intelligence that "the custom house officers are so dreadful— they rip open your trunks, pull out all your things, burn your books, take away your daguerreotypes, and even search your pockets"; and a row of groans is heard ascending from the row of state rooms, as all begin to revolve what they have in their trunks, and what they are to do in this emergency.

"Pray tell me," said I to a gentlemanly man, who had crossed four or five times, "is there really so much annoyance at the custom house?"

"Annoyance, ma'am? No, not the slightest."

"But do they really turn out the contents of the trunks, and take away people's daguerreotypes, and burn their books?"

"Nothing of the kind, ma'am. I apprehend no difficulty. I never had any. There are a few articles on which duty is charged. I have a case of cigars, for instance; I shall show them to the custom house officer, and pay the duty. If a person seems disposed to be fair, there is no difficulty. The examination of ladies' trunks is merely nominal; nothing is deranged."

So it proved. We arrived on Sunday morning; the custom house officers, very gentlemanly men, came on board; our luggage was all set out, and passed through a rapid examination, which in many cases amounted only to opening the trunk and shutting it, and all was over. The whole ceremony did not occupy two hours.

So ends this letter. You shall hear further how we landed at some future time.

[II, Letter 20]
[London] Thursday, May 12

My Dear I:—
Yesterday, what with my breakfast, lunch, and dinner, I was, as the

fashionable saying is, "fairly knocked up." This expression, which I find obtains universally here, corresponds to what we mean by being "used up." They talk of Americanisms, and I have a little innocent speculation now and then concerning Anglicisms. I certainly find several here for which I can perceive no more precedent in the well of "English undefiled," than for some of ours; for instance, this being "knocked up," which is variously inflected, as, for example, in the form of a participial adjective, as a "knocking up" affair; in the form of a noun, as when they say "such a person has got quite a knocking up," and so on.

The fact is, if we had ever had any experience in London life we should not have made three engagements in one day. To my simple eye it is quite amusing to see how they manage the social machine here. People are under such a pressure of engagements, that they go about with their lists in their pockets. If A wants to invite B to dinner, out come their respective lists. A says he has only Tuesday and Thursday open for this week. B looks down his list, and says that the days are all closed. A looks along, and says that he has no day open till next Wednesday week. B, however, is going to leave town Tuesday; so that settles the matter as to dining; so they turn back again, and try the breakfasting; for though you cannot dine in but one place a day, yet, by means of the breakfast and the lunch, you can make three social visits if you are strong enough.

Then there are evening parties, which begin at ten o'clock. The first card of the kind that was sent me, which was worded, "At home at ten o'clock," I, in my simplicity, took to be ten in the morning.

But here are people staying out night after night till two o'clock, sitting up all night in Parliament, and seeming to thrive upon it. There certainly is great apology for this in London, if it is always as dark, drizzling, and smoky in the daytime as it has been since I have been here. If I were one of the London people I would live by gaslight as they do, for the streets and houses are altogether pleasanter by gaslight than by daylight. But to ape these customs under our clear, American skies, so contrary to our whole social system, is simply ridiculous.

This morning I was exceedingly tired, and had a perfect longing to get out of London into some green fields—to get somewhere where there was nobody. So kind Mrs. B. had the carriage, and off we drove together. By and by we found ourselves out in the country, and then I wanted to get out and walk.

After a while a lady came along, riding a little donkey. These donkeys have amused me so much since I have been here! At several places on the outskirts of the city they have them standing, all girt up with saddles covered with white cloth, for ladies to ride on. One gets out of London by means of an omnibus to one of these places, and then, for a few pence, can have a ride upon one of them into the country. Mrs. B. walked by the side of the lady, and said to her something which I did not hear, and she immediately alighted and asked me with great kindness if I wanted to try the saddle; so I got upon the little beast, which was about as large as a good-sized calf, and rode a few paces to try him. It is a slow, but not unpleasant gait, and if the creature were not so insignificantly small, as to make you feel much as if you were riding upon a cat, it would be quite a pleasant affair. After dismounting I crept through a hole in a hedge, and looked for some flowers; and, in short, made the most that I could of my interview with nature, till it came time to go home to dinner, for our dinner hour at Mr. B.'s is between one and two; quite like home. In the evening we were to dine at Lord Shaftesbury's.

After napping all the afternoon we went to Grosvenor Square. There was only a small, select party, of about sixteen. Among the guests were Dr. McAll, Hebrew professor in King's College, Lord Wriothesley Russell, brother of Lord John, and one of the private chaplains of the queen, and the Archbishop of Canterbury. Dr. McAll is a millenarian. He sat next to C at table, and they had some conversation on that subject. He said those ideas had made a good deal of progress in the English mind.

While I was walking down to dinner with Lord Shaftesbury, he pointed out to me in the hall the portrait of his distinguished ancestor, Antony Ashley Cooper, Earl of Shaftesbury, whose name he bears. This ancestor, notwithstanding his sceptical philosophy, did some good things, as he was the author of the habeas corpus act.

After dinner we went back to the drawing rooms again; and while tea and coffee were being served, names were constantly being announced, till the rooms were quite full. Among the earliest who arrived was Mr. ———, a mulatto gentleman, formerly British consul at Liberia. I found him a man of considerable cultivation and intelligence, evincing much good sense in his observations.

I overheard some one saying in the crowd, "Shaftesbury has been about the chimney sweepers again in Parliament."[1] I said to Lord Shaftesbury, "I thought that matter of the chimney sweepers had been attended to long ago, and laws made about it."

"So we have made laws," said he, "but people won't keep them unless we follow them up."

He has a very prompt, cheerful way of speaking, and throws himself into every thing he talks about with great interest and zeal. He introduced me to one gentleman, I forget his name now, as the patron of the shoeblacks. On my inquiring what that meant, he said that he had started the idea of providing employment for poor street boys, by furnishing them with brushes and blacking, and forming them into regular companies of shoeblacks. Each boy has his particular stand, where he blacks the shoes of every passer by who chooses to take the trouble of putting up his foot and paying his twopence. Lord Shaftesbury also presented me to a lady who had been a very successful teacher in the ragged schools; also to a gentleman who, he said, had been very active in the London city missions. Some very ingenious work done in the ragged schools was set on the table for the company to examine, and excited much interest.

I talked a little while with Lord Wriothesley Russell. From him we derived the idea that the queen was particularly careful in the training and religious instruction of her children. He said that she claimed that the young prince should be left entirely to his parents, in regard to his religious instruction, till he was seven years of age; but that, on examining him at that time, they were equally surprised and delighted with his knowledge of the Scriptures. I must remark here, that such an example as the queen sets in the education of her children makes itself felt through all the families of the kingdom. Domesticity is now the fashion in high life. I have had occasion to see, in many instances, how carefully ladies of rank instruct their children. This argues more favorably for the continuance of English institutions than any thing I have seen. If the next generation of those who are born to rank and power are educated, in the words of Fenelon, to consider these things "as a ministry," which they hold for the benefit of the poor, the problem of life in England will become easier of solution. Such are Lord Shaftesbury's views, and as he throws them out with unceasing fervor in his conversation and conduct, they cannot but powerfully affect not only his own circle, but all circles through the kingdom. Lady Shaftesbury is a beautiful and interesting woman, and warmly enters into the benevolent plans of her husband. A gentleman and lady with whom I travelled said that Lord and Lady Shaftesbury had visited in person the most forlorn and wretched parts of London, that they might get, by their own eyesight, a more correct gauge of the misery to be relieved. I did not see Lord Shaftesbury's children; but, from the crayon likenesses which hung upon the walls, they must be a family of uncommon beauty.

I talked a little while with the Bishop of Tuam. I was the more interested to do so because he was from that part of Ireland which Sibyl Jones has spoken of as being in so particularly miserable a condition. I said, "How are you doing now, in that part of the country? There has been a great deal of misery there, I hear." He said, "There has been, but we have just turned the corner, and now I hope we shall see better days. The condition of the people has been improved by emigration and other causes, till the evils have been brought within reach, and we feel that there is hope of effecting a permanent improvement."

While I was sitting talking, Lord Shaftesbury brought a gentleman and lady, whom he introduced as Lord Chief Justice Campbell and Lady Strathheden. Lord Campbell is a man of most dignified and imposing personal presence; tall, with a large frame, a fine, high forehead, and strongly marked features. Naturally enough, I did not suppose them to be husband and wife, and when I discovered that they were so, expressed a good deal of surprise at their difference of titles; to which she replied, that she did not wonder we Americans were sometimes puzzled among the number of titles. She seemed quite interested to inquire into our manner of living and customs, and how they struck me as compared with theirs. The letter of Mrs. Tyler[2] was much talked of, and some asked me if I supposed Mrs. Tyler really wrote it, expressing a little civil surprise at the style. I told them that I had heard it said that it must have been written by some of the gentlemen in the family, because it was generally understood that Mrs. Tyler was a very ladylike person. Some said, "It does us no harm to be reminded of our deficiencies; we need all the responsibility that can be put upon us." Others said, "It is certain we have many defects"; but Lord John Campbell said, "There is this difference between our evils and those of slavery: ours exist contrary to law; those are upheld by law."

I did not get any opportunity of conversing with the Archbishop of Canterbury, though this is the second time I have been in company with him. He is a most prepossessing man in his appearance—simple, courteous, mild, and affable. He was formerly Bishop of Chester, and is now Primate of all England.

It is some indication of the tendency of things in a country to notice what kind of men are patronized and promoted to the high places of the church. Sumner is a man refined, gentle, affable, scholarly, thoroughly evangelical in sentiment; to render him into American phraseology, he is in doctrine what we should call a moderate New School man. He has been a most industrious writer; one of his principal works is his Commentary on the New Testament, in several volumes; a work most admirably adapted for popular use, combining practical devotion with critical accuracy to an uncommon degree. He has also published a work on the Evidences of Christianity, in which he sets forth some evidences of the genuineness of the gospel narrative, which could only have been conceived by a mind of peculiar delicacy, and which are quite interesting and original. He has also written a work on Biblical Geology, which is highly spoken of by Sir Charles Lyell and others. If I may believe accounts that I hear, this mild and moderate man has shown a most admirable firmness and facility in guiding the ship of the establishment in some critical and perilous places of late years. I should add that he is warmly interested in all the efforts now making for the good of the poor.

Among other persons of distinction, this evening, I noticed Lord and Lady Palmerston.

A lady asked me this evening what I thought of the beauty of the ladies of the English aristocracy: she was a Scotch lady, by the by; so the question was a fair one. I replied, that certainly report had not exaggerated their charms. Then came a home question—how the ladies of England compared with the ladies of America. "Now for it, patriotism," said I to myself; and, invoking to my aid certain fair saints of

my own country, whose faces I distinctly remembered, I assured her
that I had never seen more beautiful women than I had in America.
Grieved was I to be obliged to add, "But your ladies keep their beauty
much later and longer." This fact stares one in the face in every company; one meets ladies past fifty, glowing, radiant, and blooming,
with a freshness of complexion and fulness of outline refreshing to
contemplate. What can be the reason? Tell us, Muses and Graces,
what can it be? Is it the conservative power of sea fogs and coal
smoke—the same cause that keeps the turf green, and makes the holly
and ivy flourish? How comes it that our married ladies dwindle, fade,
and grow thin—that their noses incline to sharpness, and their elbows
to angularity, just at the time of life when their island sisters round out
into a comfortable and becoming amplitude and fulness? If it is the
fog and the sea coal, why, then, I am afraid we never shall come up
with them. But perhaps there may be other causes why a country
which starts some of the most beautiful girls in the world produces so
few beautiful women. Have not our close-heated stove rooms something to do with it? Have not the immense amount of hot biscuits,
hot corn cakes, and other compounds got up with the acrid poison of
saleratus, something to do with it? Above all, has not our climate, with
its alternate extremes of heat and cold, a tendency to induce habits of
in-door indolence? Climate, certainly, has a great deal to do with it;
ours is evidently more trying and more exhausting; and because it is
so, we should not pile upon its back errors of dress and diet which are
avoided by our neighbors. They keep their beauty, because they keep
their health. It has been as remarkable as any thing to me, since I have
been here, that I do not constantly, as at home, hear one and another
spoken of as in miserable health, as very delicate, &c. Health seems to
be the rule, and not the exception. For my part, I must say, the most
favorable omen that I know of for female beauty in America is, the
multiplication of water cure establishments, where our ladies, if they
get nothing else, do gain some ideas as to the necessity of fresh air, regular exercise, simple diet, and the laws of hygiene in general.

There is one thing more which goes a long way towards the continued health of these English ladies, and therefore towards their
beauty; and that is, the quietude and perpetuity of their domestic institutions. They do not, like us, fade their cheeks lying awake nights

ruminating the awful question who shall do the washing next week,
or who shall take the chambermaid's place, who is going to be married, or that of the cook, who has signified her intention of parting
with the mistress. Their hospitality is never embarrassed by the consideration that their whole kitchen cabinet may desert at the moment
that their guests arrive. They are not obliged to choose between
washing their own dishes, or having their cut glass, silver, and china
left to the mercy of a foreigner, who has never done any thing but field
work. And last, not least, they are not possessed with that ambition to
do the impossible in all branches, which, I believe, is the death of a
third of the women in America. What is there ever read of in books,
or described in foreign travel, as attained by people in possession of
every means and appliance, which our women will not undertake, sin-
gle-handed, in spite of every providential indication to the contrary?
Who is not cognizant of dinner parties invited, in which the lady of
the house has figured successively as confectioner, cook, dining-room
girl, and, lastly, rushed up stairs to bathe her glowing cheeks, smooth
her hair, draw on satin dress and kid gloves, and appear in the drawing room as if nothing were the matter? Certainly the undaunted
bravery of our American females can never enough be admired. Other
women can play gracefully the head of the establishment; but who,
like them, could be head, hand, and foot, all at once?

As I have spoken of stoves, I will here remark that I have not yet
seen one in England; neither, so far as I can remember, have I seen a
house warmed by a furnace. Bright coal fires, in grates of polished
steel, are as yet the lares and penates of old England. If I am inclined
to mourn over any defection in my own country, it is the closing up
of the cheerful open fire, with its bright lights and dancing shadows,
and the planting on our domestic hearth of that sullen, stifling
gnome, the air-tight. I agree with Hawthorne in thinking the movement fatal to patriotism; for who would fight for an air-tight!

I have run on a good way beyond our evening company; so good
by for the present.

[II, Letter 28]
May 28

My Dear Cousin:—

This morning Lord Shaftesbury came according to appointment, to take me to see the Model Lodging Houses. He remarked that it would be impossible to give me the full effect of seeing them, unless I could first visit the dens of filth, disease, and degradation, in which the poor of London formerly were lodged. With a good deal of satisfaction he told me that the American minister, Mr. Ingersoll, previous to leaving London, had requested the police to take him over the dirtiest and most unwholesome parts of it, that he might see the lowest as well as the highest sphere of London life. After this, however, the policeman took him through the baths, wash houses, and model lodging houses, which we were going to visit, and he expressed himself both surprised and delighted with the improvement that had been made.

We first visited the lodging house for single men in Charles Street, Drury Lane. This was one of the first experiments made in this line, and to effect the thing in the most economical manner possible, three old houses were bought and thrown into one, and fitted up for the purpose. On the ground floor we saw the superintendent's apartment, and a large, long sitting room, furnished with benches and clean, scoured tables, where the inmates were, some of them, reading books or papers: the day being wet, perhaps, kept them from their work. In the kitchen were ample cooking accommodations, and each inmate, as I understand, cooks for himself. Lord Shaftesbury said, that something like a common table had been tried, but that it was found altogether easier or more satisfactory for each one to suit himself. On this floor, also, was a bathing room, and a well-selected library of useful reading books, history, travels, &c. On the next floor were the dormitories—a great hall divided by board partitions into little sleeping cells about eight feet square, each containing a neat bed, chair, and stand. The partition does not extend quite up to the wall, and by this means while each inmate enjoys the privacy of a small room, he has all the comfort of breathing the air of the whole hall.

A working man returning from his daily toil to this place, can first enjoy the comfort of a bath; then, going into the kitchen, make his cup of tea or coffee, and sitting down at one of the clean, scoured tables in the sitting room, sip his tea, and look over a book. Or a friendly company may prepare their supper and sit down to tea together. Lord Shaftesbury said that the effect produced on the men by such an arrangement was wonderful. They became decent, decorous, and self-respecting. They passed rules of order for their community. They subscribed for their library from their own earnings, and the books are mostly of their own selection. "It is remarkable," said his lordship, "that of their own accord they decided to reject every profane, indecent, or immoral work. It showed," he said, "how strong are the influences of the surroundings in reforming or ruining the character." It should be remarked that all these advantages are enjoyed for the same price charged by the most crowded and filthy of lodging houses, namely, fourpence per night, or two shillings per week. The building will accommodate eighty-two. The operation supports itself handsomely.

I should remark, by the by, that in order to test more fully the practicability of the thing, this was accomplished in one of the worst neighborhoods in London.

From these we proceeded to view a more perfect specimen of the same sort in the Model Lodging House of George Street, Bloomsbury Square, a house which was built *de novo*, for the purpose of perfectly illustrating the principle. This house accommodates one hundred and four working men, and combines every thing essential or valuable in such an establishment—complete ventilation and drainage; the use of a distinct living room; a kitchen and a wash house, a bath, and an ample supply of water, and all the conveniences which, while promoting the physical comfort of the inmates, tend to increase their self-respect, and elevate them in the scale of moral and intellectual beings. The arrangement of the principal apartments are such as to insure economy as well as domestic comfort, the kitchen and wash house being furnished with every requisite convenience, including a bath supplied with hot and cold water; also a separate and well-ventilated safe for the food of each inmate. Under the care of the superintendent is a small, but well-selected library.

The common room, thirty-three feet long, twenty-three feet wide, and ten feet nine inches high, is paved with white tiles, laid on brick arches, and on each side are two rows of tables with seats; at the fireplace is a constant supply of hot water, and above it are the rules of the establishment. The staircase, which occupies the centre of the building, is of stone. The dormitories, eight in number, ten feet high, are subdivided with movable wood partitions six feet nine inches high; each compartment, enclosed by its own door, is fitted up with a bed, chair, and clothes box. A shaft is carried up at the end of every room, the ventilation through it being assisted by the introduction of gas, which lights the apartment. A similar shaft is carried up the staircase, supplying fresh air to the dormitories, with a provision for warming it, if necessary. The washing closets on each floor are fitted up with slate, having japanned iron basins, and water laid on.

During the fearful ravages of the cholera in this immediate neighborhood, not one case occurred in this house among its one hundred and four inmates.

From this place we proceeded to one, if any thing, more interesting to me. This was upon the same principle appropriated to the lodgment of single women. When one considers the defenceless condition of single women, who labor for their own subsistence in a large city, how easily they are imposed upon and oppressed, and how quickly a constitution may be destroyed for want of pure air, fresh water, and other common necessaries of life, one fully appreciates the worth of a large and beautiful building, which provides for this oppressed, fragile class.

The Thanksgiving Model Buildings at Port Pool Lane, Gray's Inn, are so called because they were built with a thank-offering collected in the various religious societies of London, as an appropriate expression of their gratitude to God for the removal of the cholera. This block of buildings has in it accommodations for twenty families, and one hundred and twenty-eight single women; together with a public wash house, and a large cellar, in which are stored away the goods of those women who live by the huckster's trade.

The hundred and twenty-eight single women, of whom the majority are supposed to be poor needlewomen, occupy sixty-four rooms in a building of four stories, divided by a central staircase; a corridor on either side forms a lobby to eight rooms, each twelve feet six inches long, by nine feet six inches wide, sufficiently large for two persons. They are fitted up with two bedsteads, a table, chairs, and a washing stand. The charge is one shilling per week for each person, or two shillings per room.

Lord Shaftesbury took me into one of the rooms, where was an aged female partially bedridden, who maintained herself by sewing. The room was the picture of neatness and comfort; a good supply of hot and cold water was furnished in it. Her work was spread out by her upon the bed, together with her Bible and hymn book; she looked cheerful and comfortable. She seemed pleased to see Lord Shaftesbury, whom she had evidently seen many times before, as his is a familiar countenance in all these places. She expressed the most fervent thankfulness for the quiet, order, and comfort of her pleasant lodgings, comparing them very feelingly with what used to be her condition before any such place had been provided.

From this place we drove to the Streatham Street Lodging House for families, of which the following is an outside view.[3] This building is, in the first place, fire proof; in the second, the separation in the parts belonging to different families is rendered complete and perfect by the use of hollow brick for the partitions, which entirely prevents, as I am told, the transmission of sound.

The accompanying print shows the plan of one tenement.

By means of the sleeping closet adjoining the living room, each dwelling affords three good sleeping apartments. The meat safe preserves provisions. The dust flue is so arranged that all the sweepings of the house, and all the refuse of the cookery, have only to be thrown down to disappear forever; while the sink is supplied to an unlimited extent with hot and cold water. These galleries, into which every tenement opens, run round the inside of the hollow court which the building encloses, and afford an admirable play-place for the little children, out of the dangers and temptations of the street, and in view of their respective mothers. The foregoing print, representing the inner half of the quadrangle, shows the arrangement of the galleries.

"Now," said Lord Shaftesbury, as he was showing me through these tenements, which were models of neatness and good keeping, "you must bear in mind that these are tenanted by the very people who once were living in the dirtiest and filthiest lodging houses; people whom the world said, it did no good to try to help; that they liked to be dirty better than clean, and would be dirty under any circumstances." He added the following anecdote to show the effect of poor lodgings in degrading the character. A fine young man, of some considerable taste and talent, obtained his living by designing patterns for wall paper. A long and expensive illness so reduced his circumstances, that he was obliged to remove to one of these low, filthy lodging houses already alluded to. From that time he became an altered man; his wife said that he lost all energy, all taste in designing, love of reading, and fondness for his family; began to frequent drinking shops, and was visibly on the road to ruin. Hearing of these lodging houses, he succeeded in renting a tenement in one of them, for the same sum which he had paid for the miserable dwelling. Under the influence of a neat, airy, pleasant, domestic home, the man's better nature again awoke, his health improved, he ceased to crave ardent spirits, and his former ingenuity in his profession returned.

"Now, this shows," said Lord Shaftesbury, "that hundreds may have been ruined simply by living in miserable dwellings." I looked into this young man's tenement; it was not only neat, but ornamented with a great variety of engravings tastefully disposed upon the wall. On my expressing my pleasure in this circumstance, he added, "It is one of the pleasantest features of the case, to notice how soon they began to ornament their little dwellings; some have cages with singing birds, and some pots of flowering plants; some, pictures and engravings."

"And are these buildings successful in a pecuniary point of view?" I said. "Do they pay their own way?"

"Yes," he replied, "they do. I consider that these buildings, if they have done nothing more, have established two points: first, that the poor do not prefer dirt and disorder, where it is possible for them to secure neatness and order; and second, that buildings with every proper accommodation can be afforded at a price which will support an establishment."

Said I, "Are people imitating these lodging houses very rapidly?"

"To a great extent they are," he replied, "but not so much as I desire. Buildings on these principles have been erected in the principal towns of England and Scotland. The state of the miserable dwellings, courts,

alleys, &c., is the consequence of the neglect of former days, when spec-
ulators and builders were allowed to do as they liked, and run up hovels, where the working man, whose house must be regulated, not by his
choice, but by his work, was compelled then, as he is now, to live,
however narrow, unhealthy, or repulsive the place might be. This was
called `the liberty of the subject.'" It has been one of Lord Shaftes-
bury's most arduous parliamentary labors to bring the lodging houses
under governmental regulation. He told me that he introduced a bill
to this effect in the House of Commons, while a member, as Lord
Ashley, and that just as it had passed through the House of Commons, he entered the House of Lords, as Lord Shaftesbury, and so had
the satisfaction of carrying the bill to its completion in that house,
where it passed in the year 1851. The provisions of this bill require
every keeper of a lodging house to register his name at the Metropol-
itan Police Office, under a penalty of a fine of five pounds for every
lodger received before this is done. After having given notice to the
police, they are not allowed to receive lodgers until the officers have
inspected the house, to see whether it accords with the required conditions. These conditions are, that the walls and ceilings be white-
washed; that the floors, stairs, beds, and bed clothes are clean; that
there be some mode of ventilating every room; that each house be
provided with every accommodation for promoting decency and
neatness; that the drains and cesspools are perfect; the yards properly
paved, so as to run dry; and that each house has a supply of water,
with conveniences for cooking and washing; and finally, that no person with an infectious disease is inhabiting the house. It is enacted,
moreover, that only so many shall be placed in a room as shall be permitted by the commissioners of the police; and it is made an indispensable condition to the fitness of a house, that the proprietor
should hang up in every room a card, properly signed by the police
inspector, stating the precise number who are allowed to be lodged
there. The law also strictly forbids persons of different sexes occupy-
ing the same room, except in case of married people with children under ten years of age: more than one married couple may not inhabit
the same apartment, without the provision of a screen to secure privacy. It is also forbidden to use the kitchens, sculleries, or cellars for
sleeping rooms, unless specially permitted by the police. The keeper

of the house is required thoroughly to whitewash the walls and ceilings twice a year, and to cleanse the drains and cesspools whenever required by the police. In case of sickness, notice must be immediately given to the police, and such measures pursued, for preventing infection, as may be deemed judicious by the inspector.

The commissioner of police reports to the secretary of state systematically as to the results of this system. After looking at these things, we proceeded to view one of the model washing houses, which had been erected for the convenience of poor women. We entered a large hall, which was divided by low wood partitions into small apartments, in each of which a woman was washing. The whole process of washing clothes in two or three waters, and boiling them, can be effected without moving from the spot, or changing the tub. Each successive water is let out at the bottom, while fresh is let on from the top. When the clothes are ready to be boiled, a wooden cover is placed over them, and a stream of scalding steam is directed into the tub, by turning a stop cock; this boils the water in a few moments, effectually cleansing the clothes; they are then whirled in a hollow cylinder till nearly dry, after which they are drawn through two rollers covered with flannel, which presses every remaining particle of water out of them. The clothes are then hung upon frames, which shut into large closets, and are dried by steam in a very short space of time.

Lord Shaftesbury, pointing out the partitions, said, "This is an arrangement of delicacy to save their feelings: their clothes are sometimes so old and shabby they do not want to show them, poor things." I thought this feature worthy of special notice.

In addition to all these improvements for the laboring classes, very large bathing establishments have been set up expressly for the use of the working classes. To show the popularity and effectiveness of this movement, five hundred and fifty thousand baths were given in three houses during the year 1850. These bathing establishments for the working classes are rapidly increasing in every part of the kingdom.

When we returned to our carriage after this survey, I remarked to Lord Shaftesbury that the combined influence of these causes must have wrought a considerable change in the city. He answered, with energy, "You can have no idea. Whole streets and districts have been revolutionized by it. The people who were formerly savage and ferocious, because they supposed themselves despised and abandoned, are now perfectly quiet and docile. I can assure you that Lady Shaftesbury has walked alone, with no attendant but a little child, through streets in London where, years ago, a well-dressed man could not have passed safely without an escort of the police."

I said to him that I saw nothing now, with all the improvements they were making throughout the kingdom, to prevent their working classes from becoming quite as prosperous as ours, except the want of a temperance reformation.

He assented with earnestness. He believed, he said, that the amount spent in liquors of various kinds, which do no good, but much injury, was enough to furnish every laborer's dwelling, not only with comforts, but with elegances. "But then," he said, "one thing is to be considered: a reform of the dwellings will do a great deal towards promoting a temperance reformation. A man who lives in a close, unwholesome dwelling, deprived of the natural stimulus of fresh air and pure water, comes into a morbid and unhealthy state; he craves stimulants to support the sinking of his vital powers, caused by these unhealthy influences." There is certainly a great deal of truth in this; and I think that, in America, we should add to the force of our Maine law by adopting some of the restrictions of the Lodging House act.

I have addressed this letter to you, my dear cousin, on account of the deep interest you have taken in the condition of the poor and perishing in the city of New York. While making these examinations, these questions occurred to my mind: Could our rich Christian men employ their capital in a more evangelical manner, or more adorn the city of New York, than by raising a large and beautiful lodging house, which should give the means of health, comfort, and vigor to thousands of poor needlewomen? The same query may be repeated concerning all the other lodging houses I have mentioned. Furthermore, should not a movement for the registration and inspection of common lodging houses keep pace with efforts to suppress the sale of spirits? The poison of these dismal haunts creates a craving for stimulants, which constantly tends to break over and evade law.

9

Julia Ward Howe

ೀ

Julia Ward Howe (1819–1910), poet, biographer of Margaret Fuller, author of *Sex and Education* (1874), *Modern Society* (1881), and "The Battle Hymn of the Republic," traveled to Cuba in 1859 and published an account of this experience entitled *A Trip to Cuba* (1860). As her *Reminiscences, 1819–1899* (1899) records, she traveled to Europe on five occasions between 1853 and 1877, first on her wedding journey and later in connection with causes, including women's rights, for which she worked tirelessly both at home and abroad. She organized a Woman's Peace Congress in London, lectured in Italy on suffrage, spoke in Paris on women's associations in America, and presided over a Parisian Congress of Women's Rights.

Having traveled to Greece in 1867 by way of London, Paris, and Rome, Howe published *From the Oak to the Olive: Records of a Pleasant Journey* (with the subtitle on the fly leaf printed as *A Plain Record of a Pleasant Journey*) in 1868. Eschewing antebellum epistolary conventions, her text is organized chronologically, geographically, and topically, with chapters designated by place names and topics rather than by numbers. Two of the following excerpts in this selection, "Preliminaries" and an untitled conclusion, constitute the frame for the text. The first excerpt, entitled "Preliminaries," questions the legitimacy of travel writing produced on assignment for newspaper publishers (an increasingly common phenomenon), and the conclusion offers the conventional apology of the antebellum travel account, but in the coda of the text rather than in the preface, where it typically appears. The other excerpts in this selection are Howe's accounts of the voyage; of Paris, Rome, Capri, and works of art; and of an encounter with a harem, a subject of particular interest to publishers. The excerpts reveal the ongoing preoccupations of American travelers to Europe after the Civil War: foreign opinions of America (in this case the prosecution of the Civil War); Paris as a temptress; the state of Rome and the American artist's proper relationship to it; the annoying behavior of beggars; and fascination with Oriental women.

From the Oak to the Olive

Preliminaries

Not being, at this moment, in the pay of any press, whether foreign or domestic, I will not, at this my third landing in English country, be in haste to accomplish the correspondent's office of extroversion, and to expose all the inner processes of thought and of nature to the gaze of an imaginary public, often, alas! a delusory one, and difficult to be met with. No individual editor, nor joint stock company, bespoke my emotions before my departure. I am, therefore, under no obligation to furnish for the market, with the elements of time and of postage unhandsomely curtailed. Instead, then, of that breathless steeple chase after the butterfly of the moment, with whose risks and hurry I am intimately acquainted, I feel myself enabled to look around me at every step which I shall take on paper, and to represent, in my small literary operations, the three dimensions of time, instead of the flat disc of the present.

And first as to my pronoun. The augmentative *We* is essential for newspaper writing, because people are liable to be horsewhipped for what they put in the sacred columns of a daily journal. *We* may represent a vague number of individuals, less inviting to, and safer from, the cowhide, than the provoking *egomet ipse*. Or perhaps the *We* derives from the New Testament incorporation of devils, whose name was legion, for we are many. In the Fichtean philosophy, also, there are three pronouns comprised in the personal unity whose corporeal effort applies this pen to this paper, to wit, the *I* absolute, the *I* limited, and the *I* resulting from the union of these two. So that a philosopher may say *we* as well as a monarch or a penny-a-liner. Yet I, at the present moment, incline to fall back upon my record of baptism, and to confront the white sheet, whose blankness I trust to overcome, in the character of an agent one and indivisible.

Nor let it be supposed that these preliminary remarks undervalue the merits and dignity of those who write for ready money, whose meals and travels are at the expense of mysterious corporations, the very cocktail which fringes their daily experience being thrown in as a brightener of their wits and fancies. Thus would I, too, have written, had anybody ordered me to do so. I can hurry up my hot cakes like another, when there is any one to pay for them. But, leisure being accorded me, I shall stand with my tablets in the marketplace, hoping in the end to receive my penny, upon a footing of equality with those who have borne the burden and heat of the day.

With the rights of translation, however, already arranged for in the Russian, Sclavonian, Hindustanee, and Fijian dialects, I reserve to myself the right to convert my pronoun, and to write a chapter in *we* whenever the individual *I* shall seem to be insufficient. With these little points agreed upon beforehand, to prevent mistakes—since a book always represents a bargain—I will enter, without further delay, upon what I intend as a very brief but cogent chronicle of a third visit to Europe, the first two having attained no personal record.

The Voyage

The steamer voyage is now become a fact so trite and familiar as to call for no special illustration at these or any other hands. [. . .]

Our company is a small one, after the debarkation at Halifax, where sixty-five passengers leave us—among whom are some of the most strenuous *euchreists*. The remaining thirty-six are composed partly of our own country people—of whom praise or blame would be impertinent in this connection—partly of the Anglo-Saxon of the day, in the pre-puritan variety. Of the latter, as of the former, we will waive all discriminating mention, having porrigated to them the dexter of good-will, with no hint of aboriginal tomahawks to be exhumed hereafter. Some traits, however, of the *Anglais de voyage*, as seen on his return from an American trip, may be vaguely given, without personality or fear of offence.

The higher in grade the culture of the European traveller in America, the more reverently does he speak of what he has seen and learned. To the gentle-hearted, childhood and its defects are no less sacred than age and its decrepitude; withal, much dearer, because full of hope and of promise. The French barber sneezes out "Paris" at every step taken on the new land. That is the utmost his ratiocination can do; he can perceive that Boston, Washington, Chicago, are not Paris. The French exquisite flirts, flatters the individual, and depreciates the commonwealth. The English bagman hazards the glibbest sentences as to the falsity of the whole American foundation. Not much behind him lags the fox-hunting squire. The folly and uselessness of our late war supply the theme of diatribes as eloquent as twenty-*five* letters can make them. Obliging *aperçus* of the degradation and misery in store for us are vouchsafed at every opportunity. But it is when primogeniture is touched upon, or the neutrality of England in the late war criticised, that the bellowing of the sacred bulls becomes a brazen thunder. After listening to their voluminous complaints of the shortcomings of western civilization, we are tempted to go back to a set of questions asked and answered many centuries ago.

"What went ye out into the wilderness for to see? A man clothed in soft raiment? Behold, they that live delicately dwell in kings' houses. But what went ye out for to see? A prophet? Yea, I say unto you, And more than a prophet." For the prophet only foretells what is to be, but the prophetic nation is working out and fulfilling the prophet's future.

Peace, however, peace between us and them. Let the bagman return to his business, the squire to his five-barred gate. We wish them nothing worse than to stay at home, once they have got there. Not thus do the Goldwin Smiths, the Liulph Stanleys, take the altitude of things under a new horizon. They have those tools and appliances of scientific thought which build just theories and strait conclusions. The imperfection and the value of human phenomena are too well understood by them to allow them to place all of the values in the old world, and all of the imperfections in the new. And, *apropos* of this, we have an antidote to all the poison of gratuitous malignity in the shape of M. Auguste Laugel's thorough and appreciative treatise entitled The United States during the War.[1] From depths of misconception which we cannot fathom we turn to his pages, and see the truths of our record and of our conviction set forth with a simplicity and elegance which should give his work a permanent value. To Americans it must be dear as a righteous judgment; to Europeans as a vindication of their power of judging. [. . .]

Paris and Thence

In Paris the fate of Greece still pursues us. Two days the rigid veteran[2] will grant; no more—the rest promised when the Eastern business shall have been settled. But those two days suffice to undo our immortal souls so far as shop windows can do this. The shining sins and vanities of the world are so insidiously set forth in this Jesuits' college of Satan, that you catch the contagion of folly and extravagance as you pace the streets, or saunter through the brilliant arcades. Your purveyor makes a Sybarite of you, through the inevitable instrumentality of breakfast and dinner. Your clothier, from boots to bonnet, seduces you into putting the agreeable before the useful. For if you purchase the latter, you will be moved to buy by the former, and use becomes an after-thought to your itching desire and disturbed conscience. Paris is a sweating furnace in which human beings would turn life everlasting into gold, provided it were a negotiable value. You, who escape its allurements solvent, with a franc or two in your pocket, and your resources for a year to come not mortgaged, should after your own manner cause *Te Deum* to be sung or celebrated. Strongly impressed at the time, moved towards every acquisitive villany, not excluding shop-lifting nor the picking of pockets, I now regard with a sort of indignation those silken snares, those diamond, jet, and crystal allurements, which so nearly brought my self-restraint, and with it my self-respect, to ruin. Everything in Paris said to me, "Shine, dye your hair, rouge your cheeks, beggar your purse with real diamonds, or your pride with false ones. But shine, and, if necessary, beg or steal." Nothing said, "Be sober, be vigilant, because your adversary, like a roaring lion," etc., etc. What a deliverer was therefore the stern Crete-bound veteran, who cut the Gordian knot of enchantment with, "Pack and begone." And having ended that inevitable protest against his barbarity with which women requite the offices of true friendship, I now turn my wrath against false, fair Paris, and cry, "Avoid thee, *scelestissima!* Away from me, *nequissima!* I will none of thee; not a franc, not an obolus. Avoid thee! *Nolo ornari!*" [. . .]

Rome

With feelings much mingled, I approach, for the third time, the city of Rome. I pause to collect the experience of sixteen years, the period

intervening between my second visit and the present.[3] I left Rome, after those days, with entire determination, but with infinite reluctance.
America seemed the place of exile, Rome the home of sympathy and
comfort. To console myself for the termination of my travels, I undertook a mental pilgrimage, which unfolded to me something of the
spirit of that older world, of which I had found the form so congenial.
To the course of private experience were added great public lessons.
Among these I may name the sublime failure of John Brown, the sorrow and success of the late war. And now I must confess that, after so
many intense and vivid pages of life, this visit to Rome, once a theme
of fervent and solemn desire, becomes a mere page of embellishment
in a serious and instructive volume. So, while my countrymen and
women, and the Roman world in general, hang intent upon the pages
of the picture-book, let me resume my graver argument, and ask and
answer such questions of the present as may seem useful and not un-
genial.

The Roman problem has for the American thinker two clauses:
first, that of state and society; secondly, that of his personal relation to
the same. Arriving here, and becoming in some degree acquainted
with things as they are, he asks, first, What is the theory of this society, and how long will it continue? Secondly, What do my countrymen who consent to pass their lives here gain? What do they give up?
I cannot answer either of these questions exhaustively. The first would
lead me far into social theorizing; the second into some ungracious
criticism. So a word, a friendly one must stand for good intentions
where wisdom is at fault.

The theory of this society in policy and religion is that of a sym-
bolism whose remote significance has long been lost sight of and forgotten. Here the rulers, whose derived power should represent the
consensus of the people, affect to be greater than those who constitute
them, and the petty statue, raised by the great artist for the convenience and instruction of the crowd, spurns at the solid basis of the
heaven-born planet, without which it could not stand. Rank here is
not a mere convenience and classification for the encouragement of
virtue and promotion of order. Rank here takes the place of virtue,
and repression, its tool, takes the place of order. A paralysis of thought
characterizes the whole community, for thought deprived of its legit-

imate results is like the human race debarred from its productive functions—it becomes effete, and soon extinct.

Abject poverty and rudeness characterize the lower class (*basso ceto*), bad taste and want of education the middle, utter arrogance and superficiality the upper class. The distinctions between one set of human beings and another are held to be absolute, and the inferiority of opportunity, carefully preserved and exaggerated, is regarded as intrinsic, not accidental. Vain is it to plead the democratic allowances of the Catholic church. The equality of man before God is here purely abstract and disembodied. The name of God, on the contrary, is invoked to authorize the most flagrant inequalization that ignorance can prepare and institutions uphold. The finest churches, the fairest galleries, you will say, are open to the poorest as to the richest. This is true. But the man's mind is the castle and edifice of his life. Look at these rough and ragged people, unwashed, uncombed, untaught. See how little sensible they are of the decencies and amenities of life. Search their faces for an intelligent smile, a glance that recognizes beauty or fitness in any of the stately circumstances that surround them. They are kept like human cattle, and have been so kept for centuries. And their dominants suppose themselves to be of one sort, and these of another. But give us absolutism, and take away education, even in rich and roomy America, and what shall we have? The cruel and arrogant slaveholder, the vulgar and miserable poor white, the wronged and degraded negro. The three classes of men exist in all constituted society. Absolutism allows them to exist only in this false form.

This race is not a poor, but a robust and kindly one. Inclining more to artistic illustration than to abstract thought, its gifts, in the hierarchy of the nations, are eminent and precious. Like the modern Greek, the modern Celt, and the modern negro, the Italian peasant asks a century or two of education towards modern ideas. And all that can be said of his want of comprehension only makes it the more evident that the sooner we begin, the better.

It should not need, to Americans or Englishmen, to set out any formal argument against absolutism. Among them it has long since been tried and judged. Enough of its advocacy only remains to present that opposition which is the necessary basis of action. And yet a word to my countrymen and countrywomen, who, lingering on the edge of the vase, are lured by its sweets, and fall into its imprisonment. It is a false, false superiority to which you are striving to join yourself. A prince of puppets is not a prince, but a puppet; a superfluous duke is no dux; a titular count does not count. Dresses, jewels, and equipages of tasteless extravagance; the sickly smile of disdain for simple people; the clinging together, by turns eager and haughty, of a clique that becomes daily smaller in intention, and whose true decline consists in its numerical increase—do not dream that these lift you in any true way—in any true sense. For Italians to believe that it does, is natural; for Englishmen to believe it, is discreditable; for Americans, disgraceful. [. . .]

Works of Art

[. . .] Art is, of course, the only solid object which an American can bring forward to justify a prolonged residence in Rome. Art, health, and official duty, are among the valid reasons which bring our countrymen abroad. Two of these admit of no argument. The sick have a right, other things permitting, to go where they can be bettered; a duty perhaps, to go where the sum of their waning years and wasting activities admits of multiplication. Those who live abroad as ministers and consuls have a twofold opportunity of benefiting their country. If honest and able, they may benefit her by their presence in foreign lands; if unworthy and incompetent, by their absence from home. But our artists are those whose expatriation gives us most to think about. They take leave of us either in the first bloom or in the full maturity of their powers. The ease of living in Southern Europe, the abundance of models and of works of art, the picturesque charms of nature and of scenery, detain them forever from us, and, save for an abstract sentiment, which itself weakens with every year, the sacred tie of country is severed. Its sensibilities play no part in these lives devoted to painting and modelling.

Now, an eminent gift for art is an exceptional circumstance. He who has it weds his profession, leaves father and mother, and goes where his slowly-unfolding destiny seems to call him. Against such a course we have no word to say. It presents itself as a necessary conclusion to earnest and noble men, who love not their native country less, but their votive country more. Of the first and its customs they would still say—

> "I cannot but remember such things were
> That were most precious to me."

Yet of this career, so often coveted by those to whom its attainment does not open, I cannot speak in terms of supreme recognition. The office of art is always as precious as its true ministers are rare. But the relative importance of sculptural and pictorial art is not to-day what it was in days of less thought, of smaller culture. Every one who likes the Bible to-day, likes it best without illustrations. Were Christ here to speak anew, he would speak without parables. In ruder times, heavenly fancies could only be illustrated on the one hand, received on the other, through the mediation of a personal embodiment. Only through human sympathy was the assent to divine truth obtained. The necessity which added a feminine personality to the worship of Christ, and completed the divided Godhead by making it female as well as male, was a philosophical one, but not recognized as such. The device of the Virgin was its practical result, counterbalancing the partiality of the one-sided personal *culte* of the Savior. Modern religious thought gets far beyond this, makes in spiritual things no distinction of male and female, and does not apply sex to the Divine, save in the most vague and poetic sense. The inner convictions of heart and conscience may now be spoken in plain prose, or sung in ringing verse. The *vates*, prophet or reformer, may proclaim his system and publish his belief; and his audience will best apprehend it in its simplest and most direct form. The wide spaces of the new continent allow room for the most precious practical experimentation; and speculative and theoretical liberty keep pace with liberty of action. The only absolute restraint, the best one, is a moral one. "Thou shalt not" applies only to what is intrinsically inhuman and profane. And now, there is no need to puzzle simple souls with a marble gospel. Faith needs not to digest whole side-walls of saints and madonnas, who once stood for something, no one now knows what. The Italian school was to art what the Greek school was to literature—an original creation and beginning. But life has surpassed Plato and Aristotle. We are forced to piece their short experiences, and to say to both, "You are matchless, but insufficient." And so, though Raphael's art remains immortal and unsurpassed, we are forced to say of his thought, "It is too small." No one can settle, govern, or moralize a country by it. It will not even suffice to reform Italy. The golden transfigurations hang quiet on the walls, and let pope and cardinal do their worst. We want a world peopled with faithful and intelligent men and women. The Prometheus of the present day is needed rather to animate statues than to make them. [. . .]

Capri

I have a fresh chapter of torment for a new Dante, if such an one could be induced to apply to me. I will not expatiate, nor exhale any Francesca episodes, any "*Lasciate ogni spiranza!*" I will be succinct and business-like, furnishing the outlines from which some more leisurely artist, better paid and employed, shall do his hell-painting.

We leave enchanting Naples—tear ourselves from our hotel, whose very impositions grow dear to us; the precious window, too, which shows the bay and Capri, and close at hand the boats, the fish-market, and the chairs on which the populace sit at eventide to eat oysters and drink mineral water. A small boat takes us to a very small steamer, on whose deck we pay ten francs each to a stout young man, in appearance much like a southern poor Buckra, who departs in another small boat as soon as he has plundered us. The voyage to Capri is cool and reasonably smooth. A pleasant chance companion, bound to the same port, beguiles the time for us. We exchange our intellectual small wares with a certain good will, which remains the best part of the bargain. When quite near the island, the small steamer pauses, and lowers a boat in which we descend to view the famous Blue Grotto. At the entrance, we are warned to stoop as low as possible. We do so, and still the entrance seems dangerous. With some scratching and pushing, however, the boat goes through, and the lovers of blue feast their eyes with the tender color. The water is ultramarine, and the roof sapphire. The place seems a toy of nature—a forced detention of a single ray of the spectrum. Dyes change with the fashion; the blue of our youth does not color our daughter's silks and ribbons. The purples of ten years ago cannot be met with to-day. But this blue is constant, and therefore perfect.

Our enjoyment of it, however, is marred by an old beast in human form who rushes at us, and insists upon being paid two francs for diving. He promises us that he will show us wondrous things—that he will fill the azure cave with silver sparkles. Wearied with his screeching, and a little deluded by his promises, we weakly offer him a franc and a half; whereupon he throws off some superfluous clothing, and softly glides into the deep, without so much as a single sparkle. He certainly presents an odd appearance; his weird legs look as if twisted out of silver; his back is dark upon the water. But the refreshing bath he takes is so little worth thirty sous to us that we feel tempted to harpoon him as he dodges about, sure that, if pierced, he can shed nothing more solid than humbug. On our return to the steamer we pay two francs each for this melancholy expedition, and presently make the little harbor of Capri.

And here the promised Hell begins. The way to it, remember, is always pleasant. No sooner does our boat touch the land than a nest of human rattlesnakes begins to coil and hiss about us, each trying to carry us off; each pouring into our ears discordant, rapid jargon. "My donkey, siora." "And mine." "And mine." "How much will you give?" "Will you go up to Tiberio?" But all this with more repetition and less music than a chorus of Handel's or an aria of Sebastian Bach. "My donkey," flourish; "My do-n-onkey," high soprano variation; "My donkey," good grumbling contralto. "How much?" "How much?" "How much?" "How much?" shriek all in chorus. And you, the unhappy star in this hell opera, begin with uncertain utterance— "Let me see, good people. One at a time. What is just will pay"—the *motivo* also repeated; chorus renewed— "Money"; "Three francs"; "Four francs"; "Five francs"; "A *bottiglia*"; "A *buona mano*." "A *buona mano*?" Good hand—would one could administer it in the right way, in the right place! By this time each of you occupies the warm saddle of a donkey, and at one P.M., less twenty, the thermometer at 90 Fahrenheit or more, and being warned to reach the steamer by three P.M., at latest, the punishment of all your past, and most of your future sins begins.

Facile descensus Averni. Yes; but the *ascensus?* To climb so high after Tiberio, who went so low! For this is the ruined palace of Tiberius Caesar himself, which you go to seek and see, if possible. He still plagues the world, as he would have wished to do. Your expedition in search of his stony vestiges is a long network of torment, spun by you, the donkey, and the donkey-driver, undisguised Apollo standing by to weld the golden chains by which you suffer. As often as you seem to approach the object, a new *détour* leads you at a zigzag from the straight direction. But this is little. At every turn in the road a beggar, in some variety, addresses you. Now a deformed wretch shows you his twisted limbs, and shrieks, "*co cosa, siora.*" Now, a wholesome-looking mother, with a small child, asks a contribution to the wants of "*questa creatura.*" Now, a grandam, with blackened face and bleached hair, hobbles after you. Children oppress you with flowers, women with oranges—all in view of the largest *quid* for the smallest *quo.* You grow afraid to look in a pretty face or return a civil nod, lest the eternal signal of beggary should make itself manifest. And such women and children!—every one a picture. Such intense eyes, such sun-ripened complexions! I take note of them, handsome devils that they are, all foreordained as a part of my fiery probation. For all this time I am making a steep ascent. Sometimes the donkey takes me up a flight of stone steps, clutching at each with an uncertain quiver, but stimulated by the nasal "n—a—a—a," which follows him from the woman who by turns coaxes and threatens him. Now we clamber along a narrow ledge, whose height causes my dizzy head to swim; there is nothing but special providence between me and perdition. A little girl, six years of age, pulls my donkey by the head; a dignified matron behind me holds the whip. The little girl leads carelessly, and I quake and grow hot and cold with terror; but it is of no use. The matron will not take the rein; her office is to flog, and she will do nought else. And the sun?—the sun works his miracles upon us until we wish ourselves as well off as the Niobides, who, at least, look cool. Finally, after an hour of jolting, roasting, quivering, and general exasperation, we reach the top. Here we are passively lifted from our donkeys; we mechanically follow our guide through a white-washed wine-shop into a small outer space, with a low wall around it, over which we are invited to look down some hundreds of feet into the sea. This is called the Leap of Tiberio: from this height, says the barefooted old vagabond who guides us, he pitched his victims into the deep. The descent here is as straight as the wall of a house. Farther on, we find some very fragmentary ruins, in the usual Roman style. Among them is a good mosaic pavement, with some vaults and broken columns. A sloping way is shown us, carefully paved, and with a groove on either side. Into this, say they, fitted the wheels of a certain chariot, in which guests were invited to seat themselves. The chariot, guided by two cords, then started to go down to the sea. But at a certain moment the vehicle was arrested by a sudden shock. Those within it were precipitated into the water, after which the cords comfortably drew the chariot back.

[. . .] Finally, I exhort all good Christians to beware of Capri, and on no account to throw away a trip thither, but to undertake the same as a penance, for the mortification of the flesh and the good of the immortal soul. The island is to-day in as heathen a condition as Tiberius himself could wish; only from a golden, it has descended to the perpetual invoking of a copper rain. That the Beggar's Opera should have been written out of the kingdom of Naples is a matter of reasonable astonishment to the logically inferring mind. I could improvise it myself on the spur of the moment, making a heroine out of the black-eyed woman who drove my animal— black-haired also, and with a scarlet cotton handkerchief bound around her head in careless picturesqueness. Gold ear-rings and necklace had she who screamed and begged so for a penny more than her due. And when I cried aloud in fear, she replied, "*Non abbia timor—donkey molt' avezzo*"; which diverted my mind and caused me to laugh. As we went up and as we went down, she encountered all her friends and gossips in holiday attire; for yesterday was *Festa*, and to-day, consequently, is *festa* also—a saint's day leaving many small arrearages to settle, in the shape of headache, fight, and so on, so that one does not comfortably get to work again until the third day. This fact of the antecedent *festa* accounted for the unusual amount of good clothes displayed throughout the island. Our eyes certainly profited by it, and possibly our purses; for we just remember that one or two groups in velvet jackets and gold necklaces did not beg. [. . .]

Greece and the Voyage Thither

[. . .] Our first view of the pacha's *harem* showed us a dozen or more women crouching on the deck of the Turkish steamer, their heads and faces bundled up with white muslin veils, which concealed hair, forehead, mouth, and chin, leaving exposed to view only the triangle of the eyes and nose. Several children were there, who at first sight all appeared equally dirty and ill-dressed. We were afterwards able to distinguish differences between them.

The women and children came on board in a body, and took up a position on the starboard side of the deck. With them came an old man-servant, in a long garment of whitish woollen cloth, who defined their boundaries by piling up certain bales of property. In the space thus marked off, mattresses were at once laid down and spread with coverlets; for these women were to pass night as well as day on deck. Five ladies of the pacha's family at once intrenched themselves in one of the small cabins below, where, with five children, they continued for the remainder of the voyage, without exercise or ventilation. Too sacred to be seen by human eyes, these ladies made us aware of their presence by the sound of their incessant chattering, by the odor of their tobacco, and by the screaming of one of their little ones, an infant of eight months.

When these things had been accomplished, our captain sent word to the pacha that he was ready to depart. The great man's easy-chair— by no means a splendid one—was then carried on board, and the great man himself, accompanied by his son-in-law and his dragoman, came among us. He was a short, stout person, some fifty years of age, and wore a dark military coat, with a gold stripe on the shoulder, and lilac trousers. His dragoman was a Greek. He and his suite smoked vigorously; and stared somewhat, as, with the neophyte on one side and the little Austrian lady on the other, I walked up and down the deck. The women and the old servant all slept *à la belle étoile*. The pacha and his officers had state-rooms in the saloon; the other men were in the third cabin. I forgot to say that at Corfu we left Count Lunzi and his amiable daughter, whose gracious manners and good English did credit to Mrs. Hills's excellent tuition, which the young lady had enjoyed for some years at her well-known school in Athens.[4]

When we came on deck the next morning, we found some of the Turkish women still recumbent, others seated upon their mattresses. Two of the children, a girl of ten years and a boy of twelve, went about under orders, and carried dishes and water-vessels between the cabin and the deck. We afterwards learned that these were Albanian slaves. The girl was named Haspir, the boy Ali. The first had large dark eyes and a melancholy expression of countenance; the boy also had Oriental eyes, whose mischievous twinkle was tempered by the gravity of his situation. The old servant, whom they called Baba, ate his breakfast in a corner. He had a miscellaneous looking dish of fish, bread, and olives. The women fed chiefly, as far as I could judge, on cucumbers and radishes, which they held and munched. Water was given from a brazen pitcher, of a pattern decidedly Oriental. Coffee was served to the invisible family in the small cabin. I did not see the women on deck partake of it. But from this time the scope of my observations was limited. A canvas partition, made fast to the mast overhead, now intervened, to preserve this portion of the *harem* from the pollution of external regards. Henceforth, we had glimpses of its members only when a lurch of the steamer swayed the canvas wall far out of equilibrium. The *far niente* seemed to be their fate, without alternative. Nor book nor needle had they. The children came outside, and peeped at us. Baba, grim guardian of the household, sat or squatted among his bales, oftenest quite unoccupied, but sometimes smoking, or chattering with the children. I took my modest drawing-book, and, with unsteady hand, began to sketch him in pen and ink. He soon divined my occupation, and kept as still as a mouse until by a sign I released him, when he begged, in the same language, to see what I had drawn. I next tried to get a *croquis* of a pretty little girl who played about, wearing a pink wadded sack over a gown and trousers of common flowered calico, buff and brown. She was disposed to wriggle out of sight; but Baba threatened her, and she was still.

Presently, the slave-boy, Ali, came up from the select cabin below, bearing in his arms an ill-conditioned little creature, two years of age, who had come on board in a cashmere pelisse lined with fur, a pink wadded underjacket, and a pair of trousers of dirty common calico. He had now discarded the fur-pelisse. On his round little head he wore a cap of pink cashmere, soiled and defaced, with a large gold coin attached to it. A natural weakness drew me towards the little wretch, whom I tried to caress. Ali patted him tenderly, and said, "Pacha." This was indeed the youngest member, save one, of the pacha's family—the true baby being the infant secluded down stairs, whose frequent cries appealed in vain for change of air and of scene. The two-year-old had already the title of bey.

"Can a baby a bey be?" I asked, provoking the disgust which a pun is sure to awaken in those who have not made it.

We met the pacha at meals, interchanging mute salutations. He had a pleasant, helpless sort of smile, and ate according to the ortho-dox standard of nicety. On deck some attendant constantly brought him a pipe composed of a large knob of amber, which served as a mouth piece, and a reed some eight inches in length, bearing a lighted cigar.

As we sat much in our round house, it was inevitable that I should at last establish communication with him through the mediation of a young Greek passenger, who spoke both Turkish and French.

It was from the pacha that I learned that Haspir and Ali were slaves. The little girl whom I had sketched was his daughter. I in-quired about a girl somewhat younger, who played with this one. The pacha signified that he had given the mother of his daughter to one of his men, and that the second little girl was born of this connection. The two younger children already spoken of were born of another mother, probably each of a different one.

"O Christian marriage!" I thought, as I looked on this miscella-neous and inorganic family, "let us not complain of thy burdens."

With us the birth of a child is the strongest bond of union between its parents; with the Oriental it is the signal for separation. No society will ever permanently increase whose structure rests on an architecture so feeble. The Turkish empire might spread by conquest and thrive by plunder. But at home it can never compete with nations in which family life has individuality of centre and equality of obligation. With Greeks and Albanians to work for them, and pay them tribute, the Turks are able to attain a certain wealth. It is the wealth, however, which impoverishes mankind, exhausting the sources of industry and of enterprise. Let the Turk live upon what he can earn, and we shall hear little of him.

The women sometimes struggled out from their canvas enclosure, and went below on various errands. On these occasions they were enveloped in a straight striped covering, white and red, much like a summer counterpane. This was thrown over the head, held together between the teeth, and reached to the feet. It left in view their muslin head-dresses, and calico trousers, gathered at the ankle, nothing more. A few were barefoot—one or two only wore stockings. Most of them were shod with *brodequins*, of a size usually worn by men.

At a late hour in the afternoon, Ali brought to their enclosure a round metal dish of stewed meat, cut in small pieces for the convenience of those whose customs are present proof that fingers were made before knives and forks. A great dish of rice simultaneously made its appearance. Baba chattered very much, Ali made himself busy, and a little internal commotion became perceptible behind the canvas wall.

My opportunity of observing Turkish manners was as brief as it was limited. Having taken the Moslems on board on Monday, well towards evening, the Wednesday following saw, at ten A.M., my exit from the steamer. For we were now in the harbor of Syra. [. . .]

Copy is exhausted, say the printers. Perhaps patience gave out first. My MS. is at end—not handsomely rounded off, nor even shortened by a surgical amputation, but broken at some point in which facts left no room for words. Observation became absorbing, and description was adjourned, as it now proves, forever. The few sentences which I shall add to what is already written will merely apologize for my sudden disappearance, lest the clown's "Here we are" should find a comic *pendant* in my "Here we are not."

I have only to say that I have endeavored in good faith to set down this simple and hurried record of a journey crowded with interests and pleasures. I was afraid to receive so freely of these without attempting to give what I could in return, under the advantages and disadvantages of immediate transcription. In sketches executed upon the spot, one hopes that the vividness of the impression under which one labors may atone for the want of finish and of elaboration. If read at all, these notes may be called to account for many insufficiencies. Some pages may appear careless, some sentences Quixotic. I am still inclined to think that with more leisure and deliberation I should not have done the work as well. I should, perhaps, like Tintoretto, have occupied acres and acres of attention with superfluous delineation, putting, as he did, my own portrait in the corner. Rejoice, therefore, good reader, in my limitations. They are your enfranchisement.

Touching Quixotism, I will plead guilty to the sounding of various parleys before some stately buildings and unshaken fortresses. "Who is this that blows so sharp a summons?" may the inmates ask. I may answer, "One who believes in the twelve legions of angels that wait upon the endeavors of faithful souls." Should they further threaten or deride, I will borrow Elizabeth Browning's sweet refrain—

"I am no trumpet, but a reed,"

—and trust not to become a broken one.

Conscious of my many shortcomings, and asking attention only for the message I have tried to bring, I ask also for that charity which recognizes that good will is the best part of action, and good faith the first condition of knowledge.

10

Helen Hunt Jackson

૨௦

Helen Maria Hunt Jackson (1831–1885), journalist and novelist best known for championing the American Indian in *A Century of Dishonor* (1881) and *Ramona* (1884), also published sonnets and lyrics, children's books, and a travel book entitled *Bits of Travel. By H. H.* (1872), which chronicles her European travels in 1868 and 1869. The first half of her account, comprised of her travels through the Valley of Gastein, the Ampezzo Pass, Albano, Salzburg, Rome, and Venice, takes the form of a third-person narrative, while the second half of her account, "Encyclicals of a Traveller," takes the conventional form of letters, which are dated and addressed to friends at home. One of those letters, excerpted here, covers seven days in Rome.

Like many travel writers laboring against the exhaustion of the genre in the face of repeated accounts of visits to the obligatory tourist meccas, "H. H." (her signature prior to marriage) adopts strategies to enliven her narrative. She interjects irreverent remarks about hallowed tourist shrines, the foibles of Catholicism, and the tyranny of guide books—a frequent lament of travelers. Making sport of the conventions of the travel genre, she plays with the dilemmas of travel writing, but like many other post–Civil War travelers to Europe, she nonetheless creates a fairly tedious account.

Bits of Travel

Dear People:

Will you be relieved, I wonder, or appalled, when I tell you that I have decided not to try to send you more than seven days in this letter! Such a seven days as it was, though; if I could only have photographed the seven sunshines, each bluer and whiter and yellower than the one before it! Spring is spring nowhere but here, I begin to suspect. No matter if a possible fever does lurk in every golden hour, and a certain weariness and lassitude in every whiff of the hot southwind, you don't care; you glance up and down and run swiftly into the sunny spots with no more care than the lizards, who outstrip you, do your best.

Well, it is to be a week that you are to spend with me, and you came a week ago last Thursday morning, February 4, and I said, "Good, you are just in time for a delightful excursion to the Palace of the Caesars, with the Archaeologicals, this afternoon"—so we set off, P—— and I in a little low carriage, and the rest of you on your broomsticks in the air, as you always go nowadays with me everywhere. When we got to the door of the enclosure, there was the Archaeological Society at bay! door shut! the old gray hat of John Henry Parker[1] bobbing up and down above its worthy wearer's excitement and indignation, as he was parleying with the custode, and explaining to the crowd of Britishers that, owing to an unfortunate misunderstanding, we could not go in. There had been some mistake, some informality; of course there had, and Mr. Parker, being by nature a blunderer, had made it. Then danced up the gay Signor L—— with his violets in his button-hole, and his little cane—ineffable mixture of infant, archaeologist, and Marble Faun; and he chuckles in his broken English over Mr. Parker's blunder, and says, "O, I am so *e*mused to see such many people so *deesappointed !*" We laugh till we are ashamed, and have to slink behind other people not to be seen. The crowd is quite large, fifty or sixty people—some drive off; some follow Mr. Parker, who dashes across the road, past the Basilica of Constantine, with its three grand old arches, and in among the blocks of everybody's house, and everybody's temple, and everybody's road, all lying about in centuries of confusion, between the Basilica and the Coliseum. We saunter along after them, but not of them, and finally sit down on what was a doorstep, I dare say, in the days when Romulus went to late suppers; and there we talk, and knock the sacred bits of marble with our parasols and canes, just as if we had hobnobbed with ancients all our lives. At last Signor L—— says "This is too stoopeed; we will not do it more; let us go into the Coliseum." So he shook hands with Mr. John Henry Parker as respectfully as if he believed he had not been in the least to blame for the *contretemps*, and off we went into the Coliseum, which had all that while seemed to be beckoning us with its gray arms. You all know just how it looks, I knew that before I came; but how it feels, that is something which don't photograph!—the unspeakable quiet; the dance of lights and shade in and out of the arches; the distance and the nearness of the Gothic spaces of sky, set in settings of stone, and looking like sapphire gates on which, if you had but wings, you might knock and find them opening to you! The noise of the city comes in muffled and dulled, you hardly hear it, and, if you do, you can hardly remember what it means; you are more tranquil than you supposed this world would ever let you become. I have wondered if one could not even sit still under one of those arches and be happily and unconsciously changed into wallflower or moss, without a pang of death! The wallflowers look perverse enough to have been the result of some such uncanny spell cast over human beings; they hang and wave and flaunt everywhere but where you can reach them—great blazes of yellow darting and swaying like fires on the very tops of the most inaccessible places. By and by there will be more, I see, lower down; but at first, while they are a marvel, in these early days of February, they are only in spots where no human hand can touch them. We went up to the third tier, and out through one of the openings, and sat down; my feet were in a fragrant bush, looking and smelling like the old-fashioned "southernwood" in country gardens. Below us, the mass of mingled earth and ruin was a sharp precipice; we dared not look over. Just on the edge, a smilax vine tauntingly held up a cluster of claret beads—I thought them seeds; the Archaeologist said they were buds, and, before I could stop him, had picked them, to prove his theory true. I felt like throwing them on the ground, as King David did the water for which a life had been risked; instead of that, we quarrelled still longer over them, neither of us knowing enough to prove ourself right, and when I got home I found they had fallen out of my bouquet.

Suddenly we heard a sound of chanting below. There was a procession, going from shrine to shrine, kneeling down before each one, and chanting their prayers; there were a dozen men shrouded from head to foot in coarse brown cloth, like linen—only two small holes left for the eyes. "These are they" who beg from door to door, shaking a little tin cup on every threshold, speaking no word, and turning away almost instantly if nothing is given them. I have been told that they are many of them noblemen who do this—some of them as a penance, which is imposed by their confessor, and they have to walk the streets till they have got a certain sum; some of them belong to a fraternity or society, and are pledged to do this so many days in the year. They are uncanny objects to meet in the street. For two days after this scene in the Coliseum I saw them repeatedly, in different parts of the city; in fact, one of them walked by my side one morning as I was going to my Italian lesson, and I saw that his eyes were black and fiery, and his feet were white and finely veined. (Their feet are bare, with only a leather sandal.) A monk went before them, with a cross, and some twenty or thirty poor people had joined the procession. They all fell on their knees, and crossed themselves, and chanted aloud before each shrine. One poor man, who had a white beard fit for a patriarch, carried a sort of square board, perhaps some relic; at the end of each prayer, he threw himself forward full length on this board, face down, for a second, and seemed to be kissing the earth. Meekly, at a little distance, followed another smaller procession, all women. A nun carrying a smaller cross, a few sisters walking on each side of her, and a dozen poor women following; they kept in the rear, and knelt at a respectful distance from the monks and the men, but joined in all the prayers. O, you can have no conception of the wild sense of yearning tender pity which sweeps over you sometimes in looking on such a scene. You think you cannot bear it one minute longer! You must spring down among them and say, "Poor souls, poor souls, this is nothing; do look up, and see the sun." I watched Signor L——'s face while all this was going on, but I could not fathom his expression. I could see nothing beyond a sense of the picturesque additions which the veiled figures and the chanting and the high black crosses made to our view, as we looked down on it all from the upper chambers of the air; and yet he is a Roman Catholic—so good a one that he has for five years gone, every spring, into a convent for *eight days of entire silence*. Think of that! Not one word to a human being for eight days! There are some of us who would go mad on the seventh, if not sooner. It seemed malicious in the sun to hurry down on this particular afternoon, as he had not hurried on the day before, but I am sure he set an hour earlier! We were suddenly frightened by seeing that arch after arch began to lie in shadow, and that Mount Gennaro was turning pink; we almost ran down the stairs, for you must know that nobody may see sunsets from the Coliseum. As for that matter, it is at risk of your life you see them anywhere in this land of malaria, but in the neighborhood of the Coliseum it is worst of all; so this was the end of the first of our seven days, dear people.

Then came the Saturday on which we started out early for the *Baths of Caracalla*. You *would* have the Guide-Book carried along, you remember? and I called up to you, in the air, as we drove, that you might read it for yourselves; that I would not be tormented with its husks of information; that all I cared to know about this most wonderful ruin was that it was begun only two hundred years after Christ, and that emperor after emperor kept adding and improving till it grew to be one hundred and forty thousand square yards big, and sixteen hundred people could bathe there at once. I don't know whether the historians mention about *towels!* perhaps they didn't mind drying off in the sun! If they had much such sun as this Saturday's, it would have been easy (and perfect bliss besides). There were great halls for exercises; great round rooms big enough for churches, where a thousand or so took a vapor-bath if they liked. Then there were the cold rooms and the hot rooms, and the porticos, and the tribunes and the galleries, and the walls were painted and the floors were mosaic, and everywhere there were grand statues, so that the naked men could never have found themselves or each other beautiful. And, I don't suppose there was a Roman of renown for five centuries who didn't have his turn in the tubs! That was the way it began, but now you see it is quite another sort of affair. You cannot follow out the plan of it, even if you keep Murray's map under your nose every step of the way, and break your shins, in consequence, over the great clutter of old stones lying about you everywhere; so presently you reflect that it doesn't make the least difference to you which room was the "Cella Frigidaria," and which the "Cella Calidaria"; and as soon as you settle that, you can be happy. Then you can wander through great-walled square after square, and see on which floor there are most daisies; they are like fields now—what were the old floors—thick grass, ivies, vines, thistles. (Ah, the beauty of a Roman thistle! Some day I'll try to tell you just how they look; they are almost the most beautiful of the road-side things here.) All about you are these jagged broken walls, which look as if they might topple over any minute; where windows used to be are irregular great gaps, with vines growing in them; and presently, as you get used to looking up higher and higher, till you see the tops of the walls, you see what seems to be another earth, midway between you and the sky, and there are small trees growing, and vines and bushes hanging over the edges and reaching down to meet their kindred who are climbing up from below. Then it first dawns upon you what gigantic ruins these are, and by that time the custode knows you are quite ready to scramble up to the top; so he comes along with his key and unlocks a door in the wall, and there in the wall is built a narrow ladder of a staircase, up and up and up which you go, and when you come out at top you find that the "other earth," whose fringes you had seen hanging over, is a magic wild garden, on the tops of the old walls, with here and there a bit of what was *roof* in Caesar's day, but is now more solid ground than the rest. Then you sit down on the safest-looking spot you can find, and lean up against a great stone, and think you will never go away. You dare not look over; too dizzy by half. I did wish I knew how high these walls were, but of course *that* wasn't "put down" in Murray. The few rare bits of knowledge that I do hanker after never *are* in that unpleasant red book. But I can tell you a little by this; looking over into the great chamber where I had been picking daisies, I could see no daisies, only dark, still, solemn green. In another room men were at work digging down, down for what they might find; they had struck the floor, but from our height it looked like a shapeless dark hole, and the men looked like children.

Here too were the yellow wallflowers, setting their torches where only the wind could reach them. O the cruel lure of a flower you cannot possibly touch! I shall remember some of *these* wallflowers as long as I live; and those I pick I shall forget, I suppose, though I nurture them tenderly for many days in my room.

We were so blessed in the day we took to see these ruins, that we were absolutely alone there: only one stuffy old Englishman came, and he did not stay; he wheezed up the staircase, and almost as soon as he caught sight of us he went down, looking frightened to death at the thought of two independent American women sitting with no hats on their heads, alone, on the top of the walls of the Baths of Caracalla!

But I forgot to say that besides the wonderfulness of being on the top of these walls, and scrambling about dizzily on the brink of jagged unroofed chambers, where such thickets of laurestinus and myrtle and all other green-leaved things that grow so hide the real edge that you feel as if the tiny brown path before you might be an illusion and a snare, and the next step would be your last; besides all this, you look off over all Rome, and all the wonderful hills which encircle the plain—hills so unlike any others I have ever seen that I do not know how to describe them. It is not their height—they are not very high; it is not their shape—their outlines are not unique; and perhaps I have seen other hills as pink and purple and gray and blue; but their beauty is like a subtle beauty in some faces, which cannot vindicate its claim by a feature or a tint, but which ravishes you, and holds you forever! The artists say it is atmosphere. There is an atmosphere to faces too; so I think perhaps there can be no better word for it than that.

Now have I given you a shadow of an idea of what it is like to roam about for four hours in and on the Baths of Caracalla? I am afraid I have not; and what is still more stupid of me, I skipped over from Thursday to Saturday, and never let you stir out of the house on Friday, which was the day for the Villa Pamfili Doria; and there we went and saw the whole of it, and picked anemones—yes, purple and white anemones and painted crocuses on the 5th of February. [. . .]

On Sunday we went to church at San Pietro in Montorio. We didn't hear much of a sermon, to be sure, nor stay through the services, because the church was very cold. But we made up for it by going into the cloister of the convent adjoining, and going into the little temple which somebody built over the very spot on which Peter was crucified. You don't doubt about that spot, do you? What is the use? And then wait till you hear the circumstantial evidence, i.e., we saw the very hole in which the cross rested! What more could one have! It is in a crypt (that is Roman Catholic short for a dark, damp cellar) under the temple, and there is an iron grating over the hole, and a sacred lamp perpetually burning in it. The old monk who showed us in had a long stick, hollow at one end, which he poked down and twisted round and round a few times at the bottom of the hole, and brought it up full of sacred earth, and then held it out to me, just as butter-men hold out to you the samples of their butter from the bottom of the tub. I realized afterwards that I ought to have taken the earth and carried it away as a relic; but I only stared at it and him and said nothing, and he put it back again with a sigh. However, he liked our franc just as well as if we had been Christians.

The cloister was the most shut-up spot I ever saw: high walls, brick and stone pavement; only the sky for relief, and that looked so far off it would very soon have discouraged you more than it would have comforted you, if you had been shut up there; in the middle, the cold, white, still, round temple with a dome, and a row of gray pillars around it. I thought it very beautiful, and was quite surprised to find it one of the things set down in Murray as proper to be admired. A few little weeds were struggling up between the stones in this cloister, and I thought if we did not escape pretty soon I should find my Picciola.[2] The poor monk looked wistfully after us as he let us out. I suppose he goes out too when he likes, but that can't make much difference if you know you must go back at night. O, I long to get out of hearing of the clank of these chains!

This church and convent stand on the top of one of the highest hills; behind the church, a few rods farther on the road, is the fountain Paolina—such an ugly thing; all but the water, which is beautiful and makes you leap about to look at it—three great streams rushing out of a wall into a semicircular basin; while the wall and the basin and every head and corner and post are so ugly, it only shows what water is, that it can be so beautiful in spite of them. Some pope—a Paul, I suppose—made the fountain more than two hundred years ago; that is quite modern here, in fact, a mere thing of yesterday. The water comes all the way from the lake of Bracciano, and after this one brief minute of jollity and beauty plunges down into the city, and does—what do you think?—turns all the flour-mills! How it must chafe when it remembers its frolic in the pope's fountain, to which it can never, never get back!

From the plateau in front of this fountain, and in front of the church, is a grand view of Rome—the entire campagna and the mountains. It was so warm that we sat down on the grass and looked and looked. The gay Roman people were flocking up and down, keeping their out-of-doors Sunday. Poor souls, it is no wonder this becomes part of their religion! Three women sat in a group by the roadside, with huge piles of some sort of salad, which they were getting ready for market. They ate almost more than they put into the basket; munch, munch, munch—away they ate and talked, and talked and ate, and laughed, as if clear, cold, raw spinach were the most delicious thing in the world. Before we went home, we took a turn in the Coliseum, which was sunny, and had more flowers in it than on Friday; from the topmost pinnacle they brought down asphodel to me, and when I saw that, I was sorry I had been so unsocial as to choose sitting alone in my old arch, with my feet in the southernwood bush, rather than climbing up with them. And here is the end of the fourth lesson.

Now Monday can be told in few words, because it is only the Villa Pamfili Doria over again. We went early and we stayed so late that we were half sure we should wake up with fever the next morning; and all that time we were picking anemones and lovely green things to make into bouquets to throw at the Carnival on Tuesday. Yes, absolutely to throw anemones at the Carnival! Now that it is over, I see that it partook of the nature of sacrilege, but at the time it seemed to me wise and good. O, such a basketful as I brought home! And the next morning I spent two hours and a half tying them up into lovely wild-looking bunches; snowdrops mixed with them, and great ivy-leaves set round like a bouquet-holder. I felt afraid I had left no anemones for anybody else, and thought I had enough to make at least a dozen bouquets, and, after all, I had only seven! Then I had a basket full of other flowers, and I had a white cape trimmed with purple, and a fine wire mask—and L—— had a white cape trimmed with blue, and a wire mask, and a big basket of flowers; and Tuesday afternoon we set out with Marianina, our beautiful little serving-maid, bright and early, after lunch, for the Carnival. You must know that all this week Miss S—— and I had been the owners of half a balcony on the Corso, and L—— had been the owner of a seat in a fine balcony with other friends, and yet we had been only twice to look on, and found the whole thing so stupid, and the horse-race so cruel, that we did not care to go again. But at the last minute I was seized with a sudden desire to enter into it wildly for an hour or two on the last day, and see if I could by clear, sheer force of will compel myself to be amused! Would you believe it? In less than ten minutes after I took my stand on that balcony and spread my flowers out before me, and began to pelt people, I was just as excited as if I had been the granddaughter of Julius Caesar himself! I hit everybody I aimed at, and I caught every bouquet that was thrown at me, and I worked for three hours harder than I ever worked anywhere except in Dio Lewis's gymnasium! It sounds silly. I am half ashamed to tell of it except that it would be a pity not to let you have the laugh at me, and you can't laugh harder than I do to think of it; for a woman of—well, of my age! to be heartily amused for two solid hours throwing bouquets to a crowd, and being pelted back by bouquets and sugar-plums! It sounds like a sharp, short attack of being crazy. But I did it. Some of the bonbons were very pretty, but I threw them all down again to other people. My anemones, though, I did not shower down promiscuously, you may be very sure; our balcony was low enough for us to see the faces of the people perfectly, and I threw anemones to none excepting those who looked as if they knew the difference between anemones and miserable bought flowers on wires. Then, when it grew dark, everybody lit candles, and we had a few minutes' fun with those. The people from below threw bouquets and hit them and put them out, and the people from above knocked them out of your hands, and the people from the next balcony switched them out with their handkerchiefs, and everybody screamed out, "Senza moccoli, senza moccoli," and as you looked up and down the Corso, the dancing lights were like a shower of stars blown about in the wind. But this lasted only a little while and few people in the street had candles; so that it was quite unlike what it used to be in old times.

In fact, the whole thing from beginning to end has been no carnival at all, they say. The Romans do not choose to be amused any longer. There are too many sons in prison, too many waiting for one more chance to fight; a hairdresser said to L—— one night in a half-frightened whisper, when she asked him why the Romans did not give themselves up to the Carnival as they used, "The whole city is in anger, miss!" Even in the little contact which we have with the Romans we see smoulderings of the fire. I can't help wishing they would wait till this mild, gentle, good old Pius is peacefully put away under (or in) his sarcophagus.[3] He cannot live long; I do not want him to be disturbed. After that, I could stay and fight myself to set this poor people free. [. . .]

Now I have made these days so long, that of the next one I can tell you nothing, except that it was just as sunshiny and warm as the rest, and we went to another villa—the Villa Wolkonsky. Here are old Roman aqueducts, covered with ivies whose stems are larger than my wrist, and which branch and spread like trees! And here is an old tomb, which in the time of Nero one Mr. Claudius built for himself in a fine, conspicuous situation, as he supposed, and put his family names on the front; but now his tomb door is many feet underground, and the curious few go down into his tomb, and tumble about the bones of his kindred, as much as they like. A Russian princess owns this villa, but has not lived in it for five years; so in what is she better, said we, than American princesses who own no villa?

What do you think of this for a week? We don't live quite so fast every week, but then we might, if it never rained, and if we were never tired; so the Roman calendar becomes, you see, quite another thing when you count the days in Rome. In spite of it all, however, I am hankering after a hill country with only its own legitimate dead about! Not that I mean to reflect on the family records of the Caesars and Antonines; but I think it chokes the air a little too much to dig down into so many layers of sepulchre. Sufficient unto a century is the dead thereof. I shall like Switzerland better than Rome, and I shall say a new kind of prayer at night when I get into a country where I can go to bed once more with my window wide open.[4]

Good by now, dear souls, one and all. Tell me all the smallest things you do, and keep a little green spot in your every-day hearts for me.

11

Kate Field

❧

Mary Katherine Keemle Field (1838–1896), known as Kate Field in her professional roles as journalist, lecturer, author, and actor, first traveled to Europe at the age of eighteen. Living for varying periods in Paris, Rome, and Florence, she formed friendships with such distinguished people as Anthony Trollope, Robert Browning, George Eliot, and Charlotte Cushman.

Field published several books as well as numerous travel letters, opinion pieces, and sketches in the *Boston Courier*, the *Springfield Republican*, and the *Atlantic Monthly*, and founded a newspaper, *Kate Field's Washington* (1890–1895). One of her travel accounts, *Ten Days in Spain* (1875), records her trip to Spain during the revolution of 1873. Her other travel account, *Hap-Hazard* (1873), a gathering of material from her travels in 1872, reproduced from the *New York Tribune, Every Saturday*, and the *American Register* of Paris, is dedicated to "all young women in search of careers or titled husbands." *Hap-Hazard* includes a prefatory apology and a declaration of purpose: "[T]he contents of this volume lay no claim to profundity. If their perusal entertains the American at home, and leads the American abroad to commit one folly the less, my highest ambition will be realized."

While the volume suggests an epistolary form in an occasional place name and date, it is in fact a collection of essays divided into two parts. Part 1, entitled "Leaves from a Lecturer's Note-Book," consists of essays prompted largely by travel in the United States on the lyceum circuit; Part 2, entitled "Americans Abroad," contains essays describing travel in England and Germany. The first excerpt in this selection is from Part 1, and the others are from Part 2.

Field's account exemplifies the practice of converting travel writing that is ostensibly about foreign lands into disquisitions and reflections on the United States, at a time when the usual European travel itinerary had become tiresome material. The matter of America, the subtext of antebellum American travel writing, becomes the text; geographical travel to foreign locales becomes, overtly, psychological and philosophical travel into the heart of America. Her account illustrates, as well, the anti-tourism expressed as disdain for one's traveling compatriots that constitutes a theme in travel writing, and shows the topical nature of the travel genre and how it was used by the female traveler who chose to address women's issues.

Hap-Hazard

A Lecture on Masks

[. . .] Anything more utterly senseless than the Carnival Corso at Rome is inconceivable. To pelt people with flour and *confetti;* to hurl flowers at the heads of passers-by; to converse with any mask offering the right hand of fellowship; to drive up and down, on the last night of the Carnival, with a lighted taper in one hand and a wet towel in the other, striving to put out every approaching taper while endeavoring to rescue your own from a similar fate, accompanying the effort with screams of "*Senza moccolo*"; to go home at midnight singing Rossini's *Buona Sera*—are freaks purely idiotic in themselves, yet thoroughly in harmony with a phase of human nature that rarely receives just treatment. The Italians are able to enjoy this extreme of liberty because their instincts rarely permit them to overstep bounds of propriety. Drunkenness and vulgarity of language and manner are specialties of such nations as lay claim to superior virtue.

What champagne is to supper, masked balls are to carnivals. They are the keystone to the arch of folly, and the person who has never worn a mask in the spirit of a mask has failed to experience one of the most novel and most exhilarating of sensations. There is not its equivalent in the known world. To woman the mask is the first taste of paradise. Behind it she is exempted from all rules of etiquette, and for the only time in her life has an advantage over men. Old and young enjoy equal privileges, all may go and come without the intervention of pantaloons, and for once the burden of "waiting to be asked" is shifted to manly shoulders. Woman can actually roam at discretion among a wilderness of swallow-tails, without recognition and without reproach. Put on a mask and she may be herself; take it off and she must be somebody else. How much more honest is the mask!

To completely lose one's self-consciousness and to pass unknown among unmasked friends and foes is as refreshing as to be dropped into a foreign country in full possession of a clairvoyant knowledge of its inhabitants. It is the nearest possible approach to wearing an invisible cap. Students of human nature may gaze into eyes with impunity, and read a deal of truth that would otherwise remain undisclosed. A clever masker can discover more real character in a few minutes than would be developed in years of casual acquaintance, and conversation may be sentimental or piquant without fear of a construction *au pied de la lettre.* What an intense satisfaction! Who does not at times long to insist that the moon is made of green cheese, that the world is filled with sawdust, that

> "All friendship is feigning,
> All loving mere folly;
> Then heigh, ho! the holly!
> This life is most jolly,"

and on these themes compose variations as endless as any dreamed of by Henri Herz?[1] Where else but at a masked ball can these variations be executed? In this country the genius of masked balls is not understood. Men and women, when addressed by maskers, draw themselves up to the full height of their dignity, and look unutterable don't-approach-me-ism. This is taking masked balls in vain. We Americans entertain the idea that, intrinsically wrong, they must be solemnly attended under protest. There is no *juste milieu* of deportment. One sees the extremes of decorum and "loudness," but seldom that halfway-betweenity which is the charm of Southern nations. We have not yet learned the art of properly misbehaving ourselves, an art only acquired by ladies and gentlemen. It is strange, too, how the majority of Americans lose their natural intelligence the moment they enter the magic circles of masks. There is a monosyllabic spell upon them, and "yes" and "no," followed by a wretched smile, constitute their stock of mother-wit. Any one has brains enough to go to a "German," but every one cannot attend masked balls with impunity. *Esprit* and grace of manner are indispensable to the carrying out of this amusement. Few of us are

> "Wise enough to play the fool";
> For, "to do that well craves a kind of wit";
> You "must observe their mood on whom" you "jest,"
> The quality of person and the time;

[. . .]

An After-Dinner Speech

Toast: "The Ladies"

When one of England's most distinguished physicians first urged me to return thanks for the toast last given, I declined. I never had done such a thing, and thought that I never could. Then I remembered that to the skilful treatment of this same physician I owed the restoration of that "most excellent thing in woman," a voice, which, if not "low" at present, will be shortly; and it seemed ungrateful not to make some slight return for so signal a service. The claim was none the less valid for being indirect; and as this is the age of revolution, as humanity is stronger than caste or sex, as Royalty shakes hands with Democracy by acknowledging allegiance to the republic of letters, I asked myself why, after all, women should not be heard as well as seen at public dinners. It is true that an august body of men—of course I can mean none other than the House of Commons—quotes St. Paul as though saints were their perennial guides, philosophers, and friends; and declares that women should keep silence, conveniently forgetting that St. Paul is addressing the women of Corinth, according to the law of A.D. 59; that elsewhere he contradicts himself; and that the proper reading is, "Let your women keep silence in the churches." If honorable M.P.'s persist in proving their intimate acquaintance with Scripture by misquoting it when they desire to keep lovely woman in her proper sphere, they should first descry strangers in the ladies' gallery, and order their summary ejection. But now, although at this post-prandial hour we are all supposed to be incapable of reasoning, let us try to be logical. Women sing in public, act in public, read in public; why, then, should they not speak? Why should it be considered feminine for a woman to interpret Shakespeare's ideas, and unfeminine to interpret her own—provided she has any? It seems to me that if public speaking be tolerated at all—which is doubtful, especially at dinners—it should be from the lips of women, and for this reason. Ever since the subsidence of chaos, men have been talking. For six thousand years, at least, they have, to use an Americanism, "stumped" creation, and impressed the world with their views on all subjects; but as there is as much sex in mind as there is in matter, we have seen everything in profile. Now, an artist will tell you that no two sides of the same face are exactly alike. I pray you, therefore, let us have the other profile, whereby we may see the entire face, gaze into telltale eyes, and thus get at the soul of all things. Taking for granted all that is known and said about women, they ought to make more attractive speakers than men. I do not think they are, so far; but they ought to be, and these are my data. Women are born more grace- ful; they have the great gift of beauty and the great privilege of dress. Hence, they are a greater gratification to the eye, and the majority of people hear with their eyes. Women are more impulsive, more sym- pathetic, more persuasive; therefore are they more likely to touch the heart; and when you have made an audience feel, half the battle is won. Pray, who does the greater part of speaking in private—Mr. or Mrs. Caudle?[2] Were I a man, I should hail public speaking as a bless- ing in disguise. When Vesuvius is in a state of eruption, Aetna is quiet. Fluency of diction is a desideratum in speaking. If tradition be cor- rect, women are not lacking in this requirement. Indeed, it has been seriously questioned whether women partake of celestial joys, for the reason that once upon a time there was silence in heaven for the space of half an hour. Then, if precedent be required, women can trace back their rights in this respect much further than men, for Eve was the original orator. It is to her persuasive pleading that we owe all knowl- edge. Miriam was among the first to prophesy; Deborah was elevated to the dignity of judge of Israel; Greek oracles proceeded from the lips of women; and the greatest orators of Hellas did not scorn to be taught their art by the sex they regarded with contempt. Socrates learned rhetoric from Aspasia; and it was to their mother, Cornelia, that the Gracchi owed their eloquence. And, if modern examples are asked for, I can only reply, that not many evenings since I heard six Englishwomen—the majority of them young, and two of them very pretty—speak at Hanover Square Rooms in a manner that might be imitated with advantage by the gentlemen in the House of Commons, who recently referred to them as creatures of sentiment. If it be al- lowed, then, that women may speak in public, it seems to me no more than just that one of my sex should return hearty thanks to the man- aging committee of this dinner, for treating them as though they were not too good for human nature's daily food. It is useless to talk of the equality of the sexes, so long as men sit down to turtle soup in one room, and women stand up to tea and sandwiches in another, waiting with becoming humility for admission to a Barmecide feast[3] of reason and flow of soul. I never knew a woman who did not protest against a senseless custom which deprives public dinners of half their utility as well as all their brilliancy; for, as the object of these dinners is the raising of money, their managers show little discernment in ignoring sisters of charity, who, in my country, are as effective in opening the purses as they are in touching the hearts of their lay brothers.

In conclusion, therefore, and in the name of the ladies, I thank you for the cordial manner in which the toast has been proposed and received, and trust that the managing committee may never regret having recognized women as creatures with appetites.

Festival of the London Hospital for Throat Diseases,
Willis's Rooms, May, 1872.

Specimen Americans

Ems, June 17, 1872.

I am asked to do what is an intolerable bore. I am asked to sketch my European experiences at a season of the year when the very word "experiences" sends one's mental thermometer to fever heat, and from the hottest place in Germany, where writing is not only impossible, but strictly prohibited by the medical faculty. Is this Christian? Is this doing unto others as one would wish to be done by? Were I not a little lower than the angels, I should answer as briefly and as obstinately as his Holiness the Pope—*Non possumus;* but being not only an angel but a woman ("and therefore incapable of saying 'no,'" asserts public opinion), I promise, while attempting to gratify an inhuman request, to be as inconsequent as Mrs. Nickleby, as stupid as Mrs. Raddles's girl Betsy, as sleepy as the fat boy Joe, and as unintelligible as Flora in "Little Dorrit." Like the once famous President of the once Confederate States, "all I ask is to be let alone"; and if a hapless being is roused in her sleepy lair at Ems, the consequences of an act unparalleled in its rashness must be assumed. No one is capable of an idea in this sleepy hollow. Had Rip Van Winkle gone to sleep here, he *never* would have waked. If in the dim past you ever had an idea, you forget it on arriving, and helplessly turn your brain out to grass as of no further use.

I am requested to say something about Americans abroad. Well, I am sorry to make the confession, but either there are a great many fools in America, or all the fools in America visit Europe. I have not yet arrived at a definite conclusion on the subject, for truth is said to lie in a well, and a great deal of rope is required to get at it; but judging from the fact that I never met such peculiar specimens at home as I meet or hear of abroad, I am inclined to believe that a large proportion of our idiots seek an asylum on this side of the Atlantic. Perhaps this is the retort courteous we make to Europe for sending us her adventurers, thieves, and burglars. If this be so, Europe has a decided advantage, for whereas her exports steal our property and tarnish our good name, the American exports give an impetus to trade by throwing away their own money in a manner that would astonish Croesus. Travelling on the Continent is rendered wellnigh insufferable on account of a folly that has thoroughly corrupted innkeepers, servants, and tradesmen. The mischief, begun years ago by the English, has been aggravated to a pitch beyond which human endurance, to say nothing of mortal pockets, can no further go. Strangely enough, petroleum and our terrible civil war are the principal causes of this growing evil. All the "shoddy," all the *nouveaux riches*, rush to Europe for the purpose of spending their rapidly acquired and frequently ill-gotten fortunes, and, stupidly imagining that fine feathers make fine birds, indulge in the wildest extravagance, to the intense satisfaction of trade and the disgust of disinterested common-sense. Speak English upon entering a shop on the Continent, and prices are increased one third. Let it be known that you are American, and they are doubled. Not long since I priced a trinket, and, speaking French, was supposed by the illiterate shopkeeper to be a European. Returning the next day with the determination of purchasing the bawble on account of its cheapness, I found a Frenchman examining it, evidently with intent to buy. Observing that I was about to withdraw, the Frenchman raised his hat, and, making a profound bow, declared that he did not intend to purchase, adding, "Madame est Américaine. C'est le pays des richesses et des jolies femmes"; after which genteel impertinence he retired, and the shopkeeper, forgetting that he had seen me before, doubled the price of the desired article! "The people of the Continent are very fond of you Americans, because, you see, you are all rich," said an Englishwoman to me in a railway carriage. It was useless to deny the soft impeachment, as, not unlike some of her countrymen and women, she had arrived at certain conclusions, and no mortal argument could induce her to depart from them. This opinion is not without foundation; for what think you of a man who, upon having bills presented to him, no matter by whom, extends a handful of gold and requests his creditors to help themselves? This is done over and over again. The folly of a few is the curse of many. Fancy an American girl with one hundred dresses, an allowance of two hundred francs a month for bonbons, and bills for gloves amounting to hundreds of francs! So convinced are Europeans of our inexhaustible wealth, that noblemen see in American girls heiresses from whom to obtain the means of repairing fortunes shattered by dissipation or gradual decay. They offer titles for gold, believing that no republican woman can resist a coronet. It would be funny, were it not disgusting, to note how, in a garrison town like Vienna, aristocratic officers in search of large incomes flock about Americans, as bees buzz about flowers from which they hope to extract honey. That certain girls have sold themselves for titles is not strange when their previous lives are scrutinized, as, in most instances, they have been educated in French convents, and are no more American than the Parisians themselves. Nevertheless, it is sad that such things should be. From these examples the cynic turns upon you, saying, "Look at your republican virtue! Look at your contempt for rank!" forgetting the millions of real Americans in the backslidings of a minority. According to my theory—and practice—no American should seek introduction to European courts. If he be a true republican he must disbelieve in the principle of caste, and, therefore, should not go where he is not received upon terms of equality. If Americans *are* presented at court and *do* exhibit a weakness for rank, they are hypocrites, and deserve to be despised by Europeans as the worst of flunkies. A people who do not live up to their professions of faith merit the contempt of the world.

The great mistake made by Europeans is judging Americans by themselves. Here wealth is confined for the most part to the aristocracy, consequently those who travel represent a much higher average of social culture than is likely to be found among a corresponding number of Americans. The vulgar and illiterate of other nations—

unless a percentage of well-to-do English be excepted—are poor, and remain at home. The same class of people among us are often the richest, and are therefore much more largely represented abroad than our aristocracy of intellect and breeding. In fact, the best Americans can rarely afford to make a journey which is yearly becoming more and more expensive, and which demands an amount of time that workers are not able to give. When I tell English people that the most brilliant women I know never leave their quiet New England homes, they exclaim, "Why I thought all Americans travelled!" As a nation we do travel more than any other, but the proportion of culture is less than among European travellers. Foreigners make no such nice distinctions. A hotel on the Continent will shelter, at one time during the season, a dozen Americans, six English, three Russians, two French, and one Prussian. The Russians, Prussians, and French almost invariably belong to the nobility, and generally inherit good breeding, if they do not brains. Most of the English belong to the aristocracy or gentry; while probably nine out of the dozen Americans are persons of no distinction whatever. The European observer, especially if he be English, picks out the least attractive of our people, and then and there concludes that Americans are the vulgarest and most ostentatious of people. There never was a more unjust criticism. Take the same class in any other country—exclusive of France and Italy, where good breeding is as common to the servant as to the master—and the Americans will be immeasurably superior, for the reason that we are more versatile, have seen more of the world, can more readily adapt ourselves to surroundings—either good or bad—and, owing to universal education, have a far higher average of intelligence. After all, the marvel is, not that there are so many uncouth Americans, but that there are so few. The greatest proof of our superiority is that the roughest man will not be lacking in the greatest essential of civilization—respect for women. The breeding of the Latin races is, as a rule, skin deep. "Your men must be very chivalrous," said a clever Englishman, the other day. "I happened to be walking recently in a German town during a heavy rain, when a gentleman and lady, without an umbrella, approached an omnibus that was about to start. Seeing every seat occupied, the gentleman, who spoke German perfectly and who was undoubtedly of Teutonic origin, asked whether any one would kindly give up his seat to a lady. No one replied, no one moved. 'Well,' exclaimed the German, walking off indignantly, 'it is very evident that there is no American among you.' He has either travelled or lived in America," said the Englishman. "Or married an American woman," I suggested. That American men should extend civilities in public conveyances and elsewhere to unknown women strikes Europeans either as the height of gallantry or the height of absurdity. It depends upon the individual's estimate of women.

Heat and Impudence

Ems, June 20, 1872.

In my previous letter I spoke of being sleepy; at this present moment I am both sleepy and warm, and long for a return to the original costume worn before that fall which has resulted unpleasantly in so many ways, obliging us to know something, for example, whether it agrees with us or not, and forcing us women quite out of our wits, at least twice a year, in our search for clothes. What bliss Heaven will be! There, according to painters, fashions are as everlasting as eternity; and if we are among the select few, who, like Raphael's angels, finish behind the ears, we shall be bothered with nothing but a pair of wings. However, on the whole, I'd rather there were a little more of me. I've a weakness for drapery; and it would be a great bore to wrap one's self up in one's dignity, with nothing but intellect to fall back upon. Then I'm fond of singing; and how horrible to have an ear for music with no possible means of cultivating it! with so much spare time, I mean spare eternity, too!

I remarked that I was warm. I am, and all the mind I possess, that has not become gelatinous, dwells fondly upon one of Sydney Smith's[4] clever sayings. By the way, now that he and Tom Hood and Douglas Jerrold[5] are dead, nobody in England says anything witty. "Very high and low temperature," declares Sydney Smith, "extinguishes all human sympathy and relations. It is impossible to feel affection beyond seventy-eight degrees or below twenty degrees of Fahrenheit; human nature is too solid or too liquid beyond these limits. Man only lives to shiver or perspire." At present I am too liquid to feel. My only sympathy is with the brilliant Englishman, who, writing from the House of Commons, in an atmosphere scorchingly hot and laden with the shattered remains of a murdered Ballot Bill says, "I am so sick of the links and fetters of civilized life that it would be unsafe to trust myself to the chalybeate[6] pools of a German Sylvan. It would be dangerous to—disrobe, for I should simply take to the wooded mountains, and reassert the original dignity and freedom of savage life!" What must be the temperature of London, when a sober Englishman waxes desperate? Misfortunes never come singly. I've added to the horrors of my situation by upsetting a full bottle of ink on an immaculate floor! What this means in the bill I shudder—no, I can't shudder—I perspire to think. I've washed it up with my best handkerchief, but the "damned spot" will not "out," and, like the stain on Bluebeard's key, must a fearful tale unfold.

"But about Americans abroad." Well, in preaching a sermon it is useless to praise the saints. One must abuse the sinners in order to draw a moral. This is what sinners were made for, and by the same token, sinners must be the burden of my letter. "*Plus on aime moins on juge*," declares Balzac; and though Balzac has told many fearful truths, it seems to me that this is but a half-truth, many lovers and all critics judging most severely where they are most interested. If I did not sincerely love America, the actions of its people would be as indifferent to me as those of other countries; it is because I desire to see our Republic as much respected abroad as it deserves, that I am keenly alive to all shortcomings. When a Frenchman glares impudently at a woman, or a German swallows both knife and fork in the process of eating, or an Englishman bullies his inferiors, and is "umble" in the presence of those above him in rank, I am disgusted, but not personally concerned. Let an American give offence, and I feel in a measure responsible for his conduct; for remember that our nation is a child, in fact is but just born, and in European opinion is on trial. As the prevailing governments of the Old World are more or less despotic and thoroughly aristocratic, they look with no love upon a republic whose success is a menace to divine right and the degrading spirit of caste. Singularly ignorant of all that concerns us, not thinking it worth while to study either people or institutions, all their traditions and prejudices are against us, and they are only too happy when individual examples confirm previous conclusions. Therefore it is important that Americans abroad should honorably represent their country. Each man and woman is a bit of the Republic, is scanned and discussed as such, condemned or praised as such. European radicals, anxious for the coming of the universal republic, look to us for practical evidence of what they so earnestly and unselfishly preach. They grow faint-hearted upon finding folly and vice combined with a total indifference to the propagation of the form of government which the most advanced minds believe to be best for humanity. If Americans abroad fully realized their influence, either for good or evil, there would be much less cause for adverse criticism than there is at present. Many come over for the purpose of what is elegantly termed "a spree." Out-Frenchifying fast-Parisians, they do everything that public opinion restrains them from doing at home, and, returning to America accomplished in little but vice, graft French manners on republican principles, with bad results to the tree of liberty. Bear in mind that I am dealing with our sinners, not our many saints. The men go all lengths; the women go as far as they dare, sometimes farther. Paris is the chosen rendezvous, not because of a bright sun and many works of art, but because vice and folly need not be sought. They come without bidding, and stay by you as long as there is a franc left in your pocket.

And the flattery one is obliged to endure in Paris! It must avail, otherwise it would not be universal. When I think that Americans receive it not only with toleration but pleasure, I wonder what has come over the people since the landing of the Pilgrims. If a Frenchwoman smiles, and compliments Monsieur on the shape of his hand, Monsieur is so charmed with her bright eyes and pretty lies as to pay any amount she chooses to ask for the gloves. The amount of whipped syllabub administered to us women is positively appalling! If you try on boots you are overpowered with eulogies over your *petit pied*. The more you don't like the boot, and the more the shopkeeper wants to get rid of it, the smaller and more beautiful is your *petit pied*. Listen to the following dialogue between myself and a bootmaker:

"I do not like the boot. It does not fit."

"*Mais, pardon, madame*, it exactly suits your little foot."

"It does nothing of the sort. It is too long and narrow."

"On the contrary, madame, I assure you that nothing could be better. Perhaps it is a trifle long, but your foot is so little that—"

"I repeat that the boot is too long and narrow."

"Pardon, madame, but if you observe closely you will see that your little foot—"

"Let me hear no more nonsense about my little foot, which isn't little. You know perfectly well that the boot does not fit; and unless you show me another pair I shall go without any."

"*Bien, madame*, on the whole you are right. I think that the only way to fit you properly is to take your measure."

And this change of base is made, without a blush, in the coolest possible manner! The man lied as long as he could, and, when he found it impossible to get rid of the ready-made boots, told the truth. This is my experience in everything. Send for a woman who deals in *lingerie*, and before showing you what you desire, she will exhibit Valenciennes dresses for one thousand francs, you knowing that, if beaten down with infinite labor, she will take six hundred. "But the collars," you say, impatiently. "In one moment, madame. Here is a lovely fichu." "Not to-day. The collars." "Will madame please cast her eye over this exquisite bit of lace?" "The collars." "Pardon, madame; but gaze upon these beautifully embroidered handkerchiefs." And so you will be politely bullied into examining everything that you do not want or ought not to buy. Finding it useless to display her wares, the woman at last produces the collars, which are not pretty and are not what you want. She employs much rhetoric to make you believe that never were there such beautiful collars, nor collars so becoming. Remain obdurate, and the wretched creature at last says, "There are moments when my selection of collars is not very good; this is one of them. When madame returns I promise to suit her exactly, for now I see what she requires!" Again not a blush, and the woman leaves with a smile and a bland *bonjour*. There are people who, if not fooled into buying, receive the lies with perfect equanimity. It may be unamiable, but I cannot; and I believe that fewer Americans would be cheated if more resented the attempts in this direction.

Then when it comes to dressmakers, no words can describe the acting that takes place. If you possess good points, they are descanted upon in all their length, breadth, and thickness. If you possess none, they are invented. You are a model for a sculptor; you are *distinguée* beyond princesses; you have eyes beaming with intelligence; you are so *spirituelle* as, from sympathy, to furnish wit to all with whom you come in contact; you are, you are, you are—until you feel like presenting a pistol at their long heads, and exclaiming, "Dead silence or your dead bodies!" But, as I remarked before, it answers admirably as a rule. I've seen women accept this adulation with delight, and as a consequence order dresses they did not want and at which their husbands growled. Human nature is excessively frail, particularly when it comes to Paris. There all your weaknesses break out, and, like the measles, come to the surface. Many saints would be full-grown sinners if they only had the opportunity that Paris affords for the development of latent capacities.

To return to dressmakers. Americans ruin them by paying fabulous amounts. Because clothes at the highest prices are not, on account of the tariff, as expensive as at home, American women rarely dispute a bill, and are laughed at by the very persons who realize enormous profits from their folly. For six perfectly plain underwaists, worth at the most six francs apiece, and for two similar waists trimmed with lace, worth fifteen francs apiece, I was recently charged by a fashionable modiste *one hundred and forty francs!* On looking at the bill I murmured, then counted out the money, and was about to pay it when I concluded to express my indignation, and note the result. It was received with perfect composure, as though in no way surprising. "I shall not pay this outrageous bill," I declared. "Very well," quietly rejoined the enemy; "when madame returns she will make some arrangement." Is not this dishonesty enough to spoil Anglo-Saxon tempers? It is quite time for me to return to America. I can't make matters better, and they make me much worse. But fancy fighting my battles o'er again in the present state of the thermometer! Into what apoplectic dangers have I rushed!

Sour Grapes and Snobbery

Ems, June 25, 1872.
[. . .] Rain reminds me of England; England recalls snobs; and snobs bring me back to our old subject of Americans abroad; for in this letter I shall deal with snobs. [. . .]

The only snobs in the world are English and American. The word is purely English, and has been adopted by us to supply a limited demand. That such monstrosities as snobs should arise in a republic is the penalty we pay for being Anglo-Saxon. With Anglo-Saxon virtues we inherit Anglo-Saxon vices, that break out in degenerate specimens of the American race. Where there is an oligarchy, as in England, and where trade is despised as the unpardonable sin—unless it be rich enough to retire and marry into the nobility—of course there must be snobs as long as human nature is weak enough to desire to be grander than it is. But with us, snobbery is sublimely ridiculous. When I see men and women who never had any grandfathers—at least none worth speaking of—who rose from nothing, and whose elevation is due to the institutions of our country—when, I repeat, I see such people going about Europe abusing the generous hand that has uplifted them, declaring that there is too much liberty in America, that the people (pray who are they but the people?) should be taught their place, that we need a strong government (like Napoleon's), and that America will not be a fit residence for ladies and gentlemen until we have it, I think of serpents warmed into life only to sting their benefactor. Treachery more foul is not conceivable; yet there are quite a number of such traitors—so many as to have often been quoted by foreigners in proof of the rottenness of democracy; so many as to have caused Sir Charles Dilke, in his admirable book of travels called "Greater Britain," to make them the subject of an excoriating paragraph. "Many American men and women," he says, "who have too little nobility of soul to be patriots, and too little understanding to see that theirs is already, in many points, the master country of the globe, come to you and bewail the fate which has caused them to be born citizens of a republic, and dwellers in a country where men call vices by their names. The least educated of their countrymen, the only grossly vulgar class that America brings forth, they fly to Europe 'to escape democracy' and pass their lives in Paris, Pau, or Nice, living libels on the country they are believed to represent." These are the Americans who were Louis Napoleon's warmest partisans. An adventurer himself, Napoleon received all Americans who could open his court doors with a golden key. Whether they spoke good English or bad, whether they were knaves or fools, made little difference to the hero of Sedan, so long as they spent money in Paris, and displayed beauty and toilets at the Tuileries. "I would give half my fortune to see Louis back on the throne of France," said an American woman, not long ago, calling the ex-Emperor "Louis" in order to prove her intimacy. This style of American is so frequently found living abroad, that I was more grieved than surprised when a French republican said to me recently, "You are the only American republican I ever met." "How many Americans have you met?" "A dozen." These libels cannot exist in America because they *are* libels; and certainly we are well rid of them and their offspring, who are apt to possess the vices of both hemispheres and the virtues of neither. "European Americans are a bad lot," exclaimed an Oxford professor not long since. "They do neither you nor me any credit." "When an American comes to us from the United States," said a Cambridge man shortly after, "he is likely to be a good fellow and clever; but when he comes from Europe he is a poor creature and generally a snob; he tries to pass for an Englishman; and one man was awfully cut up the other day when I told him that I knew him to be an American by his accent. He was trying to talk cockney!"

If these Transatlantic snobs only knew how they are despised by all whose opinion is worth having! They are despised by the very persons who repeat their remarks derogatory to the United States; for Europeans know the difference between gold and pinchbeck, and England has no toleration for republican flunkies. "I wish you'd write about a certain set of your country people who come to Europe and court our aristocracy," said a clever Englishman last winter. "They make themselves very contemptible, never deigning to mention any one who has not a handle to his name, always informing you of the grand houses to which they are invited, and taking good care to display cards upon which there are coronets. They immediately put their servants in livery, and get up coats of arms with mottoes in Latin—a language that half of them do not understand. There have been American Ministers here who were snobs of the first quality." Think of being told this, not by one person, but by many! Elsewhere I have heard similar complaints of the snobbishness of American officials abroad. This is intolerable and not to be endured. No citizen should receive an appointment abroad who is not a radical democrat and proof against rank, the slightest evidence of snobbishness being sufficient cause for removal from office. What private individuals do concerns themselves, but what officials do concerns the nation.

On the whole, the women are greater fools than the men in this worship of rank, which is *rank* worship, for the reason, perhaps, that women are more given to kneeling. Prudhomme, I believe, has said, "*Les grands ne nous paraissent grands que parce que nous sommes à genoux.*" "I became quite disgusted with the girls on our steamer," confessed a young American who crossed the Atlantic in a month that shall be nameless. "There happened to be on board the son of an English baronet; and though he was an ordinary fellow, not half as nice as some of us, the girls vied with one another in attracting his attention, leaving us out in the cold." This is a fine return for the respect and devotion of American men; always excepting advanced, liberal Englishmen, there are no men in the world for whom our women should entertain such regard as for Americans. Here, on the Continent, women are considered inferiors and regard themselves in that light; in Germany, they are domestic animals and drudges; among the Latin races they are intended to minister to man's pleasure, nothing more. It is only the exceptional Frenchman or Italian who believes in the virtue of woman; yet there are American girls who prefer foreign men to our own, and, knowing, if they choose to think, that no Frenchman and few Englishmen would marry a poor American girl, actually tie themselves for life to men whose views in regard to women ought to be thoroughly revolting. And by marrying foreigners, they actually give up American citizenship! It is outrageous, and the law ought to be changed. Still, if an American woman will be insane enough to marry a European, perhaps it is well that she should take the consequences.

There is another class of our people as rabidly pro-American as the other is anti-American. Everything is wrong on this side of the water. We are altogether perfect; the rest of creation has nothing to teach us. No people but ourselves are fit for a republic. The French are all mad, and Louis Napoleon was good enough for them; they are thoroughly corrupt and ought to be exterminated. The art of Europe is unattractive. No scenery is equal to our own. Of the two extremes, the latter is preferable, because it is compatible with manliness; but both are bad enough. Europe can teach us much if we are sufficiently intelligent to learn, but neither the snob nor the spread-eagle American is likely to benefit his country by the observations he makes on the institutions of the Old World. The sooner both types are educated off the surface of the earth, the better for the Republic.

Of the many hundreds of thoughtful men and women I say nothing, because saints, like good wine, need no bush. [. . .]

European *Versus* American Women

London, August 5.

One day more, and my stay in Europe will be over. One day more, and I shall be pacing the singularly unstable deck of that most untrustworthy and restless of animals, an Atlantic steamer. I am glad and sorry: glad to be going home, glad to once more take up the thread of an active existence; sorry to leave friends that I may never meet again. Europe is very interesting. In fact, if you have money, it is, in some respects, fascinating. If you possess nice tastes, it is delightful to be in the focus of culture, realizing that you are obtaining the best that the world affords. If you love art, it is a comfort and a perpetual study to be within seeing distance of famous galleries. If you love music, it refreshes the soul to hear the greatest masters, not occasionally, as in America, but daily, should you desire it. If you love society, your money will enable you to obtain it. Your appointments will be *comme il faut;* entertaining will be easier than at home, in consequence of trained servants; your groom will know his business; saddle-horses will be thoroughly broken; the roads over which you ride and drive will have the smoothness of a thousand years of travel. Be a cultivated American, with plenty of money, and Europe affords luxuries that a young country cannot furnish, although in the material comforts of housekeeping the Old World can in no way compare with the New. Be a cultivated, rich American, with no regard for aught but self, with a contempt for the people and a disbelief in republican institutions, and of course you'll prefer this side of the Atlantic to the other. Be a cultivated American, loving your country, not so much because it is your country as because you realize that it is, after all, the most enlightened of countries, offering the greatest good to the greatest number, allowing a freedom of thought and action quite foreign to the genius of older nations, and you will never call Europe "home." Europe is the place to visit: America is the place to live and work in. There is the widest field for activity and for intelligence, there you breathe the purest air, there you are least trammelled by conventionalities, there you have the fairest chance of being a whole man, and, yet more, a whole woman. As a woman, I cannot be too grateful to those stern Puritans who, in the Mayflower, braved the dangers of an almost unknown sea. The more I think of their courage, the more I respect them; the more I think of their effect upon civilization, the more I rejoice at being born after their advent. If you are a duchess, or, what is almost the equivalent, an American woman of wealth and position, Europe will give you so much as to cause the unthinking to ask, "What more would you have?" Go below the highest classes, and the reverse of the medal is soon seen. Say what they please, woman as woman is not respected here. Be a *grande dame*, and you are courted, admired, treated with deference, because you are a *grande dame*. You go about with carriage and footmen, which paraphernalia denote position or power. Go about on your two feet, and you will soon discover that to be a woman is, on the Continent, outside of Germany, to be an object of insulting interest, a creature whom no man is bound to respect. In Germany men do not insult women: they simply regard them as inferiors. Women carrying the heaviest loads while husbands are comparatively free from burdens, or women yoked with dogs or cows, is no uncommon spectacle. In France, though women are the more industrious half of the population, though they, as a rule, are cleverer than the men, though they show the greater aptitude in managing business, men speak of them lightly, and see in them probable or possible *filles de joie*. I have a very great regard for Frenchwomen; I don't believe them to be naturally corrupt; and regenerated France will mean a proper appreciation of women, according to them that equality which is their due. Of Frenchmen, the less said the better. There are noble exceptions who prove that corruption is more a fashion than a necessity; and when women are strong enough to dictate terms, Americans will readily sympathize with this same abused France. I don't mean shop-keeping or Imperial France, mind you. Both are beyond redemption.

The great comfort of America is that a woman is not always made to feel her sex. She really is allowed to exist as a human being, not, unfortunately, with all the liberty of a man, but still with so much more than elsewhere as by comparison to be free. In Europe, I never lose the sense of sex. You will be told that it is highly improper for a young lady to walk alone in London; that she thereby subjects herself to insult. This is nonsense. For eight months I have walked about London daily, sometimes going through the Seven Dials, and have never met with anything disagreeable; but then I have always dressed plainly, and have always assumed a severe cast of countenance, as though bound on affairs of state. I can't say that I have ever enjoyed these walks, on account of doing what no Englishwoman of position would dare to do for fear of shocking that amiable person, Mrs. Grundy. There is little pleasure, either, in walking about a town if you may not saunter and gaze; but my experience teaches me that, outside of Paris, which is incorrigible, it is generally a woman's own fault if she is spoken to in the street by strange men, and I heartily wish that, instead of immediately adopting European customs, American women would persist in preserving their own, and thus set a good example to the rest of creation. Unmarried women in Europe are suppressed to an intolerable extent. To me, they and their dreadful maids are the most forlorn as well as the absurdest of sights. German and English girls have often come to me complaining of their fate, saying that it was well-nigh maddening, and that they envied me my liberty. "But why not strike out for yourselves?" I have asked. "It is all very well to say 'Strike out'; but suppose your parents won't let you? Or suppose, if they do, all your acquaintance talk about you and take away your character? What is there left but submission? Thank your stars that you are American!" What *can* one say in reply? I feel sorry for them, deplore with them, and remain silent; for it takes more than ordinary courage to brave public opinion, however idiotic it may be, and from ordinary persons you cannot expect extraordinary deeds. I think that I should break chains, even were I European; still, I might be too cowardly. But the absurdity of the whole thing is, that the morals of these people are so elastic as to rather like in strangers what they condemn in their own young women! To receive, to entertain, seem to them *comme il faut* in me. They come—men and women—quickly enough when asked, and exclaim, "How nice!" Young men say, "Why cannot there be the

same freedom and friendliness of intercourse between unmarried
English men and women as in America? You cannot imagine how refreshing it is to enjoy a woman's acquaintance without fear and without reproach. The repression system renders English girls, if not stupid, at least self-conscious and uninteresting, and they are simply
intolerable as companions until after marriage, when, if there be anything clever in them, an assured position and contact with the world
brings it out." This is what liberal Englishmen say, because they are
Anglo-Saxon and believe in women. Of course, Continental men
think the freedom of American women either immoral or indelicate,
and assert that if no evil arises it is because of the absence of passion
in the American race; that such a condition of society is absolutely impossible in France. I know of no more hot-blooded people than the
Southerners of our own country. I deny that Americans, North or
South, are cold. The great difference is, not one of race, but of custom
and education. I do not think that American men are naturally better
than other men; Heaven knows the majority of those who visit Paris
are not. They happen to be born in a more enlightened hemisphere
and are surrounded by purer influences; that is all. While the learned
professors of Harvard University are shaking their wise heads, and
denying the possibility of admitting girls to their classes, predicting all
sorts of horrible results from the association of the sexes, Oberlin and
Antioch Colleges in Ohio, and Michigan University, demonstrate by
practical experience how utterly foolish are these medieval night-
mares. What Cambridge is to the West, Europe is to Cambridge. The
East seems to be a synonyme for whatever is retrograde. Wyoming
Territory sets an example to States founded before it was dreamed of.

Education being what it is, I am not attracted to Englishwomen,
married or unmarried. Englishwomen generally will not compare favorably with American, but there are exceptions greatly to the advantage of England. We have had no poet equal to Mrs. Browning, no
novelist approaching George Eliot, no scientist the peer of Mrs.
Somerville, no actress like Mrs. Siddons. There are a few women in
society far more cultivated than any leading women of fashion in
America; but when this is said, all is said. Englishwomen as a class are
dead to vivacity, tact, taste in dress, the art of pleasing, everything approaching fascination and general intelligence. In these qualities

American women outshine all others, and in beauty their superiority is universally acknowledged. But the exceptional Englishwomen are very interesting, and I have found friends here among my own sex that I leave with deep regret, knowing that I shall never look upon their like again. Englishwomen are sometimes beautiful; then they are extremely so; but the beauty is much more frequently statuesque than picturesque. There is an absence of mobility of feature and variety of expression that renders them less attractive than they otherwise would be. Indifference and listlessness of manner are considered high style, when with us they would be regarded as a defect in breeding. To try to please everybody is democratic; to be indifferent to everybody is aristocratic: consequently, Americans, men and women, are the best bred people in the world. I say this thoroughly aware of the extraordinary specimens who often visit Europe, in some instances making it their home, and of the absence in the majority of that extreme polish inherited by a percentage of the upper classes of England. Unpolished, the Englishman is a boor, and the Englishwoman a bore.

Take us for all in all, we have the best of it, and to that best I return with grateful delight. With all its faults, our Republic is the hope of the world.

12

Lucy Seaman Bainbridge

❧

Lucy Elizabeth Seaman Bainbridge (1842–1928) was a philanthropic, social, and religious activist who worked in numerous causes, ranging from caring for the wounded in the Civil War to lecturing across the United States for the Presbyterian Board of Foreign Missions. She published *Helping the Helpless in Lower New York* (1917), the story of her work with the poor; *Jewels from the Orient* (1920), the record of her second journey around the world; and *Yesterdays* (1924), her autobiographical reminiscences.

Bainbridge first traveled abroad, in Europe and the Near East, upon her marriage in 1866 to a Baptist clergyman. Later, in 1879, she undertook her first journey around the world, visiting missions in Turkey, Palestine, Egypt, India, Burma, and China. Two books of travel grew from this two-year expedition: *Round the World* (1881) and *Round-the-World Letters: Five Hundred and Forty-Two Pages of Charming Pen Pictures by the Way. A Graphic Portrayal of Scenes, Incidents and Adventures of a Two Years' Tour of the World* (1882). The latter volume, from which the following selection is taken, is a collection of letters originally written for the *Providence Daily Journal*. The letters were subsequently edited and expanded with selections from Bainbridge's notebooks and her contributions to a Cincinnati newspaper. Bainbridge begins her preface with a quotation from Lord Bacon: "Some books are to be tasted, others to be swallowed, and some few to be chewed and digested." She continues, "Because of the first part of this statement of the great authority I may venture to place this book before the public. There may be nothing to chew and digest, possibly nothing to swallow; but I believe there is something to taste."

Bainbridge's account begins in San Francisco, where she started her journey to Japan, China, Burma, India, Egypt, Turkey, Palestine, Greece, Germany, Switzerland, France, and England. The following excerpts are the opening paragraphs of Chapter 1, where she rationalizes her travel; Chapter 9, where she enters the interior of China after telling of her travels across the United States to San Francisco and then to Japan; and Chapter 14, where, in the seventh of eight chapters devoted to China, she details the condition of women. Joining other women whose accounts of travels attend particularly to women and to the domestic in foreign lands, Bainbridge includes the situation and home life of Chinese women. As do other travelers, Bainbridge places herself at the center of her worldview and constructs the Chinese as the deviation from the Western norm.

Round-the-World Letters

The poet Gray, almost a hundred years ago, writing to a friend, said, "Do you not think a man may be the wiser—I had almost said the better—for going a hundred or two miles from home, and that the mind has more in it than most people seem to think, if only we would furnish the apartments?" Yes! we respond, it makes a man wiser—and a woman too—to get beyond, at times, the narrow limits of their own home and neighborhood. Wiser, in that the one who leaves the horizon of our clique, our family, and our church society, at least learns this lesson by contact with the outside world, the emptiness of his own brain mansion, and that there are stores of unassorted rubbish in many of its apartments. There is nothing like travel to teach one to appreciate the right of opinion in others and bring one to realize what a mote he really is in the vast shifting sands of the humanity of our great world. Realizing all this and that there was unoccupied room in our mental habitation, and need of more and better furnishings, we decided upon a two years' course of study in the school of travel, taking special pains to learn something from experience of the countries and customs of the people of the extreme East, yet hoping to gain many lessons of life, day by day, in a journey all the way round the world.

"Well!" said an old friend, "you've had schoolin' privileges—I don't see no use for people to go gadden about railroads and steamboats to get more larnin'; it wa'n't so in my day. I can't see why folks fool their money away on travellin'. Now if you was agoin' to sell somethin' or buy stuff to sell it agin, and could make money by goin', I'd say all right. But its all out-goes, as I can see. And you mustn't to mind if I speaks my mind very plain to ye; it's my duty. A woman's business is to stay to home and look after things and save. Now there was my dear departed wife Saray 'Liza—she was always a helpin' me to save. Nobody could beat her a making soap, be it hard or soft, and we never, none of us, used a whole candle till every scrap and bit was all burnt up. You never see me take my time for going about to see nonsense, I tell ye, or a studyin' foreign ways, in them old times. I had plenty to do when I had a little restin' spell, to watch round the auctions and bid in some calico or gingham for the women folks to make dresses of. It was handy havin' wife and our five girls wear gowns just alike. When one got wored out it helped to mend up the other ones, and I always had a good piece of it for a handkercher. Well," sighed the old gentleman, "times is changed! There ain't none of my daughters as savin' as me; their heads are full of notions like the rest. My girls are a paintin' old jugs and saucers, and talkin' about art, and wantin' to go to Europe.

"Why can't people be satisfied to stay at home and keep to the good old ways!" Nevertheless—off! [. . .]

[Chapter 9]

"To give room for wandering is it, the world was made so wide?" Even Goethe could not have fully realized the wideness of it; no one can until he may reach this flowery kingdom, and try the wandering here. "Quiet life at Chefoo!" Forsooth! That is very well while there is danger of malarial fever; but who could rest quietly with the fever of sight-seeing surging in the veins, and a missionary party of ladies ready for their last itinerating tour of the season to the women of the eastern Shantung villages, especially when one of that party was an old friend, the latch-string of whose home in Tungchau-fu had been hung out for our party years before?

Therefore in a "togeow" we started for the village of Gonyu, where the party were waiting our coming. But do you ask, "What is a togeow?" Some call it mule-litter, but would that I had the power of pen and pencil to describe it and its various motions so that you might fully realize this mode of travel, and your sympathies would ever be enlisted in behalf of those missionaries who have no other means of locomotion. It is simply a long, narrow box, the lower part board, the upper part canvas. The front end is uncovered, and there are two small openings—one on either side.

There is sufficient height for one to sit or lie on bedding placed on the floor and not touch the roof. This box is fastened to two long poles, and the poles are attached by means of a heavy wood—sawhorse sort of—harness to the backs of two vicious, obstinate, kicking, backing mules, one between the poles in front, and the other in the rear. The front mule wears a jingling bell which he rings at every step, and would not consent to budge without. The beast behind never steps with the one in front, and generally wishes to show his own independence of character by trying to take another path now and then. A muleteer walks along side all the way, talking, yelling, and whipping the half-starved animals. There is no smooth hard road. Up and down, over ditches and over stones, here and there and everywhere they find a path which is the highway between Chefoo and Tungchan-fu, a distance of fifty-five miles. The togeow motions are numerous and peculiar. There is the rocking motion, very like in its effects to the swell of the sea; there is the bottle-washing motion, at which time you are not sure but that your heart and stomach and lungs are having an "all hands around," and have decided to change places. But last there is the churn motion; there is a good deal of this; the mules are fond of it—more so than you are, and—well! suffice it to say with every bone and muscle in a state of revolt, I was glad to ride in through the entrance-way to the court-yard of the Chinese inn, and spy the faces of my friends peering out of the doorway in their endeavor to see if the jingling of the mule-bells announced my coming.

Do you catch at the words court-yard and entrance-way, and imagine this missionary party ensconced in luxury and elegance *à la* "Palace Hotel"?

"Ah!" you say with a sigh, "that is the way my contribution of two whole cents a week is spent, is it?"

Yes! and I wish that every grumbler at missions was obliged to stay in this elegant Chinese inn an entire week. The parlor—for we were so extravagant as to occupy a suite of rooms—was ten by twelve feet, and furnished with a table, a narrow bench, and one carved chair—like the table, being more remarkable for filthiness than beauty. The floor was of hard beaten earth, and had been swept, probably when the inn was first built many years ago; but never since. The walls were frescoed with smut and smoke. A heavy drapery was festooned from the cornstalk-rafters, and the weavers dropped down, now and then, to see what was going on. The sleeping apartment had two beds or kangs. They are built into the room; are of brick and mortar, and are really ovens; for in cold weather a fire is built underneath, and on the heated top the Chinese sleep rolled in a single blanket. This kang in a

native home serves as sitting-room by day and bed at night, and often
is the dining-place for the whole family. The bedding which had made
the mule-litter endurable, was placed on the kang. It was getting toward night, and a servant brought in a light: a saucer of oil in which
floated a burning wick. It served to make the darkness more real.
Tired men and hungry beasts are crowding into the yard; animals are
feeding at the stalls; packs and litters are in the centre, and night has
come. But what a night! There were forty-seven donkeys, by actual
count, beside many mules in that court-yard. The plaintive wail of
those much-abused animals, who were too hungry to sleep and too
sleepy to eat, and who knew that this was their only time to do both;
the heavy breathing of muleteers and the gay, sprightly actions of the
small inhabitants between the kang and its matting cover, who came
out for a night's revelry, all conspired to banish sleep. Of the visits to
adjoining villages, and the preaching of women to other women; of
the medicine given the sick; the kind ministry of that noble band of
American sisters I will not speak here, but reserve such story for my
Glimpses into Mission Life. I would that every christian woman in the
home-land could have had, with me, this brief insight into woman's
work for woman in China. The country through eastern Shantung is
undulating, and there were glimpses along our journey through it of
the blue water of the sea or gulf, and of distant mountains, some of
which were lightly coated with green; but, as a whole, the landscape
was barren and dreary. Even the river-beds were dry until the summer
rains should fill them, and there was an utter lack of forests, and,
when compared with Japan, there was nothing worthy the name of
tree. No vine-covered farm-houses with pretty gardens, and clustered
out-buildings are to be seen; the people hive together in walled villages, with tiny streets, and crumbling stony houses, and go out to till
the soil.

Tung-chau-fu is a very old city, and its age may be known in a
queer way. The streets, many of them, are paved with worn-out mill-
stones; as it takes many years for a family to wear out the mill with
which they grind their corn and millet, that place must be aged to be
paved with so many of these smooth, round stones. Travellers do not
go to Tung-chau-fu. There are few sights there of general interest, and
the missionaries never see "globe-trotters." A visitor is a rarity, and

hence is fully appreciated. Among the pleasanter recollections of our world tour, will ever be the days in the mission homes of that lonely place, the quiet tea-picnics on Pebbly Beach, where all gathered at the close of the hot day to take supper together under the shadow of the high cliffs close to the sea. Year after year those devoted men and women from their Southern and Northern homes in America work on with no other society, not even such as is had at the port-cities, and with nothing tangible binding them to their own native land but the coming of the mail every fortnight. On a rugged bluff overlooking the ocean which unites them by its ceaseless motion to their country, to which their hearts were ever turning, and overlooking, on the other side, the city of their life's work and sacrifice, lie nearly a score of missionary men and women. Some of the stones which mark these graves are defaced and upset by malicious natives. Trees there are none; and but few shrubs grow in this lonely, unprotected cemetery. "Gone Home" are the fitting words on one of the stones. Yes! but not to that earthly company, that home beyond the restless waters, "where chance and change are busy ever," but to the home eternal, true, where "they shall go no more out forever."

When our journey was planned two years ago, it was found impossible to put Peking in at its best season, which is the last of September and all of October. To reach India at the right season and have time enough for its many sights, we must leave our cool harbor at Chefoo for the south by September first. Travellers who "do the world" in eighty days or even a year do not take Peking into their route. But having reached the flowery kingdom, *the* nation of all the world—all outside being barbarians—we felt we must visit the great capital where the Emperor, the son of Heaven, resides, even if we could not go in cool pleasant weather. True the mercury was in the nineties, and the sun getting hotter every day. Friends warned and advised: "You may never come back alive," said they. "The rains are coming on, and the roads will be impassable; or if the summer deluge holds off, you will be smothered by the terrible dust-storms. Everybody will be out of the city. There is more perspiration than inspiration in such a journey now." But in the face of all these warnings we went. Mr. B. having reached Chefoo June 22d, after the completion of his extensive interior journeying, we started June 23d in the steamer *Hae Shin*, for Tientsin. In less than twenty-four hours of sea voyaging, beyond the Shantung cliffs, we were at the long line of sand, which makes the bar at the mouth of the Peiho river. We must wait all day for the flood-tide to enable us to cross. The steamer was luxurious in its accommodations, the American captain excellent company, and though the sun was hot, the day was soon passed, and at six P.M. we steamed over the bar and past the mud dwellings and the forts of Taku.

Sitting on the forward deck and chatting with the captain we noticed that the bow of the steamer was sinking. Instantly the order was given to run her up on the muddy bank. The forward compartment was found to be full of water, the vessel in some unknown way having sprung a leak in crossing the bar. It was a very enjoyable accident, as far as we were concerned. We simply gathered up our traps and took a boat-ride in the darkness, lighted now and then by vivid flashes of heat lightning, to another steamer at anchor waiting for the daylight. The muddy Peiho is narrow and tortuous. It is marvelous how any large vessel can be made to swing around the sharp bends of this river. "It often happens" said the captain, "that a steamer will run into the mud wall of a Chinaman's abode on the edge of the bank, and all at once he will find his earthly house crumbling into the mud, and no damage done to the prow." It is fifty-one miles from Taku to Tientsin by the river, and the captain must be on the alert every foot of the way.

Tientsin is the outer portal, as it were, for the great capital. By direct line, Peking is little over eighty miles away; but by the winding, twisting river, it is one hundred and eighty. Prince Kung, the uncle of the present boy-Emperor, is the leading representative of the Mauchu race. Though the regency is nominally in the hands of the Empress dowager, Prince Kung holds the reins of Imperial power.

Li-Hung-Chang, viceroy of Chili, is the most influential Chinaman in the Empire. He represents the party who look more favorably on the coming of foreigners and foreign ways. He owns the largest share in the prosperous line of steamers along the coast, called the China Merchants' Steam Navigation Company. In one of these steamers, the *Hae Shin*, we came from Chefoo. He owns the only telegraph line in the Empire, extending from the Peiho forts to his home at Tientsin, and has startled even the most progressive of his native friends in arranging a dinner party where his wife presided and enter-tained Mrs. Grant and other foreign ladies.

At Tientsin we have reached the end of steam-navigation, save the one steam-yacht owned by this viceroy, and seen occasionally on these waters. Hence this is the end of civilized forms of travel. The river is crowded full with junks of all descriptions, mandarin and house-boats, one of which our missionary friends helped us to arrange for our up-stream journey. It was quite a different thing from going aboard a palace car with convenient lunch stations. A wooden kang and table, a small charcoal stove without fuel, with plenty of water-bugs, were all the boatmen furnished. We prepared to set up house-keeping on a small scale. The outfit was in this wise: A basket of char-coal and kindlings made of dried corn-stalks, filtered water in bottles, a teakettle and saucepan, canned meats, fruits, bread, etc., bedding, camp-chairs, and a candlestick, and we were ready to start with our heathen crew, who knew not a word of our tongue, and we had mas-tered just two words of theirs.

By sculling and pushing, the boat was gotten past the long rows of junks, the bridges of boats; past the scene of the terrible Tientsin mas-sacre.[1] There was no wind, the tide and current against us, so the crew harnessed themselves into a long rope attached to the top of the mast, and walked along the edge of the muddy river or up on the bank: thus slowly we went along up the stream. It is a very monotonous journey. Everything is dirt color. Mud-water, mud villages, mud-colored men, nearly naked, and burned brown from constant work in the sun. They were trying hard to keep their fields of corn and millet, which were parched and dry, from dying before the summer rains come. It was slow, hard work to irrigate by dipping leaky buckets down to the river and pulling them up and emptying on to the thirsty soil.

The morning of the fifth day from Tientsin found us at Tung Chow. Here again we found most delightful friends, one of whom was a play-mate and school friend in Cleveland many years ago. After a Sabbath's rest we exchanged boat-riding for donkeys. The distance to Peking from this city is nearly fifteen miles, and a stone road, once a wonder-ful highway, connects the two cities. The road was constructed nearly two hundred years ago, and was made by throwing the dirt up from both sides to the centre, making the real roadway an embankment about five feet high and twenty-five feet wide. The stones, which are from six to eight feet long by two feet broad, were laid upon a surface of cement, and originally fitted close together. The almost ceaseless travel of heavy carts has worn down the stones, with deep ruts between. To jolt along as the Chinese do in a springless cart, would be simply torture. Along this way are many very costly private cemeteries and graves, surrounded by a horseshoe of earth— "to ward off the evil spirits which come down from the north." With a cool breeze and no mud or dust—as a light rain had fallen the night before, the heat was not intolerable.

Suddenly our donkeys were stopped. Alone on this highway, in broad daylight, we were confronted by a Chinaman who held before us a white envelope bearing our name. What did it mean? Was it an arrest? Were we to be quarantined? Had the Chinese government concluded to try its hand at annulling old treaties, and we heathen Americans not allowed to enter the Imperial city? Not a word said the Chinaman. We broke the seal to read our fate.

"*American Legation, Peking:* Mr. Seward would be most happy to entertain us during our stay in the capital. If we had made other engagements, he should certainly expect us for part of our visit at least." But of where we went and what we saw I will write by next steamer.

Life everywhere is made up of little things. This is especially true with women; hence if I write of trivial matters, leaving to others of the opposite sex the broad, comprehensive opinions of peoples and politics, it must be remembered that the writer is looking at the world with a woman's eyes. After years of dealing with butcher, grocer, and the milkman, it is a matter of real interest to a housewife how these things are managed round on the other side of the world. A family comes to Chefoo for the summer, and needs to be supplied daily with good milk. There are no milk stores, no carts passing by full of shining, well-filled cans. Foreigners who own a cow have no milk to spare. Then how are they to manage it? A native will agree to bring them a cattie of milk in a bottle twice a day—a cattie is one and one-third pounds, or less than a quart. For this he expects to receive fifteen cents, or one hundred and fifty cash. But the new-comer soon finds that he is paying for a very diluted article, and falls in with the customs of those who have learned thoroughly the elasticity of a Chinese milkman's conscience. He insists that the cow be driven to his door twice a day and milked before his eyes. Round from house to house the poor animal goes, and is milked at every place. The price is the same. A few years ago in Shanghai, before the Europeans had imported so many foreign cows, they were wholly supplied with buffalo milk. The animal would be driven to the door, John would hold up his bottle to prove to his lady customer that there was not a drop of water in it, and then proceed to milk. Just as he was ready to fill the bottle, he would slyly touch the flank of the animal, which had all the while been nervously eying the foreigner; the hind legs would fly up, the beast start, and the lady retreat a little. John, meanwhile, pours the milk into another bottle a third full of water, and hands to his customer, who congratulates herself upon being able to secure such pure milk.

> In ways that are dark and tricks that are vain,
> The heathen Chinese *is* peculiar.—*Bret Harte*

When reasoned with upon the adulteration of milk, for which so good a price is paid, he will reply in "pigeon English," "Allo that man must wanchee that milk; spose no got must catchee; spose no can catchee, maskee must makee." Which being translated is: "Every body must have milk; if I have not got it, I must get it, even if I must make it." A Chinese cow will give only about three catties a day. A buffalo at the best less than half what a foreign cow gives.

Even dairy butter in Shanghai is worth one dollar a pound. California butter put up in glass jars, of two pounds each, sells on an average at fifty cents a pound. Butter from Denmark in hermetically sealed cans is worth sixty cents. The best beef for steaks and roasting can be bought from eight to twelve cents a pound. The best mutton is about thirteen cents. Sausage keeps at twenty-five the year through. Eggs are as low as eight cents a dozen part of the year in Shanghai. Turkeys are brought largely from Manilla, and range in price from four to eight dollars each, so that only the wealthy resident of China can afford a real Thanksgiving Day dinner.

The place to buy pongee is at Chefoo. Not in some large, elegant establishment with inviting show-windows on a broad and pleasant street, as in the home land, but through narrow winding alleys with hardly room for our chair-bearers to pass the line of donkeys and men, we sought out the finest pongee store. We crowded along past open sheds where naked blacksmiths were plying their craft; past rows of stores, the entire stock of which was ranged on narrow shelves facing the street, or laid out on the ground in front; past groups of men squatting on the ground around a huge bowl of food from which they were filling their own smaller dish as fast as it was emptied; past naked children playing in the dirt, whose only attire was an ear-ring or bracelet. The butcher and jeweller, the maker and mender, were all so wedged in together it was not easy to tell one shop from another. But my guide motioned the bearers to halt, and we entered a narrow door-way into a small room lined with shelves and filled with bundles of cotton goods. Through an adjoining court decorated with sunflowers, we reached another small room filled with Suchow silks. Still on through another dirty court to a third building, where were bundles of pongee. There is no counter; only a small table and two carved chairs. A twenty-yard piece of the best quality is five and a half dollars. I hand the dealer six Mexican dollars, and tell him I do not want my change in Chinese cash. He shakes his head doubtfully, but returns with an old handkerchief in the corner of which are tied up a few coins. There are a few francs bearing the face of Napoleon III, an English shilling, and several Japanese ten-cent pieces.

The currency of China is a mystery. People talk about an article being worth so many taels; but there is no such coin as a tael. It is simply the word to denote an ounce of silver Chinese weight; and such an ounce is a third heavier than our own. A solid chunk of silver, called a "shoe of silver," or "sycee," weighs from forty-eight to fifty-two Chinese ounces. There is a slight value added for the purest quality of silver and a corresponding depreciation for lower grades. About fourteen hundred and fifty copper cash equal a tael; and one thousand are reckoned as the value of a dollar. Of course this is constantly fluctuating. When receiving the change for a dollar, by actual count there will be only nine hundred and ninety odd cash, because these coppers are strung on strings of a hundred each, and the deficit represents the value of the tow cord. The cash of Peking will not pass in Shanghai, and vice versa. In many cities there are also tiaow notes, issued by bankers; these are worth a few cash each, but only pass in their own immediate locality. Four or five dollars worth of this iron and copper coin is as much as a man can carry. When a countryman goes to market with produce, the poor donkey gets no rest on the return home, the weight of the cash being fully equal to that of the load taken to town.

One of the institutions of China, which would delight a housewife in America, is the travelling tinker. He works by the day and boards himself for forty cents; and this includes tools as well as skill. Shattered umbrellas, leaky tins, broken dishes and glass ware are marvelously made whole again by ingenious Chinese. Sewing women work for one quarter of the tinker's price. Their stitches are neat, but the work is handled in such back-handed fashion, and they are so slow, that a quick Yankee woman would be driven to desperation before a week was out. Everything must be cut, planned and explained by European brains and hands. Another business in China is that of peddling Davis' Pain Killer. There are natives in Chefoo who lay in the immense stock of one whole bottle, and then go about the streets advertising their wonderful cure-all, giving their patrons one application and a "hard rub" for two cents. Of course the price of an internal dose depends on the quantity swallowed.

Many of those who are watching for the day of enlightenment in China—a day when superstition shall no longer forbid railroads and telegraphs; a day when the immense resources of iron and coal, silver and gold shall be developed, are encouraged by the publication of a Chinese book, of which you may have heard. It is written by a native who was sent from the custom's service to attend the Centennial in America. He has seen the world with less prejudice and narrowness than could be expected of such a visitor. Li-Hung-Chang has given the book prestige by writing the preface and using his influence against many who were opposed to its being published. It is bound in four volumes, which are all tied together into one stiff cover by imperial yellow strings. The first volume gives a brief account of United States history, and tells the story of the Boston tea. Then country by country he describes the Centennial. He is especially interested in machinery, and says that "the United States excels all nations in the amount, variety and excellence of machines." The Corliss engine overawed him, as it did many another spectator. "It was a great wonder that one man could manage it." The second volume treats of Philadelphia, its institutions, asylums and mint. He describes the process of coining, and advocates the establishment of a mint in China. Hartford and Washington are well spoken of, but "the great Capitol being beyond the power of his pen to portray." In writing of New York city, he speaks of the advantages of female education. He argues that if a mother knows how to read she can teach the boys at home, and thus, as in America, they can enter the schools with much already learned at seven years of age, and thus save expense of public funds. The third volume treats of London and Paris. The fourth is a diary of the journey from day to day.

An exceedingly hopeful circumstance, especially to mission work, has but very recently occurred in Tientsin in the home of the viceroy. The wife of Li-Hung-Chang was taken very ill. Chinese doctors exhausted their skill upon her, but her case was to them a hopeless one. She must die. The viceroy was in great grief. A consul met him and inquired as to the cause of his sadness, and on learning of Lady Li's illness suggested the calling in of a European physician. He had more confidence in foreign medicines and skill than had other high Chinese, but could he so shock the nation's sentiment and prejudices as to call in a foreigner to his home? No! He refused the suggestion. But at night the sufferings of his wife moved him to desperation of sympathy. The English doctor was sent for, and came. On hearing the case, the physician felt that Lady Li could be helped, but Chinese proprieties would be too greatly shocked if he were to give her the necessary personal attentions. A Methodist young lady, who had thoroughly qualified herself to receive the title of M.D., was summoned from Peking. Mounting her horse, which had carried her on many a deed of mercy, she galloped down to Tientsin and took her place by the bedside of Lady Li as nurse and physician. Her patient is rapidly recovering. The viceroy shows his delight by giving money and the use of a building—an old temple—for a foreign dispensary and hospital.

Will not the single ladies who read this and often say "What shall I do for the world's good?" think of the vast opportunities opening up to minister to the souls and bodies of two hundred millions of women in China? If you cannot go, help those who do go, and show the same spirit of consecration in the labor which is at hand. Let none say,

"There is no work for *me* to do."

> "If you cannot cross the ocean,
> And the heathen lands explore,
> You may find the heathen nearer,
> You may help them at your door."

[Chapter 14]

In my last, I gave you a peep into the house of one of the wealthy and more progressive Chinamen of Foochow. But it was not a fair type of the home life, even among the wealthy. Our host does not formally profess Christianity, yet he has by social intercourse with missionaries caught somewhat of the spirit they manifest, and his home is the purer and brighter for it. Woman's lot in China is dreary and unenviable in the palace or the mud hut. The iron bars of custom and superstition environ her upon every side. She enters the household an unwelcome guest and is taught, from childhood up, that

> "Woman is but dust.
> A soulless toy for tyrants' lust!"

At the age of six or eight, according to the fortune of the family, her feet must be bandaged and compressed, a terribly painful process to be endured for years. Without this crippling she cannot expect to ever become the legal wife of any man of education or position; she can never be a lady; but upon her would fall the menial services, the carrying of the sewerage to the fields, or perchance the father or elder brother will raise money, for some time of need, by selling her to some one of the numerous houses of hell to be seen in every Chinese city. Man holds the power of life and death over the female members of his household in China.

That you may gain a more correct idea of the inner life of the middle classes, let me give you a glimpse into a house I visited, which, I am told, is a fair specimen of thousands, yes, hundreds of thousands of homes in China. A high wall shuts in the premises upon all sides. The brain of a Chinese woman has not even the sights of the street to feed upon. The house consists of a series of rooms and courts. The best apartment faces the large open court towards the entrance. It was decorated with roll pictures and furnished with carved chairs and tables, every nook and cranny of which were covered with a thick film of dust. The family consisted of a widowed mother and nine sons, with their wives and children, the mother being at the head of the establishment, and holding almost unlimited power over the nine daughters-in-law and the grandchildren. Upon each side of the central rooms and courts were ten sleeping apartments, about eighteen feet square. One small window near the ceiling and the door were the only means of ventilation. Boxes and bureau, a god-shelf, dried herbs and trumpery of all sorts lined the sides of the room, while the huge bedstead, with its framework covered with netting, took up a third of the space. Within it, across the back, was a shelf for bedding; thus the bed served a triple use: it was a clothes-press and sitting place by day, and sleeping place for one entire family by night. On the frame in front was pasted an ugly red paper picture, and hanging below it a sword made of cash (the Chinese iron and copper coin) strung together.

"What are those decorations for?" I asked.

"Tell her," said daughter-in-law number one to my friend who was interpreting, "tell her they are only the children's toys."

"No!" interrupted number four, "tell her the truth."

"Yes," chimed in numbers five and eight, "If you say it's only a toy we shall have bad luck; we put the sword and the ugly picture over our beds to frighten the evil spirits away."

Number six, being an invalid, begged that we would come to her room, that she too might see the foreign lady from the far-off country of the flowery flag. We found her in the small back room, without sunshine or society, without books or a knowledge to read if she had them, without the solace of the Christian's faith. Her emaciated form and hollow eyes showed that consumption had fastened its death-grip upon her. At one side of the dining-room was a huge box covered with a faded blanket. The chickens hopped about it, picking up the stray crumbs; an old hen was perched on top of it. The sides were well fastened to the walls by festoons of cobwebs.

"What a strange thing that is," I said, "it looks like a coffin!"

"Yes," replied my friend, "it is, and the deceased father of all these sons is within it. He died nearly four years ago, and has been here ever since. The family is waiting for a lucky day in which to bury him."

At a little table in the kitchen sat the old wife, busy making up money out of silver paper for the use of her lord in the world to which he has gone.

Paper money and bills of exchange, paper horses and carriages and clothing are made up and burned for the dead. The ashes remain on earth, but the spiritual part goes to the spirit world, they say, and is magnified a thousandfold, and becomes the property of the deceased. In Canton, the other day, I was invited to lunch with the family of General Pang, who has charge of the coast defences of this district. The house was of the same general sort as the one just described, with the addition of a garden of stiff plants in quaint jars, rather more carving and dirt and dust. There were five wives, elaborately gotten up with paint and powder, but only the wife number one and the mother-in-law sat at the table with us. The other wives and all the children with numerous servants looked on from the sides of the room, occasionally joining in the conversation.

While writing of these Chinese homes, let me tell you of the way in which one of these husbands in high position in Canton showed his affection in time of distress. He was not a progressive man like the viceroy at the north, yet being so far away from royalty, and the great capital, and having been thrown into relations with foreigners for many years, he decided to call in an English physician for one of his household. It was not his better half, but "the fifth or sixth," that was beyond the power of Chinese quackery. The doctor told me that his experience was this: in the middle of the night the sedan-chair and outrunners in scarlet-fringed hats, boys with gongs carrying a red umbrella, the insignia of the owner's position, were sent to the house. Wife number two has been jealous of number four, and in a frenzy concluded not to live any longer, and had taken a dose of opium. Chinese skill having been exhausted, the doctor of the foreign settlement arrives and is met in the inner parlor by the smiling husband, who insists upon showing his courtesy with sweetmeats and a smoke. It would be the height of rudeness for the doctor to refer first to the sick woman. After half an hour of smoking and chatting the mandarin happens to remember that "one of the vile creatures of the inner apartment" is not well. Servants show the stranger to the room—the husband's dignity would not allow him to do this. During the delay the poor creature has died, and the doctor with his medicines retreated from the scene. Of course he does not receive pay for this visit. It is considered ample compensation to have thus been honored by a mandarin. What more could a miserable foreigner desire?

This is just a glimpse into the home life of China. Heathen households, not homes, they are. I thank God that the same Christianity which has elevated woman and brightened and sweetened the home life of other lands, is at work here and there in China.

13

Elizabeth Cochrane Seaman

જ⁀

Elizabeth Cochrane Seaman (1865–1922) is better known as Nellie Bly. When she was twenty years old, she was hired by the editor of the *Pittsburgh Dispatch*, who, impressed with her reply to an article that opposed suffrage, sent her to Mexico in 1886 as a correspondent. Her reports on poverty and political corruption lead to her expulsion by the Mexican government. As an investigative reporter for Pulitzer's *World*, she donned disguises, had herself committed to an asylum on Blackwell's Island, and wrote exposés of various scandals, prompting reform of asylums, sweatshops, and women's prisons. She collected her investigative reports in two books, *Ten Days in a Mad-House* (1887) and *Six Months in Mexico* (1888).

Nellie Bly initiated a new kind of heroism for the female traveler. She set a new standard for women in the area of travel—the challenge of speed, displacing the challenges of discovery and adventure. In 1889, Joseph Pulitzer sent her around the world to beat the eighty-day record of Jules Verne's fictional hero, Phileas Fogg, making her travels front-page news in the *New York World.*

Nellie Bly left Hoboken on Thursday, 14 November 1889, at 9:40:30 and returned to Jersey on 25 January 1890. Bly precisely concludes in "The Record," in *Nellie Bly's Book: Around the World in Seventy-Two Days* (1890): "Total time occupied in tour, 1,734 hours and 11 minutes, being 72 days, 6 hours and 11 minutes. Average rate of speed per hour, exclusive of stops, 22.47 miles. Average rate of speed, including stops, 28.71 miles per hour." She began her travels around the world by way of Southampton, France (where she visited Jules Verne), and Italy; passed through Aden, Columbo, Singapore, Hong Kong, and Tokyo; and returned home, a heroine, by way of San Francisco and Chicago. In celebration and adulation, songs and dances were dedicated to her, toys were named for her, parades were held in her honor.

Unknown to Bly, her famous travel stunt, which resulted in *Nellie Bly's Book*, inspired a similar stunt by Elizabeth Bisland Wetmore. In competition with Nellie Bly and on assignment for *Cosmopolitan*, Wetmore left home within hours of Bly, traveled to San Francisco, circumnavigated the globe in seventy-six days, and, like Bly, published an account of her exploits.[1] Having thought that she was competing only against time, Bly was shocked to be told when she arrived in Hong Kong, "The other woman . . . is going to win. She left here three days ago."

Bly's travel account, together with Bisland's, constructs a new Olympics for the female traveler, a race against the clock. The race unwittingly parodies the stereotypical American tourist rushing from place to place in a mad quest for culture. Her account incorporates, as well, an interest in the *lone* female traveler, a device that is brought into play in several earlier accounts of travel by women and that evokes the specter of female vulnerability.[2] In a new departure in the publication and commercialization of travel books, the flyleafs of Bly's text are printed with advertisements for the paraphernalia of her trip, such as her Ghormley gown and her Cheque Bank Checks, precursors of traveler's checks, "the Cheapest, Safest and Best form for Travelers to carry their Money, for they are available as READY CASH in every town in the Civilized World, and are far superior to Letters of Credit." The excerpts in this selection are taken from Chapter 1, where Bly describes the occasion of her trip, and Chapter 15, where Bly shows her descriptive abilities as a travel writer.

Nellie Bly's Book

[Chapter 1]

A Proposal to Girdle the Earth

What gave me the idea?

It is sometimes difficult to tell exactly what gives birth to an idea. Ideas are the chief stock in trade of newspaper writers and generally they are the scarcest stock in market, but they do come occasionally.

This idea came to me one Sunday. I had spent a greater part of the day and half the night vainly trying to fasten on some idea for a newspaper article. It was my custom to think up ideas on Sunday and lay them before my editor for his approval or disapproval on Monday. But ideas did not come that day and three o'clock in the morning found me weary and with an aching head tossing about in my bed. At last tired and provoked at my slowness in finding a subject, something for the week's work, I thought fretfully:

"I wish I was at the other end of the earth!"

"And why not?" the thought came: "I need a vacation; why not take a trip around the world?"

It is easy to see how one thought followed another. The idea of a trip around the world pleased me and I added: "If I could do it as quickly as Phileas Fogg did, I should go."

Then I wondered if it were possible to do the trip in eighty days and afterwards I went easily off to sleep with the determination to know before I saw my bed again if Phileas Fogg's record could be broken.

I went to a steamship company's office that day and made a selection of time tables. Anxiously I sat down and went over them and if I had found the elixir of life I should not have felt better than I did when I conceived a hope that a tour of the world might be made in even less than eighty days.

I approached my editor rather timidly on the subject. I was afraid that he would think the idea too wild and visionary.

"Have you any ideas?" he asked, as I sat down by his desk.

"One," I answered quietly.

He sat toying with his pens, waiting for me to continue, so I blurted out:

"I want to go around the world!"

"Well?" he said, inquiringly looking up with a faint smile in his kind eyes.

"I want to go around in eighty days or less. I think I can beat Phileas Fogg's record. May I try it?"

To my dismay he told me that in the office they had thought of this same idea before, and the intention was to send a man. However he offered me the consolation that he would favor my going, and then we went to talk with the business manager about it.

"It is impossible for you to do it," was the terrible verdict. "In the first place you are a woman and would need a protector, and even if it were possible for you to travel alone you would need to carry so much baggage that it would detain you in making rapid changes. Besides you speak nothing but English, so there is no use talking about it; no one but a man can do this."

"Very well," I said angrily, "Start the man and I'll start the same day for some other newspaper and beat him."

"I believe you would," he said slowly. I would not say that this had any influence on their decision, but I do know that before we parted I was made happy by the promise that if any one was commissioned to make the trip, I should be that one.

After I had made my arrangements to go, other important projects for gathering news came up, and this rather visionary idea was put aside for a while.

One cold, wet evening, a year after this discussion, I received a little note asking me to come to the office at once. A summons, late in the afternoon, was such an unusual thing to me that I was to be excused if I spent all my time on the way to the office wondering what I was to be scolded for.

I went in and sat down beside the editor waiting for him to speak. He looked up from the paper on which he was writing and asked quietly: "Can you start around the world day after to-morrow?"

"I can start this minute," I answered, quickly trying to stop the rapid beating of my heart.

"We did think of starting you on the City of Paris to-morrow morning, so as to give you ample time to catch the mail train out of London. There is a chance if the Augusta Victoria, which sails the morning afterwards, has rough weather of your failing to connect with the mail train."

"I will take my chances on the Augusta Victoria, and save one extra day," I said.

The next morning I went to Ghormley, the fashionable dressmaker, to order a dress. It was after eleven o'clock when I got there and it took but very few moments to tell him what I wanted.

I always have a comfortable feeling that nothing is impossible if one applies a certain amount of energy in the right direction. When I want things done, which is always at the last moment, and I am met with such an answer: "It's too late. I hardly think it can be done"; I simply say:

"Nonsense! If you want to do it, you can do it. The question is, do you want to do it?"

I have never met the man or woman yet who was not aroused by that answer into doing their very best.

If we want good work from others or wish to accomplish anything ourselves, it will never do to harbor a doubt as to the result of an enterprise.

So, when I went to Ghormley's, I said to him:

"I want a dress by this evening."

"Very well," he answered as unconcernedly, as if it were an everyday thing for a young woman to order a gown on a few hours' notice.

"I want a dress that will stand constant wear for three months," I added, and then let the responsibility rest on him.

Bringing out several different materials he threw them in artistic folds over a small table, studying the effect in a pier glass before which he stood.

He did not become nervous or hurried. All the time that he was trying the different effects of the materials, he kept up a lively and half humorous conversation. In a few moments he had selected a plain blue broadcloth and a quiet plaid camel's-hair as the most durable and suitable combination for a traveling gown.

Before I left, probably one o'clock, I had my first fitting. When I returned at five o'clock for a second fitting, the dress was finished. I considered this promptness and speed a good omen and quite in keeping with the project.

After leaving Ghormley's I went to a shop and ordered an ulster. Then going to another dressmaker's, I ordered a lighter dress to carry with me to be worn in the land where I would find summer.

I bought one hand-bag with the determination to confine my baggage to its limit.

That night there was nothing to do but write to my few friends a line of farewell and to pack the hand-bag.

Packing that bag was the most difficult undertaking of my life; there was so much to go into such little space.

I got everything in at last except the extra dress. Then the question resolved itself into this: I must either add a parcel to my baggage or go around the world in and with one dress. I always hated parcels so I sacrificed the dress, but I brought out a last summer's silk bodice and after considerable squeezing managed to crush it into the hand-bag.

I think that I went away one of the most superstitious of girls. My editor had told me the day before the trip had been decided upon of an inauspicious dream he had had. It seemed that I came to him and told him I was going to run a race. Doubting my ability as a runner, he thought he turned his back so that he should not witness the race. He heard the band play, as it does on such occasions, and heard the applause that greeted the finish. Then I came to him with my eyes filled with tears and said: "I have lost the race."

"I can translate that dream," I said, when he finished; "I will start to secure some news and some one else will beat me."

When I was told the next day that I was to go around the world I felt a prophetic awe steal over me. I feared that Time would win the race and that I should not make the tour in eighty days or less.

Nor was my health good when I was told to go around the world in the shortest time possible at that season of the year. For almost a year I had been a daily sufferer from headache, and only the week previous I had consulted a number of eminent physicians fearing that my health was becoming impaired by too constant application to work. I had been doing newspaper work for almost three years, during which time I had not enjoyed one day's vacation. It is not surprising then that I looked on this trip as a most delightful and much needed rest.

The evening before I started I went to the office and was given £200 in English gold and Bank of England notes. The gold I carried in my pocket. The Bank of England notes were placed in a chamois-skin bag which I tied around my neck. Besides this I took some American gold and paper money to use at different ports as a test to see if American money was known outside of America.

Down in the bottom of my hand-bag was a special passport, number 247, signed by James G. Blaine, Secretary of State. Someone suggested that a revolver would be a good companion piece for the passport, but I had such a strong belief in the world's greeting me as I greeted it, that I refused to arm myself. I knew if my conduct was proper I should always find men ready to protect me, let them be Americans, English, French, German or anything else.

It is quite possible to buy tickets in New York for the entire trip, but I thought that I might be compelled to change my route at almost any point, so the only transportation I had provided on leaving New York was my ticket to London.

When I went to the office to say good-bye, I found that no itinerary had been made of my contemplated trip and there was some doubt as to whether the mail train which I expected to take to Brindisi, left London every Friday night. Nor did we know whether the week of my expected arrival in London was the one in which it connected with the ship for India or the ship for China. In fact when I arrived at Brindisi and found the ship was bound for Australia, I was the most surprised girl in the world.

I followed a man who had been sent to a steamship company's office to try to make out a schedule and help them arrange one as best they could on this side of the water. How near it came to being correct can be seen later on.

I have been asked very often since my return how many changes of clothing I took in my solitary hand-bag. Some have thought I took but one; others think I carried silk which occupies but little space, and others have asked if I did not buy what I needed at the different ports.

One never knows the capacity of an ordinary hand-satchel until dire necessity compels the exercise of all one's ingenuity to reduce every thing to the smallest possible compass. In mine I was able to pack two traveling caps, three veils, a pair of slippers, a complete outfit of toilet articles, ink-stand, pens, pencils, and copy-paper, pins, needles and thread, a dressing gown, a tennis blazer, a small flask and a drinking cup, several complete changes of underwear, a liberal supply of handkerchiefs and fresh ruchings and most bulky and uncompromising of all, a jar of cold cream to keep my face from chapping in the varied climates I should encounter.

That jar of cold cream was the bane of my existence. It seemed to take up more room than everything else in the bag and was always getting into just the place that would keep me from closing the satchel. Over my arm I carried a silk waterproof, the only provision I made against rainy weather. After-experience showed me that I had taken too much rather than too little baggage. At every port where I stopped at I could have bought anything from a ready-made dress down, except possibly at Aden, and as I did not visit the shops there I cannot speak from knowledge.

The possibilities of having any laundry work done during my rapid progress was one which had troubled me a good deal before starting. I had equipped myself on the theory that only once or twice in my journey would I be able to secure the services of a laundress. I knew that on the railways it would be impossible, but the longest railroad travel was the two days spent between London and Brindisi, and the four days between San Francisco and New York. On the Atlantic steamers they do no washing. On the Peninsular and Oriental steamers—which everyone calls the P. & O. boats—between Brindisi and China, the quartermaster turns out each day a wash that would astonish the largest laundry in America. Even if no laundry work was done on the ships, there are at all of the ports where they stop plenty of experts waiting to show what Orientals can do in the washing line.

Six hours is ample time for them to perform their labors and when they make a promise to have work done in a certain time, they are prompt to the minute. Probably it is because they have no use for clothes themselves, but appreciate at its full value the money they are to receive for their labor. Their charges, compared with laundry prices in New York, are wonderfully low.

So much for my preparations. It will be seen that if one is traveling simply for the sake of traveling and not for the purpose of impressing one's fellow passengers, the problem of baggage becomes a very simple one. On one occasion—in Hong Kong, where I was asked to an official dinner—I regretted not having an evening dress with me, but the loss of that dinner was a very small matter when compared with the responsibilities and worries I escaped by not having a lot of trunks and boxes to look after.

[Chapter 15]

One Hundred and Twenty Hours in Japan

After seeing Hong Kong with its wharfs crowded with dirty boats manned by still dirtier people, and its streets packed with a filthy crowd, Yokohama has a cleaned-up Sunday appearance. Travelers are taken from the ships, which anchor some distance out in the bay, to the land in small steam launches. The first-class hotels in the different ports have their individual launches, but like American hotel omnibuses, while being run by the hotel to assist in procuring patrons, the traveler pays for them just the same.

An import as well as an export duty is charged in Japan, but we passed the custom inspectors unmolested. I found the Japanese jinricksha men a gratifying improvement upon those I had seen from Ceylon to China. They presented no sight of filthy rags, nor naked bodies, nor smell of grease. Clad in neat navy-blue garments, their little pudgy legs encased in unwrinkled tights, the upper half of their bodies in short, loose jackets with wide flowing sleeves; their clean, good-natured faces, peeping from beneath comical mushroom-shaped hats; their blue-black wiry locks cropped just above the nape of the neck, they offered a striking contrast to the jinricksha men of other countries. Their crests were embroidered upon the back and sleeves of their top garment as are the crests of every man, woman and child in Japan.

Rain the night previous had left the streets muddy and the air cool and crisp, but the sun creeping through the mistiness of early morning, fell upon us with most gratifying warmth. Wrapping our knees with rugs the ricksha men started off in a lively trot to the Pacific Mail and O. and O. Companies' office, where I met discourteous people for the first time since I left the P. & O. "Victoria." And these were Americans, too. The most generous excuse that can be offered for them is that they have held their positions so long that they feel they are masters, instead of a steamship company's servants. A man going into the office to buy a ticket to America, was answered in the following manner by one of the head men:

"You'll have to come back later if you want a ticket. I'm going to lunch now."

I stayed at the Grand Hotel while in Japan. It is a large building, with long verandas, wide halls and airy rooms, commanding an exquisite view of the lake in front. Barring an enormous and monotonous collection of rats, the Grand would be considered a good hotel even in America. The food is splendid and the service excellent. The "Japs," noiseless, swift, anxious to please, stand at the head of all the servants I encountered from New York to New York; and then they look so neat in their blue tights and white linen jackets.

I always have an inclination to laugh when I look at the Japanese men in their native dress. Their legs are small and their trousers are skin tight. The upper garment, with its great wide sleeves, is as loose as the lower is tight. When they finish their "get up" by placing their dishpan shaped hat upon their heads, the wonder grows how such small legs can carry it all! Stick two straws in one end of a potato, a mushroom in the other, set it up on the straws and you have a Japanese in outline. Talk about French heels! The Japanese sandal is a small board elevated on two pieces of thin wood fully five inches in height. They make the people look exactly as if they were on stilts. These queer shoes are fastened to the foot by a single strap running between toes number one and two, the wearer when walking necessarily maintaining a sliding instead of an up and down movement, in order to keep the shoe on.

On a cold day one would imagine the Japanese were a nation of armless people. They fold their arms up in their long, loose sleeves. A Japanese woman's sleeves are to her what a boy's pockets are to him. Her cards, money, combs, hair pins, ornaments and rice paper are carried in her sleeves. Her rice paper is her handkerchief, and she notes with horror and disgust that after using we return our handkerchiefs to our pockets. I think the Japanese women carry everything in their sleeves, even their hearts. Not that they are fickle—none are more true, more devoted, more loyal, more constant than Japanese women—but they are so guileless and artless that almost any one, if opportunity offers, can pick at their trusting hearts.

If I loved and married, I would say to my mate: "Come, I know where Eden is," and like Edwin Arnold,* desert the land of my birth for Japan, the land of love—beauty—poetry—cleanliness. I somehow always connected Japan and its people with China and its people, believing the one no improvement on the other. I could not have made a greater mistake. Japan is beautiful. Its women are charmingly sweet. I know little about the men except that they do not go far as we judge manly beauty, being undersized, dark, and far from prepossessing. They have the reputation of being extremely clever, so I do not speak of them as a whole, only of those I came in contact with. I saw one, a giant in frame, a god in features; but he was a public wrestler.

The Japanese are the direct opposite to the Chinese. The Japanese are the cleanliest people on earth, the Chinese are the filthiest; the Japanese are always happy and cheerful, the Chinese are always grumpy and morose; the Japanese are the most graceful of people, the Chinese the most awkward; the Japanese have few vices, the Chinese have all the vices in the world; in short, the Japanese are the most delightful of people, the Chinese the most disagreeable.

The majority of the Europeans live on the bluff in low white bungalows, with great rooms and breezy verandas, built in the hearts of

---

* Sir Edwin Arnold (1832–1904), poet, scholar, editor of the *Daily Telegraph* of London, and author of *The Light of Asia* (1879), an epic poem that tells of the life and teachings of the Buddha.

Oriental gardens, where one can have an unsurpassed view of the Mississippi bay, or can play tennis or cricket, or loll in hammocks, guarded from public gaze by luxurious green hedges. The Japanese homes form a great contrast to the bungalows. They are daintily small, like play houses indeed, built of a thin shingle-like board, fine in texture. Chimneys and fire places are unknown. The first wall is set back, allowing the upper floor and side walls to extend over the lower flooring, making it a portico built in instead of on the house. Light window frames, with their minute openings covered with fine rice paper instead of glass, are the doors and windows in one. They do not swing open and shut as do our doors, nor do they move up and down like our windows, but slide like rolling doors. They form the partitions of the houses inside and can be removed at any time, throwing the floor into one room.

They have two very pretty customs in Japan. The one is decorating their houses in honor of the new year, and the other celebrating the blossoming of the cherry trees. Bamboo saplings covered with light airy foliage and pinioned so as to incline towards the middle of the street, where meeting they form an arch, make very effective decorations. Rice trimmings mixed with sea-weed, orange, lobster and ferns are hung over every door to insure a plentiful year, while as sentinels on either side are large tubs, in which are three thick bamboo stalks, with small evergreen trees for background.

In the cool of the evening we went to a house that had been specially engaged to see the dancing, or *geisha*, girls. At the door we saw all the wooden shoes of the household, and we were asked to take off our shoes before entering, a proceeding rather disliked by some of the party, who refused absolutely to do as requested. We effected a compromise, however, by putting cloth slippers over our shoes. The second floor had been converted into one room, with nothing in it except the matting covering the floor and a Japanese screen here and there. We sat upon the floor, for chairs there are none in Japan, but the exquisite matting is padded until it is as soft as velvet. It was laughable to see us trying to sit down, and yet more so to see us endeavor to find a posture of ease for our limbs. We were about as graceful as an elephant dancing. A smiling woman in a black kimono set several round and square charcoal boxes containing burning charcoal before us. These are the only Japanese stoves. Afterwards she brought a tray containing a number of long-stemmed pipes—Japanese women smoke constantly—a pot of tea and several small cups.

Impatiently I awaited the *geisha* girls. In the tiny maidens glided at last, clad in exquisite trailing angel-sleeved kimonos. The girls bow gracefully, bending down until their heads touch their knees, then kneeling before us murmur gently a greeting which sounds like "*Kombanwa!*" drawing in their breath with a long, hissing suction, which is a token of great honor. The musicians sat down on the floor and began an alarming din upon *samisens,* drums and gongs, singing meanwhile through their pretty noses. If the noses were not so pretty I am sure the music would be unbearable to one who has ever heard a chest note. The *geisha* girls stand posed with open fan in hand above their heads, ready to begin the dance. They are very short, with the slenderest of slender waists. Their soft and tender eyes are made blacker by painted lashes and brows; their midnight hair, stiffened with a gummy wash, is most wonderfully dressed in large coils and ornamented with gold and silver flowers and gilt paper pom-pons. The younger the girl the more gay is her hair. Their kimonos, of the most exquisite material, trail all around them, and are loosely held together at the waist with an obi-sash; their long flowing sleeves fall back, showing their dimpled arms and baby hands. Upon their tiny feet they wear cunning white linen socks cut with a place for the great toe. When they go out they wear wooden sandals. The Japanese are the only women I ever saw who could rouge and powder and be not repulsive, but the more charming because of it. They powder their faces and have a way of reddening their under lip just at the tip that gives them a most tempting look. The lips look like two luxurious cherries. The musicians begin a long chanting strain, and these bits of beauty begin the dance. With a grace, simply enchanting, they twirl their little fans, sway their dainty bodies in a hundred different poses, each one more intoxicating than the other, all the while looking so childish and shy, with an innocent smile lurking about their lips, dimpling their soft cheeks, and their black eyes twinkling with the pleasure of the dance. After the dance the *geisha* girls made friends with me, examining, with surprised delight, my dress, my bracelets, my rings, my boots—to them the most wonderful and extraordinary things—my hair, my gloves, indeed they missed very little, and they approved of all. They said I was very sweet, and urged me to come again, and in honor of the custom of my land—the Japanese never kiss—they pressed their soft, pouting lips to mine in parting.

Japanese women know nothing whatever of bonnets, and may they never! On rainy days they tie white scarfs over their wonderful hair-dressing, but at other times, they waddle bareheaded, with fan and umbrella, along the streets on their wooden clogs. They have absolutely no furniture. Their bed is a piece of matting, their pillows, narrow blocks of wood, probably six inches in length, two wide and six high. They rest the back of the neck on the velvet covered top, so their wonderful hair remains dressed for weeks at a time. Their tea and pipe always stand beside them, so they can partake of their comforts the last thing before sleep and the first thing after.

A Japanese reporter from Tokio came to interview me, his newspaper having translated and published the story of my visit to Jules Verne. Carefully he read the questions which he wished to ask me. They were written at intervals on long rolls of foolscap, the space to be filled in as I answered. I thought it ridiculous until I returned and became an interviewee. Then I concluded it would be humane for us to adopt the Japanese system of interviewing.

I went to Kamakura to see the great bronze god, the image of buddha, familiarly called Diabutsu. It stands in a verdant valley at the foot of two mountains. It was built in 1250 by Ono Goroyemon, a famous bronze caster and is fifty feet in height; it is sitting Japanese style, ninety-eight feet being its waist circumference; the face is eight feet long, the eye is four feet, the ear six feet six and one-half inches, the nose three feet eight and one-half inches, the mouth is three feet two and one-half inches, the diameter of the lap is thirty-six feet, and the circumference of the thumb is over three feet. I had my photograph taken sitting on its thumb with two friends, one of whom offered $50,000 for the god. Years ago at the feast of the god sacrifices were made to Diabutsu. Quite frequently the hollow interior would be heated to a white heat, and hundreds of victims were cast into the seething furnace in honor of the god. It is different now, sacrifices being no longer the custom, and the hollow interior is harmlessly fitted up with tiny altars and a ladder stairway by which visitors can climb up into Diabutsu's eye, and from that height view the surrounding lovely country. We also visited a very pretty temple near by, saw a famous fan tree and a lotus-pond, and spent some time at a most delightful tea-house, where two little "Jap" girls served us with tea and sweets. I also spent one day at Tokio, where I saw the Mikado's Japanese and European castles, which are enclosed by a fifty foot stone wall and three wide moats. The people in Tokio are trying to ape the style of the Europeans. I saw several men in native costume riding bicycles. Their roads are superb. There is a street car line in Tokio, a novelty in the East, and carriages of all descriptions. The European clothing sent to Japan is at least ready-made, if not second hand. One woman I saw was considered very stylish. The bodice of a European dress she wore had been cut to fit a slender, tapering waist. The Japanese never saw a corset and their waists are enormous. The woman was able to fasten one button at the neck, and from that point the bodice was permitted to spread. She was considered very swell. At dinner one night I saw a "Jap" woman in a low cut evening dress, with nothing but white socks on her feet.

It would fill a large book if I attempted to describe all I saw during my stay in Japan. Going to the great Shiba temple, I saw a forest of superb trees. At the carved gate leading to the temple were hundreds of stone and bronze lanterns, which alone were worth a fortune. On either side of the gate were gigantic carved images of ferocious aspect. They were covered with wads of chewed paper. When I remarked that the school children must make very free with the images, a gentleman explained that the Japanese believed if they chewed paper and threw it at these gods and it stuck their prayers would be answered, if not, their prayers would pass unheeded. A great many prayers must have been answered. At another gate I saw the most disreputable looking god. It had no nose. The Japanese believe if they have a pain or ache and they rub their hands over the face of that god, and then where the pain is located, they will straightway be cured. I can't say whether it cured them or not, but I know they rubbed away the nose of the god.

The Japanese are very progressive people. They cling to their religion and their modes of life, which in many ways are superior to ours, but they readily adopt any trade or habit that is an improvement upon their own. Finding the European male attire more serviceable than their native dress for some trades they promptly adopted it. The women tested the European dress, and finding it barbarously uncomfortable and inartistic went back to their exquisite kimonos, retaining the use of European underwear, which they found more healthful and comfortable than the utter absence of it, to which they had been accustomed. The best proof of the comfort of kimonos lies in the fact that the European residents have adopted them entirely for indoor wear. Only their long subjection to fashion prevents their wearing them in public. Japanese patriotism should serve as a model for us careless Americans. No foreigner can go to Japan and monopolize a trade. It is true that a little while ago they were totally ignorant of modern conveniences. They knew nothing of railroads, or street cars, or engines, or electric lighting. They were too clever though to waste their wits in efforts to rediscover inventions known to other nations, but they had to have them. Straightway they sent to other countries for men who understood the secret of such things, and at fabulous prices and under contracts of three, five and occasionally ten years duration, brought them to their land. They were set to work, the work they had been hired to do, and with them toiled steadily and watchfully the cleverest of Japanese. When the contract is up it is no longer necessary to fill the coffers of a foreigner. The employe was released, and their own man, fully qualified for the work, stepped into the position. And so in this way they command all business in their country.

Kimonos are made in three parts, each part an inch or so longer than the other. I saw a kimono a Japanese woman bought for the holidays. It was a soft, gray silk *crêpe*, with pink peach blossoms dotting it here and there. The whole was lined with the softest pink silk, and the hem, which trails, was thickly padded with a delicate perfume sachet. The underclothing was of the flimsiest white silk. The whole thing cost sixty dollars, a dollar and a half of which paid for the making. Japanese clothing is sewed with what we call a basting stitch, but it is as durable as it could be if sewed with the smallest of stitches. Japanese women have mirrors in which they view their numerous charms. Their mirrors are round, highly polished steel plates, and they know nothing whatever of glass mirrors. All the women carry silk card cases in their long sleeves, in which are their own diminutive cards.

English is taught in the Japan schools and so is gracefulness. The girls are taught graceful movements, how to receive, entertain and part with visitors, how to serve tea and sweets gracefully, and the proper and graceful way to use chopsticks. It is a pretty sight to see a lovely woman use chopsticks. At a tea-house or at an ordinary dinner a long paper laid at one's place contains a pair of chopsticks, probably twelve inches in length, but no thicker than the thinner size of lead pencils. The sticks are usually whittled in one piece and split only half apart to prove that they have never been used. Every one breaks the sticks apart before eating, and after the meal they are destroyed.

An American resident of Japan told me of his going to see a cremation. The Japanese graveyard is a strange affair, with headstones set close together, leaving the space for the graves less than the size of a baby's grave in America. As soon as the breath has left a body it is undressed and doubled up, head to feet, and is made to go in a very small bamboo box built in imitation of a Japanese house. This house may cost a great deal of money. It is carried along the streets on two poles to the place where it is to be cremated, where it is given in charge of the cremator, and the friends go back to their homes until the following day, when they return for the ashes, which are generally placed in an urn and buried. The American, of whom I spoke, made arrangements with a cremator, and, accompanied by a friend, walked to the place in the country and waited out of sight until the mourners had vanished before they dared to draw near enough to see the cremation. They had walked quite a distance, dinnerless, and he said, naively, that the odor was like that of veal, and it made him ravenously hungry.

A small hole about three feet long is made in the earth and in it the fire is built. When it was the proper heat the box was set over it, and in an instant it was consumed. The body released from its doubled position straightened out. The lower half being over the fire was soon cremated, excepting the feet and knee joints. The man in charge carefully pulled the upper part of the body over the fire, and with the same large fork put the half-consumed feet and knee-joints under the arms. In less than an hour all that remained of the body was a few ashes in the bottom of the pit. While the cremator was explaining it all to the gentleman he repeatedly filled his little pipe and lit it with the fire from the burning body. At his urgent request the gentleman consented to take tea with him when his task was done. They entered his neat little home while he jumped into a boiling bath in the open garden, from which he emerged later as red as a lobster. Meanwhile his charming and pretty daughters were dispensing the hospitalities of their home to their guests, and the father, desirous of enjoying their society, came and stood in the doorway, talking to them and watching them eat while he wiped his naked body with a towel!

The prettiest sight in Japan, I think, is the native streets in the afternoons. Men, women and children turn out to play shuttle-cock and fly kites. Can you imagine what an enchanting sight it is to see pretty women with cherry lips, black bright eyes, ornamented, glistening hair, exquisitely graceful gowns, tidy white-stockinged feet thrust into wooden sandals, dimpled cheeks, dimpled arms, dimpled baby hands, lovely, innocent, artless, happy, playing shuttle-cock in the streets of Yokohama?

Japanese children are unlike any other children I ever saw at play. They always look happy and never seem to quarrel or cry. Little Japanese girls, elevated on wooden sandals and with babies almost as large as themselves tied on their backs, play shuttle-cock with an abandon that is terrifying until one grows confident of the fact that they move with as much agility as they could if their little backs were free from nursemaid burdens. Japanese babies are such comical little fellows. They wear such wonderfully padded clothing that they are as shapeless as a feather pillow. Others may think, as I did, that the funny little shaven spots on their heads was a queer style of ornamentation, but it is not. I am assured the spots are shaven to keep their baby heads cool.

The Japanese are not only pretty and artistic but most obliging. A friend of mine who guided us in Japan had a Kodak, and whenever we came upon an interesting group he was always taking snap shots. No one objected, and especially were the children pleasant about being photographed. When he placed them in position, or asked them to stand as they were, they would pose like little drum-majors until he gave them permission to move.

The only regret of my trip, and one I can never cease to deplore, was that in my hasty departure I forgot to take a Kodak. On every ship and at every port I met others—and envied them—with Kodaks.

They could photograph everything that pleased them; the light in those lands is excellent, and many were the pleasant mementos of their acquaintances and themselves they carried home on their plates. I met a German who was spending two years going around the world and he carried two Kodaks, a large and a small size, and his collection of photographs was the most interesting I ever saw. At the different ports he had professional photographers develop his plates.

The Japanese thoughtfully reserve a trade for their blind. They are all taught massage bathing, and none but the blind are allowed to follow this calling. These people go through the streets uttering to a plaintive melody these words:

"I'll give you a bath from head to toe for two cents."

At Uyeno park, where they point out a tree planted by General Grant when on his tour around the world, I saw a most amusing monkey which belonged to the very interesting menagerie. It was very large and had a scarlet face and gray fur. It was chained to the fence, and when one of the young men in our party went up and talked to him the monkey looked very sagacious and wise. In the little crowd that gathered around, quite out of the monkey's reach, was a young Jap, who, in a spirit of mischief, tossed a pebble at the red-faced mystery, who turned with a grieved and inquiring air to my friend.

"Go for him," my friend responded, sympathetically, to the look, and the monkey turned and with its utmost strength endeavored to free itself so it could obey the bidding. The Jap made his escape and the monkey quieted down, looking expressively at the place where the Jap had stood and then at my friend for approval, which he obtained. The keeper gave the monkey its dinner, which consisted of two large boiled sweet potatoes. My friend broke one in two and the monkey greedily ate the inside, placing the remainder with the other potato on the fence between his feet. Suddenly he looked up, and as quick as a flash he flung, with his entire force, which was something terrific, the remaining potato at the head of some one in the crowd. There was some loud screaming and a scattering, but the potato missing all heads, went crashing with such force against a board fence that every particle of it remained sticking there in one shapeless splotch. The Jap, who had tossed the pebble at the monkey, and so earned his enmity, quietly shrunk away with a whitened face. He had returned unnoticed by all except the monkey, who tried to revenge himself with the potato. I admired the monkey's cleverness so much that I would have tried to buy him if I had not already owned one.

In Yokohama, I went to the Hundred Steps, at the top of which lives a Japanese belle, Oyuchisan, who is the theme for artist and poet, and the admiration of tourists. One of the pleasant events of my stay was the luncheon given for me on the Omaha, the American war vessel lying at Yokohama. I took several drives, enjoying the novelty of having a Japanese running by the horses' heads all the while. I ate rice and eel. I visited the curio shops, one of which is built in imitation of a Japanese house, and was charmed with the exquisite art I saw therein; in short, I found nothing but what delighted the finer senses while in Japan.

14

Fanny Bullock Workman

Fanny Bullock Workman (1859–1925), a pioneer mountaineer who twice broke women's altitude records only to be charged with mendacity, typifies the "New Woman" as traveler in the late Victorian era. She pedaled a bicycle (or a "rover") nearly twenty thousand miles, packing a Kodak, and eventually became famous as a Himalayan mountaineer. She visited Karkoram eight times between 1898 and 1912, where she was photographed in 1912 with a "Votes for Women" placard. She traveled with her husband, with whom she coauthored eight accounts of her travels in Algeria, Iberia, the Himalayas, India, the Hispar, and the peaks and glaciers of Nun Kun.

The excerpts in this selection are from Chapters 3, 17, 18, 19, and the Conclusion of Workman's first book of travels, *Algerian Memories; A Bicycle Tour over the Atlas to the Sahara* (1895). They chronicle the hazards of travel by bicycle; document the treatment of women, the measure of civilization *vs.* barbarism in the western mind; and capture the taste for novelty, excitement, and adventure that drove the exploits of some female travelers and the publication of their travel accounts at the turn of the century.

Algerian Memories

[Chapter 3]
Oran to Affreville over the Ouarsenes

While at Oran, among other preparations for the tour we tried to find suitable maps of the country. Bicycle maps, so far as we could learn, did not exist, neither were good road maps to be had. We had to content ourselves with a very ordinary, not too accurate, general map published in Paris, which answered the purpose fairly well, though defective in details. When, on various occasions, we attempted to supplement its deficiencies by inquiries as to the existence, character and condition of roads, we found that information on such topics was difficult to obtain in Algeria, and, when obtained, was in very few cases reliable. Even a prominent bicyclist in Algiers, when consulted in regard to the road from Batna to Biskra, gave a description which proved to be wide of the facts, as afterwards experienced.

The noon of February 21st saw us strapping on the last packages. Salem, the handsome Arab porter, took the final orders about forwarding our trunk, and accompanied by the good wishes of the proprietor and a group of natives and Europeans, who appeared interested in our undertaking, we wheeled the rovers out of the courtyard of the "Continental," and mounted for our journey of over fifteen hundred miles through Algeria.

It seemed a wonderful ride, that first afternoon run of eighty-one kilometres from Oran to Perregaux. That was probably because it was the first ride in Africa, for, when analysed, it was, except for being rather more novel, very like a half-day's spin in France or Italy. The country was rolling, the air mild, trees and flowers in bloom, the roads fine, and offering the advantage of not being cut up by vehicles. After leaving Oran we met only Arabs and negroes, on foot, or riding on donkeys and horses. We delighted them and they charmed us, and it was with mutual satisfaction that the American and Arab met *en route* that day.

They were good-natured and orderly, and, when we several times rode through large companies of them, although they laughed and accosted us, they did so civilly, and were neither rude nor coarse. Even when their animals, frightened at the unusual sight, shied up a bank or into a field, they took it in good humour. Once an Arab was thrown from his horse, but he did not seem disturbed by the mishap. We were struck with the difference in temperament between the Arab and the Sicilian, as we recalled the various occasions on which, when in Sicily, we had been the unintentional cause of unhorsing the latter, who, although not apparently injured by the fall, would usually curse us vociferously with fierce gesticulations, as we rode on.

It has been our experience that horses, oxen and mules are much more liable to be frightened by a woman on a bicycle than by a man. Dogs also bark at the former more frequently. It may be that dogs, which seem to regard themselves as a sort of special police, consider women out of place on a wheel, and in need of correction.

In Sicily and Southern Italy, on dismounting in a town, we were immediately surrounded by a motley and noisy rabble, which accompanied us until we left it. On similar occasions, in Algeria, a few Arabs would gather slowly about at a respectful distance, evidently interested, but entirely silent and undemonstrative, never offering to touch the machines. The Arab, as a rule, is lazy and not fond of work or overexertion, yet he sometimes displays both activity and endurance. On that ride to Perregaux a young man ran along with us for two kilometres or more, as we rode at a fairly rapid pace.

We reached Perregaux, a town of fifty-eight hundred inhabitants, about six o'clock, and found a very comfortable inn, where a passable dinner of six courses was served for two francs each. A *table d'hôte* of some pretension was generally attainable, even in small places, where the other accommodations were of the simplest character, at about the price mentioned. Occasionally a charge of three and a-half francs would appear upon the bill, which did not necessarily imply that the dinner was any better, but might rather be taken as an indication that the attention of the hostess had been called to the practice prevalent in Europe, of making a higher charge to English travellers than to those of other nationalities. What the charge would have been had she known we were Americans, we would not venture to guess. Suffice it to say, it is always to the advantage of his purse, if an American abroad can pass for an Englishman, which, on the ordinary routes of travel, it is next to impossible for him to do.

As is the case in the south of France, the inns of Algeria are frequently kept or managed by women, and the chambers are cared for by men, who make excellent chambermaids. While yet uninitiated in the customs of the country, we sought one evening the bureau of an inn, and asked an intelligent-looking woman sitting there, where the host was. "C'est moi," was the reply, and she proved fully equal to the demands of her position.

Soon after leaving Oran, opportunities of verifying the truth of the captain's statement about dogs[1] began to present themselves, and long before our Algerian tour was finished, we were thoroughly convinced that the facts, in this instance at least, had been correctly stated. As we passed farmhouses and native habitations, the dogs would rush out at us, sometimes singly, sometimes in twos and threes, barking furiously, snapping and showing their teeth in a most threatening manner. These dogs are shaggy, gaunt, wolfish-looking beasts, with long, sharp noses and glaring eyes, are taught to be suspicious of strangers, and are rendered more savage by being half-starved. The most ferocious are kept chained or shut up during the day, but it is never safe to approach a house unless armed with a stout cane. What would have happened to us had we not been provided with steel-cored whips, it is not difficult to predict. To say the least, we should speedily have become candidates for the Pasteur treatment. To increase the efficiency of these, we had taken the precaution to fasten good-sized shot on the snappers. This worked well on the dogs, but was detrimental to the whips, as the weight of the shot under constant use caused the snappers to break off. The idea then occurred to us to provide the lower end of the whips with six wire barbs similar to those used on barbed fence wire, each projecting three-eighths of an inch. One blow with the whip thus armed was usually sufficient. The barking would change instantly into a short, sharp yelp, and the dog would slink off conquered. The sudden transition from an attitude of confident attack to one of ignominious defeat was most amusing.

Later on, between Algiers and Constantine, as we were passing an Arab village a little off the road, one evening after dark, we were startled by a tremendous barking. Of a sudden, at least fifty dogs broke out in full chorus and barked as if they would tear everything around them to pieces. Whether we were the cause of the deafening din we did not know, nor did we know whether they were chained, but the prospect of being attacked in the dark by these howling fiends was not reassuring. They did not molest us, and we once more breathed freely as the sounds grew fainter behind us.

The further journey to Affreville was uneventful. Between the towns only Arabs were seen. On market days we met them in large numbers, going into or out of the town where the market was held. Most of them were on foot, but the richer class rode on horses or mules.

In the Ouarsenes mountains we passed over long reaches of sparsely-inhabited country, where not even the usual shepherd boy was visible. Coming around the barren mountain side, into view of the plains of the Chelif, a remarkable landscape lay spread before us. On one side, the mountains overhanging in jagged outlines the valley stood out clear but black as midnight, shadowed by heavy clouds, while beyond, the wide plain swept for miles, an oasis of spring green illuminated by softest sunlight.

The African lights were a constant delight, whether studied on cloudless or overcast days. Except near the coast, fogs were rare, as were low tones in colour, clear outlines, sharp contrasts and strong colours prevailing. [. . .]

[Chapter 17]

Femmes Kabyles

As the advance of a nation in modern ideas may be judged by the position occupied by its women, Germany being a notable exception, so we may form some conception of the degree of civilisation existing in the Kabylie at the present time, by a brief consideration of some of the customs pertaining to the women.

Writers, guide-books and the French tell us that the women of the Kabylie occupy a high position, and one much more favoured than that of Arab women; but those who have seen them in their homes do not all agree with this opinion. As a proof of her emancipated position, it is urged that the Kabyle usually has only one wife. The fact is true, but it may be accounted for on economic grounds rather than as being due to moral principle. Nothing in the laws or religion forbids his having as many wives as he can support, and those who do business in Algiers in winter, and return for agricultural pursuits in summer, generally follow Oriental custom and have a wife in each place. Again, it is said the Kabyle woman goes with uncovered face. This is simply in accordance with long established custom, for from time immemorial only the wives of marabouts have covered their faces. One must look deeper than this and see how man regards woman, and how woman regards herself in Kabylie land.

The opinion the Kabyle holds of woman may be seen in the following remarks made by a native to a French captain:

"When two children are born, you would surely have me show more joy at the birth of the one that will be able, gun in hand, to defend his tribe, than at that of the other, who at the best will only be fit to make bad *couscous?*"

"But," replied the captain, "these daughters you so despise are in reality bargains, since, at the age of ten or twelve years, you sell them for a good price."

"Yes, but they do not give me the influence in the council that being the father of four or five well-grown sons does. Besides, our laws make a difference between the adult male and female—for example, a wife cannot kill her husband, whereas a husband may kill his wife if he deems it necessary."

The birth of a son is a cause of great rejoicing and is announced by loud outcries from the women of the village, to which the men respond by discharging guns. After this proceeding, jewels, perfumes, cosmetics and stuffs are brought as presents to the mother. A few days later a *fête* is given. The mother, with great pride, decorates her brow with the "thabezinth," a circular silver or metal brooch, about four inches in diameter, set with coral, which she wears a year and then removes, placing it again on her forehead only in the event of another son being born.

On the contrary, the newly-born girl opens her eyes on a world opposed to her advent. Her birth is celebrated in a very quiet manner, and only by the family circle—as the Arab would say, without noise. No presents are given. Women having daughters may wear the thabezinth also, but only as a breast ornament.

As the girl grows out of infancy, her education amounts to little. She does sometimes attend the village school, but exceptionally. Kabyle parents are opposed to having their daughters educated *à la française*—that is in school—for the reason that it lessens their chances of marriage, no Kabyle desiring a wife who has been to school, however little she may have learned. Not long since, a chief lamented bitterly his folly in allowing his daughters to attend school, as he had not been able to procure husbands for them, and they, at the age of twenty-five, were still on his hands. Their chances of matrimony were indeed small at that age—*vieilles filles* of fifteen years' standing.

At twelve years, an age when girls in civilised countries begin to study, the Kabyle girl, without even rudimentary knowledge, with all the innocence and ignorance of childhood, is sold to her husband by her father, who considers himself very fortunate if her charms bring him five hundred francs, the average price being two hundred and fifty.

A friend of the bridegroom makes the arrangements with the bride's father, and when all is satisfactorily settled, the future husband and his friends run about the village firing guns to announce the happy news. This is the first the girl knows of the matter, about which she is in no way consulted. A second interview follows, in which the lover pays a part or the whole of the purchase-money through an agent.

Marrying a wife is expensive in this land. Besides paying for her, the husband is expected to present her with a *panier de la fiancée*, consisting of seventy different essences, medicines and cosmetics. At the preliminary meetings neither bride nor bridegroom are present.

Nor are they present at the marriage ceremony. Before pronouncing the absent couple man and wife, the marabout, in the presence of the family and friends, reads the following enlightened words from the Koran: "Men are superior to women, because the qualities which God has given them elevate them above women, and because they use their money for the marriage dowry of women. Virtuous women are obedient and subdued." The advice is given to a man about to enter the matrimonial state—to reprimand his wife if he fears disobedience on her part, to beat her if she disobeys, but from the moment that she obeys, to cease quarrelling with her.

After the ceremony the bride, for the first time, appears on the scene, dressed in her richest garments, and closely veiled. She mounts a mule and is conducted to her husband's house. At the door, where he awaits her, a vase of water is handed her, with which she sprinkles the assembled people. This is a very ancient custom, the significance of which is now unknown. A basket containing *couscous*, nuts and cakes is next handed her while sitting upon the mule, and these she throws to the crowd. In the basket is an ankle bracelet, which she keeps, this being a symbol of the chain of wedlock she has assumed.

At her entrance on married life, the Kabyle woman is often a pretty creature, but under the weight of domestic cares she soon grows old. Her duties, besides childbearing, comprise all the housework, the weaving of cloth, the making of *couscous* and, hardest of all, the daily bringing up of the water for household use, from springs on the mountain side or in the valley below the village.

At certain hours every day lines of women may be seen, with heavy earthen water-jars on their backs, toiling slowly up the narrow, almost perpendicular, paths to their houses, clad in a large white tunic, fastened on each shoulder with heavy silver pins, and held at the waist by a woollen belt, with legs and feet bare, except for three or four ankle bracelets, their long arms thrown backward supporting the amphora. They are eminently classic in appearance, though barbarous in their thraldom.

For this life of continued drudgery she is rewarded by being permitted to eat in the presence of her husband, and when time and care have rendered her no longer attractive to her lord, she is replaced by a younger, fairer rival, who kindly accepts her services as servant.

The condition of the Kabyle women to-day, but slightly better than that of the Mauresques, is about what it was a hundred years ago, and what it may perhaps be a hundred years hence, for they are utterly without hope and have themselves no power to better their condition. The idea that they have a better position than Arab women doubtless comes from a misapprehension of existing circumstances.

It is believed, by those who have studied the matter, that in the time of the Berbers women held a higher place than now, and that their position became debased after the adoption of Islamism.

The Koran permits the Kabyle, as well as others, to have as many wives as he chooses, but he rarely avails himself of this permission, at least during the early years of married life, for the reason that it costs much to buy a wife and more to support her.

[Chapter 18]

A Day in the African Alps—The Col de Tirourda

The town of Fort National stands on the crest of a long narrow *crête* running parallel with the Djurjura, with a commanding view of the country on both sides. The town is mostly French, and presents nothing of especial interest except the Wednesday market. The fort, on a hill overhanging the town, is quite an imposing structure, suitable to the importance of the place as a military post. It was enlarged after the insurrection of 1871. At that time it was termed by the natives, "A thorn in the eye of the Kabylie," and such they probably still consider it, as it is kept well garrisoned, and, in case of insurrection, the houses of sixty thousand Kabyles could be destroyed in a few hours by its guns.

While looking about on the afternoon after our arrival we chanced to go into the shop of the only *bijoutier* in the town, and while examining Kabyle ornaments we remarked, in the course of conversation, we should like to visit the place where they were made. The jeweller, a very friendly Kabyle, who spoke French, said it would give him much pleasure to entertain us as his guests at his house at Beni Yenni, if we would come there. He added,

"To-morrow is the beginning of the feast of the Ramadan. I am going home early in the morning to remain with my people four days. Will you not go with me?"

"No," we said, "we cannot go to-morrow, for, fair, we have arranged a trip to the Col de Tirourda. Perhaps the day after to-morrow."

"As you please. I will be there."

"But how far is Beni Yenni from here?"

"Four hours on a good mule."

As we looked at the fine form before us, wrapped in the soft folds of his burnous, which fell to his sandled feet, his face bright, his eye eager with apparently real desire to have us visit him, a strong wish to see the land of the Beni Yenni seized us, and we promised to go on the second day after.

That night it rained, as it can in the mountains, in torrents, and we feared our attempt on the Col de Tirourda from this side would prove as unsuccessful as the one proposed from Tasmalt. But at five o'clock in the morning, when a small Arab boy knocked at the door to awaken us, the brilliant African stars were palpitating in the heavens—for stars do not twinkle in Algeria—and the dark blue sky was full of mysterious premonition of a cloudless dawn.

We decided to use our cycles as far as the road would permit, and then climb the Col on foot. No one at Fort National could tell us anything about the route beyond Michelet, twenty-five kilometres distant. As we rode out of the sleeping town, past the house of the *bijoutier*, a cloaked figure appeared at the door, and the words "Je vous attendrais" greeted us. We answered, "A demain á Beni Yenni."

The road, though well made, was muddy after the rainy night and we had to ride with care, but we would not have hurried if we could on this magnificent ride from Fort National to Michelet. The road runs along a high horizontal *crête*, and as it circles in and out of the curling contour of the mountain, brings into sight peak after peak of the Djurjura, and ridge after ridge of the village-covered Kabylie. We could not help recalling the road from Sorrento to Positano and Amalfi, and that from Taormina toward Messina, not on account of any similarity in the landscape, but because each in its way is so superlatively lovely.

We passed a number of villages, and many Kabyles on the highway returning home from the market of the previous day. Most of them carried pieces of meat strung on strings, for the long fast was over and the people were about to celebrate the feast which was to follow by free indulgence in meat and *couscous*. Some of the men were without the usual cloak, being dressed only in large yellowish white shirts confined at the waist by a belt, their legs and arms bare. The only addition to this costume is the cloak ordinarily worn in cold weather, or sometimes two or three when the cold is extreme.

Michelet is a small official station consisting of a few houses and a sort of fort or strong house to which the inhabitants may fly for protection in case of necessity. Its situation, facing the highest peaks of the Djurjura, is even more beautiful than that of Fort National. Fifty villages are seen from here. On one long spur running out from the mountain we counted fifteen, the first nestling on the limit of the green, overhung by the high crags above, the last perched on the end, where it fell off sharply to the valley below.

The knowledge of the inhabitants of Michelet as to the road did not extend beyond the next station, the "Maison Cantonnière," nine kilometres farther, to which point they thought we could ride. They did not tell us that the road was unfinished, and converted by the rain of the preceding night into a sea of mud, as we found to be the case after going on a short distance. Returning to Michelet, we left the cycles at the inn and started on foot for the "Maison Cantonnière," which, by picking our way along the sides of the road, we reached in two hours.

Here we found only two tattooed, bejewelled Kabyle women, who spoke no French, and could tell us nothing about the route to the pass. We were now well up on the mountain side. The road, or the attempt at one, ceased, and we struck into a mule path, which led directly upward around the edge of the mountain. The scenery had become Alpine in character, the fertile lands were left behind, and the region grew wilder and more desolate with every step. The path was obstructed in places with *débris* and rocks, which had been loosened by the frost and rains and had rolled down from above, so that progress was oftentimes slow. In one place we had to climb over a chaos of good-sized boulders, which covered the path for two hundred feet, the result of a landslide. This was the route across the mountains which we had been told in Algiers was available to bicyclists. We found it difficult enough to follow on foot and were thankful our machines were safely housed.

A turn of the path now brought into view the village of Tirourda far below, on the top of a desolate *crête*, the last village of the Kabylie in this direction, and the last to fall into the hands of the French in 1857, noted for having been the home of the Berber prophetess, Lalla Fathma.

Built almost upon the snow-beds of the mountain, amid nature's sternest aspects, it looked more like a deserted eagle's nest than the home of man. In 1857 it and Takleh, an adjoining village belonging to the marabouts of the tribe of Illilten, were governed by Sidi Thaieb, who, with his sister Lalla Fathma, lived like a petty monarch, surrounded by every luxury. Lalla had a wide reputation as a prophetess, and was consulted by the people of the whole Kabylie.

At the approach of the French, Sidi Thaieb, whose family had for centuries governed these two villages, went to MacMahon[2] and succeeded in making an arrangement by which, in return for certain services on his part, these villages should remain unmolested. This compact would have been carried out by the French had not an unfortunate mistake occurred. Several zouaves in pursuit of some fugitives from another town came, without realising the fact, into Tirourda. The people, supposing them to come with hostile intent, fixed upon them, killing and wounding them all. A detachment of the army, which was in the neighbourhood, hearing the firing came up, and before either side was aware of it, a general engagement took place.

Lalla Fathma and her brother were taken prisoners, and their arms, clothing, furniture and jewels were confiscated. As we sit on a boulder, looking down upon lifeless Tirourda, fancy pictures the procession of three hundred men and women, with torn garments and dishevelled hair, starting down the narrow steep path on their way to the marshal's camp, following their idol seated on her mule, who, in the midst of the tumult of battle, had found time to braid carefully her jet black tresses, paint her cheeks with carmine, blacken her eyelids and stain her finger-nails with henna.

A light rustling breaks the silence. Is it the voices of the sobbing women and children driven from their homes by the relentless conqueror, or is it the spring wind playing about the jutting crags of the Pic de Tirourda?

The path became narrower and ran along dangerous precipices. Evidences of the action of frost appeared in cracks on its outer side, where the loosened edge threatened to slide off in places should any extra weight be placed upon it.

All this part of the mountain is composed of a loose, crumbling material, which at this season affords an uncertain and precarious foothold. Patches of snow lay across the path, and were seen to cover it ahead in great slanting sheets running to the edge of the cliffs. These must be crossed if we would go on.

We had now arrived within two kilometres of the goal in regard to which we had so long sought for information in vain—the Col de Tirourda—from which an extended view over the Kabylie of the country south of Djurjura of the sea, and of Algiers was to be obtained. Should we go on, or give up farther attempt? It was hard to give up now, after so much effort and being so near to success, but common prudence dictated that we go no further. We knew nothing of the character of the ground under the slanting masses of snow ahead, or what foothold they had upon the mountain. We had no Alpine-stocks, and no hobnails in our boots. Reluctantly we turned our backs upon the Col, feeling that we could at least give somewhat more information about the route than we had ever succeeded in gathering from others. The grandeur of the region, however, amply repaid all exertion, and we consoled ourselves for the failure to accomplish all we had desired, by the reflection that we were not the only tourists who had had mountain luck.

We were now thankful that the mules had failed to put in an appearance that morning at Tasmalt, for had it been otherwise, we might have been deposited with our bicycles on the top of the Col, there to wait perhaps until the snow melted.

By the time we reached Michelet again we had walked eighteen miles up and down, and were glad enough to mount and ride back over the splendid road to Fort National. Over the green setting of dozens of villages hovered in the evening light a thin blue film of smoke, a sign that the labours of the day were over and the people had gathered around their hearthstones to enjoy their evening meal. The clouds behind the mountains grew pink in sunset hues, and faded into the cold greys of crepuscule before the day's trip ended. [. . .]

[Chapter 19]

Among the Kabyles of Beni Yenni

The next morning at six two mules, accompanied by two Kabyle guides, stood in front of the Hotel des Touristes ready to take us to Beni Yenni. Women's saddles appeared to be unknown in that region, so we accepted those furnished and both rode astride, which is cer-

tainly the safest way on the steep rough paths which have to be travelled. The saddles having no stirrups, we suggested to the guides that
our comfort would be promoted if some contrivance could be
arranged by which we could brace our feet. Accordingly, a grass rope
with a loop at each end was thrown over the saddle. This answered the
purpose fairly well, but some dexterity was required to preserve a
proper equipoise of the feet.

Soon after leaving the town, the path began to descend in sharp
zigzags along the side of the Souk-el-Arba spur. To us who were unaccustomed to this manner of exercise, riding on one of these long-
legged animals down a steep grade was not wholly agreeable. Its shoulder blades moved up and down to a marvellous extent, causing a
jolting that would have done credit to any of the apparatus of a movement cure. Its body was pitched to such an incline that constant attention to the rope stirrups was necessary to prevent sliding off over
its head. Added to the unpleasant sensation of plunging downward,
the mule persisted, particularly at the sharpest curves, in walking on
the very edge of the path. The attention of the guides was called to
this fact, but from their small stock of French was gleaned only the
comforting information, "Il va bien, sur très sur."

Considering the mule was accustomed to doing just that sort of
work every day of its life, we concluded to let it go as it pleased, and
direct our efforts to holding on.

We passed through two villages built on lower projections of the
crête. As we descended, the vegetation became more luxuriant and the
path more picturesque, hedged by laurel, hazel and blackberry bushes,
and lightly shaded by the young leaves of the ash, almond and *chêne
liège*. In June the country must be a bower of green. Every few turns
the path crossed the rocky beds of cascades bounding towards the
deep valley below.

At some of the brooks women were washing clothes in the running
water, treading upon them with their feet, as is customary among the
Kabyles as well as among the Arabs, the music of the bangles upon
their ankles mingling with the babble of the water. This method of
washing does not offend the taste more than that employed in many
parts of Europe, where the articles washed are rubbed against stones
in canals and streams; but when it comes to preparing salad in the

same manner, as is also done in the Kabylie, the impression produced
on the minds is unsavoury.

Men on mules met us. How infinitely picturesque a burnoused
Oriental can look on a mule, and how amazingly commonplace a European. Lines of women, bearing amphorae filled with water, filed
slowly past, and sometimes a mother with two or three pretty children
would stand aside for us. With nature so beautiful and people so interesting, it was like a pastoral symphony composed by a musician of
ancient days.

We looked for our Kodak to photograph some of the interesting
groups, and to our dismay found it had been left behind in the hurry
of departure, which accident we have never ceased to regret, as the
best opportunity of the whole journey of photographing characteristic and peculiar types and costumes was thus lost.

On reaching the bottom of the narrow, blooming valley, a stream
was crossed and the path began immediately to ascend another *crête*.
The guides gave us to understand that climbing was less disagreeable
than descending, which proved to be the fact; but before the four
hours were over, our ambitions in regard to mule-riding were satisfied,
and we were relieved to see at last the walls of Ait l'Hassen, the largest
of the towns occupied by the Beni Yenni, gracing the height just
above.

Ait l'Hassen has about eight thousand inhabitants. Our mules clat-
tered through the narrow streets, followed by many of the inhabitants,
and soon brought us to the house of Monsieur Salem, who with his
brother stood at the door to welcome us.

The house was a low stone building with two rooms, the first of
which served as an entrance hall, the second as a living-room. Unlike
Kabyle rooms in general this was furnished with tables, chairs and
Oriental rugs, for Salem was a cosmopolitan Kabyle, went often to Algiers, had even been to Chicago, and, although he allowed his wife
and children to live in the manner of the country, permitted himself
a certain amount of civilisation, not to say luxury, in his personal surroundings. His first question was, when madame would like *déjeuner*.
If madame would name the hour it should be ready, and meantime
they would show us the town.

Sight-seeing in a Kabyle village is not arduous work, and after a house or two and the Mosque and Djemaat have been inspected, nothing remains but the people and the view. To get this last they took us to the highest point, whither a considerable number of men and children accompanied us, possibly for the purpose of affording us their protection, more probably to satisfy their curiosity, for foreigners did not visit Ait l'Hassen every day.

If Fort National is called the "Thorn in the eye of the Kabylie," the *crête* upon which the Beni Yenni villages stand might be called the flower in the heart of the Kabylie. It seems to be a centre surrounded by innumerable spurs of about its own height, while the semi-circular wall of Djurjura, towering at no great distance, adds a note of grandeur to which its sublime peaks are forever tuned. In the transparent atmosphere of the Algerian noon but a few steps appeared to separate us from the glittering summit of the Lalla Kredidja, queen of the range.

In walking about the village, the absence of women on the streets was noticeable, while children, many of them handsome, were well represented. Sleek, round-faced, shaven-headed little boys, and merry-eyed, curly-headed girls led the way, ever turning around to gaze shyly at us. The older the girls the blacker their hair, which, from infancy on, is dyed regularly, that it may acquire the degree of jettiness desired by the husband when a girl reaches the marriageable age. Many have blonde hair when born.

Arrived again at Salem's house he shut out all curious visitors and we were soon seated at table. The guides sat cross-legged on the floor at a respectful distance. Two smoking dishes of *couscous* were brought by a boy, followed by another with a plate of boiled rib of mutton cut in slices. The *couscous* we were expected to eat with wooden spoons, the round bowls of which were much too large to enter our mouths, and we soon found a certain amount of skill was required to convey the contents of the spoons to the proper destination. The mutton was eaten with the fingers. We were frequently urged to take more by Salem and his brother, who, doubtless in conformity with the customs of hospitality, took nothing themselves, but remained standing ready to serve us, and from time to time deluged our immense dishes of slowly-diminishing *couscous* with bouillon.

The mixture was not unpalatable, and in smaller portions would have been relished after the long ride; but trying to dispose of quantities large enough for all present was about as hard work as travelling on the mules. Notwithstanding our desire to do honour to the feast, our ardour began to flag.

"You do not eat," remarked Salem; "you do not love the *couscous?*"

"Yes, certainly, we love it above all else, but your portions are very large. We are not accustomed to eat so much."

"Then take a little more bouillon. That is light and nourishing."

After one more feeble attempt on the bouillon we gave it up and tried to distract the attention of our friends from ourselves by turning the conversation on their own affairs. This was not difficult, as Salem liked to talk of his experience at the World's Fair at Chicago, whither he had gone in charge of twenty Kabyles under appointment of the Government at Algiers. He seemed particularly impressed, as many a Christian also was, with the Ferris Wheel and the exhibitions in the Midway Plaisance. At length, as if in proof of the truth of his statements, he took out of the inner pockets of his voluminous outer garment a match-box bearing the stars and stripes in red, white and blue, and several other trinkets sold at the Exhibition.

"Ah," he said with enthusiasm, "Chicago est une ville magnifique, finer than Beni Yenni, yes, even finer than Algiers." Did we come from Chicago? No, we did not, and were not sure we preferred it to Beni Yenni. Then followed compliments on American cookery. What could be equal to an American steak? On that point we agreed with him, and heartily wished we had one in place of the farinaceous food before us. But the American coffee was bad, did not compare with *café maure.* We saw that Salem had good judgment, was an astute observer, and would do credit to the land that had adopted him.

The boy appearing just then with the *café maure,* our still plenteous rations of mutton and *couscous* were handed to the patient guides who, with evident appreciation of the quality of the viands, made amends for any want of capacity on our part. Salem and his brother drank coffee with us. While sipping this excellent beverage, we asked Salem where his wife was, and the other women of the family.

"Have patience," he replied. "After your coffee you shall see the women." When we had finished he led the way through a narrow lane to a rear court, where eight or ten women and girls were standing about. With the dignity of a Roman senator he pointed towards them, saying with indifference, "Voilà les femmes."

It being the feast of the Ramadan they, like all the women seen the last day or two, were adorned with ornaments. In this case many were of silver, and of rich design. Several of the women were tattooed on the forehead, cheeks and chin, and the hands of all were dyed a deep red. They stood huddled together like a group of shy cattle, children of different ages clinging to their short tunic skirts. The little ones were similarly dyed and decorated. We tried to converse with them, but they only shook their heads and simpered. "The women understand nothing," remarked Salem with scorn.

"Which is your wife?" we asked. He looked at the group a moment, then, pointing to a very witch of hideousness, replied, "Voilà ma femme."

We went with the women into a typical interior, and examined among other things the earthen dishes used in preparing *couscous.* Flour forms the basis of this national food eaten by the Kabyles and Arabs usually twice a day. The women roll the flour in their hands until it forms small agglomerations about the size of pearl barley. It is then placed in a low dish, the bottom of which is perforated with little holes, and steamed, no water being allowed to come in contact with it. The poor eat it simply with bouillon, the rich with bouillon and meat. Perhaps, had we realised at breakfast that the henna-dyed hands of Salem's wife had prepared that placed before us, we should have had still less appetite for it.

We left the women and children in their desolate house with its floor of cold earth and returned to Salem's pleasant room with its carpeting of rugs, hoping in our hearts that, if our Kabyle friend ever again should go to America, he would study the woman question as well as the culinary excellences of the United States.

Salem showed us a variety of unfinished ornaments, and explained the process of manufacture. As the people were all celebrating the *fête* we did not see them at work.

The day was passing, so we mounted our mules again and said good-bye to our kind host and Beni Yenni. His brother accompanied us on foot to Fort National. He said he must go on business, and it would give him pleasure to go with us; but we liked to imagine that

he was prompted by the chivalrous sentiment of the anaia to see that
we reached our destination in safety. [. . .]

Conclusion

At Fort National our Algerian trip practically ended, for the journey back to Algiers was over ground previously travelled, which offered nothing new. It had been a trip replete with excitement and new
experiences. The frequent rains had interfered somewhat with the ex-
ecution of what had been planned, but enough was accomplished to
repay many times all efforts and sacrifices of personal comfort, and to
show that the country was well worth visiting, both on account of its
natural beauty and the originality of its inhabitants, and also of its
wealth in remains of ancient civilisation.

When one has become blasé with years of European travel, let him
turn to Algeria and he will find there what will give him new emotions, fresh impressions, enlarge the horizon of his conceptions, and
supplement the experiences that have been elsewhere acquired.

15

Constance Fenimore Woolson

ટ**ી**

Constance Fenimore Woolson (1840–1894) first traveled to Europe in 1879, landing initially in England and then venturing to Florence, Venice, Milan, and Switzerland. She lived in various places on the continent for the rest of her life. She made a trip to the Greek Isles and Athens in 1889, and in 1890 she traveled from Athens to Cairo. Her travel sketches join a canon of short fiction and novels such as *Castle Nowhere* (1875), *For the Major* (1883), and *Dorothy and Other Italian Stories* (1895). Originally appearing in *Harper's* in 1884, 1890, and 1891, her travel writings were posthumously collected and published as *Mentone, Cairo, and Corfu* (1896).

As the title suggests, the text of Woolson's travel account is divided into three parts, each of them entirely devoid of the apology and of epistolary conventions. The first part, a fictionalized account of travel around Mentone, cleverly combats the tedium of predictable elements of travel writing. It takes such features as the reproduction of tiresome historical information and hackneyed descriptions of conventional tourist sites, places them in the mouths of characters, and in this way converts dry fact and trite observations into sources of characterization, drama, and humor. Parts 2 and 3 of the text, essays organized by topics, describe Cairo and Corfu.

The excerpt in this selection is taken from the material on Cairo. Woolson evokes the western tropes for the mystic East: mosques, bazaars, the harem, and the souvenirs that, in the semiotics of travel, stand in for the places they represent. Woolson's text reveals her knowledge of other texts of travel and her ability to refresh the threadbare conventions of the travel genre.

Mentone, Cairo, and Corfu

Cairo in 1890

"The way to Egypt is long and vexatious"—so Homer sings; and so also have sung other persons more modern. A chopping sea prevails off Crete, and whether one leaves Europe at Naples, Brindisi, or Athens, one's steamer soon reaches that beautiful island, and consumes in passing it an amount of time which is an ever-fresh surprise. Crete, with its long coast-line and soaring mountain-tops, appears to fill all that part of the sea. However, as the island is the half-way point between Europe and Africa, one can at least feel, after finally leaving it behind, that the Egyptian coast is not far distant. This coast is as indolent as that of Crete is aggressive; it does not raise its head. You are there before you see it or know it; and then, if you like, in something over three hours more you can be in Cairo.

The Cairo street of the last Paris Exhibition, familiar to many Americans, was a clever imitation. But imitations of the Orient are melancholy; you cannot transplant the sky and the light.

The real Cairo has been sacrificed to the Nile. Comparatively few among travellers in the East see the place under the best conditions; for upon their arrival they are preoccupied with the magical river voyage which beckons them southward, with the dahabeeyah or the steamer which is to carry them; and upon their return from that wonderful journey they are planning for the more difficult expedition to the Holy Land. It is safe to say that to many Americans Cairo is only a confused memory of donkeys and dragomans, mosquitoes and dervishes, and mosques, mosques, mosques! This hard season probably must be gone through by all. The wise are those who stay on after it is over, or who return; for the true impression of a place does not come when the mind is overcrowded and confused; it does not come when the body is wearied; for the descent of the vision, serenity of soul is necessary—one might even call it idleness. It is during those days when one does nothing that the reality steals noiselessly into one's comprehension, to remain there forever.

But is Cairo worth this? is asked. That depends upon the temperament. If one must have in his nature somewhere a trace of the poet to love Venice, so one must be at heart something of a painter to love Cairo.

Her colors are so softly rich, the Saracenic part of her architecture is so fantastically beautiful, the figures in her streets are so picturesque, that one who has an eye for such effects seems to himself to be living in a gallery of paintings without frames, which stretch off in vistas, melting into each other as they go. If, therefore, one loves color, if pictures are precious to him, are important, let him go to Cairo; he will find pleasure awaiting him. Flaubert said that one could imagine the pyramids, and perhaps the Sphinx, without an actual sight of them, but that what one could not in the least imagine was the expression on the face of an Oriental barber as he sits cross-legged before his door. That is Cairo exactly. You must see her with the actual eyes, and you must see her without haste. She does not reveal herself to the Cook tourist nor even to Gaze's,[1] nor to the man who is hurrying off to Athens on a fixed day which nothing can alter.

The New Quarter

(One must begin with this, and have it over.) Cairo has a population of four hundred thousand souls. The new part of the town, called Ismaïlia, has been persistently abused by almost all writers, who describe it as dusty, as shadeless, as dreary, as glaring, as hideous, as blankly and broadly empty, as adorned with half-built houses which are falling into ruin—one has read all this before arriving. But what does one find in the year of grace 1890? Streets shaded by innumerable trees; streets broad indeed, but which, instead of being dusty, are wet (and over-wet) with the constant watering; well-kept, bright-faced houses, many of them having beautiful gardens, which in January are glowing with giant poinsettas, crimson hibiscus, and purple bougainvillea—flowers which give place to richer blooms, to an almost over-luxuriance of color and perfumes, as the early spring comes on. If the streets were paved, it would be like the outlying quarters of Paris, for most of the houses are French as regards their architecture. Shadeless? It is nothing but shade. And the principal drives, too, beyond the town—the Ghezireh road, the Choubra and Gizeh roads, and the long avenue which leads to the pyramids—are deeply embowered, the great arms of the trees which border them meeting and interlacing overhead. Consider the stony streets of Italian cities (which no one abuses), and then talk of "shadeless Cairo"!

The Climate

If one wishes to spend a part of each day in the house, engaged in reading, writing, or resting; if the comfortable feeling produced by a brightly burning little fire in the cool of the evening is necessary to him for his health or his pleasure—then he should not attempt to spend the entire winter in the city of the Khedive. The mean temperature there during the cold season—that is, six weeks in January and February—is said to be 58° Fahrenheit. But this is in the open air; in the houses the temperature is not more than 54° or 52°, and often in the evening lower. The absence of fires makes all the difficulty; for out-of-doors the air may be and often is charming; but upon coming in from the bright sunshine the atmosphere of one's sitting-room and bedroom seems chilly and prison-like. There are, generally speaking, no chimneys in Cairo, even in the modern quarter. Each of the hotels has one or two open grates, but only one or two. Southern countries, however, are banded together—so it seems to the shivering Northerner—to keep up the delusion that they have no cold weather; as they have it not, why provide for it? In Italy in the winter the Italians spread rugs over their floors, hang tapestries upon their walls, pile cushions everywhere, and carpet their sofas with long-haired skins; this they call warmth. But a fireless room, with the thermometer on its walls standing at 35°, is not warm, no matter how many cushions you may put into it; and one hates to believe, too, that necessary accompaniments of health are roughened faces and frost-bitten noses, and the extreme ugliness of hands swollen and red. "Perhaps if one could have in Cairo an open hearth and three sticks, it would, with all the other pleasures which one finds here, be too much—would reach wickedness!" was a remark we heard last winter. A still more forcible exclamation issued from the lips of a pilgrim from New York one evening in January. Looking round her sitting-room upon the roses gathered that day in the open air, upon the fly-brushes and fans and Oriental decorations, this misguided person moaned, in an almost tearful voice: "Oh, for a blizzard and a *fire!*" The reasonable traveller, of course, ought to remember that with a climate which has seven months of debilitating heat, and three and a half additional months of summer weather, the attention of the natives is not strongly turned towards devices for warmth. This consideration, however, does not make the fireless rooms agreeable during the few weeks that remain.

Another surprise is the rain. "In our time it rained in Egypt," writes Strabo,[2] as though chronicling a miracle. Either the climate has changed, or Strabo was not a disciple of the realistic school, for in the January of this truthful record the rain descended in such a deluge in Cairo that the water came above the knees of the horses, and a ferry-boat was established for two days in one of the principal streets. Later the rain descended a second time with almost equal violence, and showers were by no means infrequent. (It may be mentioned in parenthesis that there was heavy rain at Luxor, four hundred and fifty miles south of Cairo, on the 19th of February.) One does not object to these rains; they are in themselves agreeable; one wishes simply to note the impudence of the widely diffused statement that Egypt is a rainless land. So far nothing has been said against the winter climate of Cairo; objection has been made merely to the fireless condition of the houses—a fault which can be remedied. But now a real enemy must be mentioned—namely, the kamsin. This is a hot wind from the south, which parches the skin and takes the life out of one; it fills the air with a thick grayness, which you cannot call mist, because it is perfectly dry, and through which the sun goes on steadily shining, with a light so weird that one can think of nothing but the feelings of the last man, or the opening of the sixth seal. The regular kamsin season does not begin before May; the occasional days of it that bring suffering to travellers occur in February, March, and April. But what are five or six days of kamsin amid four winter months whose average temperature is 58° Fahrenheit? It is human nature to detect faults in climates which have been greatly praised, just as one counts every freckle on a fair face that is celebrated for its beauty. Give Cairo a few hearth fires, and its winter climate will seem delightful; although not so perfect as that of Florida, in our country, because in Florida there are no January mosquitoes.

Mosques

It must be remembered that Cairo is Arabian. "The Nile is Egypt," says a proverb. The Nile is mythical, Pharaonic, Ptolemaic; but Cairo owes its existence solely to the Arabian conquerors of the country, who built a fortress and palace here in A.D. 969.

Very Arabian is still the call to prayer which is chanted by the muezzins from the minarets of the mosques several times during the day. We were passing through a crowded quarter near the Mooski one afternoon in January, when there was wafted across the consciousness a faint, sweet sound. It was far away, and one heard it half impatiently at first, unwilling to lift one's attention even for an instant from the motley scenes nearer at hand. But at length, teased into it by the very sweetness, we raised our eyes, and then it was seen that it came from a half-ruined minaret far above us. Round the narrow outer gallery of this slender tower a man in dark robes was pacing slowly, his arms outstretched, his face upturned to heaven. Not once did he look below as he continued his aerial round, his voice giving forth the chant which we had heard— "Allah akbar; Allah akbar; la Allah ill' Allah. Heyya alassalah!" (God is great; God is great; there is no God but God, and Mohammed is his prophet. Come to prayer.) Again, another day, in the old Touloun quarter, we heard the sound, but it was much nearer. It came from a window but little above our heads, the small mosque within the quadrangle having no minaret. This time I could note the muezzin himself. As he could not see the sky from where he stood, his eyes were closed. I have never beheld a more concentrated expression of devotion than his quiet face expressed; he might have been miles away from the throng below, instead of three feet, as his voice gave forth the same strange, sweet chant. The muezzins are often selected from the ranks of the blind, as the duties of the office are within their powers; but this singer at the low window had closed his eyes voluntarily. The last time I saw the muezzin was towards the end of the season, when the spring was far advanced. Cairo gayety was at its height, the streets were crowded with Europeans returning from the races, the new quarter was as modern as Paris. But there are minarets even in the new quarter, or near it; and on one of the highest of these turrets, outlined against the glow of the sunset, I saw the slowly pacing figure, with its arms outstretched over the city— "Allah akbar; Allah akbar; come, come to prayer."

There are over four hundred mosques in Cairo, and many of them are in a dilapidated condition. Some of these were erected by private means to perpetuate the name and good deeds of the founder and his family; then, in the course of time, owing to the extinction or to the poverty of the descendants, the endowment fund has been absorbed or turned into another channel, and the ensuing neglect has ended in ruin. When a pious Muslim of to-day wishes to perform a good work, he builds a new mosque. It would never occur to him to repair the old one near at hand, which commemorates the generosity of another man. It must be remembered that a mosque has no established congregation, whose duty it is to take care of it. A mosque, in fact, to Muslims has not an exclusively religious character. It is a place prepared for prayer, with the fountain which is necessary for the preceding ablutions required by Mohammed, and the niche towards Mecca which indicates the position which the suppliant must take; but it is also a place for meditation and repose. The poorest and most ragged Muslim has the right to enter whenever he pleases; he can say his prayers, or he can simply rest; he can quench his thirst; he can eat the food which he has brought with him; if he is tired, he can sleep. In mosques not often visited by travellers I have seen men engaged in mending their clothes, and others cooking food with a portable furnace. In the church-yard of Charlton Kings, England, there is a tombstone of the last century with an inscription which concludes as follows: "And his dieing request to his Sons and Daughters was, Never forsake the Charitys until the Poor had got their Rites." In the Cairo mosques the poor have their rites—both with the *gh* and without. The sacred character of a mosque is, in truth, only made conspicuous when unbelievers wish to enter. Then the big shuffling slippers are brought out to cover the shoes of the Christian infidels, so that they may not touch and defile the mattings reserved for the faithful.

After long neglect, something is being done at last to arrest the ruin of the more ancient of these temples. A commission has been appointed by the present government whose duty is the preservation of the monuments of Arabian art; occasionally, therefore, in a mosque one finds scaffolding in place and a general dismantlement. One can only hope for the best—in much the same spirit in which one hopes when one sees the beautiful old front of St. Mark's, Venice, gradually encroached upon by the new raw timbers. But in Cairo, at least, the work of repairing goes on very slowly; three hundred mosques, probably, out of the four hundred still remain untouched, and many of these are adorned with a delicate beauty which is unrivalled. I know no quest so enchanting as a search through the winding lanes of the old quarters for these gems of Saracenic taste, which no guide-book has as yet chronicled, no dragoman discovered. The street is so narrow that your donkey fills almost all the space; passers-by are obliged to flatten themselves against the walls in response to the Oriental adjurations of your donkey-boy behind: "Take heed, O maid!" "Your foot, O chief!" Presently you see a minaret—there is always a minaret somewhere; but it is not always easy to find the mosque to which it belongs, hidden, perhaps, as it is, behind other buildings in the crowded labyrinth. At length you observe a door with a dab or two of the well-known Saracenic honeycomb-work above it; instantly you dismount, climb the steps, and look in. You are almost sure to find treasures, either fragments of the pearly Cairo mosaic, or a wonderful ceiling, or gilded Kufic (old Arabian text) inscriptions and arabesques, or remains of the ancient colored glass which changes its tint hour by hour. Best of all, sometimes you find a space open to the sky, with a fountain in the centre, the whole surrounded by arcades of marble columns adorned with hanging lamps (or, rather, with the bronze chains which once carried the lamps), and with suspended ostrich eggs—the emblems of good-luck. One day, when my donkey was making his way through a dilapidated region, I came upon a mosque so small that it seemed hardly more than a base for its exquisite minaret, which towered to an unusual height above it. Of course I dismounted. The little mosque was open; but as it was never visited by strangers, it possessed no slippers, and without coverings of some kind it was impossible that unsanctified shoes, such as mine, should touch its matted floor; the bent, ancient guardian glared at me fiercely for the mere suggestion. One sees sometimes (even in 1890) in the eyes of old men sitting in the mosques the original spirit of Islam shining still. Once their religion commanded the sword; they would like to grasp it again, if they could. It was suggested that the matting might, for a backsheesh, be rolled up and put away, as the place was small. But the stern old keeper remained inflexible. Then the offer was made that so many piasters—ten (that is, fifty cents)—would be given to the blind. Now the blind are sacred in Cairo; this offer, therefore, was successful; all the matting was carefully rolled and stacked in a corner, the three or four Muslims present withdrew to the door, and the unbeliever was allowed to enter. She found herself in a temple of color which was incredibly rich. The floor was of delicate marble, and every inch of the walls was covered with a mosaic of porphyry and jasper, adorned with gilded inscriptions and bands of Kufic text; the tall pulpit, made of mahogany-colored wood, was carved from top to bottom in intricate designs, and ornamented with odd little plaques of fretted bronze; the sacred niche was lined with alabaster, turquoise, and gleaming mother-of-pearl; the only light came through the thick glass of the small windows far above, in downward-falling rays of crimson, violet, and gold. The old mosaic-work of the Cairo mosques is composed of small plates of marble and of mother-of-pearl arranged in geometrical designs; the delicacy of the minute cubes employed, and the intricacy of the patterns, are marvellous; the color is faint, unless turquoise has been added; but the glitter of the mother-of-pearl gives the whole an appearance like that of jewelry. Upon our departure five blind men were found drawn up in a line at the door. It would not have been difficult to collect fifty.

Another day, as my donkey was taking me under a stone arch, I saw on one side a flight of steps which seemed to say "Come!" At the top of the steps I found a picture. It was a mosque of the early pattern, with a large square court open to the sky. In the centre of this court was a well, under a marble dome, and here grew half a dozen palm-trees. Across the far end extended the sanctuary, which was approached through arcades of massive pillars painted in dark red bands. The pulpit was so old that it had lost its beauty; but the entire back wall of this Mecca side was covered with beautiful tiles of the old Cairo tints (turquoise-blue and dark blue), in designs of foliage, with here and there an entire tree. This splendid wall was in itself worth a journey. A few single tiles had been inserted at random in the great red columns, reminding one of the majolica plates which tease the eyes of those who care for such things—set impossibly high as they are—in the campaniles of old Italian churches along the Pisan coast.

It may be asked, What is the shape of a mosque—its exterior? What is it like? You are more sure about this shape before you reach the Khedive's city than you are when you have arrived there; and after you have visited three or four mosques each day for a week, the clearness of your original idea, such as it was, has vanished forever.

The mosques of Cairo are so embedded in other structures, so surrounded and pushed and elbowed by them, that you can see but little of their external form; sometimes a façade painted in stripes is visible, but often a doorway is all. One must except the mosque of Sultan Hassan (which, to some of us, is dangerously like Aristides the Just). This mosque stands by itself, so that you can, if you please, walk round it. The chief interest of the walk (for the exterior, save for the deep porch, which can hardly be called exterior, is not beautiful) lies in the thought that as the walls were constructed of stones brought from the pyramids, perhaps among them, with faces turned inward, there may be blocks of that lost outer coating of the giant tombs—a coating which was covered with hieroglyphics. Now that hieroglyphics can be read, we may some day learn the true history of these monuments by pulling down a dozen of the Cairo mosques. But unless the commission bestirs itself, that task will not be needed for the edifice of Sultan Hassan; it is coming down, piece by piece, unaided. The mosques of Cairo are not beautiful as a Greek temple or an early English cathedral is beautiful; the charm of Saracenic architecture lies more in decoration than in the management of massive forms. The genius of the Arabian builders manifested itself in ornament, in rich effects of color; they had endless caprices, endless fancies, and expressed them all—as well they might, for all were beautiful. The same free spirit carved the grotesques of the old churches of France and Germany. But the Arabians had no love for grotesques; they displayed their liberty in lovely fantasies. Their one boldness as architects was the minaret.

It is probably the most graceful tower that has ever been devised. In Cairo the rich fretwork of its decorations and the soft yellow hue of the stone of which it is constructed add to this beauty. Invariably slender, it decreases in size as it springs towards heaven, carrying lightly with it two or three external galleries, which are supported by stalactites, and ending in a miniature cupola and crescent. These stalactites (variously named, also, pendentives, recessed clusters, and honeycombed work) may be called the distinctive feature of Saracenic architecture. They were used originally as ornaments to mask the transition from a square court to the dome. But they soon took flight from that one service, and now they fill Arabian corners and angles and support Arabian curves so universally that for many of us the mere outline of one scribbled on paper brings up the whole pageant of the crescent-topped domes and towers of the East.

The Cairo mosques are said to allow the purest existing forms of Saracenic architecture. One hopes that this saying is true, for a dogmatic superlative of this sort is a rock of comfort, and one can remember it and repeat it. With the best of memories, however, one cannot intelligently see all these specimens of purity, unless, indeed, one takes up his residence in Cairo (and it is well known that when one lives in a place one never pays visits to those lions which other persons journey thousands of miles to see). Travellers, therefore, very soon choose a favorite and abide by it, vaunting it above all others, so that you hear of El Ghouri, with its striking façade and magnificent ceiling, as "the finest," and of Kalaoon as "the finest," and of Moaiyud as ditto; not to speak of those who prefer the venerable Touloun and Amer, and the undiscriminating crowd that is satisfied, and rightly, with Aristides the Just—that is, the mosque of Sultan Hassan. For myself, after acknowledging to a weakness for the mosques which are not in the guide-books, which possess no slippers, I confess that I admire most the tomb-mosque of Kait Bey. It is outside of Cairo proper, among those splendid half-ruined structures the so-called tombs of the Khalifs. It stands by itself, its chiselled dome and minaret, a lace-work in stone, clearly revealed. It would take pages to describe the fanciful beauty of every detail, both without and within, and there must, in any case, come an end of repeating the words "elegance" "mosaic," "minaret," "arabesque," "jasper," and "mother-of-pearl." The chief treasures of this mosque are two blocks of rose granite which bear the so-called impressions of the feet of Mohammed; the legend is that he rests here for a moment or two at sunset every Thursday. "How well I understand this fancy of the prophet!" exclaimed an imaginative visitor. "How I wish I could do the same!" [. . .]

One day when I was passing the hot hours in the shaded rooms of the [Gizah] museum surrounded by seated granite figures with their hands on their knees (the coolest companions I know), I heard chattering and laughter. These are unusual sounds in those echoing halls, where unconsciously everybody whispers, partly because of the echo, and partly also, I think, on account of the mystic mummy cases which

stand on end and look at one so queerly with their oblique eyes.
Presently there came into view ten or twelve Cairo ladies, followed by
eunuchs, and preceded by a guide. The eunuchs were (as eunuchs
generally are) hideous, though they represented all ages, from a tall
lank boy of seventeen to a withered old creature well beyond sixty.
The Cairo eunuchs are negroes; one distinguishes them always by the
extreme care with which they are dressed. They wear coats and
trousers of black broadcloth made in the latest European style, with
patent-leather shoes, and they are decorated with gold chains, seal
rings, and scarf-pins; they have one merit as regards their appearance—I know of but one—they do look clean. The ladies were taking
their ease; the muffling black silk outer cloaks, which all Egyptian
women of the upper class wear when they leave the house, had been
thrown aside; the white face veils had been loosened so that they
dropped below the chin. It was the hareem of the Minister for Foreign
Affairs; their carriages were waiting below. The most modest of
men—a missionary, for instance, or an entomologist—would, I suppose, have put them to flight; but as the tourist season was over, and
as it was luncheon-time for Europeans, no one appeared but myself,
and the ladies strayed hither and thither as they chose, occasionally
stopping to hear a few words of the explanations which the guide (a
woman also) was vainly trying to give before each important statue.
With one exception, these Cairo dames were, to say the least, extremely plump; their bare hands were deeply dimpled, their cheeks
round. They all had the same very white complexion without rose
tints; their features were fairly good, though rather thick; the eyes in
each case were beautiful—large, dark, lustrous, with sweeping lashes.
Their figures, under their loose garments, looked like feather pillows.
They were awkward in bearing and gait, but this might have been owing to the fact that their small plump feet (in white open-work cotton
stockings) were squeezed into very tight French slippers with abnor-
mally high heels, upon which it must have been difficult to balance so
many dimples. The one exception to the rule of billowy beauty was a
slender, even meagerly formed girl, who in America would pass perhaps for seventeen; probably she was three years younger. Her thin,
dark, restless face, with its beautiful inquiring eyes, was several times
close beside mine as we both inspected the golden bracelets and ear-

rings, the necklaces and fan, of Queen Ahhotpu, our sister in vanity of three thousand five hundred years ago. I looked more at her than I did at the jewels, and she returned my gaze; we might have had a conversation. What would I not have given to have been able to talk with her in her own tongue! After a while they all assembled in what is called the winter garden, an up-stairs apartment, where grass grows over the floor in formal little plots. Chairs were brought, and they seated themselves amid this aerial verdure to partake of sherbet, which the youngest eunuch handed about with a business-like air. While they were still here, much relaxed as regards attire and attitude, my attention was attracted by the rush through the outer room (where I myself was seated) of the four older eunuchs. They had been idling about; they had even gone down the stairs, leaving to the youngest of their number the task of serving the sherbet; but now they all appeared again, and the swiftness with which they crossed the outer room and dashed into the winter garden created a breeze. They called to their charges as they came, and there was a general smoothing down of draperies. The eunuchs, however, stood upon no ceremony; they themselves attired the ladies in the muffling cloaks, and refastened their veils securely, as a nurse dresses children, and with quite as much authority. I noticed that the handsomer faces showed no especial haste to disappear from view; but there was no real resistance; there was only a good deal of laughter.

I dare say that there was more laughter still (under the veils) when the cause of all this haste appeared, coming slowly up the stairs. It was a small man of sixty-five or seventy, one of my own countrymen, attired in a linen duster and a travel-worn high hat; his silver-haired head was bent over his guide-book, and he wore blue spectacles. I don't think he saw anything but blue antiquities, safely made of stone.

Hareem carriages (that is, ladies' carriages) in Cairo are large, heavily built broughams. The occupants wear thin white muslin or white tulle veils tied across the face under the eyes, with an upper band of the same material across the forehead; but these veils do not in reality hide the features much more closely than do the dotted black or white lace veils worn by Europeans. The muffling outer draperies, however, completely conceal the figure, and this makes the marked difference between them and their English, French, and American sisters in the other carriages near at hand. On the box of the brougham, with the coachman, the eunuch takes his place. To go out without a eunuch would be a humiliation for a Cairo wife; to her view, it would seem to say that she is not sufficiently attractive to require a guardian. The hareem carriage of a man of importance has not only its eunuch, but also its sais, or running footman; often two of them. These winged creatures precede the carriage; no matter how rapid the pace of the horses, they are always in advance, carrying, lightly poised in one hand, high in the air, a long lance-like wand. Their gait is the most beautiful motion I have ever seen. The Mercury of John of Bologna; the younger gods of Olympus—will these do for comparisons? One calls the sais winged not only because of his speed, but also on account of his large white sleeves (in English, angel sleeves), which, though lightly caught together behind, float out on each side as he runs, like actual wings. His costume is rich—a short velvet jacket thickly embroidered with gold; a red cap with long silken tassel; full white trousers which end at the knee, leaving the legs and feet bare; and a brilliant scarf encircling the small waist. These men are Nubians, and are admirably formed; often they are very handsome. Naturally one never sees an old one, and it is said that they die young. Their original office was to clear a passage for the carriage through the narrow, crowded streets; now that the streets are broader, they are not so frequently seen, though Egyptians of rank still employ them, not only for their hareem carriages, but for their own. They are occasionally seen, also, before the victoria or the landau of European residents; but in this case their Oriental dress accords ill with the stiff, tight Parisian costumes behind them. Now and then one sees them perched on the back seat of an English dog-cart, and here they look well; they always sit sidewise, with one hand on the back of the seat, as though ready at a moment's notice to spring out and begin flying again.

If the figures of the Cairo ladies are always well muffled, one has at least abundant opportunity to admire the grace and strength of the women of the working classes. When young they have a noble bearing. Their usual dress is a long gown of very dark blue cotton, a black head veil, and a thick black face veil that is kept in its place below the eyes by a gilded ornament which looks like an empty spool. Often their beautifully shaped slender feet are bare; the poorest are decked with anklets, bracelets, and necklaces of beads, imitation silver or brass. The men of the working classes wear blue gowns also, but the blue is of a much lighter hue; many of them, especially the farmers and farm laborers (called fellaheen), have wonderfully straight flat backs and broad, strong shoulders. Europeans, when walking, appear at a great disadvantage beside these loosely robed people; all their movements seem cramped when compared with the free, effortless step of the Arab beside them.

The Bazaars

One spends half one's time in the bazaars, perhaps. One admires them and adores them; but one feels that their attraction cannot be made clear to others by words. Nor can it be by the camera. There are a thousand photograph views of Cairo offered for sale, but, with the exception of an attempt at the gateway of the Khan Khaleel, not one copy of these labyrinths, which is a significant fact. Their charm comes from color, and this can be represented by the painter's brush alone. But even the painter can render it only in bits. From a selfish point of view we might perhaps be glad that there is one spot left on this earth whose characteristic aspect cannot be reproduced, either upon the wall or the pictured page, whose shimmering vistas must remain a purely personal memory. We can say to those who have in their minds the same fantastic vision. "Ah, *you* know!" But we cannot make others know. For what is the use of declaring that a collection of winding lanes, some of them not more than three feet broad, opening into and leading out of each other, unpaved, dirty, roofed far above, where the high stone houses end, with a lattice-work of old mats—what is the use of declaring that this maze is one of the most delightful places in the world? There is no use; one must see it to believe it.

We approach the bazaars by the Mooski, a street which has lost all its ancient attraction—which is, in fact, one of the most commonplace avenues I know. But near its end the enchantment begins, and whether we enter the flag bazaar, the lemon-colored-slipper bazaar, the gold-and-silver bazaar, the bazaar of the Soudan, the bazaar of silks and embroideries, the bazaar of Turkish carpets, or the lane of perfumes felicitously named by the donkey-boys the smell bazaar, we are soon in the condition of children before a magician's table. I defy any one to resist it. The most tired American business man looks about him with awakened interest, the lines of his face relax and turn into the wrinkles we associate with laughter, as he sees the small, frontless shops, the long-skirted merchants, and the sewing, embroidering, cross-legged crowd. The best way, indeed, to view the bazaars is to relax—to relax your ideas of time as well as of pace, and not be in a hurry about anything. Accompany some one who is buying, but do not buy yourself; then you can have a seat on the divan, and even (as a friend of the purchaser) one of those wee cups of black coffee which the merchant offers, and which, whether you like it or not, you take, because it belongs to the scene. Thus seated, you can look about at your ease.

In these days, when every one is rereading the *Arabian Nights*, the learned in Burton's translation, the outside public in Lady Burton's, even the most unmethodical of writers feels himself, in connection with Cairo, forced towards the inevitable allusion to Haroun. But once within the precincts of the Khan Khaleel, he does not need to have his fancy jogged by Burton or any one else; he thinks of the *Arabian Nights* instinctively, and "it's a poor tale," indeed, to quote Mrs. Poyser,[3] if he does not meet the one-eyed calendar in the very first booth. But, as has already been said, it is useless to describe. All one can do is to set down a few impressions. One of the first of these is the charming light. The sunshine of Egypt has a great radiance, but it has also—and this is especially visible when one looks across any breadth of landscape—a pleasant quality of softness; it is a radiance which is slightly hazy and slightly golden brown, being in these respects quite unlike the pellucid white light of Greece. The Greeks frown; even the youngest of the handsome men who go about in ballet-like white petticoats and the brimless cap, has the ugly little perpendicular line between the eyes, produced by a constant knitting of the brows. Like the Greek, the Egyptian also is without protection for his eyes; the dragoman wears a small shawl over the fez, which covers the back of the neck and sides of the face, the Bedouins have a hood, but the large majority of the natives are unprotected. It is said that a Mohammedan can have no brim to his turban or tarboosh, because he must place his bare forehead upon the ground when he says his prayers, and this without removing his head-gear (which would be irreverent). However this may be, he goes about in Egypt with the sun in his eyes, though, owing to the softer quality of the light, he does not frown as the Greek frowns. For those who are not Egyptians, however, the light in Cairo sometimes seems too omnipresent; then, for refuge, they can go to the bazaars. The sunshine is here cut off horizontally by thick walls, and from above it is filtered through mats, whose many interstices cause a checker of light and shade in an infinite variety of unexpected patterns on the ground. This ground is watered. Somehow the air is cool; coming in from the bright streets outside is like entering an arbor. The little shops resemble cupboards; their floors are about three feet above the street. They have no doors at the back. When the merchant wishes to close his establishment, he comes out, pulls down the lid, locks it, and goes home. A picturesque characteristic is that in many cases the wares are simply sold here; they are also made, one by one, upon the spot. You can see the brass-workers incising the arabesques of their trays; you can see the armorers making arms, the ribbon-makers making ribbons, the jewellers blowing their forges, the ivory-carvers bending over their delicate task. As soon as each article is finished, it is dusted and placed upon the little shelf above, and then the apprentice sets to work upon a new one. In addition to the light, another thing one notices is the amazing way in which the feet are used. In Cairo one soon becomes as familiar with feet as one is elsewhere with hands; it is not merely that they are bare; it is that the toes appear to be prehensile, like fingers. In the bazaars the embroiderers hold their cloth with their toes; the slipper-makers, the flag-cutters, the brass-workers, the goldsmiths, employ their second set of fingers almost as much as they employ the first. Both the hands and feet of these men are well formed, slender, and delicate, and, by the rules of their religion, they are bathed five times each day.

Mosques are near where they can get water for this duty. For the bazaars are not continuous rows of shops: one comes not infrequently upon the ornamental portal of an old Arabian dwelling-house, upon the forgotten tomb of a sheykh, with its low dome; one passes under stone arches; often one sees the doorway of a mosque. Humbleminded dogs, who look like jackals, prowl about. The populace trudges through the narrow lanes, munching sugar-cane whenever it can get it. Another favorite food is the lettuce-plant; but the leaves, which we use for salad, the Egyptians throw away; it is the stalk that attracts them.

Lettuce-stalks are not rich food, but the bazaars of the people who eat them convey, on the whole, an impression of richness; this is owing to the sumptuousness of the prayer carpets, the gold embroideries, the gleaming silks, the Oriental brass-work with sentences from the Koran, the ivory, the ostrich plumes, the little silver bottles for kohl, the inlaid daggers, the turquoises and pearls, and the beautiful gauzes, a few of them embroidered with the motto, "I do this work for you," and on the reverse side, "And this I do for God." To some persons, the far-penetrating mystic sweetness from the perfume bazaar adds an element also. Here sit the Persian merchants in their delicate silken robes; they weigh incense on tiny scales; they sort the gold-embossed vials of attar of roses; their taper fingers move about amid whimsically small cabinets and chests of drawers filled with ambrosial mysteries. There is magic in names; these merchants are doubly interesting because they come from Ispahan! Scanderoun—there is another; how it rolls off the tongue! We do not wish for exact geographical descriptions of these places; that would spoil all. We wish to chant, like Kit Marlowe's Tamburlaine (and with similar indefiniteness):

"Is it not passing brave to be a king,
And march in triumph through Persepolis?"

"So will I ride through Samarcanda streets,
. . . to Babylon, my lords; to Babylon!"

[. . .]

Souvenirs

As the warm spring closes, every one selects something to carry homeward. Leaving aside those fortunate persons who can purchase the ancient carved woodwork of an entire house, or Turkish carpets by the dozen, the rest of us keep watch of the selections of our friends while we make our own. Among these we find the jackets embroidered in silver and gold; the inevitable fez; two or three blue tiles of the thirteenth century; a water-jug, or kulleh; a fly-brush with ivory handle; attar of roses and essence of sandal-wood; Assiout ware in vases and stoups; a narghileh; the gauze scarfs embroidered with Persian benedictions; a koursi inlaid with mother-of-pearl; Arabian ink-stands—long cases of silver or brass, to be worn like a dagger in the belt; a keffiyeh, or delicate silken head-shawl with white knotted fringe; the Arabian finger-bowls; the little coffee-cups; images of Osiris from the tombs; a native bracelet and anklet; and, finally, a scarab or two, whose authenticity is always exciting, like an unsolved riddle. A picture of these mementos of Cairo would not be complete for some of us without two of those constant companions of so many long mornings—the dusty, shuffling, dragging, slipping, venerable, abominable mosque shoes.

Homeward-Bound

"We who pursue
Our business with unslackening stride,
Traverse in troops, with care-fill'd breast,
The soft Mediterranean side,
The Nile, the East,
And see all sights from pole to pole,
And glance and nod and bustle by,
And never once possess our soul
Before we die."

So chanted Matthew Arnold of the English of to-day. And if we are to believe what is preached to us and hurled at us, it is a reproach even more applicable to Americans than to the English themselves. One American traveller, however, wishes to record modestly a disbelief in the universal truth of this idea. Many of us are, indeed, haunted by our business; many of us do glance and nod and bustle by; it is a class, and a large class. But these hurried people are not all; an equal number of us, who, being less in haste, may be less conspicuous perhaps, are the most admiring travellers in the world. American are the bands who journey to Stratford-upon-Avon, and go down upon their knees—almost—when they reach the sacred spot; American are the pilgrims who pay reverent visits to all the English cathedrals, one after the other, from Carlisle to Exeter, from Durham to Canterbury. In the East, likewise, it is the transatlantic travellers who are so deeply impressed by the strangeness and beauty of the scenes about them that they forget to talk about their personal comforts (or, rather, the lack of them).

There is another matter upon which a word may be said, and this is the habit of judging the East from the stand-point of one's home customs, whether the home be American or English. It is, of course, easy to find faults in the social systems of the Oriental nations; they have laws and usages which are repugnant to all our feelings, which seem to us horrible. But it is well to remember that it is impossible to comprehend any nation not our own unless one has lived a long time among its people, and made one's self familiar with their traditions, their temperament, their history, and, above all, with the language which they speak. Anything less than this is observation from the outside alone, which is sure to be founded upon misapprehension. The French and the English are separated by merely the few miles of the Channel, and they have, to a certain extent, a common language; for though the French do not often understand English, the English very generally understand something of French. Yet it is said that these two nations have never thoroughly comprehended each other either as nations or individuals; and it is even added that, owing to their differing temperaments, they will never reach a clear appreciation of each other's merits; demerits, of course, are easier. Our own country has a language which is, on the whole, nearer the English tongue perhaps than is the speech of France; yet have we not felt now and then that English travellers have misunderstood us? If this is the case among people who are all Occidentals together, how much more difficult must be a thorough comprehension by us of those ancient nations who were old before we were born?

The East is the land of mystery. If one cares for it at all, one loves it; there is no half-way. If one does not love it, one really (though perhaps not avowedly) hates it—hates it and all its ways. But for those who love it the charm is so strong that no surprise is felt in reading or hearing of Europeans who have left all to take up a wandering existence there for long years or for life—the spirit of Browning's "What's become of Waring?"[4]

All of us cannot be Warings, however, and the time comes at last when we must take leave. The streets of Cairo have been for some time adorned with placards whose announcements begin, in large type, "Travellers returning to Europe." We are indeed far away when returning to Europe is a step towards home. We wait for the last festival—the Shem-en-Neseem, or Smelling of the Zephyr—the annual picnic day, when the people go into the country to gather flowers and breathe the soft air before the opening of the regular season for the Khamsin. Then comes the journey by railway to Alexandria. We wave a handkerchief (now fringed on all four sides by the colored threads of the laundresses) to the few friends still left behind. They respond; and so do all the Mustaphas, Achmets, and Ibrahims who have carried our parcels and trotted after our donkeys. Then we take a seat by the window, to watch for the last time the flying Egyptian landscape—the green plain, the tawny Nile, the camels on the bank, the villages, and the palm-trees, and behind them the solemn line of the desert.

At sunset the steamer passes down the harbor, and, pushing out to sea, turns westward. A faint crescent moon becomes visible over the Ras-et-Teen palace. It is the moon of Ramadan. Presently a cannon on the shore ushers in, with its distant sound, the great Mohammedan fast. [. . .]

16

Agnes McAllister

❦

Agnes McAllister (c. 1868–?) was a Methodist missionary in charge of the Garaway Mission Station on the Kroo Coast of West Africa. According to an inscription dated 14 August 1895, written by the Bishop of Africa in his own hand, McAllister was "a christian heroine" who "made a success in all departments of our mission work." "Miss Agnes," he writes, "has written a book. It is full of graphic delineations of what she saw, suffered, heard and did in the babble of heathen life and the ravages of war in which she took an active part as surgeon, nurse, and counselor."

In her autobiographical account, "A Call to the Work," that makes up Chapter 1 of *A Lone Woman in Africa: Six Years on the Kroo Coast* (1896), McAllister reports that, having first heard a call to Christ at the age of seven, she began at the age of nineteen to prepare to "take the good news of salvation to those in darkness." She sailed for Liberia on 13 December 1888, passing by way of Germany and Portugal, and "eight years and two months" later wrote *A Lone Woman in Africa*, addressed to "fellow-missionaries" at a time when "Africa is the land to which all eyes are being turned in these days."

A Lone Woman in Africa is a representative missionary account in at least two of its features. First, it is largely ethnographic, focused on the community rather than on individuals and organized into topical chapters (in this case sixteen of them) on people, languages, customs, burial rites, native theology and morals, neighboring tribes, farming, and house-building. Second, it constructs and measures Africa according to Christian norms ("O, the darkness of the heathen mind, all blinded with the superstitions of years, so incapable of comprehending the things of God at first, until these obstructions have moved out of the way!"). The following excerpt is Chapter 13 of McAllister's text.

A Lone Woman in Africa

The African Woman

When a child is born in Liberia some member of the family is sent at once to the devil-doctor to inquire who it is and what its name shall be.

The devil-doctor's deeds are all done in the dark. He goes up into the housetop, which is a small windowless attic used as a storeroom and rice granary. He takes with him the cowhorn. This he blows to call the devil; and the devil is supposed to tell who it is that has come back to this world. For the people believe that every newborn child is some deceased member of the family who has returned to life among them. It sometimes receives the same name it had before, and sometimes the name is changed.

When the devil-doctor has blown his horn long enough to call the devil and receive an answer he begins to tell whose child it is by describing the parents. Sometimes he has already heard of the birth and knows the family; but it sometimes happens that he has had to guess, in which case he often makes serious mistakes. The people do not always believe in him; but it is their custom to consult him, and it is hard to break it up.

After finding out who the parents are, and whether the child is a boy or a girl, the devil-doctor goes on to describe it. The inquirer must come prepared to pay for the information with plates, cloth, and tobacco. The devil-doctor may say, for example, that the child is (or was) the mother of a certain man named Scere. In that case she will be called *Scere-day*, or Scere's mother, *day* meaning "mother." If the child is a boy it will, perhaps, be declared to be some great man who has died; and if so the babe will be much respected.

When a son was born to Kalenky—one of our chief men—the father sent to the devil-doctor to inquire who it was that had returned to the earth. The doctor said it was a great warrior named Wear, and that they must train him for war, as he had come to protect them.

When this was told to the father he brought a gun, a powder case, a shot bag, a war dress, and a fringe for the waist made from palm leaf, charms for the head, neck, arms, waist, knees, and ankles, and another peculiar charm in the shape of a cake of soap. This last, moistened with a little water, was to be rubbed with the hands on the infant's skin. They say it toughens the skin so that no shot can pierce it; and a soldier that has this charm need not fear the enemy. All these things were brought and laid on a mat by the side of an infant but a few hours old.

I have sometimes seen infants without anything on their bodies, not even the string of beads which they think so necessary. A child usually wears one of these about its neck, several around its waist, and others on its wrists and ankles. When it is a few days old its ears are pierced, and small rings are put in, or, if the rings cannot be had, a piece of fine wire or a cotton thread.

The child is washed three and four times a day in hot water, and rubbed with a white mixture like paint. Every morning when it is washed several of the older women are called in. Some of them are very competent, and they take charge of the babe. A young mother is never left with the care of her child. These nurses may be seen any morning sitting on one of their common "chairs," which is no more than a stick of stove wood—outdoors if it is warm, otherwise in the house—with a pepper board by their side. They will rub one of their fingers in the pepper on the board, then thrust it as far down the child's throat as possible, and rub and stretch the throat thoroughly until the poor child is almost strangled and throws up all that is in its stomach. This looks like unmerciful treatment; but they believe it necessary to the child's health and strength. The child is then given an injection of some herb, and laid down to sleep on its little mat on the floor by the fire. Many infants die very young, and I fear that this severe treatment is sometimes to blame.

When the child gets to be nine or ten months old small bells are tied to its person, at its wrists, waist, and ankles. These are intended to coax it to walk. When it moves the bells will tinkle. Pleased by the sound, it will be induced to make another movement, and so will learn to go alone. The mother at this time will take her child to the devil-doctor, and he will make a charm for it which will be tied around the waist.

When the child begins to walk they put on its ankles the native "gless"—a kind of anklet made with several small bells in each ring. From six to ten of these are put on each ankle. No child is supposed to learn to walk without these assistants.

But to return to the children one sometimes sees not dressed in the usual way. I have inquired the reason of the mother when I have seen one of these babies looking so uncared for. I have been told that the child is supposed to be some one who has come from the spirit world only to find articles to carry back, and that if they should dress it or give it anything it would not stay, but would take the things and be gone. Therefore they do not give it anything to wear; and so, since it has nothing to take with it, it is obliged to stay here and grow up. They hope that thus it will change its mind and consent to live with its people.

When a girl is from six to ten years of age she wears on her forearm brass rods, sometimes simply twisted in a spiral, and sometimes bent into separate rings. These are put on halfway up to the elbow—put on with a hammer to stay. They are worn night and day until the flesh becomes sore. Then they may be taken off, for the scars will always be there to prove that she wore jewelry when she was young.

If a woman grows up without these marks on her arms it is a lasting source of annoyance to her; for if her neighbors become vexed with her and wish to insult her, they cast it up to her that her mother was a poor woman and could not afford to put jewelry upon her children. This is a great reproach to a woman, as they all aspire to be reputed wealthy.

The little girls, as soon as they are able to follow their mothers to the farm and the bush, go along to help them; and when they are quite small, not able even to walk all the way, the little daughters may be seen coming home from the farm with their mothers. After having carried one on her back most of the way, the mother will put her down to walk and give her a stick of wood to carry on her head, although she is too small to carry a wood rack, or "banna."

The mother always keeps on hand a small waterpot for her little daughter to learn to carry; and the child may often be seen coming along the road before or behind her mother, with the water splashing over her from the pot, in her first attempts to imitate her mother.

The father will make a little wood rack for her, and she will have a small fanner for fanning rice. Her highest ambitions are to beat her mother's rice, carry a big load of wood on her head, and have her own farm. Then she is considered by all to be a smart girl and fitted to make a smart wife for some man.

A girl is often betrothed at the age of seven, and sometimes while she is yet an infant in her mother's arms. She is sold to be the wife of whatever man may choose to purchase her.

At about the age of ten or twelve years she is taken to live with her betrothed's people, where she will be associated with him and learn "his fashion." She is supposed to study his wishes and live to please him. Some of the men make slaves of their wives, and do not consider that any of their wishes are to be consulted; while others are not so, but treat their wives with a great deal of respect and try to please them, so that they live very happily together.

The girls in Africa reach mature womanhood much earlier than in America. At the age of fourteen or fifteen they are married. The marriage ceremony is very simple. When a man takes his betrothed to be his wife he has a fowl killed and some rice cooked. They both partake of these, and it is understood by all that the pair are henceforth man and wife. They really have no marriage ceremony at all.

A man generally has one favorite wife, or head wife. A man may choose his own wife; but his family—which is the whole family connection—pays for her. Upon his death his women, who are family property, are divided up among the other members. The head wife has charge of all the rest, unless they refuse to submit to her, in which case they live entirely independent of her, while doing their part toward caring for the husband.

A man has from three to twelve wives, according to his wealth and importance. If a man has the reputation of being a good husband, he often gets wives without paying for them. They run away from other tribes and come to him, hoping to better their condition. But if their lot turns out to be no better than with their former husbands they often go back to them again.

A man in going off to his work in the morning is never sure that he will find his wife at home when he returns in the evening. It is a common thing for wives to run away; and she is considered a queer woman who at some time has not run away from her husband or for some reason been separated from him.

In going visiting a man generally takes one of his wives with him to carry his chair, light his pipe, get his bath water ready for him, run errands, and wait upon him generally.

Some of the women are very good housekeepers, and have a place for everything and keep everything in its place; while others, like some of our civilized women, never seem to have a place for anything and keep a very untidy house.

A good housewife in Africa will always rise before it is light enough to see well. To be sure, they have no clocks; but as the fowls sleep in the house, on a perch behind the fire, the roosters are as good as an alarm clock, for they never fail to crow at three o'clock, and again at the break of day. It is thus an easy matter to wake up at about the same time every morning—much easier than to sleep, for the hens will descend from their perch and wander about, walking over the sleepers stretched on the floor, unless some one rises and opens the door to let them out.

I know this to be a fact, for I have often slept in the native houses. One night five of us slept in a circular house fifteen feet in diameter, with twenty-one fowls on the perch, a fire burning, and the doors shut tight, so as not to allow any witch to enter. It really felt as if there were some witch inside, and I fear there was more there to harm us than there could have been outside.

The first thing in the morning after letting the chickens out is to light the fire, which has generally died out, or almost out, during the night. The next is to fill the large pot with bath water from the waterpot. While the bath water is being heated the woman refills her waterpots. Generally by the time she has this done the others are up, and she can sweep her floor. When the bath water is hot she has her bath, taking with her, it may be, her child of three years, who is washed with the same towel and water. She combs her own hair, as well as that of the child; then, putting a little native perfume on her hands, rubs some on her own face and body. The child is treated in the same way. She is then ready for the day's work.

The remnant of the evening meal is warmed up for breakfast, often a little cassada or some other vegetable being cooked to eat with it. After breakfast is eaten, if it is not the rice-planting or cutting season, the housewife takes her "banna" (wood rack) on her head, and her ax and cutlass, and with her baby on her back, goes to her vegetable farm. She weeds out some of the grass, then takes up some vegetables to carry home with her, planting new ones in their place. Then gathering a rack-full of wood she returns to the village.

Perhaps, in the meantime, one of the other wives has given the husband his morning bath, and now it is her turn to give him water for his evening bath. In warm weather he may prefer cold water; but if it is at all cool he wants his bath hot—and the natives can bathe in very hot water.

She then has her rice to beat. It has been placed in the morning in the rack over the fire to dry. She now takes it down, carefully picking up every kernel that may drop, and puts it into her mortar and, with a heavy stick about seven feet long and as large around as she can well hold in her hand, beats it till she can see the chaff coming off. She then puts it into her fanner and fans it in the wind till the loose chaff is blown away. This process of beating and fanning is repeated until all the rice is cleaned. Then she sits down and picks out all the chaff that cannot be fanned out, and the rice is ready for cooking.

In preparing a meal the rice is cooked first, and taken off the fire to simmer over some coals that are drawn out on the floor. Next, the palm butter is made and set aside to cool, for no good cook will serve food that is hot enough to burn one. Finally the vegetables are cooked. These are better eaten hot, and therefore are cooked last. This is all done over a single fire as a rule; but in some cases, when the meal is wanted in a hurry, two fires are lighted, and the dinner is soon ready.

Generally, however, there is no hurry. They do not eat the evening meal—which is dinner—until dark. If it is ready earlier they often wait around until after dark before eating it. This is the big meal of the day. When they eat a hearty meal before retiring, they do without much breakfast in the morning, and sometimes with only a very light lunch, and that not until late in the day.

In "farm-cutting" time they cook a good meal in the morning for the men, for the work is hard. After it has continued for some weeks and the men are getting tired the women prepare the breakfast and take it to the men in the field about eleven o'clock.

This period of "farm-cutting" is the woman's time to obtain a supply of wood. Every day she goes forth, and returns with all the wood she can carry, piling it away neatly in the wood rack to dry for the rainy season. The sticks are about two feet long; and most of their wood is cut from small saplings. With a cutlass, they hack the stick all around, leaving a little bit in the center which is broken off. This leaves one end of the stick of wood all slivered.

These ends are all turned out in the wood rack. When the wood is dry it lights readily, as it is always put into the fire slivered end first. A woman takes great pride in having her house well stowed with wood, and when it is done feels as happy as we do when the bins are filled with the winter's coal.

A very ambitious woman will sometimes take her cutlass and go to help her husband cut farm. But as a rule the women have nothing to do with the farm till it is time for the planting, which is all done by them.

The men build little green booths on the farm, where the pots are often taken to the farm. Sometimes members of the family sleep there, and the victuals are carried out and cooked there. The women take their babies, and everybody turns out to plant rice.

As soon as the rice is up they have to watch the ricebirds, or they will pull it all out of the ground. Then the grass begins to grow, as the ground has not been broken, and it must all be weeded out. The men generally help with this, as well as in keeping the birds from the rice.

When the rice is ripe all hands turn out to cut it, the women being quite as good at this work as the men. While the men may leave the field for other things, the women feel that they must be constantly there until the rice is all out.

When it is cut and brought to town the women begin to dance; and even before the harvest is finished the evening hours are often spent by the younger people in having a good time. But after the harvest is completed the women especially spend several weeks in dancing and feasting. Great pots of rice are cooked, and everybody enjoys himself.

The women go on dancing parties from town to town, and are entertained by their friends. Often a bullock is killed for the visitors, and they dance all night, and as much of the day as they can stand; and it is the duty of the visitors to show the same honor to the hosts when the visit is returned.

The last months of the year are spent in house building. As the native houses begin to decay in about five years much time is spent in making repairs. It is a good house, and one that has been well cared for, that will last fourteen years. The thatch used for roofing often has to be brought a long distance, and always on the head; for the people have no wagons or carts, not even a wheelbarrow, and no roads except narrow footpaths.

The men go out to the bush, cut the leaves, and start home with them, and their wives meet them on the road and carry the burden the rest of the way. The timbers of the house frame may also need to be carried a long distance, and a good wife is often seen following her husband in the road, with as heavy a load of building poles on her head as he bears on his.

When the house is up and the woodwork pretty well finished the women begin to plaster. The walls are made of narrow pieces of native plank set on end, and need a great deal of plastering on account of the numerous holes. A woman seldom plasters her house alone, but she will invite her neighbor's wife in to help her, and in turn will assist her neighbor when she may be in need. In this way the work is lightened.

The floor is the last thing to be put into a house. The women bring the mud or clay for the floor. The men often help to beat it; but it has to be washed over with a substance which they call "bleen," and this the women always do.

The women can hardly be called fishermen, as the men consider that their work. But there are many shellfish that the women gather, and a very small fish called "necklies," which they catch with a cloth. Four women go together to fish in this way. They wade out into the river until they see a school of these fish. Then they arrange the cloth in the water, two of them holding it, while the other two surround the fish and drive them into the cloth, which is then gathered up like a net, and the fish emptied out into a brass kettle or a bucket brought for the purpose. Then the cloth is let down for another draught. When they are through they divide the fish and return home. These are the smallest fish I ever saw them take for food, being not over three quarters of an inch long.

They also set traps to catch a fish resembling the eel. In time of high water they set these traps in swamps or marshy places. Crabs are often caught along with the fish, and these are generally dried and put away for the dry season, when fish are not so easily taken.

In time of war the women are the messengers, as the warriors— every man is a warrior—are not allowed to go to the enemy's town. A man's life would not be safe; but the women can go in safety, and, as a rule, they are allowed to return. Sometimes they are imprisoned; but if it is known that they have been sent by the other tribe with a message of peace they are generally well received and allowed to return to their homes in peace.

When a woman becomes old and not able to earn more than her own living the husband's attention is generally devoted to his new and younger wives, and his first wife, now being neglected, seeks a better home among her children, generally with one of her sons.

I remember one of these neglected wives, an old woman, who had lived for several years with her daughter. The daughter died, and the old woman's husband, seeing that his first wife's child had died and that she was now homeless, felt it his duty to take her back. He built a little home for her near his own, and supported her in her feeble old age.

When a woman dies all the women turn out to dance, for it is a great honor to the dead to have a good dance at the funeral. Since they all want to be buried with honors they try to be present at every dance, so that when they die themselves everybody will make an effort to be present and dance for them.

When an old person dies the natives never say that some one has witched them, but that their time is finished and God has taken them.

The women exert great influence over the men. In their palavers they do not generally call on the women to say anything unless they have a serious question to settle, when they call upon the women to help them decide.

In case of war, if all the soldiers wished to go and fight, and the women rose up and said, "No, we are not willing, you must not do so," they would all be afraid to go, fearing defeat; for they say, "Woman got witch past man," and they are afraid to displease them for fear of being witched, and so defeated or killed.

Every town has its head woman, and when any person has done what the women think deserves punishment, the men keep silence and do not interfere. I have scarcely found a single man that had courage enough to face the women at such a time and say, "This thing that you are doing is wrong; it shall not be done." I have sometimes asked why it is that the men are afraid to oppose the women, and been told, "Well, woman is the mother of man, and we ought to listen to her."

Some of the women are remarkably good speakers. Not every woman would attempt to rise in a meeting of the people to give her reasons why certain things ought or ought not to be done. But they have certain women who are recognized as public speakers.

The woman in our tribe who was considered the best speaker was called "Queede." I have seen her standing in the midst of a crowd of people seated on the ground—kings, chiefs, soldiers, and women—and talking to them with just as much earnestness and decision, and receiving as much attention, as any man I ever saw.

If the women have anything to say they meet by themselves and then appoint one or more of their best talkers to speak for them in the general council.

Woman is not the downtrodden creature in Liberia that she is in India and many other heathen lands. Yet it is harder to reach the women than the men. They do not seem to have the same desire to rise out of heathenism and receive Jesus. This may be from the fact that they have been more confined to their homes and have not seen so much of the world, and do not realize the benefits of civilization. But some of the women are coming out, and they make good workers when they are saved.

Notes

Notes for the Introduction

1. *The Art of the Novel: Critical Prefaces* (New York: Charles Scribner's Sons, 1962), 48, 56; *The Custom of the Country* (New York: Charles Scribner's Sons, 1913), 360, 382.

2. *The Fortunate Pilgrims: Americans in Italy, 1800–1860* (Cambridge, Mass.: Harvard University Press, 1964), 20.

3. Allison Lockwood, *Passionate Pilgrims: The American Traveler in Great Britain, 1800–1914* (Rutherford: Fairleigh Dickinson University Press, 1981), 283.

4. "American Girls in Europe," *North American Review* 150 (1890): 681.

5. Figures compiled from *American Travellers Abroad: A Bibliography of Accounts Published Before 1900*, ed. Harold Smith (Carbondale: The Library, Southern Illinois University, 1969). Men, in comparison, published approximately 1,605 books of foreign travel, including sailors' accounts and diplomatic memoirs, with sections on the following: 92 on travel in China; 145 on travel in Palestine; 99 on travel in India; 190 on travel in Egypt; 22 on travel in the East Indies; 118 on travel in Greece; 30 on travel in Arabia; 27 on travel in Algeria; and 57 on travel in Africa.

6. Preface to Mrs. M. and Emma Straiton, *Two Lady Tramps Abroad* (1881), iii. Straiton continues his preface, "Business men in our country can seldom take the time for foreign travel, and being myself unable to get away, I was willing to let them find their own way abroad. . . . The journey gave the materials of enjoyment and instruction for life; while the splendid health in which they returned was partial recompense to those left at home for their ten months of absence" (iii–v).

7. See *Narrative of a Voyage to the Ethiopic and South Atlantic Ocean, Indian Ocean, Chinese Sea, North and South Pacific Ocean, in the Years 1829, 1830, 1831* (New York: Harper, 1833).

8. *Memoir of Mrs. Elizabeth B. Dwight* (1840). Quoted in David Finnie, *Pioneers East: The Early American Experience in the Middle East* (Cambridge, Mass.: Harvard University Press, 1967), 204.

9. See *Tent and Harem: Notes of an Oriental Trip* (New York: Appleton, 1859).

10. See Finnie, *Pioneers East*, 160–61.

11. *Algerian Memories; a Bicycle Tour over the Atlas of the Sahara* (New York: Randolph, 1895), 32–33.

12. Paul Fussell, *Abroad: British Literary Traveling between the Wars* (New York: Oxford University Press, 1980), 39.

13. Leo Hamalian, Introduction, *Ladies on the Loose: Women Travellers of the 18th and 19th Centuries*, ed. Leo Hamalian (New York: Dodd, Mead, 1981), x.

14. Information about sailing ships is taken from Lockwood, *Passionate Pilgrims*, 147–48; 292–97.

15. Lockwood, *Passionate Pilgrims*, 297.

16. *European Leaflets for Young Ladies*, by Evangeline (New York: John F. Baldwin, Printer, 1861).

17. See Sara Mills, *Discourses of Difference: An Analysis of Women's Travel Writing and Colonialism* (London: Routledge, 1991).

18. *Disorderly Conduct: Visions of Gender in Victorian America* (New York: Oxford University Press, 1985), 176. See also Sara M. Evans, *Born for Liberty: A History of Women in America* (New York: Macmillan, 1989). For the trope of separate spheres, see Linda K. Kerber, "Separate Spheres, Female Worlds, Woman's Place: The Rhetoric of Women's History," *The Journal of American History* 75 (June 1988): 9–39.

19. Anne Firor Scott reminds us that nineteenth-century American women occupied an ideological spectrum that ranged from radical feminists on the one hand to conventional women on the other, with many women in between and many in motion, moving toward the feminist end of the spectrum. The travel books of American women show that female travelers occupy all points on the spectrum. See *Making the Invisible Woman Visible* (Urbana: University of Illinois Press, 1984), 37–63. See also Karen Blair, *The Clubwoman as Feminist: True Womanhood Redefined, 1868–1914* (New York: Holmes & Meier, 1980).

20. Paul Fussell, *Abroad*, 38.

21. *Round-the-World Letters* (Boston: Lathrop, 1882), 14–15.

22. *Two Summers in the Ice-Wilds of Eastern Karakoram* (New York: E. P. Dutton, 1914), 222–23.

23. *All in the Day's Work: An Autobiography* [1939] (Rpt. Boston: G. K. Hall, 1985), 114.

24. *Beaten Paths; or, a Woman's Vacation* (Boston: Lee and Shepard, 1874), 9–10.

25. Introduction, *Ladies on the Loose*, x.

26. Florence Harley, *The Ladies' Book of Etiquette and Manual of Politeness; Being a Complete Hand-Book for the Use of a Lady in Polite Society* (1872).

27. *A Summer in England* (1891), 6–7.

28. *The Bonds of Womanhood: "Woman's Sphere" in New England, 1780–1835* (New Haven: Yale University Press, 1977).

29. Thompson, *Beaten Paths*, 11–12.

30. Dorothy Middleton reports that British women travelers insisted on ladylike dress as well. Middleton says of Mary Kingsley that "forthright and original as she was, an arch-enemy of humbug, [she] would rather have `mounted a public scaffold' than have clothed her `earthward extremities' in these garments [trousers], and she even went so far as to insist that a skirt was more suitable for jungle travel" (*Victorian Lady Travellers* [New York: E. P. Dutton, 1965], 8). Patricia Marks charts the reaction to "mannish fashions" and "rational dress" in *Bicycles, Bangs, and Bloomers: The New Woman in the Popular Press* [Lexington: University Press of Kentucky, 1990), 147–73. See also Mary Russell, *The Blessings of a Good Thick Skirt: Women Travellers and Their World* (London: Collins, 1986), who finds that, as her title suggests, skirts were sometimes useful.

31. In 1800, there were 47,000 Free Blacks living in the North, a number that increased to 225,000 by 1860. I have compiled information about the situation of African American women from the documents and editorial commentary in *We Are Your Sisters: Black Women in the Nineteenth Century*, ed. Dorothy Sterling (New York: Norton, 1984).

32. Quoted in Sterling, *We Are Your Sisters*, 177.

33. Ibid., 146–47.

34. Ibid., 180.

35. Ibid., 207.

36. Ibid., 392.

37. Ibid., 403, 410.

38. Figures compiled from, *American Travellers Abroad*. The trajectory of published travel books (and memoirs and sailors' accounts in the case of men) across the decades of the century is as follows: before 1830, none by women and 91 by men; during the 1830s, 4 by women and 76 by men; during the 1840s, 7 by women and 148 by men; during the 1850s, 16 by women and 261 by men; during the 1860s, 13 by women and 119 by men; during the 1870s, 33 by women and 215 by men; during the 1880s, 57 by women and 320 by men; during the 1890s, 65 by women and 340 by men.

39. Baker, *Fortunate Pilgrims*, 213–24.

40. *Imperial Eyes: Travel Writing and Transculturation* (London: Routledge, 1992), 171.

41. Evans, *Born for Liberty*, 127.

42. Pratt, *Imperial Eyes*, 160–70.

43. See Percy Adams, ed. *Travel Literature through the Ages: An Anthology* (New York: Garland, 1988), xxiii; and Terry Caesar, "'Counting the Cats in Zanzibar': American Travel Abroad in American Travel Writing to 1914," *Prospects: An Annual of American Cultural Studies*, ed. Jack Salzman, vol. 13 (Cambridge: Cambridge University Press, 1988), 95–134.

44. For women's relationship to discontinuous forms, see Estelle Jelinek, *Women's Autobiography: Essays in Criticism*, ed. Estelle Jelinek (Bloomington: Indiana University Press, 1980), 19.

45. *One Way Round the World* (Indianapolis: Bowen-Merrill, 1899), 48.

46. *Bits of Travel. By H. H.* (Boston: Osgood, 1872), 244.

47. *Corona and Coronet* (1898), v–vi.

48. Estimates compiled from Smith, *American Travellers Abroad*.

49. *A Fictive People: Antebellum Economic Development and the American Reading Public* (New York: Oxford University Press, 1993), 176–79.

50. See Nina Baym, "Women and the Republic: Emma Willard's Rhetoric of History," *American Quarterly* 43 (March 1991): 1–23.

51. See Susan Coultrap-McQuin, *Doing Literary Business: American Women Writers in the Nineteenth Century* (Chapel Hill: University of North Carolina Press, 1990).

52. Preface, *Scenes in China, or Sketches of the Country, Religion, and Customs of the Chinese* (Philadelphia: American Baptist Publication Society, 1852).

53. *The Beaten Track: European Tourism, Literature, and the Ways to Culture, 1800–1918* (Oxford: Clarendon Press, 1993), 158.

54. *Peterson's Magazine* (August 1857): 315.

55. *Two Women Abroad; What They Saw and How They Lived While Traveling among the Semi-Civilized People of Morocco, the Peasants of Italy and France, As Well As the Educated Classes of Spain, Greece, and Other Countries* (Chicago: Monarch Book Co., 1897), vii.

56. *Europe Through a Woman's Eye* (Philadelphia: Lutheran Publication Society, 1883), 225.

57. *Letters from the Old World. By a Lady of New York*, 2 vols. (New York: Harpers, 1839), 124–25; *Letters from Abroad to Kindred at Home . . . by the Author of "Hope Leslie,"* 2 vols. (New York: Harper, 1841), 52–53; *Round-the-World Letters*, 164.

58. Abby Jane Morrell, *Narrative of a Voyage to the Ethiopic and South Atlantic Ocean, Indian Ocean, Chinese Sea, North and South Pacific Ocean, in the Years 1829, 1830, 1831* (New York: Harper, 1833), and Banks, *Campaigns of Curiosity: Journalistic Adventures of an American Girl in London* (Chicago: F. Tennyson Neely, 1894).

59. Buzard, *The Beaten Track*, 140, 149.

Notes for Emma Hart Willard

1. Willard's hope stands on events such as the Greek War of Independence (1821) and the Treaty of Andrianople (1829), in which Turkey recognized Greek autonomy. She was a staunch supporter of Greek independence.

2. Reference to the Revolution of 1830.

3. The ministers of Charles X (last of the Bourbon kings of France, deposed in July 1830 and followed by the July Monarchy) were challenged by liberals and by the working classes during a prolonged period of unrest.

Notes for Abby Jane Morrell

1. *A Narrative of Four Voyages to the South Sea, North & South Pacific Sea, Chinese Sea, Ethiopic and southern Atlantic ocean, Indian & Antarctic ocean. From the year 1822 to 1831.* (New York: Harper, 1832).

2. Reference to Liberia, founded in 1821 when officials of the American Colonization Society took possession of Cape Mesurado. American Black settlers were landed in 1822, the first of some 15,000 to settle in Liberia.

3. Jehudi Ashmun, agent of the American Colonization Society.

4. A cholera epidemic swept urban centers in the United States in 1832.

5. British novelists Hannah More (1745–1833) and Maria Edgeworth (1767–1849); British poet Felicia Hemans (1793–1835); American poet Lydia Sigourney (1791–1865); and American novelist Catharine Maria Sedgwick (1789–1867).

Notes for Sarah Rogers Haight

1. Quoted in Susan B. Huntington's edition of a "first series" of letters, compiled from the transcript that Haight's son, David, gathered in 1916 from slips of the *New York American* and available at the New York Public Library under the title *Travels of Sarah R. Haight through Switzerland, Austria-Hungary.*

2. David Porter (1780–1843), *Constantinople and Its Environs* (1835).

3. Opera by C. M. Weber, first performed in 1821.

4. Character in George Colman's play, *New Hay at the Old Market*

(first played in 1795), who, an actor, quotes Shakespeare when both awake and asleep.

Notes for Catharine Maria Sedgwick

1. Scottish dramatist and poet (1762–1851).

2. Henry Mackenzie (1745–1831), author of *The Man of Feeling* (1771) and other fiction.

3. Frances Trollope (1780–1863) gave great offense to Americans with her *Domestic Manners of Americans* (1832), stirring defensive responses that seep into many American accounts of travel to Great Britain.

4. William Ellery Channing (1780–1842), leading opponent of Calvinism who prepared the way for Transcendentalism and other advanced social and cultural movements.

5. William H. Prescott (1796–1859), author of several histories. Sedgwick refers here to the *History of Ferdinand and Isabella* (1838).

6. William Paley (1743–1805), exponent of theological utilitarianism and of proofs for the existence of God in the design of natural phenomena, particularly in the human body.

7. British advocates of reform.

8. Frances Trollope, Basil Hall, and eventually Charles Dickens, Frederick Marryat, Thomas Hamilton, and Charles Augustus Murray were the chief offenders.

Notes for Caroline Kirkland

1. William Wilberforce (1759–1833) and Thomas Clarkson (1760–1846) campaigned for the abolition of the slave trade, achieved in 1807, and the suppression of the institution of slavery throughout the British Empire, achieved in 1833.

2. Kirkland refers to travelers to America such as Frances Trollope and Basil Hall, whose opinions offended many Americans.

3. Because American copyright law protected only American authors, the books of English writers were unprotected and free spoil in the United States. The American law of 1891 providing international copyright ended a century of controversy.

4. Basil Hall (1788–1844), whose three-volume *Travels in North America* (1826) was roundly protested in the United States.

Notes for Margaret Fuller Ossoli

1. Laws designed to regulate Sunday activities.

2. Sobriquet applied to America and the American people.

3. The years 1848 and 1849 were marked by revolutionary outbreaks. Pope Pius IX, who reigned from 1846 to 1878, put himself at the head of a

movement for reform in order to bring about a confederation of the Italian states under papal supremacy. He was frightened, however, by the demands of the populace and fled to Gaeta in 1848, to be restored to Rome by the French in 1850, after which he remained an uncompromising conservative.

4. Nicolas Charles Victor Oudinot (1791–1863) commanded the French expedition of 1849 against Rome.

5. For Gaeta, see note 3 above.

6. King Bomba was the nickname given in Italy to Ferdinand II, King of the Two Sicilies, from his bombardment of Messina and other cities during the revolutionary activities of 1849. Charles Albert, king of Sardinia from 1831 to 1849, joined the movement of Italian independence from Austria in 1848 and, defeated at Novara, abdicated in 1849. Vincenzo Gioberti (1801–1852), an Italian philosopher and politician, was chaplain to Charles Albert of Sardinia in 1831 and became premier of Sardinia in 1848 and ambassador at Paris from 1849 to 1851. Leopold of Tuscany (1797–1870), Grand Duke of Tuscany from 1824 to 1859, granted a liberal constitution in 1847 that he abolished in 1852 under pressure from the pope and other conservatives. Joseph Wenzel Radetzsky (1766–1858), Austrian field commander, became commander in Italy in 1831 and governor of upper Italy from 1849 to 1857. Louis Bonaparte was the nephew of Napoleon I and president of France from 1848 to 1852, during the Second Republic.

7. Lewis Cass Jr. was appointed chargé d'affaires to the Papal States in 1849.

8. Richard Rush was appointed minister of France by President Polk in 1847, during the closing days of the July Monarchy. Without consultation with anyone, Rush recognized the French Republic.

9. Confidential advisers to the pope.

10. Marie Joseph, Marquis de Lafayette (1757–1834), was an enthusiast for the American Revolution, a major general under George Washington, and a leader of the moderates in the July Revolution (1830) in France. Having negotiated French aid for America during the American Revolution and having revisited the United States from 1824 to 1825, arriving to an unparalleled welcome, he became a popular symbol of the bond between France and the United States.

Notes for Nancy Prince

1. I have used *A Black Woman's Odyssey through Russia and Jamaica: The Narrative of Nancy Prince* (New York: Markus Weiner, 1990), which includes an informative introduction by Ronald G. Walters.

Notes for Harriet Beecher Stowe

1. Anthony Ashley Cooper Shaftesbury (1801–1885), seventh earl of Shaftesbury, active in movements to protect the poor and the working classes.

2. Perhaps the wife of President John Tyler, and probably a letter in response to criticism of the United States by such British travelers as Mrs. Trollope and Basil Hall.

3. In the original, an architect's print is inserted here and on two subsequent pages indicated in Stowe's text.

Notes for Julia Ward Howe

1. Historian Auguste Laugel (1830–1914) wrote *Les Etats-Unis pendant la guerre*, immediately translated into English as *The United States during the War* (Paris and New York: G. Baillière and Baillière Bros., 1866), a book that saw several editions and was preceded by "La Guerre Civile aux Etats-Unis, 1861–1863" in the *Revue des Deux Mondes* (15 October 1863). Laugel defends the prosecution of the Civil War against its foreign critics.

2. Having raised funds in Boston and New York, the Howes had undertaken this trip to come to the aid of Cretan refugees rebelling against Turkish rule. The "rigid veteran" is Howe's husband.

3. She had first visited Rome in the winter of 1850–1851.

4. Frances Mulligan Hill and Dr. John H. Hill went to Athens in 1831 to superintend schools for the Greeks. Frances founded a school for girls, supported by Emma Willard's Troy Society for the Advancement of Education in Greece, in which she trained teachers from 1834 to 1842.

Notes for Helen Hunt Jackson

1. Writer (1806–1884) on architecture and author of *The Archaeology of Rome* (1874–1876).

2. From a story (c. 1836) by Joseph Saintine about the love of a prisoner for a flower in the prison yard.

3. Although the protectorate of Napoleon III over the Papal States, delaying the annexation of the city of Rome to Italy, had ended by 1870 (a decade before Jackson published *Bits of Travel*), the papacy refused to concede the loss of its temporal power, and relations between the Italian government and the papacy remained a major problem until 1929.

4. The night air in Rome was thought to carry Roman fever, malaria.

Notes for Kate Field

1. French pianist, composer, and piano manufacturer (1806–1888).

2. Characters from D. W. Jerrold's *Mrs. Caudle's Curtain Lectures*

(1846), in which Mrs. Caudle lectures her husband on domestic subjects when he wants only to go to sleep.

3. Barmecide is a patronymic from the story of the Barber's Sixth Brother in the *Arabian Nights*, in which imaginary dishes are placed before a beggar. Thus, the phrase refers to one who offers illusory benefits.

4. Noted for drollery and wit in conversation (1771–1845).

5. Hood (1835–1874) edited a comic paper, *Fun*, and *Tom Hood's Comic Annual*. For Jerrold, see note 2 above.

6. Iron-flavored mineral springs.

Notes for Lucy Seaman Bainbridge

1. In 1870, nuns and priests and French officials were murdered in a Confucian reaction against the advance of Christians into China.

Notes for Elizabeth Cochrane Seaman

1. *A Flying Trip Around the World in Seven Stages* (New York: Harper, 1891).

2. See, for example, Lilian Leland, *Traveling Alone: A Woman's Journey Around the World* (New York: American News Co., 1890).

Notes for Fanny Bullock Workman

1. They had been advised earlier to go to Tlemcen by rail because Arab dogs, Workman writes, "are dangerous, and attack strangers in troups. This was not encouraging, particularly to a woman whose skirts had previously sustained manifold injuries at the mouths of Swiss and Italian dogs. Even the thought of our revolvers and dog-whips did not quite dispel the gloomy impression produced by this statement of the phlegmatic skipper."

2. Marie Edmé Patrice de MacMahon, governor general of Algeria from 1864–1870.

Notes for Constance Fenimore Woolson

1. Henry Gaze and Sons, a firm that published a series of travel guides.

2. Greek philosopher, historian, and geographer, 638 B.C., whose *Geographia* (seventeen books) exists in modern editions and translations.

3. Garrulous character in George Eliot's *Adam Bede* (1859).

4. One of Browning's "Dramatic Romances" (1842), in which the wandering Waring is last seen off the Illyrian coast in a light bark, sailing into the sunset.

Selected Bibliography

Primary Sources

Bainbridge, Lucy Seaman. *Round-the-World Letters: Five Hundred and Forty-Two Pages of Charming Pen Pictures by the Way. A Graphic Portrayal of Scenes, Incidents and Adventures of a Two Years' Tour of the World.* Boston: Lathrop, 1882.

Field, Kate. *Hap-Hazard.* Boston: Osgood, 1873.

[Haight, Sarah Rogers]. *Letters from the Old World. By a Lady of New York.* 2 Vols. New York: Harper.

Howe, Julia Ward. *From the Oak to the Olive: A Plain Record of a Pleasant Journey.* Boston: Lee & Shepard, 1868.

[Jackson, Helen Hunt]. *Bits of Travel. By H. H.* Boston: Osgood, 1872.

Kirkland, Mrs. [Caroline Stansbury]. *Holidays Abroad; or, Europe from the West.* New York: Baker & Scribner, 1849.

McAllister, Agnes. *A Lone Woman in Africa: Six Years on the Kroo Coast.* New York: Hunt and Eaton, 1896.

Morrell, Abby Jane. *Narrative of a Voyage to the Ethiopic and South Atlantic Ocean, Indian Ocean, Chinese Sea, North and South Pacific Ocean, in the Years 1829, 1830, 1831.* New York: Harper, 1833.

Ossoli, Margaret Fuller. *At Home and Abroad; or, Things and Thoughts in America and Europe.* Ed. Arthur B. Fuller. Boston: Roberts Bros., 1895.

[Prince, Nancy Gardner]. *A Narrative of the Life and Travels of Mrs. Nancy Prince.* Boston: N. Prince, 1850; 1853. Rpt. *A Black Woman's Odyssey through Russia and Jamaica: The Narrative of Nancy Prince.* Introduction by Ronald G. Walters. New York: Markus Weiner, 1990.

[Seaman, Elizabeth Cochrane]. *Nellie Bly's Book: Around the World in Seventy-Two Days.* New York: Pictorial Weeklies Co., 1890.

[Sedgwick, Catharine Maria]. *Letters from Abroad to Kindred at Home . . . by the Author of "Hope Leslie."* 2 Vols. New York: Harper, 1841.

Stowe, Harriet Beecher, Mrs. *Sunny Memories of Foreign Lands.* 2 Vols. Boston: Phillips, Sampson, 1854.

Willard, Emma. *Journal and Letters, from France and Great-Britain.* Troy, N.Y.: Tuttle, 1833.

Woolson, Constance Fenimore. *Mentone, Cairo, and Corfu.* New York: Harper, 1896.

Workman, Fanny Bullock, and William Hunter Workman. *Algerian Memories; A Bicycle Tour over the Atlas to the Sahara.* New York: Randolph, 1895.

Selected Secondary Sources on Individual Travelers

Adams, John R. *Harriet Beecher Stowe.* New York: Twayne, 1989.

Banning, Evelyn I. *Helen Hunt Jackson.* New York: Vanguard, 1973.

Baym, Nina. "Women and the Republic: Emma Willard's Rhetoric of History." *American Quarterly* 43 (March 1991): 1–23.

Chevigny, Bell Gale. *The Woman and the Myth: Margaret Fuller's Life and Writings.* Old Westbury, N.Y.: The Feminist Press, 1976.

Clifford, Deborah P. *Mine Eyes Have Seen the Glory: A Biography of Julia Ward Howe.* Boston: Little Brown, 1978.

Coultrap-McQuin, Susan. *Doing Literary Business: American Women Writers in the Nineteenth Century.* Chapel Hill: University of North Carolina Press, 1990. Contains information on Stowe and Jackson.

Foster, Edward Halsey. *Catharine Maria Sedgwick.* New York: Twayne, 1974.

Foster, Frances Smith. "Adding Color and Contour to Early American Self-Portraiture: Autobiographical Writings of Afro-American Women." In *Conjuring: Black Women, Fiction, and Literary Tradition,* eds. Marjorie Pryse and Hortense J. Spillers. Bloomington: Indiana University Press, 1985. Pp. 23–38. Contains information on Prince.

_____. *Written by Herself: Literary Production by African American Women, 1746–1892.* Bloomington: Indiana University Press, 1993. Contains information on Prince.

Hedrick, Joan D. *Harriet Beecher Stowe.* New York: Oxford University Press, 1993.

Kelley, Mary. "Catharine Maria Sedgwick." *Legacy* 6 (Fall 1989): 43–49.

Kroeger, Brooke. *Nellie Bly: Daredevil, Reporter, Feminist.* New York: Times Books, 1994.

Leverenz, David. *Manhood and the American Renaissance.* Ithaca: Cornell University Press, 1989. Contains information on Kirkland.

Middleton, Dorothy. *Victorian Lady Travelers.* New York: Dutton, 1965. Contains information on Workman.

Moore, Rayburn S. *Constance Fenimore Woolson.* New York: Twayne, 1963.

National Cyclopedia of American Biography. 63 vols. New York: James White, 1933. Contains information on Bainbridge (vol. 23, p. 159).

Notable American Women, 1607–1950: A Biographical Dictionary. 4 vols. Cambridge: Harvard University Press, 1971. Contains information on

Field (vol. 1, pp. 612–14), Fuller (vol. 1, pp. 678–82), Howe (vol. 2, pp. 225–29), Jackson (vol. 2, pp. 259–61), Kirkland (vol. 2, pp. 337–39), Seaman (vol. 3, 253–55), Sedgwick (vol. 3, pp. 256–58), Stowe (vol. 3, pp. 393–402), Willard (vol. 3, pp. 610–13), Woolson (vol. 3, pp. 670–71), and Workman (vol. 3, pp. 672–74).

Osborne, William S. *Caroline M. Kirkland (1801–1864).* New York: Twayne, 1972.

Pioneers of Women's Education in the United States: Emma Willard, Catherine Beecher, Mary Lyon. Ed. Willystine Goodsell. New York: McGraw-Hill, 1931.

Richards, Laura E., and Maud Howe Elliott. *Julia Ward Howe, 1819–1910.* Boston: Houghton Mifflin, 1916.

Ross, Ishbel. *Sons of Adam, Daughters of Eve.* New York: Harper Row, 1969. Contains information on Field.

Schriber, Mary Suzanne. "Julia Ward Howe and the Travel Book." *The New England Quarterly* 62 (June 1989): 264–79.

Stern, Madeleine B. *The Life of Margaret Fuller.* 2d ed. New York: Greenwood Press, 1992.

Stowe, William W. "Conventions and Voices in Margaret Fuller's Travel Writing." *American Literature* 63 (June 1991): 242–62.

Torsney, Cheryl B. *Constance Fenimore Woolson: The Grief of Artistry.* Athens: University of Georgia Press, 1989.

Walter, Ronald G. Introduction. *A Black Woman's Odyssey through Russia and Jamaica: The Narrative of Nancy Prince.* New York: Markus Wiener, 1990.

Whiting, Lilian. *Kate Field: A Record.* London: Sampson Low, Marston, 1899.

Woodward, Helen Beal. *The Bold Women.* New York: Farrar, Straus, & Young, 1953. Contains information on Field.

Selected Secondary Works on Travel Literature

American Travellers Abroad: A Bibliography of Accounts Published before 1900. Ed. Harold F. Smith. Carbondale: The Library, Southern Illinois University, 1969.

Baker, Paul R. *The Fortunate Pilgrims: Americans in Italy, 1800–1860.* Cambridge: Harvard University Press, 1964.

Buzard, James. *The Beaten Track: European Tourism, Literature, and the Ways of Culture, 1800–1918.* Oxford: Clarendon Press, 1993.

Caesar, Terry. "'Counting the Cats in Zanzibar': American Travel Abroad in American Travel Writing to 1914." *Prospects: An Annual of American Cultural Studies.* Ed. Jack Salzman. Vol. 13 (Cambridge: Cambridge University Press, 1988). Pp. 95–134.

Culler, Jonathan. "The Semiotics of Tourism." *Framing the Sign: Criticism and Its Institutions.* Oxford: Blackwell, 1988. Pp. 153–67.

Dulles, Foster Rhea. *Americans Abroad: Two Centuries of European Travel.* Ann Arbor: University of Michigan Press, 1964.

Ethnohistory 33, 2 (1986). Issue on travel literature.

Kelley, Mary. *Private Woman, Public Stage: Literary Domesticity in Nineteenth-Century America.* New York: Oxford University Press, 1984.

Ladies on the Loose: Women Travellers of the 18th and 19th Centuries. Ed. Leo Hamalian. New York: Dodd, Mead, 1981.

Lockwood, Allison. *Passionate Pilgrims: The American Traveler in Great Britain, 1800–1914.* Rutherford, N.J.: Fairleigh Dickinson University Press, 1981.

MacCannell, Dean. *The Tourist: A New Theory of the Leisure Class.* 1976; rpt. New York: Schocken, 1989.

Maiden Voyages: The Writings of Women Travelers. Eds. Larry O'Connor and Mary Morris. New York: Vintage, 1993.

Mills, Sara. *Discourses of Difference: An Analysis of Women's Travel Writing and Colonialism.* London: Routledge, 1991.

Morgan, Susan. "An Introduction to Victorian Women's Travel Writings about Southeast Asia." *Genre* 20 (Summer 1987): 189–208.

Mulvey, Christopher. *Anglo-American Landscapes: A Study of Nineteenth-Century Anglo-American Travel Literature.* Cambridge: Cambridge University Press, 1983.

_____. *Transatlantic Manners: Social Patterns in Nineteenth-Century Anglo-American Travel Literature.* Cambridge: Cambridge University Press, 1990.

Pratt, Mary Louise. *Imperial Eyes: Travel Writing and Transculturation.* London: Routledge, 1992.

Said, Edward. *Orientalism.* 1978; rpt. New York: Vintage Books, 1979.

Schriber, Mary Suzanne. "Edith Wharton and the Dog-Eared Travel Book." In *Wretched Exotic: Essays on Edith Wharton in Europe.* Eds. K. Joslin and A. Price. New York: Peter Lang, 1993. Pp. 147–64.

_____. "Edith Wharton and Travel Writing as Self-Discovery." *American Literature* 59 (May 1987): 257–67.

Schwab, Raymond. *The Oriental Renaissance: Europe's Rediscovery of India and the East, 1680–1880.* Trans. Gene Petterson-Black and Victor Reinking. New York: Columbia University Press, 1984.

Strout, Cushing. *The American Image of the Old World.* New York: Harper, 1963.

Urry, John. *The Tourist Gaze: Leisure and Travel in Contemporary Societies.* London: Sage, 1990.